ALL
ABOARD!

A·L·L

THE RAILROAD IN AMERICAN LIFE

SMITHMARK

A·BO·A·R·D!

GEORGE H. DOUGLAS

This edition published in 1996 by
SMITHMARK Publishers
a division of US Media Holdings, Inc.
16 East 32nd Street, New York, NY 10016

SMITHMARK books are available for bulk purchase for sales,
promotion, and premium use. For details, write or call the
manager of special sales, SMITHMARK Publishers
16 East 32nd Street, New York, NY 10016 (212)-532-6600.

Library of Congress data is available upon request

Printed in the United States of America

ISBN: 0-7651-9736-7

10 9 8 7 6 5 4 3 2 1

To
ROBERT W. MAYER

C·O·N·T·E·N·T·S

A·C·K·N·O·W·L·E·D·G·M·E·N·T·S

This book makes an attempt to offer one writer's social history of the railroad in America. It is not intended to be "the" social history of the railroad in America, nor indeed any kind of academic exploration of the subject. There is no attempt to present a revolutionary thesis that sees the interplay between railroads and the American people in an entirely new light. Instead it hopes to provide a context and an interpretation of a phenomenon that has been so long a part of our national consciousness that we take it wholly for granted. I have tried to show how and why the railroad became so deeply buried in our national consciousness and how it shaped our social and cultural life.

Needless to say, no book of this sort could come about without having been influenced by many works of a similar nature that have come before. A number of very fine informal histories of the railroad in America have had a strong slant toward social history—that is, they are not mainly concerned with the financial or managerial dimension of railroad history but with the human dimension, the impact of the railroad on the people it touched. Readers of this book can hardly fail to see that I have been strongly influenced by Stewart H. Holbrook's *The Story of the American Railroad*. A number of other historians, popular or otherwise, have influenced me at one time or another, including Christopher Morley, Lucius Beebe, Rogers E.M. Whitaker, individuals who have a strong and zesty interest in the human juices of railroad history.

At the same time, of course, I have been strongly indebted to the many fine historians who have devoted their careers to railroad or transportation history, especially the numerous excellent works of John F. Stover and Richard C. Overton. Readers of this book will not fail to see that I have been influenced strongly in my thinking by a number of books that also deal with the social context of the railroad, including John R. Stilgoe's *Metropolitan Corridor: Railroads and the American Scene*; Jeffrey Richards's and John MacKenzie's *The Railroad Station: A Social History*; and Leo Marx's *The Machine in the Garden.*

A number of friends and colleagues of mine have been particularly helpful at one stage or another during the writing of this book. I am especially grateful to Professor Robert M. Sutton of the department of history at the University of Illinois who read the whole of the completed manuscript and gave me the benefit of his judicious comments. Among other friends and colleagues who shared their advice with me were Robert W. Mayer, Francis W. Weeks, Clark Spence, and Thomas P. Parkinson. My long-time friend and Western historian Dee Brown shared his thoughts about the West and the railroad, not only in his fine book *Hear That Lonesome Whistle Blow: Railroads in the West*, but in many conversations over the years.

Many institutions and libraries have been exceedingly helpful to me in research for this book and my previous book *Rail City: Chicago USA*. I should make mention of the Chicago Historical Society, the Newberry Library, the DeGolyer Foundation Library, the Library of Congress, the Smithsonian Institution, the Museum of the City of New York, the New Jersey Historical Society, the University of Illinois Library, the Illinois Historical Survey, Railroadians of America, the Railway and Locomotive Historical Society and the Midwest Railway Historical Society.

While not possible to mention all of the individuals who at one time or another helped me with my research or shaped my thinking, I ought at least to cite: Herbert H. Harwood, Jr., John T. Cunningham, John H. White, Jr., William D. Middleton, Don Hofsommer, Carl W. Condit, Thomas T. Taber.

Of course my greatest debt is to the American people who shaped the railroad and gave it the distinct personality that it enjoys in North America, who celebrated the railroad in song and verse, and who learned to enjoy the freedom of travel and movement that only the railroad can provide.

I·N·T·R·O·D·U·C·T·I·O·N

Saturday, November 21, 1914, New Haven, Connecticut. A cheering throng would be on hand this day for a football game between Harvard and Yale. The Yale Bowl was to be opened and dedicated, and all of its seventy thousand seats would be occupied. Spectators would arrive from New York and Boston, and from more distant points up and down the eastern seaboard. Nearly all of these people would arrive and depart New Haven by railway train. There was, in 1914, no such thing as an interstate highway anywhere in the United States. Except for Henry Ford's spunky but flimsy Model-T, the automobile was still thought of as a rich man's toy. Only the hardiest or pluckiest of individuals would have attempted to travel over the cinder-covered roads between Boston and New Haven by automobile. There was only one way to travel in those days, only one way to travel in style, only one way to bring one's wife or girlfriend to town in fit condition to be seen—by railroad.

The Yale Bowl crowd was being served that day by the New York, New Haven & Hartford Railroad. The New Haven was in fine fettle then and in the full vigor of its youthful maturity; it was accustomed to running its trains on time, even when, as in this case, it would be required to run dozens of special trains to accommodate thousands of travelers. The New Haven was clearly ready for the job. And it was a big job. On this glorious day, the

New Haven would carry 37,500 passengers to the Yale-Harvard game, 33,468 of them during a single four-hour period. Most of these individuals were carried on special trains, but some also came on the New Haven's numerous regularly scheduled passenger trains. During the peak four-hour period, twenty-seven trains arrived from New York with 17,800 passengers; eighteen from Boston with 7,474 passengers; five from Springfield with 3,997 passengers; and three from Hartford with 1,254 passengers. There were twelve other trains with 2,943 passengers.

Such an influx may seem an inconceivable burden by the standards of passenger train operations today, but the New Haven carried off this great migration without a hitch. Days before the planned event, the railroad issued a special employees' timetable, listing all of the trains and their departure and arrival times. This multipage pamphlet also contained information for bridge tenders and tower operators along the right-of-way, for train crews, station agents, information bureaus, parcel rooms, yardmasters, switchmen, even crews of freight trains that would be called upon to weave in and out of this heavy passenger traffic. There were also instructions dealing with every imaginable emergency procedure or mishap. The special timetable gave the location of nineteen engines that would be ready and fired up at fifteen points along the way in case of mechanical breakdowns. These engines would be pointed toward New Haven for the morning rush and away from New Haven for the evening rush. The timetable also gave the location of major officials of the road—all on duty and at the ready. Roles were set out for trainmasters, road foremen of engines, master mechanics, electrical foremen, and car inspectors—all of them strategically placed along the line should their services be needed at a moment's notice.

The passengers were not forgotten in all this planning. En route to New Haven, each passenger was given a circular telling where his train would be waiting for the return trip and giving the track number, departing time, and other information. Included in this circular were a diagram of the New Haven terminal, a map of the city showing the routes between the station and the stadium, and a map of the Yale Bowl itself. (Alas, it would not be a good day for Yale fans: Harvard won 36–0.)

The care and foreplanning that went into this operation resulted in a mass operation of trains and persons that was close to perfect. All passengers inbound to the game arrived on time to within three or four minutes; sixteen trains arrived in New Haven ahead of schedule. In the outbound movement, in a one-hour period, between 5:20 P.M. and 6:20 P.M., eighteen thousand passengers were moved out of New Haven—an average of three hundred per minute. All of these passengers arrived at their destinations on time!

An exceptional operation, not encountered every day, to be sure. On the other hand, in 1914, a task of this magnitude did not daunt the railroads of the United States. When the task confronted them, they were ready for it. Railroads ran on a timetable, passengers expected to arrive at the time found in the timetable, and so they almost invariably did. The railroad was a thing built to operate with clocklike precision, and when the railroads were in their heyday all of the major carriers operated their trains according to these standards. On time, to the minute.

Time. The measurement of all human activity. Time, as measured by hours, minutes, seconds: It was discovered by the railroads in the nineteenth century, or, more precisely, made into an article of faith that energized a great industrial civilization. Before the railroads, time was nothing but an amorphous set of conventions, governed by the rising and setting of the sun, the braying of cattle in the field, the disparate practices of an agrarian way of life. Split-second timing and clocks that are set together in harmony were products of the railroad. Before 1883, there was no such thing as "Standard Time" in America, and there would have been no such thing as "Standard Time" if it had been left up to legislators or representatives of the people. The railroads developed "Standard Time," and Congress adopted the idea several decades later.

Today, of course, we sometimes lapse into a state of forgetfulness about the merits of time. Airlines, which now provide most long-distance or intercity transportation for the general public, are governed by timetables that look something like the railway timetables of old, but as their patrons are mostly aware, such documents are provided only as a kind of courtesy. They are a grim reminder of the kind of service that railroads once provided. In the golden years of railroad passenger service, a timetable was supposed to mean what was written on it. For years, the president of the New York Central railroad (like many other railroad presidents) asked to have a report on his desk the first thing in the morning revealing the arrival time of the road's luxury flyer, the Twentieth Century Limited from Chicago. The train was due into Grand Central Station at 9:00 in the morning, and so it almost always was. And 9:00 meant that—not 9:05 or 9:25. These last were disaster arrival times for those responsible for the movements of the Twentieth Century Limited. Alfred H. Smith, president of the railroad in the early 1920s, had arrival reports of the Century cabled to him when he was on vacation, and there were sure to be stern inquiries about poor performance whatever may have been the cause of it. Legend has it that on one occasion, when Mr. Smith was on safari in Africa, arrival times were brought to him by a naked tribesman, bearing telegraph receipts on the end of a pole.

In those days, it was said that the United States really worked!

It is commonplace today to believe that we live in the post–railroad age. Even though this is perhaps a thoughtless overstatement, there may also be some truth to it. For over a century, the railroad was the dynamic force giving motion and life to American society. The railroad was the agency that brought the United States of America into being. Before the 1830s, when the railroad began making its appearance, the country was a "united" nation in name only—bad roads and slow-moving canals defied all attempts to establish a working infrastructure. Travel between Boston and any interior city—Albany, New York, let us say—less than two hundred miles away would be an arduous, physically punishing journey of several days and one that would never be undertaken lightly. In a few short decades, after the coming of the railroad, such a journey could be made in a few hours of routine passage.

Ralph Waldo Emerson likened the railroad to a magician's rod—it had transformed America into a great industrial nation with merely one wave. In 1820, the United States was a disjointed nation composed of lonely and self-sufficient farmers. Its way of life was that dreamed of by Thomas Jefferson, who wished to see the "free" man relieved of the burdens of cities and crowds. But the railroad would make us something altogether different. It welded the nation together, creating an American outlook, an American point of view. And it did this in a time span that can only be considered miraculous in comparison with all previous developments of history. Wherever the railroad went, it would bring a whole new way of life into being as if by lightning. Chicago, a railroad town if ever there was one, was nothing but a few rude huts inside a wooden stockade in 1830; forty years later, it had accomplished what had taken London and Paris centuries—it had become one of the great cities of the world. A young boy tramping through the mud and through the marshes of the old Chicago, when it was called Fort Dearborn, could grow up and in his middle age dine in luxury at the Palmer House on State Street.

Everywhere the railroad went, it created something as if by magic. The British had invented the railroad, had figured out how to make it work. But they were aghast at what Americans did with their invention. Mostly using the same gauge as the British railroads, Americans were more generous with the loading gauge, making it possible to build enormous locomotives (too big to be safe, they said in England). Furthermore, these crazy Americans built lines to everywhere—even to nowhere at all. Nobody in Europe would have dreamed of building a railroad into uninhabited territory. You had to have two great metropolises—Birmingham and Manchester, let's say. But Americans believed in this agency of growth, saw it as a way of creating their civilization from nothing, and laid tracks into the wide open spaces. And then, where the railroad went, settlers immediately followed.

In essence, the railroad built the trans–Mississippi West, and created the enduring institutions of that region. So many of the towns of Kansas or South Dakota were at first nothing but places where railroad men had decided to lay out a shanty depot—throwing off a pile of lumber from some tattered work car. In the beginning, nobody wanted to get off at any of these godforsaken places—places that would sometimes get worse before they got better, becoming sinkholes of shoot-em-up anarchy before they were settled. But the railroads took care of the settlement. Not only did they bring the marshal, the minister, and the lawyer, eventually they brought the people from the East and from Europe—thousands of people who would go on to fulfillment in all walks of life.

Not only did the railroad give birth to a unified American people, by providing the only technological link between cities and towns, the railroad also established a single, integrated economy.

It made a nationwide system of manufactures possible. Before the coming of the railroads, when milady bought her dress, or master his watch, they were invariably products of some cottage industry. Or they had been imported from Europe at great expense. The railroad wedded together the factories of New England with prairie farms that raised livestock and grain. The railroads encouraged and gave birth to what we so proudly refer to as the free enterprise system.

It has often been asserted that the railroads were America's first big business. As such, they came in for more than their share of calumny in the years after the Civil War, when they had a stranglehold on shippers from the grain states, when their labor practices set a bad example for the heavy industries of the East, when railroad moguls got disgustingly rich. But Americans could forgive the railroads most of their transgressions, since all of their hopes and aspirations had been spurred by the railroad.

Furthermore, there was always something primordial about the railroads; Americans saw the railroad as inextricably bound up with their national destiny. Somehow, the railroad was an agency of freedom, and freedom was what America was all about. Even the people who worked on the railroad were seen as footloose and fancy-free; they were taken as romantic personages by small boys and starry-eyed maidens. The railroad may have been a heavy industry, and for a long time a smoky industry, but there was always something liberating about it. To be able to swing from cars moving to some other place, to sit atop a boxcar or at the throttle of a powerful locomotive, always carried with it some identification with the joyful principalities of the air. In Europe, there had been but one lot for the ordinary man—toil and drudgery. For centuries, he had been a serf, tied to the land. He could move nowhere. In the factory system of the late eighteenth century, he had gotten off the land but was tied to his workbench or some gloomy, cavernous mine. But the railroad, America's chosen industry, was something different, something infinitely more romantic and agreeable. It provided a license to move, a true declaration of independence. The railroad dramatized human freedom better than any other agency yet dreamed of by the human mind.

Americans accordingly were drawn to the railroad, magnetized by it. In so many small towns, depot square was the very locus of social activity. All the boys hung out there, as did those yearning for a better life somewhere else—a great city perhaps, a place of sophistication. The American small town was energized by the coming of the trains, whether the passing in a blaze of glory of some streaking express or the labored chug of the accommodation train with its load of newspapers or mail. There was always magic when the train came in; the moment of arrival gave poignancy and drama to the slow hours at the depot, which were witness to nothing but the ticking of the clock or the clatter of the telegraph key. Not only had the railroad brought America to life, the coming of its cars brought the small town to life every day. At Varden, Mississippi, a county seat, the district court was adjourned so that everybody—the judge, jurors, lawyers, courthouse loafers—could go down to the depot to watch the Illinois Central's crack Panama Limited go by.

By slow degrees in the nineteenth century, the railroad began to determine the character of America. It controlled the pace and quality of society in city and small town alike. The railroad gave Americans a sense of mobility, and what is more important, upward mobility. The railroad had the capacity for delivering the country boy from the farm to his hoped-for success in the city. For those who didn't go but stayed behind, the railroad was responsible for the rhythms and quality of everyday life. The railroad gave the name and meaning to such enduring attributes as "the other side of the tracks," shantytown, hobo jungle, junction, "jerk water" town, main line, "hot shot." Always the railroad was the link which joined everybody and everything together: small town, big city; the rich and the poor; the ocean and the mountains; factory town and lush resort; home and office. The railroads gave birth to suburbia, an idea which didn't even exist at the beginning of the nineteenth century. It made it possible for a man to work in the city and yet preserve at least a remnant of the Jeffersonian ideal in that little patch of green he could call his homestead with its attendant blessings of blue skies, green grass, and fresh water.

The railroad has perhaps faded from the forefront of consciousness in recent decades, but American's love of trains has never been obliterated, even as the railroad as a mode of passenger transport faded. Railroad passenger traffic has increased, not declined, on the slowpoke Amtrak, even after all the prophets insisted that people no longer wanted to travel long distances by train. On the other hand, there remains something sentimental, something dramatic, something compelling, about the railroad. People still like to watch trains go by, listen to the sound of the far-away whistle, the groans of the engines, even if the diesel locomotive has lost the flair and beauty of the iron horse.

Deep down, most American still believe the railroad made us the people we are. It gave us our desire for movement and escape to some other place. It gave birth to our sense of the diversity of places—of cities, of suburbs, of leisured resorts. Some social historians have traced the American's wanderlust to the automobile, but the automobile was a Johnny-come-lately in this game. Many developments that have been said to be the product of the automobile were tried first by the railroad. The huge malls found almost everywhere today were in fact pioneered by the railroads back in the early years of the twentieth century. The great city terminals—South Station in Boston, Grand Central in New York— were malls even before the word "mall" was brought into use. And even before these terminals were built, their predecessors had already determined the essence of life in our cities—governance of the clock, the hurried step, the quick exchange of luggage, and the electric transfer of information—this not the product of radio or television but the telegraph, an early ancillary enterprise of the railroad. The great urban terminals were our first temples of progress and achievement. They explain why Americans dress up when they go traveling (practicality might have ordained quite the opposite), why Americans are seemingly energized by travel. The railroad, after all, was the product of a new kind of energy, a kind that had not been known before. All previous forms of human endeavor had enslaved people, kept them wedded to toil. The railroad always represented the opposite. It was a form of energy suited to the appetites and dreams of a democratic people.

C·H·A·P·T·E·R 1

NEW YORK TO PHILADELPHIA IN 1820

New York and Philadelphia: They are today two of America's greatest cities, just as they were in 1820. As the crow flies, they are less than ninety miles apart, so close together that, in this age of urban sprawl and airport congestion, the idea of travel between them by air seems to be something of a sick joke. The ideal way from New York to Philadelphia is on the ground. Today, alas, that trip is often a frenzied, headlong, madcap, bumper-to-bumper relay on the New Jersey Turnpike, although more sensible travelers will choose a leisurely ride on one of Amtrak's comfortable Metroliners, suitably named to commemorate this, one of the most congested metropolitan rail corridors in the nation, if not the world.

Philadelphia and New York have so long been joined by close ties of trade and commerce that it is hard to imagine a time when travel between them was anything but routine, convenient and rapid. But things were once vastly different. In 1820, a trip between these two cities was an ordeal sufficient to cause anxiety and apprehension, typically requiring two tedious boat trips and a long bone-jarring stagecoach journey, the total of which would consume the traveler's entire day. All this on what was then considered the most modern, efficient transportation network to be found anywhere in the land.

In 1820, New York and Philadelphia were, respectively, the largest and second largest cities in North America. Not long before, during the American Revolution, Philadelphia had been the largest, but in the early years of the nineteenth century a quick spurt of commercial activity allowed New York to outpace its two long-time archrivals, Philadelphia and Boston, both of which were still known throughout the world as America's leading cities.[1]

None of these cities, of course, were giant metropolises; they were mere towns by European standards, or by the American standards of today. New York's population was 123,000, and Philadelphia's 112,000. Still, they seemed immense for a nation that was almost exclusively agricultural and whose frontier was either sparsely populated or uninhabited. One thing characterized all the major American cities in 1820: All of them were port towns—Philadelphia, New York, Boston, Baltimore, Charleston, New Orleans—all had been given their essences, their spurts of growth, by maritime commerce. All had been settled by Europeans who came to the new continent in sailing ships and who, by 1820, were still mostly living in these coastal towns or in settlements that lay nearby. Ninety percent of the people of the United States lived within a short distance of the sea. To be sure, the frontier had been moving steadily westward, and by 1820, even Illinois had been admitted as a state. But most of the land between Virginia and Illinois was crude frontier land, settled only scantily by a few isolated and tiny towns and forts.

Since the major American cities were ports, it should be obvious that most of the commerce between them was by means of sailing ships. There wasn't much even of this commerce. Philadelphia, New York, Baltimore, and Charleston were largely self-contained and independent of one another. Cotton was beginning to make its way to Boston from the South, and manufactured goods were returning, but generally, the various settled areas of the United States were freestanding and self-sufficient. Traffic between them was light, mainly because it was perilous, frightening, and uncomfortable. Anyone who ventured to travel between Boston and Charleston by sea was undertaking a voyage every bit as perilous as the voyage they had taken across the great ocean.

Thus, the colonies, like the continents, were bridged by the sea. Because they were bridged by the sea, they were, for practical purposes, cut off from one another by the sea. A classic example of the vicissitudes of sea travel in colonial times was the misfortune that befell the youthful Benjamin Franklin, who attempted to journey from Boston to Philadelphia in 1732. In crossing New York Harbor, on the way to Perth Amboy, his boat could not enter the Kill van Kull, was blown off course, and sailed far out on Long Island, resulting in thirty hours of wasted time before his vessel could tie up at Perth Amboy for the remaining land portion of his journey to Philadelphia.[2] (Surely Franklin, and others of his time, could sympathize with the discomfitures of twentieth-century air travelers!)

But what of the roads? Were there no roads? There were, and they were terrible. In the years before the Revolution, a number of old Indian trails had been widened and were euphemistically called roads, but few if any of these would qualify as roads in the modern sense. They were not hospitable to wagon or coach, only to the horseback rider or hardy wayfarer. For the most part, even the best roads before 1800 were little more than broad paths that had been cut through the woods. Typically, they were not cleared of boulders or stumps and other natural obstacles, and this made travel by means of wagons and carts nearly impossible. Occasionally, in swampy places, where mud was an impediment, logs were laid side by side to form what were then called "corduroy roads." In some places, where a way was needed to get the farmer into town to sell his produce or attend church, some further improvements might be in evidence, but nothing that would be recognized as a road today.

Generally speaking, overland travel was seldom used for the transportation of goods or household possessions. Things that were made in Philadelphia or Boston stayed there. After the Revolution, there were a few exceptions, perhaps. Traveling around the East, a few intrepid figures like Parson Weems, the vagabond book peddler who wrote a famous fictional biography of George Washington, would endure "roads horrid and suns torrid" while his wagon, loaded with books, jostled from place to place, often having to be pulled out of mud that covered the axle, stopping occasionally to bathe and wash out his clothes by some stream.

For all intents and purposes, the original thirteen colonies were as separate as countries, and passing through them was not unlike passing through the various vest-pocket principalities of old

Germany. There was not one single culture, as in the United States of today—the values, the life-style, even the physical appearance of the Virginia planter bore little if any resemblance to that of the rock-ribbed Yankee of New England or the Dutch settlers of the Hudson valley. These were separate peoples, brought together a few years before by a common hatred of English rule, but generally none were anxious to rub shoulders with the others. Even the relatively short journey between Philadelphia and New York, a territory so well homogenized today that nothing in it bears differentiation, would have been an experience in cultural diversity in the early years of the nineteenth century. In Philadelphia, the Quaker influence held strong, and one could expect to encounter the tri-cornered hat and tie wig. But the city had thousands of French residents, and a somewhat continental flavor. Crossing the Delaware River into New Jersey, the traveler would encounter small, independently owned farms, and those who toiled on them were grim faced and tight-lipped—not eager to learn the news of the cities and lands beyond. Even tiny New Jersey itself was unhomogenized in those days. The western part of the state, nearest to Penn's colony, was strongly Quaker in its flavoring; the Northeastern part of the state, in Newark and Elizabethtown, was settled by Puritans, which gave that area a feel much like that of Connecticut.

But even these generalizations are somewhat misleading. Northeast New Jersey had been settled first by the Dutch, and, as one approached New York, the Dutch influence, both in the people and in the architecture, exuded a very pronounced aroma. Towns like Communipauw and Bergen resembled villages in Holland. Here one found high-peaked gabled roofs with weathercocks, little Dutch churches, and taverns that overflowed with merrymakers on the weekend, giving bemused offense in this seat of Puritanism. Broad-hatted burghers, smoking pipes, followed oxen up and down their fields. They spoke Dutch to their neighbors, whitewashed their houses, tended flocks of geese, puttered in extraordinarily tidy gardens, and of an evening sat taciturnly looking out at the world, their plump wives knitting placidly beside them.[3]

Because of this cultural diversity, because of the inherent difficulties of communication, perhaps because of a certain stubbornness and standoffishness, most Americans in the early nineteenth century were not greatly disturbed by the fragmentation of their nation. They liked it that way. They were, to a very great extent, suspicious of their neighbors, and had no strong desire to hobnob with them. They had no urge to travel. They liked being isolated and independent; they were suspicious of unification, even though all belonged to the "United States."

The quality of intractable isolation among the American colonies had been apparent to the land's foreign rulers as far back as the seventeenth century. A royal governor of New York had dispatched the first overland mail in North America between New York and Boston in January 1673. But the Dutch, who had only recently lost their colony to England, and who would make one more attempt to possess the land known to them as New Amsterdam, didn't like the idea of commerce with the New England Yankees, so that the postal service was discontinued and not revived for many years.[4] Even in the middle of the eighteenth century, after a reasonable postal service had been established by the English crown, and brilliantly administered by Benjamin Franklin, the entire postal system in the thirteen British colonies was slow, irregular, and costly. And it could not have been otherwise, since the means of internal travel remained primitive and unreliable.

In the eighteenth century, there was no such notion as roads being built through the use of public funds, or through the agency of public planning. By tradition in most of the eastern states, "all able bodied men between sixteen and sixty years" were expected to offer at least one day a year in which they would labor with their teams on local roads, and another day on which they would work on the "King's Road" or "Great Road"—today, what we would call the county or state highway. Township supervisors could fine laggards five shillings for failure to comply with this civic responsibility, but the fine was seldom levied, and the work was invariably done in a haphazard manner, if at all. Invariably, too, all the efforts of local laborers were put into local roads of convenience, and such parts of a "King's Highway" as radiated from town, leaving the long-distance roads full of gaps and broken segments.

Shortly after the United States was established as a nation, all serious journals of public opinion, and many local newspapers, began pressing for something to be done about the pitiful state of the roads. State legislators were deluged with complaints, and newspapers peppered with "letters to the editor" complaining about the condition of the byways that were whimsically called highways. A man signing himself "A Traveller" wrote to the *New Jersey Journal* in 1792: "Thy inhabitants O State, are respectable—thy Senators wise—thy militia is formidable—and the daughters are fair; but some of thy ways are bad. Whoever travels the road from stony brook steep, to Rocky Hill, in a wheel carriage does it at the hazard of his life."[5] The same complaint could be heard everywhere in the republic, for many years to come.

In 1808, Albert Gallatin, Thomas Jefferson's sagacious and fore-sighted Swiss-born secretary of the treasury, submitted a report to the U.S. Senate proposing a comprehensive system of roads, improved waterways, and canals, and in the next few years the goal of "internal improvements" became a heated public issue. Almost immediately, however, the power of the federal government to construct internal improvements was challenged on constitutional grounds. Gallatin's useful idea surfaced again and again over the next several decades, especially after the War of 1812, when all the great public men became aware that the war effort had been severely impeded by the lack of a good transportation network. But a series of presidents—Madison, Monroe, and Jackson—all vetoed legislation providing for internal improvements on the ground that they were unconstitutional.

Nonetheless, the situation was bad enough that a few projects did manage to obtain federal funding anyway. Realizing the total isolation of the rapidly growing West from the coastal states, Congress as early as 1802 had appropriated funds for a road from Cumberland, Maryland, to Wheeling, (West) Virginia. This road, known at first as the Cumberland Road, and later as the National Road, inched itself forward by the aid of as many as fourteen special acts of Congress, although it, too, was constantly under attack, even though everybody agreed on the need for such a thorough-fare. Because the times were out of joint for such an enterprise, the road took fifteen years to get to Wheeling. It didn't arrive at its termination in Vandalia, Illinois, until 1852—a half century after its original conception![6] Regrettably, national funding of interstate roads would have to wait for the appearance of the auto-mobile.

Even though the federal government would do nothing, the transportation picture was not entirely hopeless in the early nineteenth century, and it was being relieved somewhat by the hand of private enterprise and by rapid advances in the technology of transportation. While the federal government was refusing to fund a system of internal improvements, other forces were at work which would soon ameliorate the miseries of overland travelers. The states, while themselves lacking revenues for transportation networks, did what they could. In 1792, while George Washington was still in his first term as president, the state of Pennsylvania granted a charter to a private company to build a road between Philadelphia and Lancaster. This charter opened up a major new chapter in American transportation history.

Private companies, of course, must be paid for their efforts, so the improved road to Lancaster was a "toll road"—an idea well known in Europe. When this new road was opened in 1794, it was called the Lancaster Turnpike, because along its way, every so many miles, there was a large pole or "pike" that blocked the road. At each of these gates, the traveler had to stop to pay a fee for the use of the road, and, when paid, the pike would be turned to permit passage—thus the term "turnpike." Eventually, all of the eastern states issued charters for turnpikes. Between 1801 and 1829, as many of fifty-one charters were issued, although only half of them were eventually built. The important thing about the toll roads, however, was that they did provide a means to pay for road improvements, and those were made in a systematic and orderly way.

But during this same period, the first three decades of the nineteenth century, a great deal was also being done to improve the actual means and types of conveyance. Throughout the colonial period, overland journeys were undertaken in wretched open wagons, mere carts with no springs—a means of transportation that might well have been invented by a specialist in the arts of torture. By slow degrees, more comfortable, and faster stagecoaches were developed, leading eventually to the oval-shaped "post coach" and then, finally, around 1830, to the flat-topped "Concord Coach" (so named for the New Hampshire town where it was manufactured), all built upon springs, and all designed for some degree of human comfort. In the years before the coming of railroads, stagecoach journeys were not by any means undertakings of unalloyed delight, but many of their more notorious terrors had been removed.

Far greater advances were being made in another area, howev-

er. If journeys by land were still slow and perilous, travel by inland
waters was now becoming more attractive. This was because of the
invention in the early years of the century of a practical steamboat, a technological advance that would shortly allow some of the
great American rivers of the West—the Ohio and the Mississippi—
to become veritable arteries of commerce, the kind of all-purpose
highways that had been looked for by the disappointed planners
of "national roads" and commercial turnpikes.

There had been numerous early attempts to create a successful
steamboat—the virtues and possibilities of Watt's steam engine
were well known in America, and in the 1780s and 1790s, a number of Americans were working on a multitude of different steamboat designs. One of the most active inventors was John Fitch, who
experimented with several types of boats on the Delaware River.
Among the other workers in the field was the aging Benjamin
Franklin, whose interest in all things relating to transportation was
unbounded. Franklin convinced a Maryland boat builder by the
name of James Ramsey to construct a vessel that used a steam
pump to suck water in at the bow and eject it at the stern. Then
there was Col. John Stevens of Hoboken, New Jersey, who experimented with several steamboats in the 1790s, and even conceived
the idea of using a screw propeller instead of the usual poles, ore,
and paddle wheels. The screw propeller idea was dropped, but
fortunately was revived by a later generation of marine engineers.

The first practical steamboat was the *Clermont,* designed by
Robert Fulton and launched in the spring of 1807. Fulton had
been a painter by profession, but later became interested in engineering. He had been fascinated by the ships' designs of men like
Fitch and Ramsey, and forming an alliance with the wealthy
Robert Livingston, then minister to France, he managed to purchase a steam engine and boiler from the best-known British firm
of the day, Boulton and Watt, and returned home to design a
steamboat to utilize them.

While the boat was under construction on the Hudson River at
New York, citizens arrived from everywhere to jeer "Fulton's folly,"
all convinced that no such vessel of this size (it was 140 feet long,
of sixteen-foot beam, and twenty-eight inch draft), could ever do
anything but sink or erupt in flame. On the spring day in 1807
when the *Clermont* was launched, crowds had assembled to jeer,

but they were struck dumb with amazement when the boat churned relentlessly into the river and turned northward and advanced steadily against wind and tide. As the boat plied its way up the river, it was a fearsome sight to behold, its pinewood fuel sending clouds of smoke and flashing sparks from a thirty-foot stack. It is said that this puffing monster terrified many old rivermen, some of whom jumped into the water as the *Clermont* passed, or ran their boats aground. Driving to Albany against the wind, the *Clermont* made the 150-mile trip in thirty-two hours. Here, at last, was proof positive that steamboats were successful and steam power was the wave of the future.

It hardly needs to be said that in the next few years steamboat manufacture became all the rage in the United States, a nation that was desperately looking for any means of improved transportation. And here there had been a giant leap forward all at once. Within only a few years, by 1810, steamboats could be found in considerable numbers on the Hudson and Delaware rivers, most of them brought into service to vastly upgrade the snail-paced Philadelphia–New York trade. The usefulness of steamboats would also be quickly felt upon the Western waters, but men like Fulton and Livingston, and Robert Stevens of New Jersey, who immediately attempted to seize a big initiative on the Delaware River, knew that steamboating in the busy New York to Philadelphia corridor could be made to pay handsome dividends.

So handsome were the dividends, in fact, that the Livingston-Fulton consortium appealed to the New York state legislature to offer them an exclusive charter (that is to say, monopoly) for steamboat service in New York State waters. For a number of years, competition by New Jersey vessels to the port of New York was legally banned, even though boats making the Philadelphia connection would have to ply the Raritan River of New Jersey. So lucrative was the traffic, however, that numerous newcomers to steamboating attempted to deposit passengers in New York in clear violation of the law. The Stevens family tried all sorts of ploys to evade enforcement of the monopoly, and so did a wily young ferry boat captain named Corneilus Vanderbilt, whose guile and resourcefulness knew no bounds, and who was adept at dodging New York state process servers and ramming boats of the opposition. The early years of steamboat competition were thrilling, if

not hair-raising, at least until 1824, at which time the United
States Supreme Court took from the states the power to govern
interstate commerce and sailing on coastal waters.

While the monopoly was still in effect, and even after it was broken, competition for passenger trade in the heavily traveled corridor between New York and Philadelphia was brisk and often
uproarious. The United States was rapidly growing, as were these
two cities, and the need now existed to move not a few individuals,
but scores of individuals daily. Accordingly, in 1820, in comparison with colonial times, travel between New York and Philadelphia
had become positively speedy by the standards of that time.

The means of accomplishing this voyage were fairly settled and
well publicized by 1820. The appearance of the steamboat had
shortened the trip considerably and made it far more reliable
than it had been under sail. Naturally, the New York–Philadelphia
trip was accomplished, insofar as possible, by water. This meant a
steamboat trip down New York Bay, along coastal waters between
Staten Island and New Jersey, then up the Raritan River to New
Brunswick, or a few other occasional landing spots, thence on
board stagecoaches to the Delaware River at Trenton or
Bordentown, from which the trip to Philadelphia would be completed by yet another steamboat passage.

Of course, it would also have been possible, although uncomfortable, to have made the entire trip overland. There were, by
1820, at least three "King's Highways" between New York and the
Delaware River, and numerous stage companies hustled whatever
business might be available along these roads. They also enjoyed
the patronage of a long string of rapidly mushrooming New Jersey
towns. Stagecoach travel across New Jersey was now as fast as it
would ever be.

Still, however you looked at it, stagecoach journeys were
unloved by travelers—they were slow, dusty, and confining. Many
teams of horses might be employed by numerous companies, all
racing to make the best times possible, but there was no luxury
and little comfort in this means of transportation. Passengers were
crowded in on one another, which was particularly objectionable
to women, who were never allowed to ride on the outside with the
driver, and who invariably found themselves pinched into the
smallest corner, shoved, sat upon, and jostled by every bump of
the road. Stages made regular stops at "taverns"—institutions that

at one time had a perfectly respectable reputation, but whose very name now became unsavory in the lexicon of American life. The taverns returned many passengers, especially males, to the coaches unduly under the influence of strong spirits, and thus even less suited than before to the torments of the stage wheel.

It is little wonder, then, that travelers preferred journey by water to journey by land in 1820, and in the trip between New York and Philadelphia half the distance was upon the waters—distinctly the most pleasurable part of the trip. Taking this voyage from south to north in the 1820s was Mrs. Frances Trollope, the mother of famed English novelist Anthony Trollope, and herself a distinguished writer and world traveler. The trip from Philadelphia to New York was hardly among the worst that she endured in her many travels, especially in the western states, but she did not look upon it with unalloyed delight either. She reported:

> At Trenton, the capital of New Jersey, we left our smoothly-gliding comfortable boat for the most detestable stage-coach that ever a Christian built to dislocate the joints of his fellow men. Ten of those torturing machines were crammed full of passengers who left the boat with us.[8]

There was, said Mrs. Trollope, an immediate and pronounced change in the disposition of the passengers. Young men, who had been lounging on board ship, attempting to catch the attention of young maidens, now looked more like men who had been turned on a torturer's wheel than leisured dandies preparing for a conquest. The teams of horses all started off at a gallop. This was the "King's Highway," with no foot-high tree stumps or mud quagmires; still, the journey was such that no one would choose to take it who was not under the command of necessity. Accordingly, two of the nation's largest cities, although less than a hundred miles apart, were still separated by a formidable natural barrier that continued to reinforce the notion that the United States were not really united, but rather separate mini-nations, each of markedly different style and cultural complexion.

But if that is the way things were in the 1820s, a great transportation revolution was now about to erupt. It was one that would completely alter the spirit of the nation, and bring about a long-sought unification of the American people. The innovation that would bring about these changes, was, of course, the railroad.

In 1820, there was not a single mile of railroad anywhere in the United States, and the railroad would make a slow and inauspicious start over the next two decades. Gradually, although often clouded in controversy and even scandal, it would be embraced warmly by the American people, and it would become the nation's first big business. The railroad would be the principal agency that provided the arteries and transfusion lines needed to make a once insular and isolated people into the nation of Americans we all know today.

C·H·A·P·T·E·R 2

THE COMING OF
THE IRON HORSE

It may seem remarkable today, but the railroad did not win immediate popularity in America, even though the youthful nation seemed the ideal place for this clearly revolutionary form of transportation. Here was a vast territory, with poor roads, with waterways that reached only a limited area of the country. Here were a people constantly clamoring for "internal improvements," for better means of transportation and communication. Here were a people who appreciated enterprise and invention, and who were driven to a frenzy by the introduction of Fulton's steamboat in 1807. Here were a people who eagerly embraced canals, toll roads, turnpikes, plank roads, and every other transportation fad or fancy of the day—anything that might facilitate travel and transportation—yet who for decades continued to think of railroads as the brainchild of crackpots, visionaries, and impractical dreamers. As late as 1825, there was not a stretch of railroad anywhere in the land, and no such thing as an operating railway locomotive.

There were ample reasons for America's slowness to perceive the virtues of the railroad. The concept of the railroad was a complex one, and confusing to small minds—probably to some capacious minds as well. As we understand it today, the concept "railroad" involves two separate ideas that are now joined, but which need not necessarily have been linked together. "Rail road" or "railway" means the use of specially prepared track, designed to carry heavy loads with reduced friction and making use of a system of guidance that makes it unnecessary for vehicles on such a road or way to be steered. That's one part of the equation. The other part of the equation involves propelling such vehicles by means of steam locomotion, which would permit speeds and tonnage never considered possible before the nineteenth century. But such machines of locomotion did not begin to appear until after 1800, and for a number of years there was considerable resistance to them, mainly because their early versions were crude and impractical. The development of the railroad thus meant the putting together of several technologies, none of which existed in the United States in colonial times, and of which there was little evidence either of their application or practicality.

Truth to tell, things were not really much more advanced in England at the same time, even though that nation was in the midst of its Industrial Revolution. This was probably because one side of the railroad equation—prepared track with reduced friction—was already well recognized and developed, with "railroads" functioning well under horsepower to most people's general satisfaction. Railroads in this sense were anything but new; in ancient times, near the Mediterranean, the Greeks used "rutways" to reduce friction. With the first stirrings of the Industrial Revolution in the sixteenth century, there were textbook illustrations of mines that employed railways or tramways to pull heavy weights in confined spaces, the earliest being found in Germany.[1] English writer Daniel Defoe wrote in the seventeenth century of "a great machine called a Waggon" running on an "artificial road called a Waggon-way." By this time, British mine owners had moved into the forefront of rail technology, and early in the 1600s there were several primitive types of railways that carried coal from a mine to a port or river. By 1800, there were at least two hundred miles of horse-worked track scattered throughout England, the most notable of them in the vicinity of Newcastle-upon-Tyne, where, by the middle of the eighteenth century, there were over twenty separate lines in operation. Rails for this work were being constantly improved. Cast-iron rails were used from the 1770s; a far superior wrought iron "edge rail" from the 1790s.[2]

With the uses of the horse-drawn railroad well worked out by the middle of the eighteenth century, there was not a strong impetus to make changes in a technology that was already well understood. This was true even after 1769, when James Watt patented the first efficient steam engine. Watt himself seemed to be little interested in anything other than stationary engines. He had barricaded himself behind a fortress of patents for his device, had founded a company to build and sell such engines, and was later scornful, if not downright hostile, to others who tried to experiment with steam engines that moved things from place to place. Accordingly, it was a Frenchman named Nicholas Cugnot who made the first self-propelled "steam carriage," which he operated on the streets of Paris. But one of Watt's assistants, William Murdoch by name, also experimented with steam carriages. Apparently, he succeeded in producing some small and workable models, but he was so hectored by Watt and others that he gave up the search for a truly practical railway locomotive.

The historical laurels that by rights should have gone to William Murdoch go instead to Richard Trevithick, a moody and erratic Cornishman, the son of one of Watt's principal rivals. In 1801, Trevithick made a full-size steam carriage intended to run on rails. As soon as he had finished building it, he left it to get up steam while he went to have a drink. When he got back, the boiler had overheated and the carriage was destroyed. Mercurial as he was, Trevithick abandoned the idea for a time, but returned to it in 1803 and 1804. In 1804, he made the first locomotive in the world to run on rails. The machine first turned a wheel on the Pennydarren tramroad, near Merythyr Tydvil in South Wales, on February 13, 1804. "A week later it pulled ten tons of bar-iron from the Pennydarren ironworks to the Glamorganshire Canal, nine miles away. In addition to the iron it hauled seventy sight-seers, 'drawn thither (as well as hundreds of others) by invincible curiosity.'"[3]

Those trials should have been a cause for great celebration; alas, Trevithick had not led the way to acceptance of the railroad as we know it. He had produced a true steam locomotive to be run on a rail, but he had not made a success of his experiments. His machine was too heavy for the track then available, and did considerable damage to it. Also, his locomotive did not really have an adequate boiler—engineers had not found a way to make rolling plates for highpressure boilers. Accordingly, except for a small circular demonstration line in London in 1808, Trevithick made no further progress on his invention, and died an embittered and impoverished man.

During the next few years, a number of other engineers were working on designs for locomotives, but none of them were able to spark the public's imagination or to slough off the superstition that such machines were foolish and impractical. Suddenly, however, the center of the stage was occupied by the first truly great railroad pioneer, George Stephenson (1781–1848), a once illiterate, self-taught engineer who had been born in a grimy workman's house in the colliery village of Wylam on the river Tyne, not far from Newcastle.[4] Stephenson's father had worked in the mines and tended a primitive old steam engine of the kind that most companies of the day used to pump water out of the pits. Young George Stephenson learned everything there was to know about steam engines even before the age of eighteen, at which time he first learned to read and write. After developing a reputation in the Newcastle area as an "engine doctor," as "the man to see" if anything needed fixing, Stephenson was appointed enginewright at the Killingworth Colliery in 1812. These mines had long been served by horse-drawn tramways, and Stephenson immediately found ingenious ways to improve the existing systems. But almost immediately, he began work on a steam locomotive for the line, the first of his many successes being an engine called the Blucher in 1814. (The name was taken from the duke of Wellington's then very popular Prussian comrade-in-arms.)

The British *Dictionary of National Biography* describes George Stephenson as the "inventor and founder of railways," which may seem to be rather extravagant praise. He did not personally make a great many important contributions to the development of the locomotive, and none of his locomotives were tremendous advances over those of Trevithick. Yet the laurels are apt in a larger sense. Stephenson was an able organizer, a planner of tremendous vision and ingenuity, and in the years ahead he came to dominate every phase of the railroad industry. In essence, he made the railroad concept work. His gifts as a natural prophet, gadfly, and all-purpose engineer were to prove even greater than his mechanical skills, and, as he moved into his life's work and into his mature years, he became a man of oracular authority and magisterial bearing, which enabled him, in spite of his humble birth, to mingle freely in the upper reaches of the usually class-conscious English society.

During the years when he was first becoming recognized, Stephenson had the good fortune to be aided in his endeavors by his brilliant son Robert, who had received a formal education in Edinburgh, and whose later innovations in locomotive technology led to the achievements that made British railways the envy of the world in the first half of the nineteenth century. Father and son cross-pollinated one another much in the same way as did the American father-and-son engineering team of John and Washington Roebling in a later generation.

In 1821, a group of promoters in the county of Durham were thinking of building a public tramway between the two towns of Stockton and Darlington, a tramway that would be open for general traffic—to anyone who wanted to transport merchandise, cattle, carriages, or whatever. They were thinking that their tramway would be horse drawn, of course, but they were almost immediately visited by a very persuasive and inspiring George Stephenson—still not nationally known—who somehow convinced the startled developers that one good locomotive could do the work of fifty horses. Not long after, Stephenson was appointed chief engineer of the Stockton and Darlington Railroad, and he and his son Robert, now eighteen, began supervising every phase of the work, from surveying the twenty-five-mile right-of-way to the building of locomotives. The Stockton and Darlington Railroad was officially opened on September 17, 1825, and can rightly be seen as the world's first railroad in the modern sense—the first common-carrier railroad. Stephenson established the gauge of the railroad as four feet eight-and-one-half inches, mainly because that had been the gauge that had been used on most of the colliery railroads. But that width has stuck and predominates on most of the world's railroads today.

Within a few years, the Stephensons, father and son, were engaged in constructing an even larger and more important railway, the Liverpool and Manchester, but before this project was completed, Robert Stephenson, with his advanced locomotive called Rocket, convinced all the world that railroads were the wave of the future. Within a scant few years, everyone was looking to Britain, and to the Stephensons, as the fountainhead of railway engineering know-how.

While all this was going on in England, virtually nothing had happened with the railroad concept in the United States. There was some excuse, of course. England had had several hundred years of experience with horse railways in mining areas. It was considerably ahead of North America in the use of iron, and, above all, in the use of steam engines. There had been a few stationary steam engines imported to America in the eighteenth century, and they were mostly used in ways that were already accepted in Europe. For example, a Col. John Schuyler had imported from England the first steam engine in America. He used it to pump water from his copper mine in North Arlington, in Bergen County, New Jersey, in 1753. And, of course, there was a miraculous boost to the benefits of the steam engine for transportation purposes with the appearance of Robert Fulton's *Clermont* in 1807. But somehow this inspiration did not automatically transfer itself to the railroad. The canal era was then in full swing, and many people were convinced that canals would happily overcome the obstacles to western migration and would meet whatever demand there was for the transportation of heavy freight. At this same time, plank roads and toll roads were all the rage, and were being touted as answers to all the other transportation needs. No one gave railroads a second thought, or so it seemed.

But there were a few people who had kept up with what had been going on in England and championed the cause of the railway. To a certain extent, also, there was a small amount of experience with horse-drawn railways in America going back to the eighteenth century, although these were much more primitive than in England. As early as 1764, there was a cable-operated tramway made of grooved logs in Lewiston, New York. It was apparently used to haul supplies to a military camp.[5]

Another interesting tramway was the Quincy Granite Railroad, built in 1826. Since this was a wooden track faced with iron, some historians have called it the first American railroad. It wasn't that, since it was horse drawn, and continued to be long after the coming of steam locomotives in America.[6] But the road is of considerable historical interest since it hauled much of the stone used for constructing the Bunker Hill Monument.

And there were a number of tinkerers playing around with steam carriages of one sort or another. Most of them were considered crackpots. There was, for example, Oliver Evans, a

Philadelphia blacksmith who was commissioned to build a dredge, but who developed his machine into a curious-looking amphibious craft, which he called an Orukter Amphibolos.[7] It had wheels and a propeller, but when Evans put it on the cobblestone streets of Philadelphia, the axles and the wheels collapsed.

There were a few others who could not be so immediately dismissed. One voice of authority was Col. John Stevens, a distinguished veteran of the Revolutionary War and a farsighted engineer. Even before the rage for canals and toll roads had reached its peak, Stevens was dramatically claiming the severe limitations of those means of transportation and championing steam-driven railroads instead. In 1812, even before any digging on the great Erie Canal had begun, Stevens published a pamphlet entitled *Documents Tending to Prove the Superior Advantages of Railway and Steam Carriages over Canal Navigation*. In this, the first published American work on the subject of the railroad, Stevens predicted that locomotives could be built that would attain speeds of fifty miles per hour—perhaps even one hundred miles per hour! He also asserted that transportation costs would be much cheaper than those of canals.[8]

Stevens was anything but a novice when it came to steam engines. He had already established the world's first steam ferry boat—this on the Hudson River—and another steamboat of his, the *Phoenix*, had been the first to venture into open sea. Stevens had also been one of the early entrepreneurs who sought to upgrade the transportation facilities across New Jersey between New York and Philadelphia. With his vast experience and with his sterling reputation, in the year 1815, he would appeal to the New Jersey state legislature for a charter to build a steam railway in that state. The charter was granted, but funds to actually build the railroad were not forthcoming.

In the years ahead, Stevens made himself a committee of one to sell the railroad idea to the American public. Always treated courteously, although doubtless with some snickers behind his back, he was never able to find financial backing for his projects. When Stevens heard the details of the construction of the Stockton and Darlington railway in England, he stepped up his efforts, and in 1825, built a small circular track on his estate in Hoboken, New Jersey (now the site of Stevens Institute of Technology), and ran a small experimental engine on it. Although this machine was little more than a toy, it was remarkable from an engineering point of view. It had a vertical boiler capable of reaching the astonishingly high pressure of five hundred pounds per square inch (compared to only twenty-five pounds per square inch on Trevithick's engine). This little machine, which Stevens called a "Steam Waggon," ran around its circular track at the speed of twelve miles an hour. This was the first operation of a steam carriage on a railway track in the United States.

Although John Stevens has sometimes been called the father of railroading in America, the term is apt only in the broad philosophical sense. In a few years, Stevens (who, like George Stephenson in England, was blessed with a resourceful son also to become a famous railroad pioneer) would come to play a role in the establishment of one of America's earliest railroads, the Camden and Amboy. But this was not the result of the 1825 experiment. Before the Stevenses, father and son, turned their skills to good account, there were several other major developments in American railroading, each of which have claimed the honor of being the "first" American railroad.

The first true steam locomotive to operate in the United States, although not the work of Colonel Stevens, surely did result from his well-publicized experiment. Among those who saw the light at Hoboken was one John Jervis, then chief engineer of the Delaware and Hudson Canal Company. In 1828, his company built a nine-mile stretch of track between its mines and the end of the canal at Honesdale, Pennsylvania. Like all such railroads of the time, the intent was that it should be horse operated. But the grades were steep, and Jervis wondered if he might be able to obtain a locomotive to perform the work with much greater ease. Accordingly, he sent his assistant Horatio Allen to England, and Allen watched Robert Stephenson's Rocket in action at the famous Rainhill Trials. Allen was commissioned to order two locomotives for the Delaware and Hudson Canal Co.

One of these locomotives was the Stourbridge Lion. It arrived in New York aboard the clipper ship *Columbia* on January 15, 1829, and was tried out at Honesdale on August 8, 1829, with Horatio Allen at the controls. (Historians have never been able to determine what happened to the second locomotive that was ordered.) This date marks the first running of a true railroad locomotive in the United States. The operation of the machine left much to be desired, unfortunately. It was too heavy for the track (it weighed eight tons, five more than the company had hoped for), and the experiment proved as fatal as that of Richard Trevithick's engine at the Pennydarren mine in England. The Stourbridge Lion was abandoned, put in a little shanty beside the road, and slowly disintegrated over many years, after which it was eventually sold for scrap. A fine replica of the machine (which cost the Delaware and Hudson $3,663.30, delivered) was made for Chicago's Century of Progress Exposition in 1933, and photographs show it to have been a handsome and sturdy looking piece of equipment.[9]

Even before the disappointing performance of the Stourbridge Lion, the railroad concept was beginning to cause a stir in other parts of the country, most specifically in Charleston, South Carolina, and Baltimore, Maryland. Both were port cities, and both had grown uneasy over the opening of the Erie Canal in 1825. Neither city could perceive the possibility of building a canal that would meet the needs of transportation to the west in their terrain, while the railroad concept held out at least a faint hope that they might remain competitive. Both cities began thinking of railroads as common carriers, and charters for railway lines were quickly forthcoming. Baltimore moved first, but numerous railroad historians have insisted that the tiny Charleston and Hamburg Railroad was the first in America to run a "train" of cars pulled by a steam locomotive on track specifically designed for that purpose.

The city of Baltimore has occasionally been called the "Mother of Railroads," and not without some justification. Even though the city was the starting point for the famous National Road, there were a number of prominent citizens who believed that railroads in some form provided the only answer to the city's transportation needs. And they weren't thinking of some little experimental track, or modest coal-hauling road. Instead, they were thinking of something even more ambitious than George Stephenson's Stockton and Darlington. Accordingly, a group of spirited citizens and financial backers sought, and obtained, from the Maryland legislature, a charter to build a "Baltimore and Ohio Railroad." It was a grandiose project that some people would have described as megalomanic—a railroad that would run several hundred miles, over mountains and rivers. In truth, the Baltimore and Ohio

Railroad would not reach Ohio for twenty-four years. In only a few years, however, a thirteen-mile line from Baltimore to Ellicott's Mills became a veritable cradle and showcase of early American railroading.

The backers and directors of the Baltimore and Ohio Railroad Company were thinking big in every area but one: motive power. The initial stretch of the line was planned for horsepower, and consisted of strap rails, or "snakehead rails," which seemed to rule out steam power if that was later decided upon. On the other hand, the money men in Baltimore did not have closed minds; they were willing to accept experimentation, and even before the first stretch of track was completed to Ellicott's Mills, a number of inventors were allowed to offer suggestions and try out their own pet schemes for motive power. One invention that was tried was a locomotive that was not pulled by a horse, but operated by a horse tramping on a kind of treadmill that supplied power to the axels. Evan Thomas, brother of the road's first president, Philip Thomas, built a sailing car for the rails which he called the Meteor. Needless to say, both of these systems proved to be completely impractical.

It seemed only sensible that a steam engine ought to be given a try also. Unfortunately, the track was not designed for such heavy usage. Furthermore, there were some curves on the line that were believed to be too sharp for the kinds of speeds that might be expected. But a young man newly moved to the city from New York seemed willing to see what he could do in spite of these impediments. His name was Peter Cooper, a self-made tinker, with only a year of formal education, who had spent his youth apprenticed to a carriage maker, during which time he had invented a machine for mortising the hubs of carriages. In a small iron foundry he owned in Baltimore, he put together, from extremely crude materials, a dimunitive locomotive, which he christened the Tom Thumb. Little more than a toy locomotive really, it was designed with those forbidding curves in mind—just as a demonstration model.

The Tom Thumb was only a one-horsepower engine, but in an experimental trial on August 28, 1830, it hauled a load of thirty-six people at speeds up to eighteen miles per hour. Directors of the company were duly impressed by this achievement, but there were not a few doubters. And others were downright hostile, including a number of local stagecoach operators who challenged Peter Cooper's one-horsepower engine to a race. On the appointed day, the horse-drawn carriage started off at a fast clip, but the locomotive soon built up power and speed and overtook the horse. The locomotive was well in the lead when the belt that operated the fan for the fire slipped from its pulley, and before it could be repaired, the horse won the race.[10] But the vast lead that had been built up by the tiny locomotive had not gone unappreciated by the directors of the railroad. Peter Cooper did not continue with his locomotive experiments—although he did go on to become one of the best known and most admired businessmen in America, and a candidate for the presidency late in his life! But his audacity caught the admiration of a number of other Baltimore engine builders who took the lead in transforming the Baltimore and Ohio into a true steam operated railroad during the 1830s.

Meanwhile, down in South Carolina, the Charleston and Hamburg directors were having no doubts about the usefulness of steam. They hired Horatio Allen, fresh from his experiments with the Stourbridge Lion, to build a really good steam locomotive for their road. Allen, who had consulted widely in England with the best locomotive builders of the day, commissioned the West Point Foundry in New York City (no connection of any kind with the U.S. Military Academy), to build a locomotive for him. He named it The Best Friend of Charleston. On Christmas day of 1830, with cannons firing salutes on the first car, and with 141 dignitaries riding in several trailing coaches, Allen guided his engine over the portion of the railroad that had been built up to that time. This was the first scheduled steam "train" to be operated in America.

The third center of early railroad development was, of all places, the state of New York, which seemed to have its east-west transportation problems solved with the opening of the Erie Canal. But the Erie Canal, it was quickly discovered, was not at all suitable as a passenger carrier, and had virtually no advantages over the existing stagecoach routes. This was particularly true of the easternmost segment of the canal, between Albany and Schenectady, a forty-mile time waster which consumed a traveler's entire day. (By stage coach, the distance was only seventeen miles.) Accordingly, in 1826, to make its beloved canal more accessible, the state of New York permitted the chartering of its first railroad, the Mohawk and Hudson, between Albany and Schenectady.

The road was not completed, however, until 1831. In that year, there was an inaugural run of a regular passenger train behind another West Point Foundry engine—the De Witt Clinton. Named for the principal booster of the Erie Canal and a popular governor of New York, recently deceased, the engine was, like most of the early American engines, extremely primitive. It weighed 6,758 pounds, and had four four-foot driving wheels. It had no cab, and the engineer perched on a narrow platform (for some strange reason, there was a small canopy over the fuel on the tender, but none over the engine crew.)[11] On August 13, 1831, the De Witt Clinton set off on its inaugural voyage. It was followed by a few light coaches that were really nothing more than stage coach bodies on flanged wheels, and these followed by several more plain open carriages for less dignified members of the assemblage. The little wood-burning locomotive sent a shower of flames from its smokestack, which burned holes in the clothes of travelers in the open coaches; it jerked and lurched its way down the track; but it also traversed the entire seventeen miles without any real calamity.

If America had been slow to embrace the railroad during its experimental phase, once it was learned, during the 1830s, that even the promoters of the Erie Canal were conceding the superiority of railroads as a form of passenger transit, a mild epidemic of railroad enthusiasm broke out all up and down the eastern seaboard. If cities like Baltimore and Charleston had railroads, so, too, must Philadelphia, New York, and so on. New York City's first railroad was the New York and Harlem, opened as a horse line in 1832. The horses were kept until 1837, however, so that the railroad was not one of the true railway pioneers. Still, from a historical perspective, the Harlem was an important milestone, and eventually gave the New York Central Railroad its valuable foothold in the island of Manhattan.

The year 1832 was a seminal one in American railroad history. In that year, Philadelphia also entered the competition, opening for business the Philadelphia, Germantown, and Norristown Railroad (or, more precisely, a six-mile segment of it between Philadelphia and Germantown), the road that was eventually to become one of the building blocks of the Reading Railroad. One short-term benefit of the early Pennsylvania road was that it attracted the talents of Matthias Baldwin, who was to become one of the nation's great locomotive builders. Baldwin, a former jeweler and watchmaker, had exhibited a small locomotive on a circular track in the Philadelphia Museum in 1831, and the amusement it provided to the passengers who rode in its dimunitive passenger cars (much like those that can be found in amusement or theme parks today), served as a great spark to the public's imagination.

Of most immediate significance in this watershed year of 1832 was the beginning of operations on the Camden and Amboy Railroad—a railroad that attempted to respond to the long-felt need for superior transportation across New Jersey between New York and Philadelphia. The Camden and Amboy would be a big enterprise, bigger than any of its day, and very early in its history it became a passenger carrier of epic proportions.

The history of the railroad went back a few years, to 1830, when the state of New Jersey granted a charter for the construction of a railroad between Raritan Bay and the Delaware River. The charter was granted, as was only proper, to the Stevens family of Hoboken, and the first president and chief engineer of the road was Robert Livingston Stevens, the son of Col. John Stevens. This time, however, the charter was more than just a scrap of paper. For a change, with railroad fever rampant in the land, financial backers rushed to the fore. When the subscription books were opened, the entire stock of the railroad, one million dollars, was sold in ten minutes![12]

Colonel Stevens, now eighty years old, proposed that the railroad run between New Brunswick and Trenton, the best choice no doubt, but his two sons, Robert and Edwin, decided upon South Amboy and Bordentown instead (with Camden added as an afterthought). Before any construction began, Robert Stevens set sail for England, with the intent of bringing home the best locomotive he could find. But he also had a bigger problem on his mind. Although the route that had been surveyed between Bordentown and Perth Amboy was an easy one, Stevens knew that none of the railroads existing or planned in America had the kind of rail or roadbed that could stand up to the heavy traffic he was expecting on his line. He also knew that no foundry in America was capable of turning out the kind of heavy-duty rail he needed, so he would have to order his rails in England also. While on the high seas, he gave considerable thought to the design of his rail, and borrowing a chunk of pinewood from the ship's carpenter he whittled with his jackknife the first crude T-rail—essentially the same rail design used everywhere today except for weight and height. He also carved out the first "hook-headed" spike and the "iron tongue" or fishplate used to join rails, the designs of which have also not changed essentially over the years.[13]

While in England, Stevens saw the latest engine design of Robert Stephenson, the Planet, and ordered an identical machine to be shipped to him in America. This locomotive, known as John Bull, arrived by sea at Bordentown in 1831—in crates, and completely unassembled. Stevens assigned the job of putting the ten-ton locomotive together to a twenty-two-year-old machinist named Isaac Dripps, who had never seen a steam locomotive either assembled or disassembled. Nonetheless, Dripps managed to assemble the machine and prepare it for a trial run. No tender had come with the engine, so Dripps built a small flat car and purchased from a local grocer a whiskey cask to be used as a water tank. From a Bordentown shoemaker, he ordered a leather hose to carry water to the engine's boilers.

The John Bull had its first successful trial run at Bordentown on November 12, 1831. In the meantime, several boatloads of rails had arrived from England (one cargo ship, alas, sank under its heavy load), and the railroad's thirty-six-mile main stretch between Bordentown and Perth Amboy was under swift construction. While the track was going down, Dripps and Robert Stevens adjourned to Hoboken, where they set to work building three more locomotives of their own design for the railroad. They would be big machines by comparison with the John Bull, and they would be sorely needed when the Camden and Amboy was put in full operation. One of them, appropriately named the Monster, weighed forty tons, and had forty-eight-inch driving wheels. It was to remain in service on the Camden and Amboy for many years.

The rails of the Camden and Amboy reached Perth Amboy in December 1832, and regular passenger service began immediately thereafter. The service was popular from the very beginning. Travel time between New York and Philadelphia was reduced to seven hours (sea and rail time combined). At a fare of three dollars, the Camden and Amboy carried 110,000 people during its first year of operation. The era of rail transportation had truly arrived.

On the other hand, during the 1830s, which were nothing more than an incubation period for the railroad, railroads did not make a strong impact on the American people. Since railroad mileage was small during this period, there was little cause for alarm about these little lines, and, with a few exceptions, not many complaints about their coming. Americans embraced this new form of transportation as they have most newfangled devices—as an amusing but possibly useful addition to the scheme of things.

There were opponents, to be sure. Breeders of horses, stagecoach operators, and others whose livelihood might be threatened by the iron horse put up a hue and cry for a while, although they were invariably drowned out by those actually touched by the conveniences that the railroad provided. So, too, in time, were operators or canals, toll roads, and the like, all of whom were silenced by the railraod's manifest superiority as a common carrier of passengers.

There were a few other problems in these first few years. In the early 1830s, hardly anybody in the United States had ever seen a locomotive engine, and the first appearance of the snorting, fiery beast could be a terror to some. There were a few who were reluctant to ride on such a contraption, and believed it to be the work of the devil. However quaint that reaction may seem today, it must be recalled that in 1830 few Americans had ever seen a steam engine of any kind, stationary or mobile. The steam, the smoke, the sparks emitted from the belly of the monster were quite sufficient to invoke anxiety, if not downright terror, in timid souls who drew nigh the early demonstration runs.

Troubles with the awesome physical presence of the locomotive arose long before Stephenson went to work. Legend has it that William Murdoch, the friend and assistant of Watt, who had incurred the master's wrath by experimenting with steam carriages, had a nip of trouble with the first machine he tried out. One night, after leaving his job at the Redruth mine in Cornwall, Murdoch decided to run his engine on a little lane that led out of town and toward the parish church—a lane surrounded by hedges on each side. Murdoch heated up his boiler, and his engine, fitted up with wheels to run on the ground, started up briskly with its inventor in hot pursuit. Coming down the lane was the village pastor, who fled in terror at the sight of this flaming, hissing monster. He took it to be the devil himself, or at least one of his helpers. It hardly needs be said that Murdoch's name was mud in town thereafter.

In its later guises, the railroad locomotive, forced to keep to its rail, would seem to provoke little anxiety that it would run amok and seek out innocent victims. Or so it seems from the vantage point of hindsight. Nonetheless, there were numerous broadsides, editorials, and so on lamenting that locomotives might seek out innocent women and children and perhaps carry out the work of the devil or acts of vengeance against civilization. On some early lines, such fears might have been justified. On the New York and Harlem Railroad, which was begun as a horse-drawn line running on city streets, there was fear that numerous accidents would result. And they did. Braking on the early steam cars was often not adequate, and the inevitable collisions between locomotives and pedestrians occurred. The local press made much of this, running sick jokes about the deadly new form of transportation. Cartoonists showed Bowery locomotives plowing their way through groups of men, women, and children, and occasionally took the license of showing the machines leaving their rails and chasing people down side streets.

Generally, though, when the iron horse made its first appearance in a particular locale, the reception was one of breathless expectation and delight. The backers and planners of all the early railroads saw to it that their first demonstration runs were occasions of festivity and did all that they could to stir up public enthusiasm. The first trip of the Best Friend of Charleston in South Carolina was to the tune of a brass band and the explosions of artillery fire and fireworks.

Building up suspense to a demonstration run in a place where there had been no iron horse before was half of the public relations battle. In Bordentown, New Jersey, when the John Bull arrived and was uncrated, there was much local curiosity about the iron beast during the weeks it was being assembled by Isaac Dripps. Among the village loafers and roisterers, there was considerable skepticism and scoffing. Some young wags insisted that no such machine could possibly be made to move on wheels. "Even if it is like a tea kettle," they scoffed, "and the steam has enough power to make the lid pop up and down, you can't get a kettle itself to move."

Still, for all of the skepticism, when the great day arrived for John Bull to be unleashed from its pen, everyone from miles around was on hand—the scoffers included. There were people lined up on both sides of the track, with the timid naturally seeking the back rows in anticipation of the explosion they felt sure to occur. As Dripps's fireman Ben Higgins stuffed big chunks of pinewood into the firebox and as black puffs of smoke poured from the smokestack, some may have believed that the end of the world was near. Still, they stayed, even those close up, who were being sooted up by ash. A big cheer went up from the crowd as the John Bull, pressure up, moved resolutely down the track.

Robert Stevens, talented in the ways of the yet undiscovered art of public relations, had provided long tables filled with oyster soup and other good refreshments, and even the most contemptuous scoffers filed by to partake of the celebration while John Bull was out on its track. When the locomotive returned with its single flat coach carrying a group of delighted dignitaries and officials, Colonel Stevens offered a ride to all comers. More people wanted to ride than could be taken. Even women were game, and Mr. Stevens saw to it that the first lady to board was the tremendously attractive young Madame Murat, niece by marriage to Napoleon, who was determined to be the first woman to ride on the Camden and Amboy.

Women, interestingly, were seldom among the scoffers and doubters in these early days. They usually took to the steam cars with passionate enthusiasm. Contrary to the mythology of many twentieth-century historians, women of these times were not reticent souls who did nothing but tend the hearth. When hot air balloons first came along, women were among the first to go up. The steam railway immediately fascinated them, perhaps in part because it offered some alternative to the much-despised stagecoach. On the other hand, they loved the iron horse for its own sake, and were not often among the timid and bashful. In England, in 1830, on the first public excursion of the Liverpool and Manchester Railway, among the wildly enthusiastic passengers was the celebrated actress Fanny Kemble, then playing at a

Liverpool theater. Miss Kemble was infatuated not only by the iron horse, but by its master, George Stephenson, as well. She wrote afterward to a friend:

> Now for a word or two about the master of all these marvels, with whom I am most horribly in love. He is a man from fifty to fifty-five years of age. (George Stephenson was actually forty-nine.) His face is fine, though careworn, and bears an expression of deep thoughtfulness. His mode of explaining his ideas is peculiar and very original, striking and forcible. Although his accent indicates strongly his north country birth, his language has not the slightest touch of vulgarity or coarseness. He has certainly turned my head.[14]

All this should not lead to the conclusion that travel on the early railroads was a significant advance in comfort. Some of the people who stepped on board those early trains—Fanny Kemble being one of them, no doubt—savored a touch of the hazardous, and they usually had their desires gratified. Even under the best of circumstances, the cars of the early railroads gave a very jarring ride. Sometimes they were nothing more than flatcars with seats attached. At best, they were modified stagecoaches fitted up for the rail. Brakes were very crude, and usually worked much like stage coach brakes—some crew member would put his foot on a long foot lever. But often this application didn't take hold. Many times the engineer had to wait for steam pressure to subside, if he did not first sail into some frightening collision.

Even worse from the perspective of passenger comfort, the couplings between cars were loose iron links, so that when the engine started, passengers' necks were almost dislocated, or they were thrown bodily to the floor. Furthermore, the sparks from the wood-burning locomotives would regularly land right on passengers, always exposed to the elements. Those who rode in the open cars on the first run of the De Witt Clinton spent the whole trip putting out one another's flames. On the inaugural trip of the first scheduled train on New England's earliest railroad, the Boston and Lowell, even the inside passengers got punished. Sparks blew inside and ignited ladies' satin dresses and ruined the carriage upholstery. Still, according to railroad historian Alvin Harlow, the conflagration did not seem to dampen enthusiasm.

When the first train arrived in Lowell from Boston, "the yelling, hat-waving throng on the hillside ... the fireworks, the banquet that followed, the heady stimulus of the wines and flowery speeches made the discomforts seem worth while, even though one's best clothing was flicked with spark holes."[15]

During the first decade of the railroad's existence, the railroad was mostly an object of awe, excitement, and mild trepidation. Few at the time bothered to speculate on whether railroads had a future, whether they were anything other than a novel form of amusement. Surely fewer still could have predicted that the railroad would rapidly become an American institution of earth-shattering importance and the railroad industry the greatest and most powerful in the land.

It was plain, though, that if this newfangled machine could be perfected, it would make a vast difference in the social fabric. For one truth was not doubted right from the start: The railroad was faster than any existing forms of transportation. Not only a little faster, but a great deal faster. And a perception arose among the multitudes that with a little improvement and technical development it might be made more comfortable as well.

There were, of course, doubts and admonitions about fast travel. Why was it needed? What reason to get somewhere an hour or so quicker? And what was there at the end of the line anyway? Smug, self-satisfied Bostonians, who held back for a few years and watched the goings on in Baltimore, Philadelphia, and New York, scorned the doings of these "Flying Yankees" and jibed, as Bostonians frequently have: "Why should I travel. I'm already here." (In only a few years, however, Boston was being served by not one but three railroads.)

Nevertheless, there was perhaps some unease, some vague rueful anticipation, that an instrument had been born that would in time drastically change the nature of the American landscape and the American character. In 1830, way out in Vincennes, Indiana, where nobody had seen a steam locomotive, where people only read about them in the county papers, one native Hoosier wit questioned the whole railroad frenzy with a funny broadside that nonetheless expressed the skepticism of many—skepticism that a railroad might start taking over things as they had been known and loved. Take over and take charge.

I see what will be the effect of it; that it will set the whole world a-gadding. Twenty miles an hour, sir!—Why, you will not be able to keep an apprentice boy at his work! Every Saturday evening he must have a trip to Ohio to spend a Sunday with his sweetheart. Grave plodding citizens will be flying around like comets. All local attachments will be at an end. It will encourage flightiness of intellect. Veracious people will turn into the most immeasurable liars. All conceptions will be exaggerated by the magnificant notions of distance.—Only a hundred miles off! Tut, nonsense, I'll step across madam, and bring you your fan!

... And then, sir, there will be barrels of pork, cargoes of flour, chauldrons of coal, and even lead and whiskey, and such like sober things that have been used to slow travelling—whisking away like a sky rocket. It will upset all the gravity of the nation .... Upon the whole, sir, it is a pestilential, topsy-turvy, haram-scarum whirligig. Give me the old, solemn, straight forward, regular Dutch Canal—three miles an hour for expresses, and two rod jogtrot journeys—with a yoke of oxen for heavy loads. I go for beasts of burden. It is more formative and scriptural, and suits a moral and religious people better.—None of your hop skip and jump whimsies for me.[16]

These, then, were the whimsies of the crackerbarrel philosopher in 1830. Probably not a wholly accurate expression of the American conscience. But the same chords were to be heard in the years ahead, often with darker and more ominous overtones.

C·H·A·P·T·E·R 3

THE SPREADING RAILROAD FEVER

During the 1830s, after years of public skepticism, the railroad spread rapidly throughout the eastern part of the United States. In the northeast, in settled areas, and along well-worn urban corridors, railroads quickly supplanted other forms of transportation—canals and turnpikes—which had themselves just come into existence and had only recently been touted as the final answer to the nation's transportation needs.

Canals did not, of course, wither and die right away, and many of them continued to be built in the 1830s and 1840s. The Morris Canal and the Delaware and Raritan Canal in New Jersey reached their greatest prosperity in the years immediately following the Civil War, even though the latter was in direct competition with the vigorous Camden and Amboy Railroad. In its first few decades, the railroad was mainly a passenger carrier. Its chief virtue was seen to be rapid movement of passengers who previously had to undergo the long, torturesome stage coach journeys of the early republic. Canals, on the other hand, were admirably suited to the transportation of heavy freight in large quantities, something for which the flimsily-built early railroads were unsuited.

The canals, of course, did not want to admit that they were poorly adapted to passenger travel. And, in the beginning, travel on the canal was both more comfortable and safer than on the railroad. But since travel on the canal was markedly slower, the railroad obtained an almost immediate monopoly on passenger traffic in places where canal and railroad were competitors. The Delaware and Raritan Canal, which was in direct competition with the Camden and Amboy, declared itself to have had a "banner" passenger year in 1849, when 136 persons passed through. To be sure, canals also attracted many individuals interested in excursions and pleasure boating. But that could hardly be calculated as a form of utilitarian transport. It was jocularly related that one eloping couple managed to elude an irate father by "speeding away" in a boat on the Delaware and Raritan Canal, but it later turned out that the couple only followed the waterway until they reached the nearest railway station.[1]

During the 1830s, more than three miles of railroad were built for every two miles of canal, so that by 1840 the total mileage of both systems was about equal. In 1840, the railroad industry was still in its infancy, but a great many short lines in the eastern states added up to 3,328 miles of track. In another decade, this mileage would more than double, to 8,879 miles. Yet this was only a mild beginning. Railroad mileage soared from 8,879 in 1850 to 30,626 in 1860.[2] By the time of the Civil War, the railroad was the dominant form of transportation in the United States, and, in the aggregate, the nation's largest business.

In the 1830s and 1840s, railroad fever spread dramatically around the country. During this period, New England, which at first had been wary of this upstart convenience, embraced it with unqualified enthusiasm, and within only a few years, a number of lines were built, with Boston clearly becoming the hub of what would soon be a complex railroad network. The noble heads of the Bay Colony had suffered a considerable loss of pride in the early years of the nineteenth century as other states experimented with tollways and canals, often with considerable success, whereas Massachusetts, once the leader in transportation, fell by the wayside. The state had been a pioneer with canals, constructing the Middlesex Canal between Boston and the Merrimac River from 1793 to 1803. But this canal, the purpose of which was to bring manufactured goods from New Hampshire to Boston without having to go out to sea, was a complete failure, had never accomplished its purpose, and had never made money for its stock holders.

So when the civic leaders of Boston finally took to the railroad idea, they took to it in a big way. They had at first shared the widely held superstition that steam engines would be unreliable on the kind of track with which they were already acquainted through the operation the the Quincy Granite line. But once they became convinced, they threw caution to the wind, and began railroad projects in all directions. Almost immediately, three railroads were built—the Boston and Lowell, the Boston and Providence, and the Boston and Worcester. The first was chartered in 1830; the others the following year. All three were completed and in operation within three years.

During the next several decades, most of New England, with the exception of Maine, was crosshatched with railroad lines in a configuration that is not very different from that which we know in the twentieth century. New England had three-fifths of the railroad miles constructed between 1840 and 1850, and when the 1850s began it was possible to travel from Boston to most of the cities of Massachusetts, and also to Portland, Maine, New Haven, Albany, New York, and even Montreal. It should be clear, however, that the lines of New England, for all their diversity, were seldom more than short local lines that were simply patched together, not the vast trunk systems that we are familiar with today. A trip between Boston and New Haven would invariably mean changing railroads and cars several times, often on lines that were far from cooperative with one another and gave little thought to the amenities of "through" travel. Not until after the Civil War would railroad giants appear—lines like the Boston and Maine and the New York, New Haven and Hartford, both of which were essentially amalgamations of many earlier short lines.

And this is the way it was essentially everywhere in the country during the 1830s and 1840s. Railroads were little more than local carriers, built not to carry people or goods across country, but to carry them between two points that were known to have brisk local traffic. The Boston and Lowell was built because people in Lowell wanted ready access to Boston. The same kind of need had given birth to the Camden and Amboy, the Philadelphia, Germantown, and Norristown, the New York and Harlem, the Paterson and Hudson River Railroad, the Mohawk and Hudson (which was essentially the Albany and Schenectady), and so on.

Nearly all of the railroad building of the first few decades was in the East—east of the Allegheny Mountains, that is. West of the Alleghenies, people were still traveling as they had for years— floating down the Ohio River on flatboats or steamboats, inching their way across the land by means of wagons, prairie schooners, and stage-coaches, and, of course, by horseback and on foot. There were some early railroad experiments beyond the Alleghenies, some of them as early as the 1830s, but few of these seemed to have any compelling practical justification. Ohio's first railroad was the Mad River and Lake Erie Railway, a line projected from Sandusky to Springfield that was begun in 1835. By 1840, it was only thirty miles long. It obtained a locomotive called the Sandusky which was built in Paterson, New Jersey, by The Rogers Locomotive and Machine Works, and shipped to Ohio by way of the Erie Canal and Lake Erie. A silly idea perhaps, but a historical first: This was the first locomotive to turn a wheel west of the Allegheny Mountains.

If Ohio had a railroad, Kentucky had to have one, too. A wild desire to possess a railroad seized the backwoods town of Frankfort, and construction began posthaste. The people of Frankfort had no idea why they needed a railroad or where it would go, but they had read about railroads and so felt they need-ed to have one. A line struck out for the neighboring town of Lexington—strips of iron on limestone slabs that were readily available from local quarries. The railroad was horse drawn for a few years, but then a local mechanic built a crude locomotive. None of these innovations were adequate, however, especially the limestone slabs, which cracked and eventually had to be replaced by timbers.[3] The line carried few passengers and no freight.

Building railroads on the frontier and through the backwoods to nowhere may seem like the height of folly in retrospect, and it certainly seemed so to many foreign observers at the time. On the other hand, frontiersmen were extremely proud and boastful of their place in the scheme of things, in particular the fact that they were on the cutting edge of what Americans had come to think of as progress. It quickly came to be an American trait of character that if some new advance of technology was enjoyed by some, all must enjoy it, even if the immediate practical consequences might seem downright silly. If easterners were building railroads, fron-tier towns must have them also. During the 1830s, during his famous tour of the United States, the French sage Alexis de

Tocqueville found Americans driven by a lust for equality in all things, a trait he found repellent, although he also esteemed it to be responsible for much of the country's vitality and surging dynamism.

Europeans generally never ceased to be amazed at the reckless sense of manifest destiny on the part of Americans.

These foolish Americans planned and dreamed of giant cities, roads, industries, railroads, or whatever, sheerly on the basis of some wild future expectation, not on the basis of proven fact. In England, on the other hand, nobody would ever dream of building a railroad unless the need for it were already firmly established. The first great English railroad, the Liverpool and Manchester, was an answer to a specific need: There was no easy way to get imported goods from the seaport of Liverpool to the bustling manufacturing center of Manchester. The Americans, however, would build railroads between two places, one or both of which might not exist, or, as one English wit put it, a railroad from Nowhere-in-Particular to Nowhere-at-All. In America, it was all a matter of hope and expectation. Nowhere-in-Particular was shortly expected to be Somewhere-Big. People who were "thinking big" put railroads in their plans as soon as they could. They might construct a railroad that merely connected two remote hamlets, Magpie and Hornswoggle, let us say, and then tag the words "and Western" on the end, giving birth to a very impressive sounding line: the Magpie, Hornswoggle, and Western. And the truth is, these upstart lines often did thrive and sometimes joined with other railroads to become part of a true railway system of the sort we know today. Many didn't make it, of course, but it wasn't for lack of trying.

The West, particularly, was imbued with what historian Daniel Boorstin called the "booster spirit"—which is to say it became an American characteristic that even if you started with nothing, or nearly nothing, you could find ways to puff yourself up and sell yourself or your community into something lively and impressive. A small town might thrust itself into prominence, said Boorstin, by means of a booster newspaper, or a booster college (out on the frontier, a college might be nothing but a single professor in a dilapidated building, but at least it was a college, and thus had its drawing powers), and above all by means of the activities of local businessmen, drummers of trade, civic pep groups, and all the rest.

The faith always was that since the eastern parts of the nation had arisen dramatically from primitive communities, so, too, could the latest frontier town, if the drum was beaten loudly enough. Admittedly, sometimes the booster imagination ran riot. As late as 1881, Superior City, Montana, consisted of nothing but a log house and a barn.[4] On the other hand, the power of the booster spirit can hardly be underestimated by students of American history. The people of Pig's Eye, Minnesota, used more than a little imagination when they built a "cathedral" and changed the name of their town to St. Paul. It is now the capital of the state.

This is not to say that railroad fever was due to nothing but the booster spirit in the 1830s and 1840s. The railroad had proven its merit, and there was no doubt that a form of transportation had been found that could cement together the spacious, discontinuous, and often isolated parts of a young, vast, and rapidly growing republic. Still, passion for the railroad was a major ingredient in its climb to success during these years. With its utility proven conclusively, the railroad was universally seen as vital to all economic growth and social well-being.

Consider the case of the Erie Railroad, conceived and built as a link between the Hudson River and Lake Erie, that is, between the Atlantic Ocean and the Great Lakes. The Erie was America's first real trunk railroad, the first line to realize the kind of lofty objectives that were really only boasted of in such names as "Baltimore and Ohio." From the very beginning, it was envisioned not as a local carrier but as a giant, thrusting its way westward over mountains and rivers, through difficult terrain, across the whole width of the state of New York.

Curiously, though, it was not this overreaching goal of linking the lakes to the ocean that sold the idea of the Erie to the citizens of New York. Indeed, New York already had such a link in the Erie Canal, and the canal interests would fight the coming of the "Erie Railroad" tooth and nail. But the reason the canal interests were defeated was that numerous communities along the way, communities that had no transportation at all, created such an uproar in the state legislature that the canal interests had to back down and allow the Erie Railroad to be chartered. It was obvious to all concerned that the Erie Canal, which ran through the central part of the state, did little, if anything at all for the counties of the lower tier.

The impetus for the Erie came about in a characteristically

American way. A young lady from Ramapo, New York, Mrs. Henry Pierson, was traveling through South Carolina on her honeymoon when the Best Friend of Charleston made its inaugural run. Hearing of the event in advance, she implored her husband to let her be among the passengers; the husband, as a dutiful bridegroom, consented, and the two were immediately bitten by the railroad bug. The Piersons were the first honeymooning couple to ride on a train in America. But, more importantly, they were in a better position than most people to spread the railroad idea far and wide. Mr. Pierson's father, Jeremiah Pierson, was one of the nation's first captains of industry. He owned several thousands of acres of land near Ramapo, and in the vicinity he also owned tanneries, a cotton mill, iron works, and a nail factory. He had a son-in-law named Eleazar Lord, who was one of the leading financiers in New York City. When the young Piersons returned from their honeymoon, Mrs. Pierson wasted no time painting the railroad in glowing terms to her father-in-law and brother-in-law. She was convinced that a railroad could be built across the southern tier of New York, serving all the communities therein, and that a trip between the Hudson River and Lake Erie would take a mere twenty-four hours. (She proved to be cannily prophetic: When the Erie was opened to its full length, the trip took almost exactly twenty-four hours.)

But it wasn't merely the influence of a few rich and powerful individuals that brought the Erie into being. The numerous towns along the proposed right-of-way had their say: Newspapers were filled with editorials on the need for a railroad. Men of business everywhere roared; state legislators cajoled, threatened, and ranted. In short, every art of persuasion known to democratic statecraft was eventually brought to bear on the project. So the idea, then finally the railroad itself, moved inexorably forward.

The undertaking was not an easy one. Construction was begun in 1833, but it took eighteen years for the line to be completed from Piermont on the Hudson River to Dunkirk on Lake Erie. During those years, in spite of relentless enthusiasm, the Erie was always in a peck of trouble. The terrain was difficult; there was difficulty raising money (even though Eleazer Lord was the road's first president and had plenty of clout in Wall Street); the state of New York blew hot and cold on the project, sometimes appropriating funds, sometimes backing away; there were troubles obtaining

land (railroad executives quickly found that anyone who heard
that a railroad was coming their way would ask exorbitant prices
for their farm or woodland); there was trouble obtaining decent
labor; and so on. As a business enterprise, the Erie lurched and
pitched from side to side. On more than one occasion, the treasury was empty, and during these years, the railroad went through
what turned out to be the first of many bankruptcies. Still, with
the help of its early leaders, Eleazar Lord and especially Benjamin
Loder, the Erie got built. And by and large, it was built well to the
best standards of the day. The Starrucca Viaduct, near
Susquehanna, was one of many marvels of the line. A bridge of
1,200 feet, composed of solid bluestone arches, it was built in 1847
and intended to carry diminutive locomotives and wooden cars
far above the creek and valley below. The viaduct is still in service
today, however, and is capable of carrying the loads of four-hun-
dred-ton locomotives and freight trains of 150 cars. It carries such
loads with ease, and without a tremor.

When the Erie was finished, it was called "The Work of the
Age." Not a few people likened it to the wonders of the ancient
world—the pyramids, perhaps, or the Colosseum of Rome. The
day that the railroad was opened from the Hudson River to Lake
Erie, May 14, 1851, railroad management staged what surely must
have been among the great celebrations of American history.
President Millard Fillmore was invited to attend and he did. So,
too, came governors, senators, cabinet members, bankers, prominent citizens—everybody who was anybody. Starting from
Piermont (a number of miles upriver from New York City (which
point was reached by steamboat), a series of trains festooned with
banners started out over the line and were greeted at every town
and hamlet by cheering crowds, sometimes by bands and
fireworks. The weather all day was delightful. America's elder
statesman Daniel Webster was along, and rode by himself on a
freight car—a big easy rocking chair provided for him was lashed
firmly to the floor. From this superlative vantage point, he had an
unobstructed view of some of the most lyrical scenery found anywhere in the East.[5]

The grand and tumultuous celebration that punctuated the
completion of the Erie's New York State lines was, if anything,
something of an anticlimax for Erie officials. They had been
through the same thing many times before as the railroad inched

its way westward for eighteen years. Every time the railroad arrived at a new town, the roars of approval were deafening; the mayor and President Benjamin Loder had to give a speech to the multitudes; everyone adjourned to the best inn or hotel in town for a great collation. The coming of the railroad was the grandest and most awe-inspiring event that had ever been witnessed in these towns, some of them soon to be leading cities of the area. The Erie railroad was the work of the age, and its work was to breathe life into communities that were isolated from the rest of the nation. It would link these people firmly to all their fellow citizens.

For those of us in the twentieth century who have long taken the railroad for granted, it is perhaps impossible to imagine how great an event was the coming of the railroad to the isolated communities of the early nineteenth century—an event that everyone immediately understood would change their lives and their destinies forever. Consider the coming of the railroad three years earlier to the already important town of Binghamton, which was reached on December 27, 1848. Two hundred miles of Erie had been built, making it already the longest railroad in the United States. It was a cold, snowy day, and the train, carrying dignitaries, officials of the road, and other important personages was supposed to arrive at dinnertime. A great feast had been laid out in the car house, and crowds of enthusiastic onlookers were on hand. Hours passed—seven, eight, ten o'clock in the evening came and went; the crowd thinned as some people went home to their beds. There was as yet no telegraph in operation, and some fear was expressed that something may have gone awry. Then, the great moment arrived, as described by a reporter from the *Binghamton Democrat:*

> Midnight, the sound of a distant whistle came booming down the line. Bang! Bang! went the cannon and suddenly all was excitement. Many who had gone home and retired to rest arose and repaired to the depot grounds. The cooks and waiters set themselves to the final arrangements at the long tables. The firing of cannon continued. The whistle sounded nearer and louder and the long pent-up hurrahs of the crowd, becoming more enthusiastic, altogether marred the usual midnight stillness of our quiet village. At this moment the stately train, drawn by the panting locomotives, approached and halted at the car house where the refreshments were in waiting. From 300 to 400 passengers alighted and entered

the car-house and began at once the discussion of the merits and
bounties of the table.[6]

The railroad was immediately perceived to be something of and
for the people, an instrument of utility, an instrument that would
change the way people lived and behaved. The railroad, of course,
reached out to many towns and hamlets that would not be transformed in actual fact, would perhaps remain insignificant dots on
the map for all time, perhaps would disappear, but the railroad
was universally celebrated wherever it went because it provided a
link with the wider world, an anodyne for isolation.

Scrutinized more carefully, of course, the first few decades of
railroad history held far more promise of an instantly mobile society than the technology of the day would permit. Equipment was
primitive in those times; the roadbed and the rail were often poorly constructed, passenger cars were uncomfortable, and, what is
worse, unsafe; the right-of-way more often than not was ill conceived, hastily planned and executed, so that later it would have to
be completely relaid; there were few if any standardized railway
practices and procedures (in these last two categories, American
railroads were especially inferior to those of Europe in the years
before the Civil War). Individual railroad lines were built to the
eccentric standards of their owners, many of whom were poorly
informed about the latest developments of railway technology or
were otherwise willful or stubborn. The Erie Railroad, when it was
first laid, used a six-foot gauge, mainly because when the railroad
was chartered, New York state legislators wanted to be assured that
the railroad would not "mate" with other lines beyond the border
of the state. This eventually led to financial catastrophe for the
Erie, which, in the 1870s, would have to completely rebuild its
entire line to standard gauge at great expense.

Conditions of travel on the early American railroads were primitive in the extreme, and would doubtless seem deplorable to anyone familar with the railroads of today. To be sure, in the early
days, passengers thought of this great innovation as such a vast
improvement over the already existing forms of transportation
that they gladly accepted everything that a railroad journey dished
out. Railroad travel had a touch of the exciting and the perilous
about it, and people gave up a great deal, even gladly putting life

and limb in jeopardy, to be able to get where they were going in only a fraction of the time that had been previously required.

Curiously, early trains were every bit as uncomfortable as the despised stagecoaches; it is just that they got people over their journey much quicker, and those who were intrigued by the dramatic powers of the iron horse tended to forgive discomforts that they would not have abided in stagecoaches. The discomforts and dangers were due to numerous causes. Most of the early railroads were incompetently constructed and engineered. In many places, the rails were still nothing but length of strap iron, insecurely fastened to wooden stringers. Only in rare instances was the track laid with ballast; accordingly, it was completely exposed to the vicissitudes of the weather. In the winter, the rails were liable to be dislocated by ice and snow; in the spring, the line was not infrequently buried in mud; in the summer, weeds grew between the ties, and the unballasted track bed threw up a cloud of dust, which, when combined with the smoke and sparks from the locomotives, made for a near asphyxiating ride for the long-suffering passengers.

The early passenger cars were linked together by a crude chain or bar that violently jerked the passengers whenever the train started or stopped. The right-of-way was invariably full of sharp curves and vicious bumps. When strap rails were still in use, some of these (popularly called "snakeheads") would pop up through the floorboards and gouge or impale passengers.

Derailments were frequent, so frequent in fact that some early railway tickets included a clause to the effect that passengers were liable to help put the engines or cars back on the track again. The early railroads were seldom fenced or otherwise protected—in this they differed from English railways, which, from the beginning, were well protected. Livestock frequently wandered out on the track just when a train came along, usually derailing the train and slaughtering the poor beast to the dismay of some neighboring farmer. These butcherings were considerably reduced when locomotives were finally fitted up with "cowcatchers"—an invention of the ingenious Isaac Dripps of the Camden and Amboy.

The long and short of the matter is that the early trains were definitely not safe, and people rode in them with a kind of tacit understanding that they were putting their lives in jeopardy—this

in a day long before consumer advocacy or the proliferation of liability lawsuits. The primitive early lines came in for plenty of
adverse criticism, but they continued to lay down their lines carelessly. New and better rolling stock also took long years to arrive.

The railway "accident" almost immediately became a standard
part of the American folklore. It is not possible to determine
when the first railroad fatality occurred, but we do know that on
one of the earliest runs of the Best Friend of Charleston a black
fireman was annoyed by the sound of hissing steam escaping from
the safety valve. Unseen by the engineer, he sat on the valve to
quiet the noise—much to his satisfaction until he was blown heav-
enward. Probably the first accident involving a passenger occurred
on the Camden and Amboy on November 11, 1833, when a derailment caused one passenger to be killed and a number of others
severely injured. Among the injured was "Captain Cornelius
Vanderbilt of the New Brunswick steamboat," who survived the
accident to inscribe his own notable chapter in American railroad
history. Also among the passengers, but uninjured, was former
president John Quincy Adams.[7]

Even greater than the perils of early railroad travel were the
many frustrating delays. Most of the primitive lines were single
tracked. As traffic increased, passing sidings ("turnouts" they were
then called) were provided, but often these were useless in speeding up the flow of traffic—or so it seemed to most passengers.
Train operations were governed entirely by timetables (the telegraph would be invented by Samuel F. B. Morse in 1837, but it was
not used to facilitate train movements until 1851). When, say, a
westbound train was scheduled to wait at a certain turnout until
an eastbound train arrived, it might have to sit there interminably,
even though the eastbound train might have been derailed a few
hours earlier. Delays were therefore a constant bugaboo to early
railroad travelers, and with increased traffic they tended to cancel
whatever advantages there might have been in the rapidity of train
travel.

In the early days, when lines were very short, delays were not a
matter of serious concern, but as they became longer, or were
linked together, delays became the object of serious complaint. By
1850, it was possible to travel all the way from Albany to Buffalo
through the "central" part of New York on a number of discon-
nected lines (three years later Erastus Corning would bring these

lines together in the "first" New York Central Railroad). But even though you could do it, in theory, and for a fare of only $9.75, it was not a journey to delight in.

First of all, there were as yet no such things as public timetables. Passengers might be assured by the "ticket master" at Albany that the trip to Buffalo would take fourteen hours, and that there were five trains a day each way, but they could receive no assurances when these trains might leave. Consider the case of a traveler who attempted to make this very journey on a spring day in 1850. Told by the "ticket master" that he would surely be in Buffalo the next morning, he boarded a train which departed Albany at 7 P.M. When the train arrived at Utica at 11:30 P.M., it was switched onto a sidetrack, and stayed there for two and a half hours, without anyone informing the passengers whether or when the train would move again. The journey resumed at 2 A.M., at which time the train proceeded to Rochester. Arriving there at 5 A.M., the passengers were subjected to a delay of twelve and a half hours, during which time no entreaties or enquiries of train crews elicited the slightest amount of information about what was wrong and when the train would be moving again. The train arrived in Buffalo with its agitated and incensed passengers thirty-six hours after leaving Albany.[8] Altogether, the experience was not atypical for a trip of this length in 1850.

Lengthy delays were not the only annoyance endured by early rail travelers. Passenger cars left a great deal to be desired both in terms of comfort and safety. The quality of cars improved by slow degrees, but it should be remembered that on the first railroads of Charleston, or Baltimore or Philadelphia, cars were not more elaborate than little wooden bowls fitted up with seats, and invariably exposed to the elements. Later on, railroads were using stagecoach bodies on wheels, in a design captured for posterity by the artist William Brown in his silhouette of the De Witt Clinton. Cars had to get larger than this as patronage increased, and long wooden cars developed, first with rows of seats running the width of the car (the conductor was provided with a running board along the outside to collect his fares), and later with a narrow center aisle.

Such cars were monstrously uncomfortable for many years. Seats were of wood, often with no backs. The cars themselves for a long time had no springs, and while this was the case they were not notably more comfortable than travel by a covered wagon, except that people were so thrilled with the wonder of rail trips that they overlooked this fact. Roofs were added to protect passengers from soot and ash, but for a long time they were so low that a man could hardly stand to full height in the aisle. The clerestory did not come into widespread use until after the Civil War. There were tiny windows, but the sashes were so loose that they rattled a continuous obligato in their flimsy frames. Such cars were often called "rattlers," "hyenas," or "cribs."[9]

Heating and ventilating in the early passenger cars were atrocious. Heat was generally provided in winter by a potbellied stove placed either in the center or at the end of the car. In cold weather, people attempted to place themselves as near as possible to the stove, but they were often rewarded for their efforts by roasting; those at the greatest distance from the stove froze. Similarly, in the summer months, there was no system of ventilation except open windows—when they worked. But this invariably brought in so much soot from the engine and dust from the roadbed that the value of the open window was a matter of debate. By about 1840, many cars were being built with a ventilating hole about eight to ten inches in diameter in the center of the roof. Better systems would develop slowly.

Two innovations that brought tremendous relief were the advent of coaches with springs, and a better method of linking cars together so that they did not jerk passengers when the train started up. The first need was perceived almost immediately. Only a year after it began operation, the Baltimore and Ohio's chief engineer, Jonathan Knight, stated in his report that it "had been found absolutely necessary to the comfort of passengers that carriages used for their conveyance should be mounted upon springs or some equivalent feature."[10] A link-and-pin method came into use for coupling cars and was in service until the invention of the automatic coupler after the Civil War; it was notoriously dangerous for brakemen, but it provided some of the flexibility needed to keep passengers from being thrown to the floor every time the train got underway.

Also contributing to a smoother ride for passengers after 1840 was the use of the double-truck, eight-wheeled car (the earliest cars had only four wheels). Cars immediately became longer, and took curves much more smoothly. With this and other technical innovations, and with cars becoming both longer and more stable, passengers became somewhat more complacent about the perils of riding the railroad. Truth to tell, all of the early cars, made as they were of wood, continued to be extremely unsafe. When accidents or derailments occurred, especially when the potbellied stoves were lit, the danger a conflagration was always imminent.

Still, as construction methods improved, railroads took pride in their cars, most of which they built themselves according to their own eccentric designs. They were painted in gaudy colors, as were the locomotives of the day; frequently they were given individual names. In time, railroads saw to it that their passenger cars were fitted up with their own "livery"—uniform colors and design.

Roughly by 1840, the passenger day coach took on something very much like the layout that it does today—rows of seats on either side of a center aisle. This was in distinction to the European practice, which continued to build cars with a series of isolated compartments, each of which opened up to the outside, or later to a side aisle. The American, by and large, was a gregarious fellow who loved to wander up and down the aisle (for many years, he was not permitted to pass between cars, but after the introduction of dining cars it became necessary to develop a way for him to do so). In Europe, where there were marked class distinctions, it was considered necessary to offer isolated compartments so that the gentry need not rub elbows with the common folk. Later on, of course, America, too, developed a distinction between first class and ordinary coach travel, but in the 1830s, in the age of Jackson, with its egalitarian slogans, such as "a hog is as good as a horse," and "raised in a log cabin," Americans took delight in the communal benefits of the open coach, where no one was too good to hobnob with his seatmate, and where all merriment was shared.

Some curious modifications of the railway coach evolved during the first few decades of American railroad history. One was the introduction, on several lines, most especially in the South, of cars for women. This peculiar innovation came about not for reasons of prudery, or because women needed to be spared the presence of members of the opposite sex, but because in those years a great many men smoked and an equally large number were devoted to the then very widespread practice of chewing tobacco. Railway cars could be supplied with spitoons, and invariably were, but men tended to be careless in these matters, and car floors and walls were frequently streaked with tobacco juice, which was loathsome to many women. Accordingly, a number of railroads introduced ladies' cars, where smoking and spitting were prohibited. On the other hand, no effort was made to keep ladies from having their consorts accompany them; thus men could be found streaking up the "ladies cars" as well as the regular coaches. Eventually, the ladies' cars were phased out, but in time railroads did return to the idea of confining smokers to particular sections of cars, or to whole "smoking cars."

Another kind of car that made a somewhat premature appearance in the early years of railroading was the sleeping car. As early as 1843, the Erie introduced two cars—called Diamond cars from the shape of their windows. They contained seats upholstered in black haircloth that could be converted to couches. In 1843, an Erie train run was as yet no longer than three hours, so these couches were only intended for passengers wanting to snooze. These cars were eleven feet wide, and proved to be too heavy even for the broad-gauge Erie, so they were eventually removed.[11] There would be a number of sporadic attempts to build sleeping cars over the next several decades, but the idea would not really take hold until well after the Civil War.

Still, to make travel pleasurable, railroads did continually seek to improve the technology and the fittings of passenger cars, and withal provide a certain amount of luxury. In 1853, the Hudson River Railroad created a form of compartment car or parlor car that might be suitable for daytime travel, but would provide more comforts and more luxurious surroundings. The car was divided into staterooms of eight-feet square, which were carpeted, and contained a sofa and chairs, a looking glass, and a small center table. There was a washroom in the center of the car. The concept did not spread widely at the time, but some of the amenities inspired the designs and practices of such later car manufacturers as the Wagner Palace-Car Company and the Pullman Palace-Car Company.

By and large, during the first few decades of railroad operation, passengers did not crave luxury, and the vast majority of travelers appreciated the sociable tendencies of the ordinary open car with its sprawling children, its cigar smokers and tobacco spitters, its braggarts and mashers. Most of these cars, still made of wood, and heated by individual stoves, were extraordinarily dangerous in the event of any kind of accident, but the vast majority of American travelers were grateful for getting where they wanted to go at breathtaking speeds, and they were delighted with the sociable railway cars, which had replaced the claustrophobic imprisonments they had known in stagecoach days. There was a great deal to reproach, but by and large these early passengers endured the discomforts of this still-primitive means of conveyance with good spirit and good humor.

In one sense, the technology of the American railway was developing very rapidly in these years. However many of the technological developments were more utilitarian than pragmatic. Europeans were aghast at the reckless way that American railroads were built—the poor quality of the roadbeds, the sinewy routes, the shacklike stations, the unprotected grade crossings, and so on. The best European engineers were horrified when American locomotive engineers began experimenting with engines with high boiler pressure to get their machines over the mountains. This seemed to be courting disaster. Yes, the American railroads were literally being thrown together. They were not "state-of-the-art." But they were there. By the end of the nineteenth century, the United States would have half of the railway mileage in all the world.[12]

Long before this time, however, the railroad was to become the prevailing and predominating element of the American infrastructure. Indeed, during the very first years of railroad experience on this continent, the railroad was obliged to create, and it did create, a railroad style, a railroad culture, a railroad way of doing things. If Americans lagged behind Europe in the refinements of technology, they took second place to nobody in the growth and diversity of technology, the richness of practice. Never having to stand on principle, never having to answer to higher authority, the American railway builders got the job done through trial and error, storm and stress. For the most part, they carried an admiring public along with them every step of the way.

C·H·A·P·T·E·R 4

PEOPLE UP AND DOWN THE LINE

When English author Charles Dickens visited the United States in 1842, he found a nation that was both crude and energetic, inspiriting and depressing. His recollections of the trip, assembled a few years later from letters, notes, and diaries, and published in a book called *American Notes,* struck many Americans as unjust and atrabilious, seldom giving the youthful nation the benefit of the doubt on matters of good taste. Dickens, of course, possessed a large gift for satire, and the still-underdeveloped United States provided much grist for his mill. During his sojourn in Boston, Dickens decided to pay a visit to the famous factories of Lowell, and thus made his first rail trip in the United States on the Boston and Lowell Railroad.

He was both appalled and astonished by his journey. A ride on an American railroad was a disconcerting experience for a passenger used to the amenities that were provided in Europe. He was struck by the poorly constructed coaches, which reminded him of oversized London omnibuses, kept hot by a glowing, and obviously dangerous, potbellied stove. The Boston and Lowell he found to be poorly constructed, full of twists and turns, unguarded grade crossings, flimsy trestles and bridges. "There is," he said, "a great deal of jolting, a great deal of noise, a great deal of wall, not much window, a locomotive engine, a shriek and a bell."

He found rail passengers a bit too familiar and chummy by English standards. Americans seemed to believe that it was their right to start up a conversation whenever and with whomever they liked. The conductor, or guard, or ticket taker, or whatever he was called, paid few attentions to the proprieties; he wore no uniform, walked up and down the aisle at his leisure, leaned against the wall and engaged in casual conversations with passengers. Could Americans have liked such informality and lack of decorum? Apparently, they didn't know any better, and seemed to assume that English railways were run like this.

There was, of course, no separation by social classes, although on later journeys Dickens found that some railroads provided a separate coach for blacks, "a great blundering clumsy chest, such as Gulliver set out to sea in, from the Kingdom of Brobdingnag." There was also a ladies' car, but men were apparently allowed to sit in it. He discovered that women felt entirely free to talk to any man they liked, and that if a woman expressed a preference for a particular seat, either at a window or elsewhere, her wishes would invariably be gratified. Everywhere, though, even in the "ladies' car," there was this obnoxious American habit of chewing and spitting tobacco. The floors and walls of most American passenger cars were full of telltale stains testifying to the American's lack of concern for the comforts of his fellow travelers.

If the English countryside and the railroad right-of-way was pretty, genial, homey, settled, the American landscape seemed bare, raw, unkempt—with trees that had been hacked away seemingly for no purpose, land that was ill used and ill tended. The scenery that Dickens spied from widely spaced and undersized windows he found to be depressing.

> Except when a branch road joins the main one, there is seldom more than one track of rails; so that the road is very narrow, and the view, where there is a deep cutting, by no means extensive. When there is not, the character of the scenery is always the same. Mile after mile of stunted trees; some hewn down by the axe, some blown down by the wind, some half fallen and resting on their neighbours.... Now you emerge for a few minutes on an open country, glittering with some bright lake or pool, broad as many an English river, but so small that it scarcely has a name; now catch hasty glimpses of a distant town, with its clean white houses with their cool piazzas, its prim New England church and school house:

when whir-r-r-r! almost before you have seen them, comes the same dark screen; the stunted trees, the stumps, the logs, the stagnant water—all so like the last that you seem to have been transported back again by magic.

The train calls at stations in the woods, where the wild impossibility of anybody having the smallest reason to get out, is only to be equalled by the apparently desperate hopelessness of there being anybody to get in. It rushes across the turnpike road, where there is no gate, no policeman, no signal; nothing but a rough wooden arch, on which is painted, "When the Bell Rings, Look Out for the Locomotive." On it whirls headlong, dives through the woods again, emerges in the light, clatters over frail arches, rumbles upon the heavy ground, shoots beneath a wooden bridge which intercepts the light for a second like a wink, suddenly awakens all the slumbering echoes in the main street of a large town and dashes on haphazard, pell-mell, neck-or-nothing, down the middle of the road. There—with mechanics working at their trades, and people leaning from their doors and windows, and boys flying kites and playing marbles, and men smoking, and women talking, and children crawling, and pigs burrowing, and unaccustomed horses plunging and rearing, close to the very rails—there—on, on, on—tears the mad dragon of an engine with its train of cars; scattering in all directions a shower of burning sparks from its wood fire; screeching, hissing, yelling, panting; until at last the thirsty monster stops beneath a covered way to drink....[1]

This, of course, was a pretty good description of primeval railroading in America. Ironically, when Dickens picked on the Boston and Lowell as being typical of the vast differences between railroad practices in England and the United States, he had selected a road which its builders believed followed British conventions and standards religiously. The Boston and Lowell was capitalized at $1,200,000 (quite munificent for that day and age), and materials and engineering practices were of the highest quality. Contrary to Dickens's recollections, which doubtless were an amalgam of his various railway trips in America, the Boston and Lowell had only three grade crossings in its entire length. Dickens was surely right that the scenery must have been desolate, since the line was constructed away from all towns and hamlets as a way of linking only Boston and the growing factory town of Lowell, which believed itself to be inadequately served by the Middlesex Canal.

People in the small towns between Boston and Lowell wanted nothing to do with the railroad, but farmers eagerly welcomed the idea, thinking that the railroad might be a way to get their products to market. Accordingly, between its two termini, the Boston and Lowell ran through a virtual wasteland, as Dickens made clear. Within a few years of Dickens's visit, however, new towns sprouted up along the railroad, and older towns started to stretch themselves toward the railroad, so that in a short time the Boston and Lowell had more than an adequate amount of local traffic.

One thing is certain: The traveler on an American railroad at the time of Dickens's trip in 1842, and for several decades thereafter, had a great many hardships to endure and mysterious rituals which required initiation and savvy. Where to board the train, for example. Some railroads ran down the main streets of a town and stopped at specified corners. Some railroads would stop out in the country for what seemed like no good reason whatsoever; others might make a practice of stopping when they saw a farmer waving a colored shirt, especially if he were a regular passenger. Sometimes such decisions were left up to conductors and engineers, and depended on their individual moods and whims.

The development of the railroad station is a good example of the vagaries and inconsistencies of early railroading in America. In the first few decades of railroad history, there was no firmly fixed notion of what a station should be and what functions it should perform. In many cases, railroads had no stations at all except perhaps at the ends of lines. The first railroad station built and intended as such in America was the Mount Clare station in Baltimore, built in 1830, which was nothing more than an octagonal street corner building that looked something like a tollhouse.[2] Very often, the early railroads rented space in some shop that with luck might be adjacent to the tracks. Occasionally, it was found necessary to build a small ticket booth that might be nothing more than a lean-to. Where more important way stations were needed, railroads sometimes made use of abandonded stagecoach offices. Occasionally, old houses or even hotels were used as stations. When necessary, railroads might build stations for their lines, but in the early years, when entrepreneurs had enough to think about in laying track and acquiring rolling stock, stations were invariably not places of charm or distinction. The newly built railroad "depots," so named because they served as a place where

passengers could gather as well as a place where goods and shipments might be deposited, tended to be low-slung, barnlike structures—an architectural form that continued to predominate in
small towns for most of the nineteenth century.

The railroad station also brought into existence one of the most
prominent figures in the social life of the country for over a century—the station agent. The agent was, as his title suggests, the
local representative of the railroad in all of its dealings with the
public. In the early days, and in small towns even to our own day,
he took care of everything: sold tickets to passengers, arranged for
the shipment of packages in the freight house (often a mere
appendage of the passenger station), sent messages over the telegraph after that device was introduced to the railroad scene, and
served as a communication link with train crews. In some communities he became a figure of some note, a social eminence, even a
father confessor. It was not unheard of that the station agent doubled in brass as barber, postmaster, express agent, real estate dealer, seed salesman, druggist, florist, cemetery manager, even dentist. In small-town America he was often the focal point of the
social life in these places where the coming of the accommodation train was the only event that broke up tedious and sleepy
afternoons. As such, he was the great hero of small boys and the
interlocutor of roustabouts, idlers, roisterers, and crackerbarrel
philosophers.

During the first few decades of railroading, the life of the station agent was far less diverse, his duties fewer, his status far less
enviable. For a long time, railroads dispatched trains at intervals
that were only more or less regular. No railroad ran more than
two or three passenger trains each day. There were no printed
timetables, only approximate arrival times, and these often
depended upon the arrival times of steamboats or stagecoaches in
faraway towns. The station agent usually had no information to
pass along to passengers arriving at his depot about when the next
train would actually come, only the hope and expectation that
one would be along shortly. The agent was thus in a position not
unlike our present-day airport ground representatives when an
airport is socked in by fog—he was faced with anxious, worried,
and abusive passengers who couldn't understand why he didn't
know anything. Being on the lookout for the coming of the train
was thus a constant preoccupation of the early station agent, who

had no telegraphic link with the rest of the system. For this reason, many early railroad stations were fitted up with a high pole
that the agent could ascend on ladderlike cleats, take a seat that
was fixed at the top of the pole, and peer down the tracks for the
coming of the train.[3] From this vantage point the agent could
watch for the train with a spyglass, and call down to the anxious
passengers milling below, then finally put up a great whoop when
the first puff of smoke was seen on the horizon. Doubtless these
high seats were designed as much to relieve the agent from mewl-
ing and handwringing passengers as it was to ascertain any useful
information about the movement of trains.

In time, this intolerable burden was removed from the shoulders of the station agent when railroads begin to run trains on
more regular schedules, and issued timetables for their governance. The earliest timetables were for employees only, and consisted of crude handwritten sheets. The information written on
these early timetables was studiously kept away from passengers,
since it would only have enraged them. But as equipment was
upgraded, as there were more double tracks and "turnouts" allowing trains to bypass one another, arrival times got somewhat more
reliable. Accordingly, prominent roads in the East, notably the
Baltimore and Ohio, the Erie, and the Boston and Lowell began
to post sheets of timetables (or "Arrangements of Trains" as they
were called) in their stations for the edification of travelers.[4] In a
later stage, and in a glorious public relations gesture, they began
to print convenient folder-type timetables for distribution to the
general public. Widespread use of that kind of publication would
have to wait until the U.S. railroads instituted a Standard Time
convention in 1883; before that, timetables often left passengers
more confused by the profusion of local times than if no printed
timetables had been available. Still, those that were circulated
were better than having no printed timetables at all, the situation
that had existed in the early years of railroading.

One duty that fell to the lot of the station agent at an early period was, of course, the sale of tickets. From the very beginning,
American railroads departed from the European practice of
"booking" passengers, a process by which agents merely wrote
down the names of passengers and their destinations and then
checked to see that only such passengers boarded the train.
(Between 1838 and 1842, apparently, the Reading experimented

with the British practice of "booking," but it was found to be totally unreliable at America's free-access stations, and was abandoned.) American railroads gravitated immediately toward tokens
or tickets of some kind—occasionally these would be made of met-
als such as pewter, brass, or copper, which could be reused, but
eventually the paper or cardboard ticket emerged.[5] After about
1855, such tickets began to be numbered consecutively, which
added an auditing check not only on passengers, but on ticket
agents and conductors as well.

Needless to say, even in the early days, railroads were considered "big business" by their passengers and shippers, and people
were not above trying to ride trains without paying their fare or
buying a ticket. For a number of years, at a time when tickets were
usually made of heavy paper or cardboard, and were collected by
conductors and then returned to agents to be sold again, there
were numerous possibilities for abuse. Consider how things were
on the Erie, at the time that it was the longest railroad in the
country and had several divisions. Let's say that a passenger
boarded a train somewhere in upstate New York, Hornell, for
example, and had bought a ticket for New York. The conductor
on the first leg of the trip would look at the ticket, then give it
back to the passenger, who would later be required to show it to
other conductors, and finally surrender it on the last leg of the
trip, which was the ferry boat from Piermont to New York City.
Wily passengers discovered that they could get off the train at
some stop very near the end of the rail line, buy a ticket from that
place to New York (a much less expensive ticket naturally), and
then surrender that ticket on the ferry boat. Retaining the ticket
from their original destination, they were then free to use it over
again every time they wanted to go to New York, yet pay only the
small fare from a station near the end of the line.

To counter this neat little ploy, the Erie instructed its conductors to mark their tickets with a pencil when first examined, but
this did not prove totally satisfactory; accordingly, they introduced
the idea of perforating the ticket with a ticket punch, and this
device became an integral part of railroad practice and railroad
lore in the years thereafter. It was another example of American
ingenuity at work, and the ticket punch idea later spread to other
parts of the world.

If the local agent was the most important business and public relations contact with members of the traveling public, he never quite assumed the legendary importance and dramatic appeal as the members of the operating crews—the conductor, the engineer, the brakemen, trainmen, news agents, and all others who passed through the cars on their rounds. The engineer, of course, was, from the very beginning, the most heroic and glamorous figure in railroad operations. In the early years, when the number of railroads were few, and the number of people who understood locomotives exceedingly small, the engineer seemed to be a personage of monumental importance, especially since in all likelihood he not only drove his locomotive but had built it or assembled it as well. In cases like George Stephenson on the Stockton and Darlington, the engineer seemed to be the whole railroad from top to bottom. As railroads grew, the engineer's prestigious role diminished, and he became more and more a technical functionary, but to small boys and train watchers everywhere he seemed to be the possessor of an arcane magic, the follower of some noble priestcraft. The engineer, accordingly, tended to be a highly respected member of the community throughout most of the nineteenth century and remained such until the development of the craft unions, after which, although his pay might have improved, his social status slowly sank to that of an ordinary worker. Early railroad engineers often wore top hats and cravats, but as the wage-earner atmosphere replaced the early idea that railroading was a form of romance, the engineer found himself pressed down into an ever more obscure position in the social order; he dressed in workman's clothes (albeit often with a distinctive cap), and although he continued to have status among the generality of railroad workers, his original centrality in the scheme of things was lost.

The most familiar railroad official to the average passenger back in the 1840s, as today, was the conductor. In the early days, he was sometimes referred to as the "captain," a term that persisted in use among passengers long after railroads abandonded it officially. The conductor took tickets, sold passage to those who boarded the train without tickets, supervised the other trainmen, settled arguments, disciplined unruly children, and admonished inebriated passengers—whatever was necessary to keep the passenger cars from falling into anarchy. Before the Civil War these captains or conductors dressed formally, sometimes in stovepipe hat and frock coat. In our own time, they have been consigned to standardized uniforms that accord with their diminished status (although until long into the twentieth century conductors on some roads continued to wear frock coats along with their standard-issue railroad hats—sometimes they sported flowers in their buttonholes as well).

Whatever his dress, the conductor was the man for passengers to see about everything—questions about arrival time, stoves that were too hot or too cold, stuck windows, disputes with other passengers, lost parcels or luggage, bawling infants, anything of human concern, however trivial. Naturally, the railroads in those primeval times tried to hire captains that were solid and imposing looking individuals, men of dignity and aplomb who could make their authority prevail.

A splendid example of the stuff early conductors were made of can be seen in the career of one of the Erie's early conductors, Henry Ayres—familiarly known to his passengers and to others as "Poppy Ayres." A huge, genial teddy bear of a man, weighing nearly three hundred pounds, Captain Ayres completely filled the aisle, and had to squeeze through the door, even on the cars of the broad-gauge Erie. He hovered over his passengers in a kind of benevolent menace. During the winter months, he wore a fur-trimmed overcoat and coonskin cap, which must have added considerably to his imposing girth. Ayres came to the Erie in 1841, long before the road was completed from the Atlantic to the Great Lakes, and for thirty years he was the dean of railway conductors on the Erie, if not in the entire nation.

Poppy Ayres was entitled to his title of "captain" if anybody ever was. Indeed, it was he who established the right of the conductor to control the movement of the train. During the very early years of railroading, there was no way for the conductor to communicate with the engineer if some problem or emergency arose. And with trains becoming longer, passengers more numerous and stations more frequent, this was a serious problem. To address the problem, Poppy Ayres decided to rig up a device whereby he might communicate with the engineer. He strung a rope to the locomotive and attached a stick of wood on the end of it. He told his engineer, a German named Hamel, that when he pulled the rope and the stick rapped against the cab he was to bring the train to a halt. Hamel, a stubborn fellow who firmly believed that he was in charge of the train, said nothing, but cut the rope, where-upon Ayres strung it up again. Once more it was cut, but the next time the engineer came to a stop and climbed down from his cab, Ayres was there, and told the fellow that if the rope were cut one more time or its signal not obeyed, he would have to take off his jacket and fight the issue out. The engineer, doubtless not wishing to take a thrashing from the gigantic Ayres, surrendered, and thus the precedent was established that the conductor had control over the movement of the train. Thus, too, was invented a crude early version of what later became the bell rope.[6]

To his passengers, Ayres was anything but a tough guy. He presided over his cars with a fatherly dignity, dispensing informa-tion, answering questions, giving good cheer. The story is told that one day, after the Erie train had left the docks at Piermont on its westerly jaunt, a little old lady began sobbing piteously that she had left her umbrella on the ferry boat—it was a family treasure, she said weeping, and she couldn't bear to be parted from it.

"Don't worry, Mother," said the kindly Ayres. "We'll get your umbrella back for you. I'll send for it on the telegraph." Thereupon, he reached up and did some fancy wriggling with the now vastly improved bell rope, performing some kind of ritualistic incantation. The old lady instantly brightened, but she was of course completely confused as to how an umbrella could be sent by telegraph.

Well, the telegraph was still something of a mystery in those times. A telegraph line had been strung along the Erie, but by a kind of reverse miracle, it was not until a number of years after the installation of the device that railroads found that it could be used to control the movement of trains. Erie's own superinten-dent, Charles Minot, is given credit for that discovery in 1851, fourteen years after the invention of the telegraph by Samuel F. B. Morse. In early days, trains ran strictly by the timetable on single track and would have to wait at assigned turnouts for their meet-ing times, even if the opposing train were hours late. This was pre-posterous, of course, and one day, when Minot was out on the line with his own train subjected to delay, he had the station agent wire ahead and inquire if the opposing train had arrived at the next station down the line. It hadn't, so Minot wired ahead for that train to be held when and if it arrived. He then ordered his train to proceed. This discovery was a godsend to passengers everywhere—the only mystery being why this simple discovery wasn't made years sooner.

Poppy Ayres's pretended use of the telegraph was something altogether different. No, there was no way that an umbrella could have been sent over the telegraph wires, but in the 1840s and 1850s most people didn't know what it was capable of. Ayres however knew that cabin attendants on board the ferry from New York went through the cabins after the passengers departed, and put all loose articles on board the baggage car. Thus, Poppy Ayres knew that the umbrella belonging to the old lady would be on board the train, and a short time later he appeared with it, presenting it to the lady with a theatrical flourish. The woman was so flabbergasted and overjoyed that she jumped up and gave the kindly conductor a hug and a kiss.

"For land sakes alive," she exclaimed. "Who'd ever a thunk it? I've heern 'o letters and papers bein' sent by telegrapht, but who'd 'a' thunk they could send umbrell's?"[7]

Conductors, being the principal public relations contacts with the general public in the early days, were deemed very important personages not only by the passengers, but by management as well. Strong efforts were made to see that conductors with strong human appeal were put on the cars, and, if at all possible, allowed to stay for years, and build up a wide circle of acquaintances among the traveling public along the line. During the nineteenth century, many conductors stayed on their jobs—the same trains at the same time—for years on end. Accordingly, they became figures of some social prominence.

Poppy Ayres was one such figure. Another was the legendary Asa R. Porter, for many years the conductor on the Fall River Boat train of the Old Colony Railroad. For most of the nineteenth century, the Old Colony Railroad (subsequently absorbed into the New York, New Haven, and Hartford), carried passengers between Boston and Fall River, where they would board an overnight steamboat to New York—through rail connections between New York and Boston did not exist in the beginning. For many years, the Old Colony Railroad was a legendary New England institution, and it brought into fashion scores of beaches and beauty spots of southern Massachusetts—places like Cohasset, Duxbury Beach, Nantucket, and Martha's Vineyard.

The Fall River Boat train was the most famous train in New

England in those times, and it was one of the must enduring train runs in U.S. history—it ran for ninety years, from 1847 to 1937. Asa Porter was conductor on the train from 1864 to 1896, and during his tenure is said to have entertained every president of the United States in his cars. He was one of the best known men in all New England, surely rivaling the land's native poets—the Emersons, Longfellows, Lowells, and Whittiers.

Supremely polite, impeccably groomed, always with a pink flower in the buttonhole of his frock coat, he spoke to every passenger, calling most of them by name. He was undoubtedly known to more New Englanders of that day than any other single individual. More than one time, management offered him a higher post in the company, but he was not interested; he believed that he already had the best job on the railroad.

New England newspapers called Asa Porter "the man who made the Fall River train," but passengers remember him more fondly as the man who greeted them at the old Kneeland Street depot in Boston with its ornate staircase and elaborate woodworking, always expressing interest in how they had been since last they rode the train, always remembering their names, their families, their concerns. Mary R. Gifford of the Fall River Historical Society was one of the many people with nostalgic memories of conductor Porter. "My recollections," she later wrote,

> were necessarily those of a small child, but I remember most clearly two things: his unfailing interest whenever we took his train in what we had been doing since our last trip, and the fact that his whiskers were just like my own grandfather's. He used to tell us children jokes as he punched our tickets and let the tiny pieces fall into our hands so we could see what shape they were in. A bit of the pleasure of the trip was lost when he no longer rode the train.[8]

If the conductor, or "captain," was the most familiar and revered railroad figure to travelers in those times, a number of other railroad workers were known to everybody who took the train regularly, and some of these became, in their own way, figures of legendary stature, or, at the very least, figures with their own color and aroma. There were, of course, the brakemen, invariably in the early days gaunt, intense, hardened young men, usually recruited from the working classes, and by no means aspirants to the office or the dignity of the conductor. In the primitive times at least, the brakeman's lot was far from an enviable one. Each passenger car was braked individually by turning a wheel on the top end of the car, and the brakeman had to perch there waiting for a braking signal from the engineer, sometimes enduring temperatures of ten below zero—with the train in motion! The brakeman was also responsible for the coupling of cars when trains were being assembled, and for many years, until the invention of the automatic coupler in 1868 (and for long years afterward, in fact, since most railroads did not adopt that device with alacrity), this was a terrifying and dangerous chore. The early method of linking railway cars together was by means of a link and pin, which required the brakeman to stand between two cars being pushed together by the locomotive and drop the pin into a socket at the very last second. Naturally, if he missed or the device failed in some way, he could be killed or maimed for life. Thousands of brakeman were horribly mangled or lost their lives in this manner until the automatic coupler was universally adopted (in some roads not until 1900). Still, the job of brakeman was not without its glamour, and the railroads had little difficulty finding young men willing to undertake these dangerous assignments.

Another railroad worker who rapidly became a familiar figure in American life beginning in the 1850s was the news agent, often fondly called the news butcher. For a while, the news butcher tended to be an entrepreneur; later, he became an employee of the gigantic Union News Company, which supplied him with magazines and newspapers as well as candy, soda pop, and other confections. Usually a jaunty adolescent with falsetto voice, calling out, most often in half intelligible polysyllables, "candycigarettescigars," or "newspapersmagazines," he was dramatically garbed in neat blue uniform with brass buttons and a brass nameplate on his cap announcing his noble calling as "News Agent." The lad was a model of worldly sophistication, or at least worldly aspiration, although invariably he had only recently left the farm that he now regarded, as he did his former comrades still in jeans and galluses, with ill-disguised disdain.

Not many news agents stayed in harness for many years; most of them moved on to better things, but as young and vigorous lads, usually with only a faint stubble of hair on their chins, they were invariably well liked by passengers, whose long train journeys were enlivened by this touch of youthful zest and enthusiasm. In the 1880s, Robert Louis Stevenson, making the long trek across the United States, had nothing but praise for the young pup who sold newspapers on the leg of his trip between Ogden and Sacramento. "You could hardly overpraise his services....All in the cars came to love him." Stevenson believed that the plain ordinary newsboy was a prominent personage on the railroad, particularly in the West. You could buy from him, "soap, towels, tin washing basins, tin coffee pitchers, coffee, tea, sugar, and tinned eatables, mostly hash or beans and bacon." [9]

In the more settled East, the news butcher's offerings may have been somewhat less wide-ranging, but even there this prize functionary made several passes through the cars with all kinds of offerings. He sold candy, gumdrops, magazines, local newspapers, chewing gum, ice cream cones, cigars (invariably poor in quality, old-timers have attested), souvenirs, gewgaws, and trinkets of every imaginable variety. The magazines offered to train riders under the regime of the Union News Company were most often the respectable weekly or monthly periodicals, such as *Harper's, Scribner's, Munsey's,* and the great comic weeklies *Puck* and *Judge,* with their bold cartoons in chromolithography. There was, however, nothing to keep the news butcher from selling on his own, and sub rosa, saucy romances, penny dreadfuls, and any number of other lurid soft cover books to titillate the imagination of male passengers. Probably these did not exceed in erotic daring the *Decameron* of Boccaccio, but there was said to be a fraudulent bowdlerization of *Fanny Hill,* which had not so much as a single truly bawdy line in it, but was nonetheless hawked at outrageous prices to the gleeful profit of the newsboy. The selling of faintly naughty literature on trains became a significant part of American folklore during the late nineteenth and early twentieth centuries.

The things that news butchers could sell were only limited by their imagination and ingenuity. At a time when no local stations contained newsstands or candy counters, the news butcher was the purveyor of everything bought and sold along the line. In early times, the lads sold bottled water—none too hygenic, apparently, since they often reused the bottles after only a superficial washing—but when the railroads started putting water jugs and paper cups at the ends of cars, this trade was lost. Thomas Alva Edison, who began his career as a newsboy at the age of twelve in his hometown of Port Huron, Michigan, showed the ingenuity that marked many of these peppery railroad hucksters of that age. In the baggage car, he set up a little press on which he turned out his own newspaper called the *Weekly Herald,* which consisted of tidbits received from local telegraph operators as well as scraps from bigger papers along the way. This little railroad newspaper enjoyed a brisk circulation of about eight hundred copies, and turned a profit of forty-five dollars a month for its young editor-publisher.[10]

By the 1850s, railroads were doing a great deal more to change the face of American society than carry passengers faster than any earlier mode of transportation. The railroads were king, now, and were looked to for solutions to all problems having to do with the conveyance of people, goods, and possessions—whatever needed to be moved from one place to another. Canals, where available, continued to do their work with heavy cargoes. And stagecoach lines continued in places where no railroads existed. But when the older and once highly profitable main stagecoach lines came into contact with railroads, they quickly withered and died. On the old stage line between New York and Philadelphia, the stage men had tried to compete by promising to take passengers directly to the door of their homes or to some other convenient location, but it didn't work. On the other hand, the stagecoach operators had always been good at carrying and delivering parcels, packages, foodstuffs, and other things—sometimes as a favor to their regular passengers and to others on consignment. For several decades, the railroads, so consumed with their brisk passenger business, took little interest in moving such things—it would mean adding personnel and equipment that did not appeal to them. But the need was there, so accordingly it was met, in typically American fashion, by outsiders who recognized a good opportunity when they saw it.

The kind of railroad traffic long known as "express" was curiously slow to develop, perhaps because the stagecoach operators had always done such a superb job of handling small packets, letter post, and the like. But the railroads were so vastly superior to stages except in very short distances that it is hard to fathom why the early railroad managers took no interest in this kind of business. When traffic of this sort did become prominent in the 1840s, it was developed largely by outside entrepreneurs.

The first individual to use the railroad for purposes of express was William F. Harnden, who for five years had been a conductor on the Boston and Worcester Railroad. His work, which often required sixteen hours and more a day, broke his health, so he quit. While on a vacation trip to New York, he spoke to an expatriate Bostonian named James W. Hale, who was an agent for a New York to Providence steamboat company. Hale explained to Harnden that he was constantly being asked if there was someone who could do errands or deliver packages in Boston. This convinced Harnden that a person who would develop such a service could make out quite well. Acting on the eminent good sense of the idea, Harnden made a contract with the Boston and Providence Railroad and the manager of the steamboat *John W. Richmond* plying between Providence and New York, and began making regular trips between Boston and New York. Shortly thereafter, carrying a large leather bag for packages, Harnden became the first railway expressman in the United States, personally carrying items between Boston and New York in March 1839.

During the next few years, Harnden's business increased a hundredfold. Within only a few months of beginning his business, he was employing other carriers, and had opened offices staffed with clerks in Boston and New York. The express idea attracted so much attention, even abroad, that by the early 1840s Harnden was responding to requests to set up express services on trans-Atlantic sailing ships. He had a contract with the Cunard Company to convey express items between Liverpool and Boston, and before long some of the items being expressed were very strange indeed. Among the cargoes accepted by Harnden were human beings—immigrants to the new world. Harnden booked some ten thousand immigrants from their homes in Europe to America, this by establishing agreements with the British railway lines, steamship companies, American railroads, and the Erie Canal. Many early settlers of the Midwest had thus been "shipped" to America by express!

Harnden lived only until 1845, but when he died he was the best-known expressman in the United States, if not the world. In the Mount Auburn Cemetery in Cambridge, Massachusetts, there is a sixteen-foot monument to Harnden, commemorating this "Founder of the Express Business in America." [11] Even before Harnden's death, there were other express companies doing busi-

ness with various American railroads. By the 1850s, the most dominant express business in the United States was that established by
Alvin Adams in 1840. Between that time and the Civil War, Adams
& Co. gained a near monopoly in the express business along the
eastern seaboard and in the South. But in that same period, there
were a number of other major companies in the field: the
American, the National, the United States, and Wells-Fargo & Co.
The express companies, being independent of the railroads,
could use whatever method of transportation that was needed to
get the job done—sometimes resorting to stage, horseback, mule,
pony, or dog train. Very early in their existence, these companies
established expertise in forwarding valuable or perishable freight,
or shipments of gold; they also gained considerable revenue from
the execution of papers, from writing money orders, making collections, and maintaining an order and commission business.
Express transportation by rail mostly remained in the hands of
outside businesses, and the function was only wrested away from
them by gradual degrees. During World War I, the railroads established their own express consortium, the American Railway
Express Company, which for decades thereafter maintained a near
monopoly on rail express.

In the period before the Civil War, the railroads were very slow
to perceive the vast possibilities for expansion in their services.
They were, for example, very slow to get into the business of carrying the U.S. mail. The postal service had contracts with the railroads as early as 1839, but for many years the railroads did little
more than carry sealed mailbags from one destination to another.
Later, whole mail cars were set aside for this purpose; however, it
was not until after the Civil War that anybody had the vision of
using mail cars as a place for sorting and processing mail. It was
still later before the railroads (and the Post Office Department)
saw the virtues in having "fast mail" rail service between major
population centers of the country.

So slow were the railroads in accepting and developing new
ideas for carrying things that for a long time they didn't even have
satisfactory facilities for carrying the baggage of their passengers.
It had been obvious from the start of railroad service that some
kind of provisions would have to be made for passengers' baggage
and other impedimenta; accordingly, the first regular run of a
Camden and Amboy train contained a baggage car of sorts, and

the Baltimore and Ohio put baggage cars in service immediately thereafter. But the railroads did little if anything to facilitate baggage handling, and forced its riders to sling their bags on board the baggage car, which invariably was not shielded from the elements. For a number of years, railroads admitted no liability for lost or damaged baggage, and posted notices to the effect that "All Baggage Handling Is at the Owner's Risk."

A number of passengers who had lost their bags challenged in court the railroad's refusal to accept liability for baggage, and by 1838, with railroads now having the status of common carriers in the eyes of the law, companies began to make a systematic effort to mark luggage with its intended destination. At first, they marked bags with chalk; later they provided brass checks (in duplicate—one for the customer, one for the bag), and later cheaper cardboard checks similar to those used to this day. Furthermore, they eventually hired a functionary, the baggage master, to preside over the baggage car and see that items got off at the correct destination. The baggage master, as much as any railroad worker, entered the folklore of American life under the popular nickname of "baggage smasher," a term traced by the *Dictionary of American English* to 1856.[12] So vivid were the legends about "baggage smashers" that a great many Americans firmly believed that the boys assigned to baggage cars had contests among themselves to see how far they could heave a bag, some champions being reputed to have the ability to stand at one end of the baggage van and hurl a passenger's bag against the wall at the far end.

The railroad's slowness to realize the vast potential for carrying freight seems incomprehensible to Americans of the present day. Since the railroads of our time are best known as transporters of low-grade freight, there may be some mystery as to why railroads were so slow to develop freight traffic. Again, however, it needs to be remembered that before the early nineteenth century there simply was no such thing as shipping manufactured goods and heavy articles from one part of the country to another. Philadelphia, Boston, New York, and Charleston were all self-sufficient and independent of one another, and the idea of crating up things in Boston with the idea of shipping them to Charleston (except occasionally by sea) was unknown. The railroads didn't get into the freight business in the early days simply because there was no freight business to be had.

Slowly, though, things began to change as America became an industrialized nation, and in the decade between 1850 and 1860 the railroads got some kind of preview of how things would eventually be. Still, as in the case of the express business, railroads themselves didn't take the initiative; it was outside visionaries—or people in need of service—who pointed the way. Some of these visionaries themselves got into the railroad business and fashioned freight services to meet their own needs. The coal barons of Pennsylvania built their own railroad lines when they saw that canals couldn't meet their needs and were frozen over during the winter months just when people in New York were needing fuel for their fires and local wood supplies were near exhaustion.

Or consider the case of the development of milk traffic, for over a hundred years an exceedingly important part of the revenues of many railroads. Railroad executives saw no possibilities along this line for many years, mainly because dairy producers themselves saw none. A good deal of the Erie's territory in Orange County, New York, was devoted to dairy farming, and the farmers of the region were well known for the quality of their butter. Butter was an item that could be preserved and shipped, and was shipped before the coming of the railroad. But in New York City, supplies of milk were scarce. A small number of dairies existed, but most city dwellers received their milk from cows that had been kept in brewery and distillery stables. No alternative seemed to exist, because farmers were in almost universal agreement that milk couldn't be shipped more than fifty miles, especially in hot weather.

But an agent of the Erie in Orange County named Thomas Selleck was convinced that shipping milk might be possible. In the early 1840s, he talked up the idea in New York, where parents were having to force swill milk down the throats of their children, and he talked up the idea to Orange County farmers. All laughed at him for a while, but Selleck persisted. He promised to build a railroad depot just for milk and milk products in New York. Technologies were found to keep milk cool in transit, and milk shipments to New York City began, slowly at first, but finally to flood tide. Within a scant few years, the milk depot Selleck built in New York was totally inadequate for its purposes. Within a year, the Erie was hauling between 600,000 and 700,000 quarts of milk a year. The next year (1843), the railroad was carrying to market nearly four million quarts, and by 1845, milk traffic comprised nearly two-fifths of the total freight receipts of the railroad.[13] All from a product that only a few years before was seen as inconceivable as a source of revenue.

But it would only be a few years before the effects of freight traffic on the American economy and the American nation would be a force every bit as powerful as that of our Constitution and our traditions of liberty. Very early railroads carried people wherever they went, and this induced a feel for unified nationhood in the American people. But the impact of a good form of freight transportation justified that sense of unification. When it was possible, and easy, to ship manufactured goods from Boston to Kansas, or wheat from Nebraska to Philadelphia, the United States became a national economy, and furthermore a national economy that had a particularly salubrious effect on the character of the American people.

This point was made very effectively by one of the nineteenth-century railway prophets, Thomas Curtis Clarke, in a book intended to sum up the achievements that American railroads had reached in a half century or less. "The grand function of the railway," said Clarke,

> is to change the whole basis of civilization from military to the industrial. The talent, the energy, the money, which is expended in maintaining the whole of Europe as an armed camp is here expended in building and maintaining railways, with their army of two millions of men.... By the railways, aided by telegraphs, it is easy to extend our Federal system over an entire continent, and thus dispense forever with standing armies.

For Clarke, American railways, eliminating as they do stubborn feudal economies, had not only made possible an American democracy on a high level, but they might eventually do the same thing for the entire world, most especially for pugnacious Europe, which for centuries had exhausted itself in military confrontations.

> American railways have nearly abolished landlordism in Ireland, and they will one day abolish it in England and over the continent of Europe. So long as Europe was dependent for food upon its own fields, the owner of these fields could fix his rental. This he can no

longer do, owing to the cheapness of transportation from Australia and the prairies of America....

With the wealth of the landlord his political power will pass away. The government of Europeans will pass out of the hands of the great landowners, but not into those of the rabble, as is feared. It will pass into the same hands that govern America today—the territorial democracy, the owners of small farms, and the manufacturers and merchants. When this comes to pass, attempts will be made to settle international disputes by arbitration instead of war.... Whether our Federal system will ever extend to the rest of the world, no one knows, but we do know that without railways, it would not be possible.[14]

How justified this optimism was could long occupy the attentions of historians here and abroad. We do know, in fact, that the railroad in Europe did not completely stifle the military spirit, and it did not put an end to all class struggles. Most students of history recall how the railways were harnessed to military ends by Germany in both World War I and World Wars II. And internecine struggles and class warfare did not abate. But, yes, in the United States, it was true that the railroad did hold this promise of a peaceful economy and of a larger democratic community in which farmers, mechanics, and manufacturers could be welded together in a democratic commonwealth. There was more to it all than just the railroad, of course, but for most of the nineteenth century the railroad was the American infrastructure; it was what cemented the people together; and most Americans believed that it conferred benign blessings of peace, harmony, and prosperity.

C·H·A·P·T·E·R 5

LONG SHADOWS
OF DOUBT

The railroad had been warmly embraced by the American people almost from its inception. Its utility in unifying the nation and in creating a strong national economy were apparent to nearly everyone in this age of euphoria and unbounded expectation, in this period when almost nobody questioned any of the fruits of American society, any "work of the age," any fancy of the technological imagination. Still, it must not be assumed that all Americans found the railroad untroubling or unthreatening. Yes, there were those few people in the beginning who scoffed at the very possibility of the railroad, or who believed that the iron horse was dangerous to life and limb, but these early skeptics had been swept aside in the first few years. Still, no such institution, no novel form of technology, could flourish and expand without causing serious thinkers to question the long-term effects of its development. And the early American railroads did have their more darkly reflective critics.

Of course the very fact that the railroad was an industry, a contrivance of iron, smoke, and noise, perhaps also a contrivance of financiers and of "businessmen," gave sufficient cause for doubt in a nation which had been founded as an agrarian democracy, which cherished the pastoral pleasures of wide open spaces, the absence of cities, the absence of class distinctions, and the freedom from toil, from cruel excesses of population, from the crowding in of one human habitation upon another. Thomas Jefferson, and not a few of the other founding fathers, believed that the American experiment in democracy could only work if it continued as a nation of yeoman agrarianists, each free of his neighbors, yet in harmony with them—a nation that built no cruel cities and avoided the heartless excesses associated with industrialism in Europe. Good numbers of Americans had visited England during the first stirrings of the Industrial Revolution, and they didn't like what they saw. They developed no magisterial philosophical system to denounce it as did Karl Marx a few years later, but they felt instinctively that America should not be allowed to go that route, that it should avoid the excesses of large cities, of smokestack industries, of people crowding in on one another, and probably learning to hate and despise one another.

During the early nineteenth century, few Americans thought of the railroad as being a harbinger of an industrial revolution or of any drastic change in the social order. The lines were too short, the equipment diminutive—with locomotives and cars not very much different from mechanical toys—the geographical area of the country limited in the extreme. But in a few decades, with railroads intruding everywhere, with lines being hastily laid down wherever people lived, it was clear to everybody that this was a new form of industry with the power to effect the face of the American landscape. The factories of Lowell or Paterson stayed where they were; they did not impinge on the frontier or even on the broad sunlit pastures only a few miles away; but when railroads turned up everywhere, there was considerable cause for alarm. Invariably, the railroad had come from somewhere else, and people accustomed to the farmer's or small owner's way of life still clung tenaciously to the notion that their habits, their lifestyles, their politics, should not be dictated by an industry not of their own making and outside their control. Only recently, Andrew Jackson, with his coonskin democracy, had warned his fellow citizens on the frontier of the dangers inherent in the greedy financial centers of Boston or Philadelphia, of the perils of trade and manufacturing, and here now was a rapidly growing institution that would introduce not only its own noisy physical presence but the despised grip of bankers, speculators, and other financial manipulators.

Be that as it may, Americans in general were slow to generate hostility or even suspicion of the railroad in the years before the Civil War. They remained, on the whole, upbeat and enthusiastic. In historical retrospect, they would have had ample justification for skepticism about a number of things, but railroad fever was so overpowering in those times that the very evident signs of danger or excess were mostly overlooked, except perhaps by highly perceptive and reflective individuals.

One issue that did trouble the general public in the early years, and which received a good deal of editorial comment around the country, was the safety issue. From the beginning of railway operations, accidents were frequent, and most Americans were aware that this much-venerated means of transportation was hazardous to one's health. To be sure, in the early years, most accidents were minor in nature; few resulted in the loss of life or limb. The typical accident, a simple derailment, or collision with livestock upon the tracks, tended to be more of a nuisance and cause of delay than a justification for fear and trepidation.

However, suddenly, and like an alarm bell in the night, this whole picture changed in the early 1850s. Within two weeks of one another, in the spring of 1853, two calamitous accidents took place with heavy loss of life,[1] and these accidents, which received a great deal of press coverage, marked the beginning of a long chain of railway accidents that gave the general public reasons for concern about how well railroads were built and how well they were operated. These two accidents, in fact, resulted in more fatalities than all the previous railroad accidents combined.

The first of these accidents, in which twenty-one people were killed, took place at a spot called Grand Crossing near the city of Chicago, which had just begun its meteoric rise as a railway junction. A number of lines were being quickly laid down in the Chicago area, many of them crossing one another at grade (in railroad parlance, these were called diamonds to distinguish them from grade crossings with roads and highways). The diamond known as Grand Crossing was a place where two somewhat hostile and competitive lines intersected—the Michigan Central and the Michigan Southern (later New York Central). Operational procedures and rules for such crossings existed, but they were inadequate, and not scrupulously followed by engineers who believed that trains of the other line were somehow intruders. The inevitable happened, and on April 25, 1853, numerous lives were lost in a terrible smashup.

With this catastrophe still burning in the public's imagination, only eleven days later, on the New Haven Railroad at Norwalk, a train fell through an open drawbridge, the first of a number of such accidents over a period of many years. The bridge was operated by a draw tender who controlled signals for the railroad traffic, and apparently all such warning signals were working properly; still, the engineer apparently ignored the clearly displayed warnings and drove his train off the bridge and into the Norwalk River. Forty-six people were killed in this accident.

Two accidents of such a serious magnitude and in such a short period of time had the effect of making many Americans wonder whether their railways were safe enough to ride on. In the Norwalk accident, the engineer was clearly to blame; in fact, he had to escape the clutches of a lynch mob at the scene of the accident, a fate that would befall numerous engineers—some culpable, some totally innocent—in the years ahead. But not a few editorial writers questioned whether railroads employed safe operating procedures, whether they were up to the task of meeting the challenges of their rapidly increasing traffic and volume of business. Later that same year, a number of dramatic accidents, head-on collisions due to fast running or disregard of timetable schedules, and a number of miscellaneous others—burst boilers, derailments, collisions with unfenced livestock—led to fatalities of record in such a way that the luster of railway travel was tarnished in the eyes of many Americans.

In this same decade of the 1850s, a multitude of other serious questions about railroads began to surface, many of them unsettling to the populace. Safety, of course, was a function of how railroads were built and operated, how *well* they were built and operated, but this in turn was related to deeper and more complex questions about the development, the planning, the funding, and the financing of railroads in the United States. The railroads had been organized and constructed more rapidly in America than anywhere in the world; it seemed as though every place that wanted a railroad got one. On the other hand, few had stopped to reflect on the process by which this remarkable growth took place.

In this process lay some deep dark secrets, some proverbial skele-tons in the closet.

Although this aspect of railroad development did not trouble most Americans in the early years of railroading, there was ample reason for skepticism, even alarm, over the ways in which railroads were chartered, financed, and managed. From the very first, it was clear that railroads could not be directly financed either by state or federal governments—the same constitutional roadblocks were put against public finance of railroads as had hampered the many projects to build roads and turnpikes at public expense. It was understood from the beginning that railroads would have to be financed with private funds, in clear opposition to the practice of some European countries, where governments played an impor-tant role in the planning, funding, and governing of railroads.

Private financing of American railroads seemed to be an ideal approach, and everybody was in favor of it. The only trouble was that the young republic did not yet have the kind of financing that would be needed to build the thousands of miles of railroad that were going to be needed in the United States—many of them plunging into the wilderness or the unsettled frontier. Clearly, capital to build these miles of "speculative" railroads wasn't going to come from faraway Boston or New York—at least not in the beginning. A banker might be more than willing to foot the bill for a railroad between Boston and Worcester or between New York and Philadelphia, but a railroad between two log cabin vil-lages in Indiana was something altogether different. Yet the peo-ple in Indiana and Kentucky or Illinois were thirsty for their own railroads by the 1850s—how could they be funded?

In a typical manifestation of shifty American pragmaticism, compromises were worked out, ways were found—many of them of dubious legality and propriety—to get the job done by combin-ing the initiatives of governmental action and private enterprise. Many students of American history will recall that during the 1850s the federal government sidestepped its own self-imposed prohibitions against funding "internal improvements" by making lavish land grants to railroads. Millions of acres of land in western states were lavished on the railroads, the sale of which was more than adequate to build railroad lines in those territories.

But even before the federal government got into the act, state governments had thrown all caution to the wind and found their own ways to subsidize railroad construction. They did so either by putting exceedingly liberal provisions in the charters they granted to railroad companies, by supplying money or credit to private builders of railroads, or, in a few instances, actually building railroads themselves. All of these were practices that could have been (and were) open to attack by many publicly spirited citizens.

Nearly all railroads were organized as corporations, and as such they needed charters from state legislatures. Not only were these freely granted, but they were granted with privileges that would certainly have been withheld to most other corporations. Railroad charters often contained sweeping provisions for the confiscation of land by eminent domain. They often provided for freedom from state taxation, at least for a period of time. (When the Vermont Central Railroad was established, for example, it was granted freedom from taxation for a period of ten years.) Many states granted lottery and banking privileges to railroads as they had to canals in an earlier period. Lotteries permitted railroads to tap the savings of even the smallest savers; railroad banks allowed operating companies to raise the money needed to pay their laborers, contractors, and suppliers. Some states, but not all, granted monopolies to railroads, though the very word "monopoly" was anathema to Americans even in that distant time, as it is today. Among the states that granted monopolies were New Jersey, South Carolina, Georgia, Massachusetts, Kentucky, and Louisiana. Among the most notorious of these monopoly charters was that granted to the Camden and Amboy in New Jersey, which received exclusive rail transportation rights between New York and Philadelphia, and in fact over the whole state—a very foolish action of the New Jersey legislature, which was later overturned but only after much agitation and public uproar.

These charter provisions, excessive as they may seem, were modest in comparison with direct financial aid given by the states to railroads. Even in the eastern states, where capital was not difficult of access, states were free and easy with their money where railroads were concerned. In New England, where private capital was clearly abundant, states showered largesse on many new railway lines. By the time of its completion in 1841, the Western Railroad of Massachusetts had received $4,600,000 from the state legislature, $600,000 of this being a direct investment in the stock of the company, the remainder in the form of a secured loan.[2] In Maryland, the city of Baltimore had provided most of the capital for the early Baltimore and Ohio Railroad. The state of New York, in spite of many objections from canal interests, issued bonds totaling $3,000,000 to subsidize the Erie Railroad, and by 1846 had advanced more than $9,000,000 to ten different railroad companies.[3] In the South, states lavished their funds on railroads in a positively shameless manner. In Virginia, the state agreed to accept three-fifths of its state's railroad stock. In North Carolina, by the time of the outbreak of the Civil War, state debt arising from subventions to railroads amounted to at least $9,000,000.

In spite of all the prohibitions to the contrary, during the years of intense railroad fever, a few states not only loaned money to railroads, they actually built and operated railroads themselves. When Boston saw itself falling behind the middle Atlantic states in the 1830s, there were numerous proposals that the state of Massachusetts build its own railroad lines. But these proposals were rejected in favor of private financing. New York and New Jersey also rejected this approach. On the other hand, in the South, where capital was not readily forthcoming, states like Georgia and Virginia did not shy away from spending their own public funds on building railroads. For example, in Georgia, the state built the Western and Atlantic Railroad between Atlanta and Chattanooga in the 1840s, and subsequently ran it with some degree of success. In Virginia, the state constructed a railroad across the Blue Ridge mountains as a very needed connection to its western frontier. After completion, the line was leased to the Virginia Central Railroad. Needless to say, this state investment in railroads turned out to be more than indispensible a few years later, when the largely agrarian South was forced to conduct a war with the industrialized north.

No part of the country was more wildly enthusiastic about state ownership of railroads than the states of the Midwest, which had not yet outgrown their frontier status. In 1837, the very year it was admitted as a state, Michigan initiated an ambitious program of railroad building, hoping to eventually have its own extensive network of rail lines. The project was not successful, however, and the major Michigan lines quickly fell into the hands of eastern financiers and railway entrepreneurs, mostly from Boston. Indiana and Illinois also had ambitious schemes for internal improvements in the 1830s and 1840s, and built a number of railroad lines, but the financial circumstances of both of these states were repeatedly in such a parlous state that they were eventually forced to dispose of their railroad holdings to private corporations. In time, state-owned railroads would completely disappear in the United States, although, curiously, there has been something of a return to it in the latter half of the twentieth century, when drastic abandonments of essential rail services once again brought the public sector into the business of railroad ownership.

Attempts of the federal government to aid railroads in their growing years presents a much more complicated story. Although the federal government was supposed to be precluded by the constitution from financing internal improvements (or so it had long been believed and accepted), public pressures to do something to aid railroad expansion were inexorable and irresistible. From the very beginning, in the face of incessant populist uproars, the federal government found ways to sidestep its traditional constitutional restraints. For example, many early railroads (including the Baltimore and Ohio and the Charleston and Hamburg) were aided by surveys made by government engineers. In addition, Congress passed legislation to exempt railroads from tariff duties on the iron they needed for their construction.

During the 1840s and 1850s, Congress was under unremitting public pressure to make loans to nascent railroads, especially from western states, which lacked the capital to begin construction. Such loans were not voted, but in time the federal government was prodded into another form of subsidy, namely the gift of publicly owned lands to make possible the construction of regional railroads. The idea had been bandied around for years, but it had met stiff resistance from many quarters. Finally, however, in 1850, a coalition of western and southern states combined to push through a grant for a north-south railroad extending from northern Illinois to Mobile, Alabama. By a curious twist of fate, representatives from gulf and western states did not have enough clout to push through this legislation, but they received considerable support from New York and Boston capitalists, who were now pushing lines of their own into Chicago, and saw the advantage of a north-south line in the nation's heartland.

The bill went through, and provided that federal lands in the states through which the railroad passed should be used to subsidize railway construction. This subsidy totaled 3,736,005 acres, a good deal of which the young Illinois Central Railroad sold to settlers before the completion of its originally chartered line in 1857. The railroad had cost in excess of twenty-three million dollars to build and equip; most of this money came from mortgages secured by railroad properties that had primarily consisted of federal acerage. Less than one-sixth of the capital costs came from stockholders.[4] The Illinois Central was, of course, an almost instant success. It not only provided a much needed link between North and South, but it opened to farming the fertile but hitherto neglected prairies of Illinois.

On the whole, however, most railroads in America were financed by private capital. This seemed to be the American way, and it was perhaps the only way that a vast system of railroad lines could be put together at a time when public funds were severely restricted. The initiative of private capital proved to be at one and the same time a boon and a curse to the railroad industry. At first, the only curse seemed to be that there was simply not enough capital available to build all the lines that were needed. After the Civil War, there was a large influx of British capital, which permitted the sometimes wildly speculative expansion of that period. But before that time Americans had to go it alone. At first, the only problem seemed to be that the principal financial centers of Boston, New York, and Philadelphia were wary of railroad capitalism, skeptical of the value of railroad stock, and, more importantly, not yet large enough to produce the huge amounts of capital needed.

For these and other reasons, the chief financial support for early railroads tended to come from local businessmen—merchants, farmers, small manufacturers, and people along the right-of-way who might benefit from the construction of the railroad. The Baltimore and Ohio Railroad was largely a Baltimore project pushed forward by local businessmen who saw their western trade being threatened by the Chesapeake and Ohio Canal. The Charleston and Hamburg Railroad was promoted by the Chamber of Commerce of Charleston, which hoped to take the business of the back country away from rival Savannah. Even in Boston, where there was a mild interest in railroads amongst State Street grandees, the principal support for the Boston and Lowell came from the cotton textile manufacturers of Lowell. When coal rose to prominence in the 1850s, coal barons put up the funds for railroads coming into their coalfields. For example, the Delaware, Lackawanna, and Western Railroad (and its predecessors) was largely promoted and financed by the Scranton family, who owned an iron foundry at a place called Slocum Hollow (now Scranton), Pennsylvania, and needed an outlet for their product and, subsequently, the rich anthracite fields that lay nearby.

On the other hand, it was not long before another kind of investor appeared on the scene—the kind of person whose principal interest in the railroad was not as a service entity, but as an object of speculation, control, or simply pecuniary gain. One of the first railroads, the Mohawk and Hudson, was funded chiefly by wealthy New Yorkers, who managed to get the line listed on the New York Stock Exchange as early as 1830! The cost of building the Philadelphia and Reading Railroad was largely underwritten by banking houses in New York and Philadelphia. By 1841, the Second Bank of the United States in Philadelphia owned nearly one-fourth of the stock of the Reading.[5]

By the late 1840s and early 1850s, however, there was a noticeable shift in the pattern of railroad investment. A small amount of foreign capital began to trickle in (mostly from London), but most important of all, the big financiers of State Street and Wall Street began to see that there was money to be made in railroads. Their interest was naturally applauded, although in the long run the effects of their speculations were far from salutary.

Even the more cautious English had already found to their chagrin that financial speculation in the railroad field was a harbinger of real trouble. In the 1840s, during a period of wild speculation, the British railways passed from the control of their wise old heads—men like the Stephensons—and into the hands of financial manipulators. These manipulators got the job done, to be sure: By 1840 nearly 2,400 miles of track connected London, Birmingham, Manchester, Brighton, and numerous other places. There were a great many lines put down, some prosperous, others marginal. Since there were few laws governing the capitalizing of these lines, crafty individuals, like George Hudson, the so-called "railway king," with a talent for turning "scrip into gold," managed to gain control of vast British railway mileage. Hudson made attractive profits for investors by building up a fragile house of cards, and accordingly he controlled as much as one-third of the

British railway system by 1845. He managed this by paying dividends on existing lines out of capital raised for unbuilt branches, a technique that faltered in the economic hard times of 1848. Hudson was exposed and run out of the country, but not before British railway mileage had risen to over eight thousand.[6]

In America, no single "railway king" arrived in the model of George Hudson, although shortly there would be a few pretenders to the throne. What America got instead, during the 1850s and 1860s, were not baronial lords of a railroad "system," but an assorted collection of proverbial jacks of the pack; some historians have gone so far as to proclaim that the next several generations of railroad financiers and builders were the biggest collection of rogues and rapscallions ever to trod American soil. Whatever cast of light is shed on these individuals, there can be little doubt that a number of them did incalculable harm to the railroad industry in the middle decades of the nineteenth century.

The influence of financial manipulation on the railroad industry did not become clearly evident to the wider general public until after the Civil War; but anyone who followed financial affairs closely in the 1850s should have perceived that serious troubles were at hand. The root of the problem, simply summarized, was that many railroad ventures were extremely risky, so that sophisticated and savvy capitalists (with a few notable exceptions, of course), were not tremendously eager to buy stock in railroad companies. Of course, railroads were fully understood to be the "coming thing," and capitalists wanted in on the action, but for the most part they only wanted to lend money to railroads, not to accept the risks of ownership. Accordingly, by the 1850s, it became a fixed pattern that the largest share of money needed to build or improve railroads would have to come from the bond market, not from the stock market.

For this reason, railroad stock tended to be owned not by the nation's conservative financial leaders, but by little investors, usually businessmen along the route of a particular railroad, but sometimes by anyone who had a small sum of money that they hoped to invest—even wives and widows with a little household money stashed in a cupboard. Railroad stock was usually cheap, but it seemed to hold out enormous promise of growth—in short, it seemed an ideal speculative investment.

In the 1850s, Americans first began to notice the advantages of "playing around" with stocks—an activity that previously had been limited to a few sophisticated traders. The New York Stock Exchange at Broad and Wall Street in New York suddenly became an enormous institution, although it had begun only some sixty years before as a semiformalized group of individuals who gathered in the afternoon in the shade of a buttonwood tree to buy and sell securities. For a few years during the 1850s, it seemed that all Americans were drawn to stock trading, much as they would in the fatal years of the 1920s, as a means of quick profit and gain but without fully understanding the risks involved. Since railroad stocks were cheap (in large measure because they usually were not paying good dividends), little people were avidly drawn to them.

Not perceived by the general public, however, these railroad stocks were really being manipulated by a small number of individuals who had bought them specifically for this purpose. Occasionally, a few active traders in railroad stocks were interested in controlling railroads. Some of these acted out of noble, or at least honest, motives. On the other hand, there were other stock manipulators who had no such public-spirited concern, and in fact no interest in the railroads whose stock they owned—their concern was only to manipulate railroad stocks for their own short-term gains. Since in those days there was no such thing as regulation of stock trading, these individuals could use any means fair or foul to gain their ends.

Probably the most notorious stock manipulator of the 1850s was a half-literate curmudgeon named Daniel Drew, who quickly discovered to his own delight that railroads, most specifically the Erie, seemed ready-made for his own particular brand of dirty tricks. Drew had been born in a once very rural area of Putnam County, New York, in 1797. Reared in poverty, he bought some cattle with a military bonus received from the War of 1812. Almost immediately, his large gift for sinister business practices made itself apparent. He used to drive cattle to market in New York from all over the East, and as his herds approached their final destination he had his drovers salt them well and then drink copiously, thus greatly increasing their sale weight. The notoriety of this practice later gave rise to a Wall Street term—"watered stock." Drew settled permanently in New York and began a number of shady business ventures there. Noticing that Commodore

Cornelius Vanderbilt was cleaning up with his Hudson River steamboats, Drew bought a rickety old vessel, and offered to carry passengers to Albany for a quarter of a dollar. To rid himself of this scruffy competition, the Commodore bought Drew off, the profits only spurring the latter on to further financial dealings on Wall Street. (This early skirmish between Drew and Vanderbilt, the first of many, gave the two men mixed feelings of admiration and hatred for one another.)

Drew was a tall, lanky individual, a loner type, with crude, rustic manners. He had many acquaintances but no intimates. He gave few confidences and seemed always to be running his business entirely out of his own vest pockets, and out of the vaster pockets of his great coat, which was always stuffed with notes and gold certificates. When he finally became a man to conjure with on Wall Street, he was easily recognizable for his untypical, thread-bare dress. In an age when most Wall Street financiers wore beaver hats and sported gold-headed canes, Drew wore a rumpled drover's hat and carried a frayed black umbrella. He kept a house on Bleeker Street where he seldom socialized, and could frequently be seen walking from there to the markets, just as Ebeneezer Scrooge walked to his countinghouse from his dank and dreary rooms. Drew sometimes ate at the famous Delmonico's restaurant, but always in the cheapest, downstairs part of the place, among the messenger boys and counter jumpers.

It is said that many people were beguiled by Daniel Drew's rustic manners—he was half affectionately referred to as Uncle Dan'l—but many more were upended by his pretended simplicity, which masked a Byzantine deviousness. He would tell people who asked, "I got to be a millionaire afore I knowed it, hardly," and he referred to stock shares as "sheers,"[7] but his innocence was always nothing but a pose. Somewhat less of a pose, perhaps, was a strong religious streak—he carried a Bible with him wherever he went, and quoted from it frequently, and was a regular churchgoer. Many of those who knew him described his manner and mien as that of a country deacon or undertaker. Whenever he gave to charity, it was invariably to some church or religious organization. After his fortune was seemingly secure, he donated the sum of $250,000 to found a Methodist theological seminary in New Jersey (now Drew University). It turned out that he had only given his note, and in his last years, after having suffered business reverses, the note proved worthless.[8]

Aside from business and religion, Drew seemed to have no comforts except strong liquor. He was what we would today call a closet drinker, although more appropriately an episodic drinker. Sober at most times, and never permitting anyone to see him in anything but a sober mood or frame of mind, he would occasionally lock himself up in his house on Bleeker Street, draw the shades, and go on a binge that might last as long as four days. He emerged as sober as a country judge, ready to make new killings on Wall Street.

To Drew, business meant only one thing—making money by whatever means were easy to hand. Of business ethics, he knew nothing—his methods were strictly those of guile, trickery, and chicane. By the 1850s, Drew was a major stock trader on Wall Street; indeed, he was the best known "bear" of the street. A bear in Wall Street parlance was an individual who believed that stock prices were going down, and he would sell short to profit by the losses. A bear was a pessimist, so to speak, who believed that business was going to hell—an attitude that fitted Uncle Dan'l's saturnine countenance. But Drew was never a pessimist on his own account; he was always looking for somebody else on whose misfortunes he could capitalize. He raised to a high art the practice (now illegal) of maneuvering a "bear raid," whereby prices are driven down by repeated short selling. All Drew needed to do was identify suitable victims for his special brand of trickery.

By the early 1850s, Drew had identified the woebegone Erie Railroad as his principal victim. The Erie had been finished through to its full length, but it had never escaped its early financial deprivations. It was perpetually cash poor, and it already had among the public a poor reputation for its inadequate roadbed, its unsafe rail, and its rickety, lamp-lit passenger cars. Erie stock was cheap, and what is more important, subject to violent fluctuations, so that Drew was drawn to it, not only as a way of gaining entrée into the inner circles of management, but so that he might profit directly by whatever manipulations of price he could engineer.

By 1853, Drew managed to maneuver his way onto the board of Erie, opposed only by the horrified silence of other board members, staid and conservative pillars of the financial community who had been struggling gamely to keep Erie from faltering.

Drew's appearance on the Erie's board, said historian Stewart Holbrook, was the greatest calamity ever suffered by this railroad, which had already experienced a long string of calamities. But still worse was to follow. The following year, Drew became treasurer of the company, after which its stock began to fluctuate wildly, partly because it was no longer paying dividends, but also because Drew himself was secretly manipulating the stock.

Over the next several years, the Erie dangled helplessly in the breeze, as Drew thought up new and innovative ways to empty its treasury. In 1857, desperately short of cash, and often unable to meet its payroll, the railroad turned to Drew for a loan of $1,500,000, which he tendered while taking a mortage on everything he could, and helping himself to a $25,000 finder's fee as well.[9] The year 1857 was a bad year financially for the nation, a depression year, but miraculously, Erie didn't go into bankruptcy. That unhappy event did occur in the summer of 1859, however, after which the Erie Railroad had to be completely reorganized. Needless to say, Drew, as a creditor of the old company, managed to get his hands on much of what was due him, a pittance in comparison with what he had already made as a stock manipulator.

The Erie emerged from bankruptcy three years later, and during the Civil War profited mightily like most northern railroads. But Daniel Drew remained on the board waiting to pluck the feathers of this new chicken, and in the late 1860s and early 1870s, now an old man, he once again began taking advantage of this company whose physical condition had not improved, and whose employees were frequently left unpaid. In partnership with two other rascals, Jay Gould and Jim Fisk, the Erie would be taken over the coals yet another time, in one of the most disgraceful episodes in American financial history, an epic chronicled so meticulously by the brothers Henry and Charles Francis Adams in their book *Chapters of Erie.*

It would be unfair to say that men like Drew were characteristic of the railway leaders of their day. Nor were all railroads of the pre–Civil War period so vulnerable to financial manipulation as the Erie. Some railroads were soundly financed, and there were true railway giants active in the field—men like John Edgar Thompson of the Pennsylvania, or John W. Garrett of the Baltimore and Ohio. Even Commodore Vanderbilt proved to be a competent railroad manager in spite of his own pecuniary lusts.

But the fragility of a number of railroad lines became evident to perspicacious Americans during the 1850s, and not a few fore-sighted individuals began to question where it was all going to end. Some might have excused the wild speculation and deceptive practices of men like Daniel Drew as an aberration necessary to support the rapid growth of industry. But were all men of business to be of this stripe? Were our business leaders to be no more pub-lic spirited than this? Railroads were universally believed to belong to the people; they had a semipublic status, so that whenever it was perceived that they were being milked dry for the profit of the few, when railroad equipment was falling apart, when railway workers were left unpaid, there was considerable anxiety that the public interest was not being well served, and that there was some-thing profoundly wrong with the way businesses were financed and managed. Furthermore, there was already anxiety over whether some of these distortions and ills of the capitalist system might spread to other industries and other conditions of life. Alas, in the years after the Civil War, many of these anxieties would be realized.

The inner workings of finance were mysterious and arcane to most Americans in the 1850s, and even Americans who were famil-iar with the shady dealings of a Daniel Drew were not inclined to worry about their ultimate effect on railroads. When there were criticisms expressed in the public prints about railroads, it was nearly always some other issue, most often safety, that engendered the most hostile comment. Nevertheless, there were other reserva-tions about the railroads—and what their growth might lead to—expressed by a number of other individuals, especially some of the country's best-known writers and intellectuals. Some of these thinkers expressed serious reservations about the railroad's abrupt intrusion on the American scene and its possible ill effects on American life.

The same thing had happened in England. Adverse comments about British railroads began almost immediately after the first lines were laid—usually coming from individuals who saw the rail-road as a nasty and mobile form of the Industrial Revolution. Thomas Carlyle began fulminating over the railroad shortly after the first locomotive wheels were turned, and in another genera-tion he would be joined by other writers, such as John Ruskin, who saw the railroad as an ugly manifestation of the factory system, which they believed to be a blight on English life, to say nothing of the English landscape. Carlyle and Ruskin were essentially medievalists, who saw the only road to salvation as a return to a simpler, more pastoral life-style. They were also concerned (as most American critics were not) that railroads would hasten the march of democratic man, perhaps even foment revolution; they saw the railroad as an agency that would permit idiotic ideas and foolish people to flutter aimlessly around the country expressing discontent and dissension. Thomas Carlyle, in whom rage and calumny often knew no bounds, dashed off one of his brilliant diatribes after viewing the construction of one of the early railroads. There was a beautiful hillside that he admired—shortly a railroad blasted through it with dynamite. To what end? he raged. Simply so that some fool or jackal in Birmingham could get to Leads in half the time. What was the use of it: Why did not the fool in Birmingham just stay in Birmingham as nature and the forces of the universe intended him to do? What use of all this blasting, the smoke, the noise, and the despoiling of the landscape just so that fools could prance from place to place?

No such patrician disdain for mass man would trouble America's early critics of the Industrial Revolution or the railroad—it was universally believed that industry could be safely confined to certain geographical areas, and that the railroad, noisesome as it might be, would never be able to gobble up the whole of the vast American landscape. When perforce it had to blast through some usually remote valley, there was always assurance that there were many others resting in silence and aesthetic isolation. Furthermore, there was much to be said in favor of the railroad from the beginning—the very immensity of the American nation cried out for an infrastructure to bind together its people. In England, the people were already bound together; the problem instead was that a large population with abrasive class divisions could be agitated by further spread of the Industrial Revolution, by the joining of cities and urban corridors.

But the railroad did provoke in America a certain amount of hostility for some of the same reasons that it did in England—the railroad was an "industry," after all, and a sometimes disruptive and intrusive one, and many Americans felt, even more intently than their English counterparts, that great efforts must be made to preserve a virgin continent that had not yet been despoiled by factories, by large cities, and by massive overpopulation. Many of the American founding fathers, Thomas Jefferson especially, felt that democracy as a form of government could only survive in an essentially agrarian society, as a land of yeoman farmers, each tilling his own plot of land and cultivating his own personal and eccentric life-style.

In his justly praised work in intellectual history, *The Machine in the Garden: Technology and the Pastoral Ideal in America,* Leo Marx made the point that a recurring pastoral ideal, a kind of enduring nostalgia for space and arcadian delights, has motivated the American people throughout their history. Even in the twentieth century, the dweller in an urban skyscraper apartment yearns for a sailboat, a country retreat, a hilltop paradise far from the maddening crowd's ignoble strife—even while continuing to crave the fleshpots of the city. More importantly, as soon as transportation became available, typical American city dwellers who were financially able chose to abandon the city for the suburbs, a place where their children could grow up with trees and green lawns. So the pastoral ideal is a continuing part of the American dream, whatever grotesque forms it may sometimes take. When the railroad first made its appearance, as Marx so forcefully demonstrates, there was a considerable source of anxiety that it would be an instrument, perhaps *the* instrument, whereby the noble dream of the virgin continent would eventually be destroyed.

On the other hand, Americans as a whole, even our early intellectuals, were not ill disposed to the fruits of technology, were not hostile to steam and energy, iron and machinery. Thomas Jefferson, for example, the most philosophical and the most resolutely agrarian of our early presidents, believed the factory system could work in America, even though it had been an unhealthy influence in Europe. He saw enormous hope in the newer forms of technology. All kinds of machines, he believed, when freed from the dark, crowded, plague-ridden cities of Europe, could make a contribution to a healthy American civilization and culture. He saw the machine turning millwheels, moving ships up rivers as achievements that could transform a wilderness or barren territory into a genial society.[10]

Jefferson did not live to see the dawn of the railroad era in America, but there is every reason to believe that he would have held this innovation in transportation to be a worthy addition to

American life. And so, too, did most of America's sages in the years before the Civil War, although there were also a few dissenting opinions during this period. In general, Americans continued to have a wide pragmatic streak in their character; they believed that when things really needed to get done, there should be ways to do them. Such things would be realized in good health, because the American people were healthy. Consider the case of Ralph Waldo Emerson, our great national sage and poet, who believed in the sanctity of nature, who believed that there could be a bond between nature and human character, between the physical world and the world of spirit. From the oracular authority of his pulpit in Boston, and from the safe precincts of his study in Concord, where, during the 1850s, he issued some of the most graceful and thoughtful essays ever penned on American soil, Emerson might well be expected to blast technology, particularly the railroad, much in the manner of his friend Carlyle. But he did not.

In a lecture delivered in 1844 entitled "The Young American," Emerson expressed the belief that our vast open spaces have required technology for the realization of a new, young, and vital civilization. He fully shared Jefferson's notion that the machine, freed of overpopulated and class-ridden Europe, could prove a useful agent of progress. He had special praise to offer the newer forms of transportation, the steamboat and the railroad, which he saw as annihilating distance, as drawing the American people into a unified culture. He believed that the agency of the railroad would minimize factionalism, overcome local peculiarities, open up the West, and preserve the Union—it was drawing nigh the time when Americans were beginning to speak a great deal about the need to "preserve" the Union. In an even greater leap of faith, Emerson held that technology (including the railroad) was like a divining rod, and that it could unearth the hidden graces of the landscape. "Railroad iron," he said, "was a magician's rod, in its power to evoke the sleeping energies of land and water."

Although a boundlessly optimistic man, Emerson added a certain caveat to his praise of the railroad magic. Technology, he admitted, could come into the sole possession of men who would abuse it—men of understanding rather than reason, as he put it— men who are able to manipulate knowledge, the findings of science, but have no moral goals in doing so. They can get things done, they can create the means by which society functions, without asking where society was headed, or what were the limitations of these new and ingenious forms. Technology—railroads—might fall into the hands of a generation of men who care not for civilization, men with no feel for the continuity and the lessons of history, and this could result in a dangerous downturning.

Emerson's friend and sometime Concord neighbor, Henry David Thoreau, was another who viewed the railroad with some ambiguity and puzzlement. Thoreau has been mistakenly viewed by some readers of his works, most especially readers of *Walden,* which describes the two years that he lived in semi-isolation in a small cabin on Walden Pond, as a nature lover and something of a hermit, who wanted to leave behind the mundane world of commerce for an elysian paradise. In fact, Thoreau was one of the most politically concerned and socially motivated writers of his generation, using his stay at Walden Pond merely as a window to better view the world. Like most of his contemporaries, even the so-called New England transcendentalists, he had a pragmatic strain, and possessed an interest in objects of social utility. Thus, he shared Emerson's primitive faith in the usefulness of the railroad, even though he might well have become annoyed at its presence so near his place of solitude—the Fitchburg Railroad skirted the edge of Walden Pond!

Even though the railroad could have been a nuisance to Thoreau—he might have been annoyed by the clatter of the bell, the shriek of the whistle; he might have complained of this intrusion on nature, this spread of urban life into the wilderness—instead he seemed to enjoy it. He was amused to find train crews waving to him as an old acquaintance, even a fellow worker, a track repairer perhaps. The railroad, he seemed to believe, was something of a social energizer, an anodyne to complacency and slothful habits. It had the effect of making men alert and animated, keeping them on their toes. The railroad had obviously transformed the simple America of days past into an active and vibrant society. Everywhere it went, it had changed the nature and the mood even of small-town life.

The startings and arrivals of the cars are now the epochs in the village day. They go and come with such regularity and precision, and their whistle can be heard so far, that the farmers set their clocks by them, and thus one well-conducted institution regulates a whole country. Have not men improved somewhat in punctuality since the railroad was invented? Do they not talk and think faster in the depot than they did in the stage-office? I have been astonished by the miracles it has wrought.[11]

Walden is a very moody book, and Thoreau a moody and temperamental man, so it is not surprising that his vision of the railroad is expressed in ambiguous and sometimes contradictory terms. In numerous references to the railroad, he compares it metaphorically to a fiery steed of some new mythology, or to a partridge; elsewhere he compares it to a hawk swooping down upon its prey. At times, the railroad tended to blend smoothly with the landscape, to have its own aesthetic energies, but at the very same moment Thoreau would express doubts, as in this particularly lovely verse:

> What's the railroad to me?
> I never go to see
> Where it ends.
> It fills a few hollows,
> And makes banks for the swallows,
> It sets the sand a-blowing,
> And the blackberries a-growing

On the other hand, he crosses the tracks immediately thereafter with a sense of mild annoyance. "I will not have my eyes put out and my ears spoiled by its smoke and steam and hissing."

What's the railroad to me? There are some other doubts as well. "All the Indian huckleberry hills are stripped, all the cranberry meadows are raked into the city. Up comes the cotton, down goes the cotton cloth; up goes the silk, down goes the woollen; up come the books, but down goes the wit that writes them." People's lives may be improved by rapid transportation, but they may also be drawn away to silly, frantic, and ignoble pursuits. "If all were as it seems and men made their servants for noble ends,"[12] he laments in the manner of Emerson, all would be well, but the point is we can't fathom these ends; we don't really know whether this great capacity of the railroad will be used for the advancement of civilization in the spiritual sense. It has the capacity to do so, but whether it actually will, we can only wait and see. Thoreau

is intrigued by the physical presence of the railroad, but, as he
makes so clear in his poem, "I never go to see where it ends."

Another famous American writer was much less ambivalent
about the railroad than Emerson and Thoreau, and thought that
he knew where the railroad would end, and it was not paradise. In
a remarkable satire entitled "The Celestial Railroad," which mir-
rored the allegorical techniques of Bunyan's "Pilgrim's Progress,"
Nathaniel Hawthorne laid the railroad out flat, declaring it to be a
force for the destruction of civilization. In Hawthorne's ominous
tale, a group of wayfarers await to board a train for the Celestial
City. They will get there in short order, too, as they are reminded
by the hearty Mr. Smooth-it-away, one of the directors of the railroad, a booster or salesmen type who endlessly points out how
quick and easy it is to travel by rail, and who scoffs at old fashioned pilgrims along the right-of-way who are still going by foot or
on horseback.

The narrator of the story is skeptical from the very beginning.
When the train pulls into the station, he notices with a chill that
"on its top sat a personage almost enveloped in smoke and flame,
which…appeared to gush from his own mouth and stomach, as
well as from the engine's brazen abdomen." While on his journey
to the Celestial City, the narrator has opportunities to make some
sly observations on how poorly the railroad is built, how its
bridges shake, and how the cars rattle, but he is even more per-
turbed about how the railroad has transformed the landscape,
ruining settled institutions and traditional ways of life. People who
board the train are hurried, agitated; they seem to want to drop
their values by the wayside. The bluff, optimistic Mr. Smooth-it-
away assures everyone that things are fine, but when the train
arrives at the end of its journey, depositing passengers at the bank
of a river where they are to board a steamboat for the Celestial
City on the other side, Mr. Smooth-it-away deserts his friends;
apparently he will not be going on to the Celestial City. He gives a
sinister laugh, "in the midst of which cachinnation, a smoke-
wreath issued from his mouth and nostrils, while a twinkle of lurid
flame darted out either eye, proving indubitably that his heart was
all of a red blaze."[13]

The narrator understood now; the railroad could be advertised
as providing a smooth ride to heaven, but in fact it was the work of
the devil himself. At this point, the narrator woke up—it was all

just a dream, a bad dream. But the point Hawthorne was making was perfectly clear. Progress, physical progress, so triumphantly realized in the railroad, may be nothing but a mirage. Will we let it carry us away to some shiny future that will only blow up in smoke and brimstone just when we are about to reach our goal?

Hawthorne may not have been typical of most of his fellow Americans in the 1850s; yet there must have been everywhere some of the same tincture of doubt. The railroad led away from arcadian America, from the virginal continent, to a new and shadowy nation. It would transform the American people, it would subvert their values. It would make a promise of leading to a city of wonders, to new and gleeming life-styles, but would it really lead to our salvation as a people? Hawthorne thought not, and surely a good number of his contemporaries shared these same grave doubts and dark reflections.

C·H·A·P·T·E·R 6

A NATION DIVIDED,
A NATION JOINED

In 1860, the year that Abraham Lincoln was elected president, the official census of the United States showed that the total population of the nation had reached 31,443,321. Of that total, 19,690,000 individuals lived in the North; 11,133,361 in the South, and a mere 619,000 in the West.[1] By this same year, the northeastern states of the country had been linked by a dense web of connected (but not yet integrated) rail lines. Railroad growth in the last several years had been unprecedented anywhere in the world, mileage having been virtually doubled since 1855.

As the decade of the 1860s opened, the North appeared to be in the midst of a frenzied spurt of railway construction. In 1858, the young Baltimore businessman John W. Garrett was appointed president of the Baltimore and Ohio and quickly laid plans to extend his lines beyond the Alleghenies, first by building a line up to Pittsburgh, then, through purchase of other railroads, to extend the B & O empire from Marietta, Ohio, to St. Louis. After the Civil War, he would strike out vigorously across northern Ohio and Indiana for Chicago. The already impressive Pennsylvania Railroad was expanding, too, under the leadership of J. Edgar Thompson, who purchased the Pittsburgh, Fort Wayne, and Chicago Railroad so that the Pennsylvania would have its own entrée into the windy city on Lake Michigan.

Chicago was, in fact, a good example of what the railroads were doing for the northern states in the years immediately before the Civil War. Chicago had grown from an obscure and dilapidated military post known as Fort Dearborn, which as late as 1830 had a population of no more than forty people. The Illinois River and some canals gave slight growth to the settlement in the next several decades, but it was the coming of the railroad that in a few short years raised Chicago from a rough pioneer settlement to one of the great cities of the world. Interestingly, Chicagoans wanted nothing to do with the railroad in the beginning, preferring instead the development of canals and plank roads. But the city's first mayor and greatest promoter, William Butler Ogden, obtained a charter to build a railroad from Chicago to the lead mines of Galena on the Mississippi River. This railroad, known as the Galena and Chicago Union Railroad, forerunner of the present Chicago and Northwestern Railroad, energized the citizens of sleepy Chicago as soon as its first trains began to run in 1848.[2]

Within the next three or four years, Chicago began to show signs of becoming what it would be in the years ahead—America's great railway junction. Not only was there Ogden's Galena Road, which shortly pushed its way up into Wisconsin, but the Illinois Central Railroad would construct its important Chicago Division, later to become the main line of this vital north-south carrier. Boston financier John Murray Forbes and Detroit lawyer James Frederick Joy were linking Chicago with Michigan and other points east with their Michigan Central Railroad (later part of the New York Central Railroad). Also by the early 1850s, Henry Farnum of Rock Island was laying plans for a railroad that would link Chicago with his hometown on the Mississippi River, and it would only be a matter of a few years before this railroad (the Chicago and Rock Island) would leap the Mississippi and provide rail service to the state of Iowa. It was clearly evident to any careful observer in 1860 that Chicago, linked as it was by rail to so many other places, would also be an industrial and commercial center of the first rank, contributing in the years ahead to the strength and muscle of the northern states.

In 1860, you could not ride between New York and Chicago on a single railway train, but had to make your trip, which would take several days, over the rails of interconnecting lines. Shortly after the Civil War, however, the so-called "trunkline" railroads came into existence and made travel between New York and Chicago or Washington and St. Louis a routine and everyday occurrence. The makings of the trunkline system were indeed partially in place by 1860, but not yet implemented due to the sometimes stubborn resistance of local carriers. Yet even at this time, the implications of the great eastern trunklines were obvious for all to see. A dense web of railway lines throughout the northern states had brought about a transformation of this region into a kind of national market with a cohering sense of identity. Chicago was now clearly linked to Philadelphia and New York, with these cities freely exchanging their manufactured and agricultural products. For example, by 1860, the railroads of the north had begun to participate in a large-scale transport of western grain, which was eventually loaded at eastern seaports for shipment to Europe.

More importantly, however, the railway web had firmed up and solidified what had long been thought to be a loose union of states. The northern states may well have been markedly different in character, but they were now all pulling together economically, welded by the miracle of railway transportation. A coherent national market had created a union that pragmatically now could not be broken.[3]

The situation was markedly different in the South, in the states that would soon form the Confederacy. There was a political and spiritual unity among these states that was undeniable, but economic union was something altogether different. The South did have an economic union of sorts in that the territory was almost completely agricultural, and its political advocates in Congress were always effective spokesmen for the agrarian interests of the region, whether of cotton, tobacco, or whatever. But beyond this, the South had little drawing it together economically. No better example of this can be found than in the statistics relating to railroad mileage in the South in 1860. At this time, the northern states had 20,814 railroad miles, the South a mere 9,819.[4] What is perhaps more significant, the South's railroad mileage consisted almost exclusively of small local carriers. The only thing that even faintly resembled an east-west trunkline among the numerous southern railroads was one line between Memphis and Chattanooga, with branches northward to Richmond and Norfolk and southward to Atlanta and Savannah.

This situation certainly did not bode well for a sector of the country that was about to embark on a war with the neighboring states of the North. But an even more serious problem was that the South in effect had no capacity or facilities of its own for improving railroad mileage or rolling stock. Nearly all the locomotives running on southern railroads were built in the North, as were nearly all of the South's steel rails. The southern states did not have a great many locomotives to begin with (in 1860, the Erie and Pennsylvania railroads alone owned more locomotives than all of the southern railways combined). What's more, the South had no capacity for building more locomotives in the event of war. Its only factory devoted to locomotive construction was the Tredegar Iron Works at Richmond, and when the war broke out the Confederate government converted it to the construction of shell billets and military ordnance. This defect in their ability to prosecute a civil war on a grand scale was not of course evident to most southerners (or most northerners, for that matter), mainly because there had been no previous war in history in which railroads had played a strategically important role. All of a sudden, the railroads would change the course of military history forever, although few could have foreseen this when the Civil War broke out in 1861.

In the years just before the Civil War, the statesmen of neither North nor South were spending a great deal of time thinking about the military uses of railroads or how their respective destinies would be effected by this new form of military transport. Insofar as railroads were concerned in the late 1850s, the hottest political issue had nothing to do with railroads already in existence, nothing to do with an anticipated war between the states, but rather with the much debated question of whether and where to build a railroad from the Mississippi River to California that would provide an overland link between the Atlantic and Pacific oceans. Congress had been vigorously debating the issue—called the issue of the Pacific Railroad—for some time. They discussed it with some degree of vigor ever since gold had been discovered in California in 1848, and that state admitted to the union in 1850.

As a matter of historical fact, however, the vision of a railroad spanning the entire continent of the United States was almost as old as railroads themselves. The first individual to conceive of the idea apparently was one Judge S.W. Dexter of the little hamlet of Ann Arbor, in what was then Michigan Territory, who wrote an editorial on the subject in a paper he owned, the *Weekly Immigrant,* on February 6, 1832. The idea was not given much credence at the time, but like a lot of good ideas, it never died, and intrigued a number of other visionaries in the years after. Following Dexter, there was John Plumbe, a Welch-born engineer who had surveyed several railroad lines in the East and who eventually settled in Dubuque, Iowa, where in 1838 he gathered together some influential friends and presented them with a scheme for privately building a railroad from that place to the Pacific Ocean.

Plumbe, too, was far ahead of his time, and he received few converts to his scheme. Few people thought at the time that there was any reason or practical use for a railroad to the West Coast. But shortly later, another individual, Asa Whitney by name, became the champion of a Pacific Railroad. Whitney spent ten years of his life and a small business fortune to convince people that a railroad to the Pacific coast was an absolute necessity. He conceived the idea while on a business trip to China, and became convinced that a transcontinental railroad would be the key to securing a rich Oriental trade for America. Something of a fanatic, a monomaniac, Whitney peppered Congress with proposals, memorials, addresses, and broadsides, all the while mounting a vigorous publicity campaign, especially in the big eastern cities, which he believed would profit by such a rail link to the Pacific.

Whitney did gain a certain amount of public attention for his scheme, and in several successive sessions of Congress bills were introduced to survey one or more possible rail routes to the West Coast. Fully aware that no financial backers could be found for a railroad that would pass through a vast region inhabited only by Indians and buffalo, Whitney made the very sensible suggestion that the railroad be granted a sixty-mile-wide strip of land from the Mississippi to the Pacific at the Columbia River—a plan that would supposedly allow the railroad to pay for itself by selling land, timber, and minerals and by developing cities along the way. But after ten years of effort during the 1840s, the idea remained stillborn, and Whitney retired from his crusade a beaten and broken man.

By the 1850s, however, with California now a member of the Union, the idea of a Pacific railroad was being talked up everywhere, and in fact it would be hard to find a congressman anywhere who had not gone on record as being highly enthusiastic about the basic concept. The trouble was that by the 1850s sectionalism had become rampant in the affairs of state, and politicians were drawn into self-defeating arguments about where the line should be laid. Southern senators and congressmen naturally wanted to see a line from the Old South, through Texas and on to "southern" California. They had some strong arguments to make in behalf of their plan, not all of them related to the issue of slavery. They pointed out that such a line would not have to fight the high Sierra mountains, and that it would also escape the ravages of the hostile Sioux Indians who inhabited the middle plains.

Most people in the northern states, and those associated with the strong industrial interests of the East, naturally favored some kind of route through the middle part of the country, west from Chicago or St. Louis, although a number also favored a far northern route from Lake Superior west. Even though a middle route seemed the most useful, there were bitter disputes over exactly where that route should be located. One session of Congress seemed well disposed to select a route that ran west from Chicago through Iowa and Nebraska, but the idea was blocked by Senator Thomas Hart Benton of Missouri, who would not tolerate any route that did not include St. Louis.

Since by this time hardly a statesman anywhere in the land opposed the *idea* of a transcontinental railroad, Congress in 1853 appropriated $150,000 to survey as many as six different possible routes that a railroad might take. Supervising this work was Jefferson Davis, Secretary of War in the cabinet of President Franklin Pierce, who naturally favored one of the southern routes. Still, he gave judicious consideration to all the proposed routes. But it hardly needs to be added that there were some who liked none of these routes and proposed still others—Senator Thomas Hart Benton was one of those unhappy with all proposals and personally paid for the surveying of his favorite route.

The surveys were made, there was much talk on the subject every year in Congress, but as the decade of the 1850s wore down, no agreement was reached on the subject. The southerners were becoming intransigent on the subject, as they were on every subject that had implications for their identity, their honor, and their economic survival. All legislation that affected the various national sections—South, North, and West—died a slow and painful death in the United States Senate. In the election of 1860, the

Republican party, which selected Abraham Lincoln as its candidate, took the bull by the horns and pushed a great number of issues that were of vital importance to the western states and territories, including the long-delayed Homestead issue. And among the major planks of their party platform was a proposal to build a Pacific railroad by one of the central routes. This was not simply a matter of attempting to bedevil the South: It now seemed clearly warranted by the pattern of emigration to the West, the population of the area, the steady growth of cities like Denver and San Francisco, of states like Kansas and Utah, and many new mineral discoveries along the proposed central route.[5]

Still, in that presidential year of 1860, nearly everybody realized the full immensity of effort that would be needed to bring the transcontinental railroad to fruition. With the secession of the southern states and with southern representatives withdrawn from Congress, President Lincoln was able to sign the Pacific Railroad Act on July 1, 1862, but it would be seven years before the line would be completed. The delay can largely be attributed to the Civil War, of course, since the war seriously drained the North of its resources and its desire for activity in the far West. Even Lincoln's signing of the Pacific Railroad Act, while it contained provisions for the building of such a railroad, did not provide the impetus. When the impetus came, it came not from the places that might have been expected—the industrial North and the Midwest—it came instead from a place that would not have been dreamed of a few years before: the faraway and struggle-free state of California. Once again, too, the impetus came from a hard-driving monomaniac, who had migrated to California ready to take up the holy war that Asa Whitney had recently abandoned. The transcontinental railroad needed another Asa Whitney to get the job done, and as the Civil War began he was on stage and ready for action—in California.

The name of the man was Theodore Judah, and he had just designed and built the first railroad line in California: the twenty-one-mile Sacramento Valley line between Sacramento and Folsom. Judah was not a native Californian—indeed, in the 1850s nearly all Californians had come from somewhere else. Judah hailed from Connecticut, had received engineering training at the Troy Engineering School (now Rensselaer Polytechnic Institute), had worked on several eastern railroads including the New Haven, had designed bridges, and had virtually planned and built the Niagara Gorge Railroad, considered a technological marvel in its day. In 1854, at the age of twenty-eight, with this experience under his belt, he was engaged to build a line that would run from Sacramento, the capital of California, to the mining country of the Sierra foothills.

But something big happened to Judah during his first assignment in California. He was bitten by a bug, an idea, one that would never leave him—the need to continue this line not merely a few more miles to Nevada, but all the way to the Atlantic Ocean. Apparently, this conversion came to Judah when he was doing some sideline surveying for his employers. The placer mines of California had begun to peter out, and it was thought that it might be possible to build a wagon trail to the rapidly growing silver towns of Nevada. Judah made the survey, and it occurred to him that there was no reason why his company should settle for a wagon road—they could and should build a railroad. Judah's surveys showed him that it was possible to get a railroad over the passes of the Sierra, and that once this was accomplished it could go right on to the eastern shore.

His employers thought that Judah had lost his senses, and showed not the slightest inclination to sponsor any such harebrained scheme. Not to be put off, however, Judah abandoned his surveying work, which had already convinced him of the feasibility of his scheme, and began a vigorous campaign to sell the idea to the leading citizens of his state. He went to San Francisco, which contained most of the state's moneyed citizens, but was laughed away. He went to the newspapers; he issued broadsides; he took to the platform; he bent the ear of anyone who would listen. Informally, he picked up the nickname "Crazy Judah," and a lot of people believed that here was just another madman pushing for an impractical ideal over which he had become deranged or paranoid. Another Asa Whitney.

Interestingly, there were a great many citizens in California who agreed that the idea was a good one. Railroad historian Stewart Holbrook pointed out that a smoldering interest was there. "Nearly everybody in the state had come from back East. All felt isolated from their old homes. Most were as avid as Judah for the railroad."[6] By 1859, Judah's ideas were popular enough that he was able to convene a Pacific Railroad Convention in San

Francisco, where his plans were greeted by universal acclaim. The only drawback was money. The needed capital was simply not forthcoming.

By this time, Judah was convinced, as were many in Washington, that the transcontinental railroad would only be possible with financial aid from the federal government. Accordingly, loaded with facts, surveys, and testimonials, Judah traveled to Washington, where he was warmly received by both houses of Congress. Sympathy for the project was almost universal at this time, and only the antipathy between the northern and southern sections prevented the immediate enactment of a Pacific Railway bill. Everybody was listening; Judah was even appointed secretary of the Pacific Railroad Committee of the House, given an office, which he turned into what he called "The Pacific Railroad Museum." He went on to charm senators and congressmen, newspaper editors, visitors, callers, and plain citizens, nearly all of whom went away convinced that Judah had an unshakable and irrefutable idea.

Because of the sectional strife, the railway bill did not get through Congress in 1859, so Judah went back to California hoping to be able to bring back more detailed surveys, and perhaps to find citizens of his adoptive state willing to put up some capital. San Francisco once again proved stubborn and unmovable, but eventually Judah found a few who would listen in Sacramento, where he had begun his railroad activity in the state. He called a meeting that was attended by about a dozen businessmen, and here he began to encounter at least a modicum of interest. Among those who began to see the light were four individuals who, thanks to Judah, would go on to become among the most legendary figures in California history. They were a dry goods merchant named Charles Crocker, a wholesale grocer named Leland Stanford, and two partners in a local hardware store, Mark Hopkins and Collis P. Huntington.

Judah began to hang around the Huntington and Hopkins hardware store at 52 K Street in Sacramento, where he could always be assured of the sympathetic ear of the proprietors and almost everyone else who happened to drop in. In time, Judah knew that he had identified his financial backers in the persons of Huntington, Hopkins, Stanford, and Crocker. None of them were wealthy men, only prosperous, although in only a matter of a few years Judah's vision would make of them some of the wealthiest men in the nation. Curiously, none of these merchants were themselves men of keen vision or imagination. So Judah did not even attempt to push on them his transcontinental vision, but only something with an immediate profit connected with it—a railroad to the silver mines of Nevada, which would give its proprietors a monopoly on the brisk trade with that area. Judah kept his counsel, with the transcontinental scheme concealed in the background, and finally obtained a modest backing from these modest merchants for a railroad to Nevada—a railroad that would be cheap and quick. Judah knew that the larger scheme would have to await action from Washington. Now, alas, the Civil War was imminent, so it was obvious that starting out with this short line to Nevada was the only practical possibility, at least for the time being.

Accordingly, it would be a long time before the saga of the transcontinental railroad would unfold—Theodore Judah would have to cool his heels for a few years while the nation back East recovered from the first traumas of war, and Collis P. Huntington, Leland Stanford, Charles Crocker, and Mark Hopkins would remain for a few more years small town merchants in Sacramento, California. California would be untouched by the Civil War, of course, but east of the Mississippi River there was no time to think of anything else; the transcontinental railroad remained an important vision but one that would have to wait the action of the federal government. Now there was the more pressing question of whether the Union could even survive.

After the firing on Fort Sumter in April 1861, after the secession of the southern states from the Union, there was no doubt that this splitting of a nation would have large implications for transportation, most especially for the railroads. The railroad history of the time would be every bit as important an epic as that of the transcontinental line, and in the short run it would have more earth-shattering consequences for all Americans. In retrospect, the Civil War has been called the first great railway war, and so it was; on the other hand, few officials and few military men understood in 1861 exactly how crucial the railroads would be to the outcome. All were aware that railroad lines and railroad equipment would be a major objective of military action, but few perceived the extent to which they would seal the fate of the conflict.

Still, the military importance of the railroads was apparent even before the war began. In 1859, at the time of John Brown's famous raid at Harper's Ferry, the Baltimore and Ohio Railroad was suddenly confronted with the fact that it possessed a rail line that straddled the states of North and South and would perpetually be in the line of fire, would itself become something of a battleground. In 1859, an eastbound Baltimore and Ohio train found itself waylaid by a group of armed abolitionists who took shots at various members of the crew before allowing the train to pass. It was a mild skirmish in view of what would transpire in the next few years, but it was an act which vividly brought home to the minds of railroad men the fact that railroads that ran through the war zone would themselves be targets during all military exploits.

Not all railroads would be adversely affected by the war. A number of the northern railroads, including the Erie and the Pennsylvania, profited mightily during the war years and were never subjected to plunder. But roads like the Baltimore and Ohio and the Louisville and Nashville that sat astride some area of conflict frequently found themselves in an unmanageable condition and sometimes broken, truncated, or completely paralyzed. Naturally, parts of the border railroads would pass from the dominance of one army or the other depending on the fortunes of war. At times, they were allowed to keep operating by both sides because they were important to both. But in the final analysis, the outcome of the war was not determined by who held this or that border railroad; it was determined by a reality much bigger and more fundamental.

This reality was that the North was far more populous than the South, far more industrialized, and much more cohesive as an economic unit. The railroads had had a great deal to do with making it that way. Even before the war began, the northern railroads were quickly approaching trunkline status. They had almost completely knocked out all other forms of transportation. When the war came, the South would be deprived of the older forms of transport on which it had depended much more heavily than the railroad—river traffic, most especially. The South continued to depend very heavily on the Mississippi River for much of its economy, and even though it would do a great deal to hold its part of the river during the war, the river's undependability for north-south transportation had the effect of wedding the states of the middle border to the North and the East. Thus, when railroads reached Chicago and St. Louis, it was foreordained that these cities would be sending their goods East by railway, not down through the Confederacy on the Mississippi River. Accordingly, the states of the new middle border were pulled relentlessly into the Union—even Missouri, with all of its southern sympathizers, was economically drawn to the northern group of states.

From a railroad point of view, the North was clearly in a superb position to wage war over a vast geographical area. Not only did it have the railroad mileage, it had nearly all of the railroad industries—the facilities for making rails, locomotives, and rolling stock. Over seventy-five percent of the locomotives being built in the United States in 1860 came from two cities in the North—Philadelphia, where the Baldwin Locomotive Works was the nation's largest single builder of locomotives, and Paterson, New Jersey, showing an even bigger volume of production with three major locomotive builders, the Rogers Locomotive and Machine Works, Danforth, Cooke, and Company, and the New Jersey Locomotive Company. During the Civil War, the Rogers Locomotive and Machine Works, with over one thousand employees, would turn out ten to twelve locomotives a month, and the three Paterson locomotive plants together produced the unbelievable number of one locomotive every working day during the high tide of industrial prosperity during the Civil War.[7]

In contrast to all this might and muscle, the South had—nothing! Southern railroads owned locomotives, most of which had been made in the North, but they had virtually no capacity for building their own. Their most productive plant, the Tredegar Iron Works at Richmond, had produced some forty locomotives by the beginning of the war,[8] but this factory would have to be converted to producing military hardware almost immediately. In contrast, by 1862, both the Baldwin and Rogers locomotive works had produced one thousand locomotives each, and were moving ahead full force, building new and better locomotives for the military.

The disparity in the number of cars was equally dramatic. The average number of railway cars (passenger and freight) owned by all southern railroads was not much over two hundred. The largest collection of cars possessed by any southern railroad was 849 (on the South Carolina Railroad). The strategically important Western and Atlantic had 726. But in the north, these numbers would have been considered paltry in the extreme. The Delaware, Lackawanna, and Western, not yet built to its full length between New York and Buffalo, possessed more than 4,000 cars. Even the Michigan Central, strictly a regional carrier, owned about 2,500.[9]

An even more desperate problem in the South would be the shortage of rail and the inability to produce more of it. No new rail was produced in the Confederacy after 1861, and very little could be imported. A few of the southern railroads had facilities for rerolling worn iron, and a little of this work was done, but not an amount sufficient to be a factor in the war effort. Furthermore, even the rail that was in good condition was being lost by attrition. During the war, the Confederate Navy Department seized a great deal of rail for use in armor plating its ships in a forlorn effort to break the blockade of southern ports. Eventually, the South was driven to cannibalizing its own rails—tearing up the tracks of little used branch lines or railroads that were perceived to be of small use in any military campaign.

In one important area, the Confederacy did have an edge where railroad operation was concerned. Confederate military men almost immediately grasped the strategic importance of railroads to the war effort, and even though they were in possession of relatively short lines, sometimes with different gauges and sometimes with poor exchange points, the railroads of the South were immediately and well mobilized for war, in spite of the fact that the railroads of the South remained in private hands and were never effectively dominated by the poorly centralized Confederate government. The impetus was there from the citizenry, however, and when the government did set up a Railroad Bureau, it managed to evoke a spirit of cooperation from the many small railroad owners and managers.

Above all, what seemed to characterize the South in the first few years of the war—in the railroad field as on the battlefield—was a kind of boldness and daring. It has been one of the platitudes of history that Confederate generals were more inspired and resourceful than those of the Union Army, and so it seemed in the beginning. In the last few years of the war, certain Union generals, most notably William Tecumseh Sherman, developed a more systematic and comprehensive notion of the railroad uses of war than any that had existed in the South, and this resulted in a deft and precise plan for leaving the southern railroads impotent as the war ground to a halt. But in the early part of the war the Union generals never seemed to grasp the full potential and strategic importance of the railroad.

And, yes, in terms of boldness the Confederate generals clearly took all the prizes in the early years of the war. With the war only days old, at a time when the government in Washington and the rebel government as well were still expecting railroads to continue with the usual functions of delivering the federal mails, and so on, Thomas Jonathan (later "Stonewall") Jackson seized forty engines and three hundred cars belonging to the Baltimore and Ohio. The B&O did not link up with the southern railroads that Jackson wanted to supply, but he was able to get at least a dozen of these commandeered locomotives to the South using horses and sweating recruits to haul them up hill and down dale on country roads. In these same early exploits, Jackson burned as many bridges and destroyed as much rail property of border railroads as he could possibly manage.

Confederate generals were certainly quick to realize the importance of railroads to logistics and supply. They were the discoverers of the idea that it was possible to rapidly transfer whole armies from one theater of operation to another. The first such important transfer was the movement of the infantry of General Bragg's Army of Tennessee from Tupelo, Mississippi, to Chattanooga, Tennessee, in the summer of 1862. A year later, another such mass movement allowed the Confederate armies to be decisive at the battle of Chickamauga. This was a movement of Longstreet's First Corps from northern Virginia to reinforce the Army of Tennessee, then in north Georgia, just below Chattanooga. Traveling a distance of nine hundred miles over single track railroads with diverse gauges and with no physical connections between lines, Longstreet managed to bring five brigades into play on the last and decisive day of the battle.

In the North, the importance of railroads was not disregarded, although Union generals took a more desultory attitude toward their various uses, and the leaden-footed bureaucracy of the U.S. government took a long time deciding how, whether, and for what purpose it should use the many miles of railroad in its territory. President Lincoln and other officials in Washington were aware of the strategic importance of railroads, of course. The railroads' very physical presence was a source of deep anxiety in the nation's capital. When the war began, the only railway line out of Washington to the North was the Baltimore and Ohio's branch to Baltimore (Baltimore was itself a city with many southern sympathizers, and Washington had more than a few skeptics of the loyalty of that city, its railroad, and its railroad officials— probably unjustified, since President Garrett was completely committed to the Union and continued to operate his railroad in behalf of the Union throughout the war.) Furthermore, Washington was ringed by Confederate railroads—on any good day, a rebel line could be seen in operation across the Potomac River in Virginia. So Lincoln and all of his advisers were completely convinced that dominating railroad lines would be a vital objective of the war.

The government rapidly acted on this conviction. From the very beginning of the war, first by a proclamation of President Lincoln, and then by an act of Congress on January 31, 1862, the United States government seized the authority to take over and operate the railways in any way that it saw fit. (Such sweeping authority was never sought by the Confederate government, and probably could not have been obtained.) In truth, the federal government never exercised this power to the full, and "because of the prompt and efficient working" of the railroads it was never exercised at all except in the military theater of operations. The power the government did possess, it implemented tactfully. In 1861, Thomas A. Scott of the Pennsylvania Railroad, with the assistance of Andrew Carnegie, was supervising "Government Railways and Telegraphs," but with the assumption that railroads would mostly continue their nonmilitary functions, which throughout most of the North they did.

It was not until 1862 that the government appointed a real czar to run the railroads in their military dimension. The individual chosen by Secretary of War Edwin M. Stanton to perform this function was Daniel C. McCallum, a robust Scot who had shown unusual administrative and engineering talent as general superintendent of the Erie. A supreme organizer with a reputation for strict discipline, he proved himself to be a more efficient bureaucrat than any of those who directed the railroad effort in the South (although the South also had some strong leaders in the area). Starting as a colonel, McCallum rose to be a brigadier general, a position that doubtless gave him a little clout with nonrailroad generals. For much of the war, McCallum shared responsibility with Herman Haupt, an engineer with a strict military background, who was a West Point graduate possessed of a magical gift for building bridges and getting wrecked tracks back in service.[10]

With McCallum in the office and Haupt mostly in the field, the railway generals had to buckle down to the job of "educating" the field commanders on the value and uses of the iron horse in waging a new kind of warfare. This was no easy chore in the beginning. The commanders, especially of the Army of the Potomac, were not quick learners. Officers would sometimes make outlandish demands on the operators of the railroads in the war zone. One officer held a train all night on the main track of a rail line supplying the Army in Virginia so that his wife might enjoy a night's rest in a nearby farmhouse. After the battle of Bull Run, Herman Haupt was threatened with arrest by General Samuel Sturgis, who had taken possession of railroad trains and held them for use in a short march (which was not needed) when they should have been sent forward to support General Pope's Union Army of Virginia. In this, Sturgis was later adjudged to be insubordinate and in direct violation of an order from Chief of Staff Halleck that "no military officer will attempt to interfere with the running of trains."[11]

For a long time—much too long a time—the field commanders of the Union Army could not be convinced of one important principle of railway operation, that the main thing is to keep cars rolling and to load and unload them quickly. Several years of the war passed before officers learned the stupidity of using freight cars as ministorage depots. They had been thinking of the railroad only in terms of whatever short-term local need that they might have had, an attitude that once caused the assistant secretary of war to telegram Haupt, advising him to "be as patient as possible with the Generals. Some of them will trouble you more than they will the enemy." Alas, for a long time, this was to be the agony of the Union Army.

Slowly but surely, under the leadership of McCallum and Haupt, the men in blue got the knack of it. A corps of some seventeen thousand railway military men was finally built up, and eventually they learned the art of keeping supply lines open and trains moving to the places where they were needed. This corps also became phenomenally good at rebuilding bridges, replacing tracks torn up by the opposing forces, and knowing when and where to apply destructive force to the railroad facilities of the enemy. When General Sherman, with the administrative help of McCallum, planned the campaign for Atlanta, the Union Army knew how to wage a railroad war, how to restore track, build bridges, and fix tunnels, bringing 100,000 men and 35,000 animals into the most decisive battle of the war over a single-track railway line. Then, during Sherman's famous march to the sea and similar exploits, Sherman completely smashed Confederate railways so they could no longer be used for purposes of war. But, of course, he did so only when he knew for a certainty that he would not need these roads himself. In this famous march, Sherman correctly perceived that now the railroad would only be of use to his enemies, so he effectively laid waste to it.

The Civil War years provided markedly different experiences to the railroads of the North and South, and also to the citizens of the two struggling sectors. The North was never really threatened by the war, even during the few vigorous forays into the area, such as that of the Gettysburg campaign. The railroads of the North by and large were well protected and continued doing business as usual with no interference from the Confederacy. Railroads of New England, incipient trunklines like the Erie and the Pennsylvania, all aided the war effort and carried millions of passengers during the war years, and nearly all of them continued to grow and prosper during this time. Even the threadbare Erie, with both Vanderbilt and Daniel Drew on its board of directors, paid dividends (and paid its employees) during these trying times. Passenger and freight business rose to a high tide. All the northern roads profited handsomely by carrying troops to battle. In 1862, the Pennsylvania alone carried 108,524 troops, providing an income of $379,393.21—yet this was a mere fourteen percent of its passenger business during that same year.[12]

Partly because most of its major railroads continued to operate, the North encountered few drastic shortages during the war. Agricultural products flowed out of the Midwest. Factories in New England, Pennsylvania, and New Jersey continued to ship products all over the Union. Families with small children could count on making a safe trip from Pittsburgh to Philadelphia or from Albany to New York without hindrance from the war machine. The coalfields of Pennsylvania still supplied fuel for the stoves of

New Yorkers. Freight business rose to unprecedented levels, and only a small proportion of that business was part of the military effort. The major express companies carried on their functions unabated. The huge Adams Express Company paid enormous dividends during the war, and shipped parcels everywhere that railroads went—even to the South during most of the war, although there it took on the local designation of "Southern Express." Among the more lugubrious (but nonetheless highly profitable) chores of the express companies was the shipment of the coffins of soldiers killed in battle. The railroads and the express companies for the most part handled this function with care, with accuracy, and with dignity.

Since the North was structurally a unified nation, and became more so during the war, its economy continued to prosper. In the South, the people were vitalized and inspirited by their nation and their crusade, but their economy slowly and steadily deteriorated. The conditions of their railroads illustrate this to perfection. Passenger travel by train in the South continued throughout the war, and in the beginning there was much of it. The Scarlett O'Haras and Melanie Hamiltons of the old plantations would bolt off by train to meet their cavaliers as they returned from the field of battle swathed in bandages. Sometimes, they might take the train from the deep South to Chattanooga or Richmond to accompany the remains of their loved ones.

But southern rail travel was hardly luxurious, comfortable, or even safe in 1861, and it would deteriorate rapidly. Coaches were invariably of poor quality, and soon most would be impressed for military service, and those remaining for public use became progressively more rickety. There was no such thing as a sleeping car anywhere in the Confederacy. Railroad travel was painfully slow. By far the fastest passenger service in the South was provided by the Louisville and Nashville, which occasionally attained speeds of forty miles an hour. But the Nashville and Chattanooga required nine and a half hours to travel 151 miles; passenger trains in South Carolina were forbidden to exceed twenty-five miles per hour.[13] Throughout the war, timetables were printed showing ever slower schedules for passenger trains, and even these times were often not met. Since there were few actual physical connections between lines, and a multiplicity of gauges, making transfers from one railroad to another for long-distance travel was a daunting experience.

And there were plenty of other problems for rail passengers in
the South. Passenger fares increased drastically, with no improvement in service. Because of the numerous time zones in several
sovereign states and municipalities, timetables were often documents of baroque complexity or unintelligibility. Railroad stations
were small and ill suited to the growing passenger traffic. There
were long queues at ticket windows, and crowded and insufferable
waiting rooms. Many passengers might have to wait hours for a
train with no place whatsoever to sit. Most railroads were forced to
place some embargo on the shipment of civilian freight, so getting
goods around the South during the war was painful, although
never completely impossible. Eventually, shipment priorities were
settled upon, but it became harder and harder for people in the
South to get manufacturered products from somewhere else.

All this had the effect of forcing the populace of the
Confederacy back on the homespun. Some well-to-do individuals
were able to obtain imported goods from blockade runners or war
profiteers—the Scarlet O'Haras of the world may well have been
able to obtain bonnets from Paris for a while. But as the northern
stranglehold was exercised on the South, even wealthy individuals
were forced more to accept whatever home-crafted substitutes
were available. They could no longer expect to receive shoes from
New England or New Jersey, and they had neither the resources
nor the leisure to develop substitutes for the sources of supply
they had once depended on.

Even though plantation owners were able to employ slave labor
to provide certain creature comforts, the supply of labor in the
South was always dangerously low; accordingly, the economy seldom had the opportunity to reinvigorate itself. Curiously, one of
the few areas where the labor pool was adequate was the railroad
industry, which the government wisely protected through draft
exemptions for railway workers. Northern railroads had more
severe railroad labor problems because of less generous exemptions, but, as the war continued, the southern railroads also had
trouble finding able-bodied men.

Southern railroads did not hesitate to make extensive use of
slaves during the Civil War. In some instances, railroads themselves owned slaves. The South Carolina Railroad alone owned
ninety slaves in 1859, before the war began. During the war, all the
Georgia railroads owned slaves and used them in a number of dif-

ferent capacities. Other railroads, particularly in Virginia, hired slaves from their owners, and regularly advertised for hired slave labor in southern papers. The Virginia and Tennessee regularly employed over three hundred such "rented" workers.[14] Most slaves on southern railways were relatively well treated and cared for. On the whole, they were good and reliable workers. Mostly, they held menial positions as toters and track workers, but a few held skilled positions as clerks, sometimes as brakemen or firemen (never engineers).

White workers were fairly well paid during the emergency, although probably not quite as well as similar workers in the North. An accommodation conductor on the Virginia Central made $70 a month. Express passenger conductors on the Richmond and Danville earned $81.20 per month. Expert machinists were well compensated during the war, receiving a daily wage of two to three dollars or even more. The treasurer of the Richmond and Danville Railroad received an annual salary of $1,375.

Among the generality of its railroad workers, the southern cause undoubtedly inspired more loyalty, more devotion, and more sheer perspiration than any lines of the North during the same period. Probably no railroad legend of the Civil War is more keenly remembered than the famous Andrews raid of 1862, which has been retold countless times and even made into several movies. The story has been lovingly maintained in the South as an example of southern ingenuity and prowess. When a group of Yankee spies under the direction of one Captain James J. Andrews stole a train on the Western and Atlantic at Big Shanty (now Kennesaw), Georgia, with the idea of racing to Chattanooga, burning bridges, ripping up rail, and blowing up tunnels, the exploit was foiled by an indefatigable Western and Atlantic conductor, W. A. Fuller, who followed first on foot, then on a handcar, then in several locomotives. Truth to tell, Andrews was undone by bad weather, by heavy rail traffic, by a single-track bottleneck, by trains not on schedule, and by other vicissitudes of southern railroading as much as he was by Fuller.[15] But the event was one brief, bright, gleaming moment—never to be forgotten in the annals of the Confederacy and of Civil War railroading.

There were two legendary locomotives involved in the great chase—sometimes referred to as "the great locomotive chase."

They were the wood-burning "Atlantic"-style General (the locomotive that gave the title to Buster Keaton's famous movie of the
same name), which had been stolen by Andrews at Big Shanty,
and the Texas, another primitive machine, which provided the
final instrument of Conductor Fuller's victory. Both these engines
were subsequently restored, and for years hardly ever missed an
exposition of any importance, especially in the South. The
General found its final resting place in the Big Shanty Museum in
Kennesaw. The more important Texas, ensign of southern pride,
which in its chase is supposed to have reached the unbelievable
speed of sixty miles per hour on the rickety Western and Atlantic
track, can be seen in the Cyclorama Building in Atlanta. Both
engines are objects of immense southern pride, as well they
should be. On the other hand, when one looks at the builder's
nameplate on each of these locomotives, a significant truth is
revealed. The General was built in 1856 by the Rogers Locomotive
and Machine Works—in Paterson, New Jersey. The epic Texas was
built, also in 1856, by Danforth, Cooke, and Company—also in
Paterson, New Jersey. Therein lies the principal clue to the outcome of the American Civil War.

In the spring of 1865, the Civil War ground to its lugubrious
conclusion, with both sides exhausted, the South in virtual desola-
tion. Railroad activity punctuated the final moments of the war, as
Jefferson Davis and his cabinet fled Richmond by train in advance
of Grant's army, clutching a small cache of Confederate records
and documents. Davis had hoped to travel to Texas and fight on,
but he was captured in Georgia, and later spent two years in
prison, although he was never tried. Abraham Lincoln, felled by
an assassin's bullet, returned home to Springfield in a flag-draped
funeral train, which made many stops during its one-week trip.
The late president's body was taken out to lie in state in all of the
large cities through which it passed. It was a final journey suitable
for the tragedies of Aeschylus or Sophocles.

But far to the west, even as Lincoln's body was being viewed by
thousands of mourners, a real monument of railway achievement
was being built to this frontier president who had fought so hard
during his political career to keep the blight of slavery from
spreading to the western territories. Lincoln continued to support
the transcontinental railroad during his tenure in office, and even
before his death the completion of this all-important link was a

virtual certainty. Within four years, the Atlantic Ocean and the Pacific Ocean would finally be joined by rail.

The story of the transcontinental railroad is one of epic proportions, but it is far from being an unblemished chapter in American history. With the war over, and the Gilded Age now at hand, large endeavors of this sort were frequently tainted by motives of greed, plunder, and avarice. Men of the better sort were crowded from the stage, while crude, unprincipled robber barons came into the ascendancy. If such men had also been men of vision or men of superlative technical skill, there might have been sufficient justification for them, but with few exceptions, although bold and audacious, they were inept and unsuited to the task that lay before them. Unfortunately, before work began in earnest on the transcontinental line, Theodore Judah was dead, a victim of yellow fever as he crossed the isthmus of Panama on one of his many trips between Washington and California. Although an idealist and man of strong conviction, he had already been euchred out of his share of the Central Pacific Railway by the hardware store bunch—Stanford, Huntington, Crocker, and Hopkins. These individuals, in whom the flame of duty and service burned at low ebb, and who originally saw the railroad only as a device to allow them to get their hands on Nevada silver, suddenly came to envision the transcontinental scheme as the large (and highly profitable) enterprise that Judah had already perceived it to be.

What had brought the light of conversion to the Sacramento merchants were the terms of the Pacific Railway Act of 1862, which called for generous (some would say too generous) land grants to the two railroads that would be built from the East and West to link the continent. The terms called for the companies to receive a right-of-way strip for their line (and whatever they needed for rail yards, sidings, and other facilities), as well as five alternate land sections (a section was 640 acres) on each side of the track. In addition, the federal government offered loans to the railroads—from $16,000 per mile of track in the lowlands to $48,000 a mile in mountainous regions—these funds taking the form of low-interest bonds. At this time, the land parcels did not seem extravagant because most of the territory was uninhabited except by Indians. But the belief was that the land grants would make a profit for the railroad, which was having to pay a stiff penalty for developing through desolate regions. The railroads could sell their sections to homesteaders and others, which would also have the effect of bringing settlement to the area—a major goal and objective of the federal government at that time.

The two railroads that were set to bring this project to fruition were the Central Pacific, now entirely in the hands of the "Big Four" of California, and the Union Pacific, chartered by Congress in 1862 and controlled by 162 commissioners whose job it was to get the railroad's stock sold and the management organized. Almost from the start, the Union Pacific's management was sluggish and inept. The company fell into the hands of a bibulous ex-doctor of medicine named Dr. Thomas C. Durant and an eccentric booster and breast beater named George Francis Train. Neither were suited to railway management. The Central Pacific was to be better served by the "Big Four," who, if never paragons of virtue, at least worked well in partnership and never lost sight of their main objectives once they got in gear. Leland Stanford, the politician and once governor of California, was the front man, and president of the road; Charles Crocker was the General Manager, a born organizer who got the job done; the parsimonious Mark Hopkins kept watch over the books; C. P. Huntington, the real brains of the group, served as the "outside man" and carried on negotiations with Washington and the financial centers of the East.

The Union Pacific didn't go anywhere for a few years, until the federal government began to put pressure on and until the company was forced to acquire a really good engineer in the person of General Grenville M. Dodge, one of Sherman's Civil War railroad men. For several years, the Union Pacific, which was supposed to be striking out to the West from Omaha, had to cool its heels while Dr. Durant cagily speculated on what route to take through nearby suburban territory, allowing him to make the best use of his land grants. Naturally, he wanted to locate his railroad next to the most valuable or highly developed land that he could get his claws on. After Dodge was on the scene, however, work began to proceed in a more orderly manner.

Financially, the Union Pacific shortly fell under the sway of a Massachusetts manufacturer of shovels named Oakes Ames, whose original interest in the railroad was the opportunity it provided as a large consumer of shovels. Ames and his brother Oliver, the so-called "Boston crowd," became the chief financial wizards of the Union Pacific. They were especially well fixed to do the Union Pacific some good because Oakes Ames was a member of Congress (between 1863 and 1873), and a member of the committee on railroads. Not only did Ames sell stock in the railroad to fellow members of Congress at bargain prices, he was able to facilitate a scheme, originally thought up by Train and Durant, to have the actual construction of the railroad carried out by a dummy company called the Credit Mobilier. This company could be awarded fat contracts, while the railroad itself grew deeper into debt. The Credit Mobilier Scandal, when it finally broke in the 1870s, ruined the careers not only of the Ames Brothers, but of numerous members of Congress, including Vice President Schulyer Colfax. It was the biggest scandal to break over the federal government prior to the Teapot Dome Scandal of the 1920s, and painted a grim picture of the voracious appetites of men of affairs in the post–Civil War era.

Not that things were enormously better at the Central Pacific. The Big Four had their own dummy construction company, which drained their railroad of some sixty million dollars. Furthermore, the gentlemen from Sacramento, so far away from the centers of power in the East, had their own brand of tricks. They had bogus surveys produced that showed the Sierra mountains beginning much farther west than they actually did, thus fleecing the government out of the $48,000-a-mile rate for mountain construction, while the line was actually being built over flat land. When the "Big Four" died, each had amassed fortunes of at least forty million dollars, a good deal of it ill-gotten gain. In extracting these fortunes, they had saddled their company with a massive debt, which had to be borne by the government and local communities for many years to come.

The story of the building of the transcontinental railroad has been told in many books, with special reference to the financial buccaneers who made the undertaking infamous to several generations of Americans. Sometimes neglected is the all-too-human side of the story, the saga of the thousands upon thousands of individuals who toiled for years to lay the rails, of the human habitations they left behind and the storm and stress involved in their

Herculean effort. It is a tale no more pretty than that of the financial freebooters, but perhaps more indicative of the color and the zest of the America of that day.

Almost all of the labor involved in building the Union Pacific and the Central Pacific was provided by human toilers and draft animals; steam shovels were introduced only in the final weeks of the construction. Accordingly, the route was cleared, the roadbed was built, and the ties and rails were laid by huge armies of workers—armies large enough to create whole communities as they moved forward, and, in their wake, no small amount of conflict, uproar, and dissension. Much of the conflict was due to the presence on the plains of the Sioux Indians, who had not the slightest intention of giving up their land to the settlers and their iron horse.

On the Union Pacific under the guiding hand of General Grenville Dodge, the work took on all the flavor of a military operation, which in a sense it was. A good number of the track laborers were veterans of the recent war, some had been with Sherman in Georgia. Their rifles were at the ready in case they had to deal with hostile Indians—and they often did. By far the largest contingent of Dodge's army were Irish paddies, some of whom had worked earlier on the Erie and the Illinois Central after having fled the Irish potato famines of the 1840s. These laborers were top rate—when they were working—but they were a constant source of trouble in their free time. While toiling on the Erie, the Irish track laborers had proven to be extremely volatile, although they added their own color and charm to railway life. In their free hours, they caroused; luckily, out on the vast plains of Nebraska, there were few settlements to plunder. Still, the Irish remained volatile, although it has long been acknowledged that the American railroads could hardly have been built without them.

Whenever Dodge's "army" had to lay down their picks and shovels, when winter blizzards came sweeping down the plains, mobs of unruly individuals had to be plunked down in temporary settlements, in crude shacks and tents. These were the fabled "railroad" towns of dark repute, so often memorialized in the movies and in pulp fiction. When the winter season came on in 1866, the Union Pacific had already passed the long-awaited 100th meridian—247 miles west of Omaha—and gotten to a spot 43 miles farther west.

They called this place North Platte, and decided to settle down for the most savage part of winter. Tents and shacks were put up, and because North Platte was the temporary end of the rail line it became a brisk and often violent starting off point for overland traffic to the West. Mormon emigrants arrived; a few of them pressed onward; others stuck to their tents awaiting the arrival of spring. Gathering about were every manner of Indian fighter, gold seeker, homesteader, and roustabout. Freight shipments piled up under sailcloth until they could be moved out by wagon train.

In a matter of only a few weeks a hundred jerry-built structures had blighted the area—saloons, bordellos, hotels, warehouses, stables. The huge army of boisterous workers was inevitably followed by the usual assortment of gamblers, shoot-em-up boys, whiskey salesmen, and miscellaneous troublemakers. A correspondent for the *New York Times* deftly characterized the atmosphere:

> The larger part of the floating population is made up of desperados who spend their time in gambling of all kinds, from cards to keno to faro. Day and night the saloons are in full blast, and sums of money varying from five dollars to fifty and even one hundred change hands with a rapidity astonishing to one who is not accustomed to the recklessness which their wild frontier life invariably begets.

A reporter for the *Missouri Democrat*, Henry Morton Stanley, dropped in on the scene in early Spring when construction was about to begin again. "Every gambler in the Union," he wrote,

> seems to have steered his course for North Platte, and every known game under the sun is played here. The days of Pike's Peak and California are revived. Every house is a saloon, and every saloon is a gambling den. Revolvers are in great requisition. Beardless youths imitate to the life the peculiar swagger of the devil-may-care bullwacker and blackleg.[16]

When things got moving again settlements like North Platte were left behind, but new ones in imitation would spring up wherever the railroad went. Soon there would be Cheyenne in Wyoming and Julesburg in Colorado. Furthermore, the noisy multitudes could always keep up with the progress of the railroad, some of them traveling in the wooden coaches and chuck wagons, which daily trailed along as part of the sustaining work train. Pimps, prostitutes, gamblers and gunslingers were right behind the location of the day's construction, thus giving ample warrant to the sobriquet "hell on wheels" for the work trains, a term still enshrined in the American language.

Construction of the Central Pacific, while no less arduous, was a good deal less tumultuous. Indian raids were fewer—the Big Four, to their credit, attempted to mollify the Indians in their territory, giving them passes to ride the trains and allowing them to hitch rides whenever they liked. More importantly, Charlie Crocker had found an ingenius solution to his labor problems. California, of course, was not endowed with a huge labor force. Such workers as Crocker was able to induce to work on the railroad only seemed to want transportation to the silver mines, after which they would vanish. At one time, there was talk of importing workers from Mexico, but that goal never materialized. Crocker then thought of the Chinese, but he was scoffed at—the Chinese were too frail for this hard labor, it was said. "But hadn't they built the Chinese wall?" asked Crocker. In desperation, a group of fifty Chinese were given a chance, and proved themselves to be workers of extraordinary ability. The cry went out for more, and in a matter of months, thousands of Chinese were on the job building the Central Pacific. It was reported that by 1865 some four thousand men were toiling on the Central Pacific, nine-tenths of them Chinese.

A number of Chinese had come to California in the wake of the gold rush of 1849.[17] Most of them had been warmly embraced in this labor-starved state, a great many working as cooks, butlers, laundrymen, gardeners, but some as mine and factory workers. On the railroad they proved to be wonder workers. So good were they, in fact, that Charlie Crocker sent agents to China to recruit thousands more for work on the Central Pacific. Surely the Chinese laborers were taken advantage of—they were paid a mere thirty to thirty-five dollars a month—but they made a singular contribution to the building of the transcontinental railroad. The thousands of Chinese track workers also quickly became a colorful and readily identifiable feature of the Western railway scene. They could easily be spotted anywhere in their blue-dyed pajamas, their pigtails, and their umbrella-shaped basket hats. They added a calm and steady influence on a volatile environment. In contrast to General Grenville Dodge's uproarious army veterans to the east, the Chinese worked sober and caused no headaches for their bosses. They drank tea and subsisted on a diet of rice, and none of their pitifully low wages wound up in the hands of card sharks, harlots, or whiskey sellers.

During the last few years of work on the transcontinental railroad, or, more precisely, the two railroads that were to be linked, the effort took on the appearance of a race.[18] And it was a race, since the railroads were being paid for construction by the mile and each would ultimately stand to gain by possession of whatever land acreage they could capture. In the end, the Union Pacific would stretch 1,095 miles west from Omaha, the Central Pacific 690 miles east from Sacramento. The Central Pacific had the worst of it, since for years it had had to inch its way over the perilous Sierra Nevada mountains. When finally liberated from that burden, the Central Pacific began to build with breakneck speed across Nevada. With ever larger crews in the field, the competing railroads upped their rate from two miles a day, to five, then to seven. Finally, in one stupendous effort, on a single day, April 28, 1869, the Central Pacific laid ten miles of track between sunrise and sunset—this to settle a thousand-dollar bet between Charlie Crocker of the Central Pacific and Dr. Thomas Durant of the Union Pacific.

In early May, the work slowed down and the two armies of workers came in sight of one another. General Dodge's Irishmen didn't like the look of Crocker's Chinese and hurled boulders down on them. The Chinese, for their part, did not cotton to the noisy Irishmen. By common consent among the officials, the meeting place for the two railroads was to be a waterless basin of sagebrush just north of the Great Salt Lake in Utah. It was called Promontory Point. The CP got there first, on April 30, and stopped working. A great ceremony had been planned for May 8, but had to be postponed for two days since a washout on the Central Pacific held up a train carrying President Leland Stanford and other dignitaries. The whole nation, perhaps the whole world, was watching. Eastern newspapers had been writing about the great moment for months; everyone was in a state of suspended animation. The Western Union Company had prepared a nationwide telegraph hookup to alert the world that the last spike of the transcontinental railroad had been driven in.

On the morning of May 10, everything was in readiness. Blue-clad Chinese workmen laid the last ties and rails, bolted on the fishplates, and drove in all but the last few spikes. The ceremony was scheduled for noon. At about 10 A.M., two Union Pacific trains carrying officials and dignitaries pulled up. In the lead was coal-burning engine No. 119. At 11:15, the Central Pacific's train, drawn by the wood-burning locomotive Jupiter discharged President Leland Stanford and other officials. There was much handshaking and considerable quibbling over protocol. Stanford had brought along two golden spikes, a silver spike, a collection of other ceremonial spikes, a silver-plated sledgehammer, and a laurel tie. President Durant, mightily indisposed after imbibing heavily of champagne in his private car the evening before, was only anxious for the affair to be over.

Telegraph operator W. N. Shilling stood at the ready, his line open and expectant. Soldiers of the Twenty-First Infantry formed a double line facing the tracks at parade rest. Up stepped Leland Stanford with his silver-plated sledgehammer. He swung at the golden spike, and missed. Up swaggered Dr. Durant. Another blow. Another miss. A contemptuous jeer rang out from the Irish laborers nearby. The bosses were no good with a hammer, it was plain to see. Soon, however, all the ceremonial spikes were driven in (it is not clear who actually drove in the golden spike), and the two locomotives eased forward and touched each other.

It was a great moment in American history. When the news came through, a hundred guns were fired in salute in City Hall Park in New York. Bells rang in Independence Hall in Philadelphia. The time was 12:47 P.M., May 10, 1869—2:47 P.M. on the East Coast. At the precise moment, telegrapher Shilling had touched his key and tapped out one word. By now, only one word was needed—"Done."

Among the earliest regularly scheduled passenger trains in America were those of the Camden and Amboy Railroad of New Jersey. Here locomotive "John Bull," built in 1831, pulls early-vintage coaches, built in 1836 *(New Jersey Historical Society)*.

Primeval railroading. This picturesquely gothic station of the Boston and Maine Railroad in Salem, Massachusetts., was built in 1847. Could it be that the famous witches there might have taken comfort from the eerie looking solid masonry polygonal towers *(Essex Institute)*?

Annapolis Junction, Maryland, as it appeared during the Civil War. The leisurely ambience reflected here nonetheless expresses the centrality of the "railroad depot" in most American towns during the nineteenth century *(Smithsonian)*.

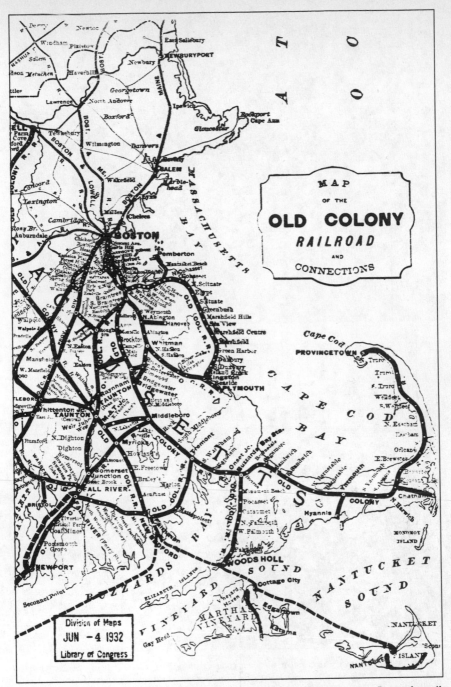

For a better part of a century the railroad *was* the American infrastructure. It was the rail-road that held the people, the towns, the nation together, as is evidenced by this map of the Old Colony Railroad in Rhode Island and eastern Massachusetts. The Old Colony began operations in 1845 *(Library of Congress)*.

ABOVE: A rather rowdy incursion into a private railway car traveling on the Northern Pacific in 1888. A figment of some artist's imagination no doubt, but characteristic of what people feared might happen when they rode the steam cars beyond the Mississippi (*Illustrated Police News*).

BELOW: The departure of trains into the hinterlands was always a moment of high drama in the old West. This pen and ink sketch from *Harper's Weekly* in 1870 shows the departure of an immigrant train for Colorado (*University of Illinois Library*).

The railroad brought civility, then luxury to the West. No train exuded greater luxury and panache than the *Overland Limited*, which traversed the rails of the Chicago and Northwestern and the Union Pacific between Chicago and San Francisco *(Author's collection).*

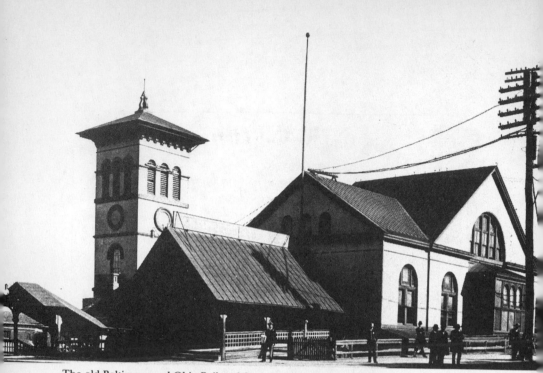

The old Baltimore and Ohio Railroad Station in Washington, D.C., built in 1851. This simple but stately building in the Italian villa style was the place where Abraham Lincoln arrived in Washington to take up the presidency *(Smithsonian)*.

Railroad construction in the West. The tracks went down just ahead of the trains and wild frontier towns sprang up in their wake. Indians and buffalo provided reminders that the wilderness had not yet been tamed. But railway passengers traveling across the continent would have been disheartened if they did not see these evidences of the "real" West *(Illinois State Library)*.

LEFT: The Illinois Central Railroad was the most mammoth railroad undertaking of the 1850s. Perhaps no railroad in American history was more clearly responsible for the growth of its territory. The railroad land office enticed people from all over the world with broadsides like this from 1867 (*Illinois Central Gulf*).

BELOW: The sign says "R.R. Eating House," and the railway eating stop was a major American institution before the coming of the dining cars. Eating houses continued to be important in the West well into the twentieth century. This house on the Union Pacific is seen through the lens of noted photographer A. J. Russell (*National Geographic Society*).

Few individuals played a more important role in the history of railroading than George Mortimer Pullman, inventor of the sleeping car. Before the advent of the Pullman car and Pullman protocols of service, lengthy railroad travel was an arduous and unpleasant experience. Pullman made travel synonymous with luxury and comfort *(Library of Congress)*.

"In the Waiting Room," a travel poster of the Frisco Line in 1899. Railroads turned out thousands of travel posters, everything from the sentimental to the purely utilitarian. Not lacking in ingenuity, the Frisco had actually produced a poster within a poster *(Library of Congress)*.

Union Pacific tracklayers at Laramie, Wyoming, in a photograph by A. J. Russell. There are quite a few hardened Civil War veterans in this assemblage; indeed, work on the western railroads was one of the rewards of being a veteran of the Union army *(Union Pacific Museum)*.

The old-style Pullman berths became the stuff of legends. Open-berth cars, many of which were still in service in the 1950s, leant themselves to a peculiarly American style of familiarity—as well as sometimes to the ribald and the risible *(University of Illinois Library)*.

In the early days of railroading the conductor (or Captain as he was sometimes called) was a social functionary of no small importance. Shown here is Augustus S. Messer, conductor of the New Haven Railroad's legendary *Flying Dude* from 1890 to 1904 *(Author's collection)*.

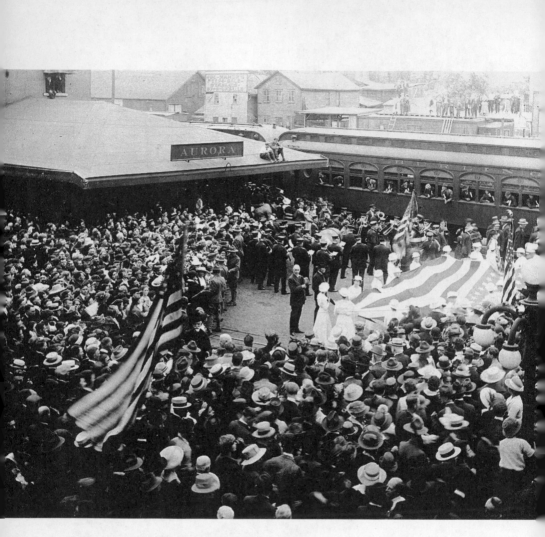

For years the railroad station was the focal point of activity and a stage for human events both great and small. It is September 13, 1917, and, it seems, the whole town of Aurora, Illinois, has turned out to bid the boys farewell as they leave for the sodden battlefields of France *(Burlington Northern)*.

C·H·A·P·T·E·R 7

THE GILDED AGE: BURNISHED AND TARNISHED

In the year 1876, the United States would celebrate its one hundredth birthday. By that year, few of the nation's founding fathers would recognize either the society, the economy, the mood, or the ways of life that had sprung with such violent suddenness from the simple agrarian roots of the original thirteen colonies. In the years immediately after the Civil War, an older, more stately, more temperate America moved toward a nation of bustle, of struggle, of industrial muscle. The frontier everywhere was giving way to vigorous settlement; small towns were growing into larger towns; these towns in turn would often become cities, some of the great cities of the world. The whole nation had now been spanned by the railroad. Power mills which had once sprung up at the waterfalls were now superseded by smokestack industries giving employment to a rising tide of a generation of European immigrants, people who had come to the new world to improve their lot. The population of the nation would reach fifty million by 1880, and many of the country's new citizens, as well as many of the older ones as well, were mystified, traumatized, and agonized by the seemingly ungovernable growth in the scale of the new industrial commonwealth.

If there were painful side effects to the enormous expansion of the economy, they were largely ignored in the exuberant mood of steady expansion. The word "progress" was heard everywhere, and Americans were seldom skeptical of the dynamic thrust of an economy that seemed always to be on the upswing, always leading to higher wages, to ever-increasing opportunities, to an expansion in the number of available goods and services, to a steady improvement in the quality of life. Walt Whitman, whose voice could be heard above all others singing the praises of this new vibrant, progressive, material America, saw the reborn United States in terms of the richness of all the possibilities available to this open-ended republic:

> Here first the duties of to-day, the lessons of the concrete,
> Wealth, order, travel, shelter, products, plenty;
> As of the building of some varied, vast, perpetual edifice,
> Whence to arise inevitable in time, the towering roofs, the lamps,
> The solid-planted spires tall shooting to the stars.

Of course, it was also Whitman's belief that the only justification of a great material society was that it should serve as the underpinning of a great spiritual society, and there were many of a more somber cast of mind who entertained strong doubts, and believed that this new America was being thrown together without design and without forethought. This age of the telegraph, of gas lamps, of speeding railroad trains, of abundant consumer goods, of access to fortune, was also the age of the get-rich-quick schemer, of the robber baron; and in the West, of the land grabber, the sharpshooter, the cattle rustler, and the Indian fighter. It was an age of child labor, of unsanitary and overcrowed cities, of ill-treated immigrant labor, of corrupt and impotent government and courts of law. But everything moved so fast, the breath of fresh air so quickly washed away abuses, and fortunes were so quickly won that few Americans were disposed to question the dogma of progress. Progress and abundance constituted the religion of the day, and few were willing to doubt their authority.

But if there were undercurrents of corruption and decadence in the so-called Gilded Age, the contrasting evidence of progress and material good health was so dramatic that the prophets of gloom and doom had little impact on the reflective thought of the time. This was true of the railroads. Even before the Civil War, they had been the biggest business in America, and in the 1870s and 1880s their growth would be astronomical. At the start of the

Civil War, there were but 31,000 miles of track in the United States, nearly all of them east of the Mississippi River. Between that time and 1914, railway mileage increased to 252,000, most of the growth occurring in the 1870s and 1880s.[1]

Increase in mileage was only one side of the picture. Even more important was the vast improvement in the management and technical resources of the railroads. In the 1870s, railroads were not only becoming bigger, they were becoming better.

Already established lines in the East were double tracking their lines for faster travel; they were laying out new rights-of-way to eliminate sharp curves and roundabout routes. They were ordering new equipment, better and stronger locomotives, and passenger cars made of steel (though the transformation here was not sudden—many major railroads were still using wooden coaches as late as World War I and even after). Safety became the watchword of the day, and all manner of new safety devices were introduced during the 1870s and 1880s. Eli Hamilton Janney patented the first of his automatic couplers in 1868, a device that would save the lives of thousands of brakemen in the years ahead.

Even more important to the general public was the introduction of the air brake by George Westinghouse in 1868. This invention (subsequently fortified by patents on at least twenty improvements), made it possible for railroads to run faster and heavier trains than those equipped with risky hand brakes, which had to be turned by brakemen on each individual car. Alas, it took many years for all railroads to adopt the air brake. Commodore Vanderbilt reportedly said to Westinghouse, "Do you mean to tell me, young man, that a train weighing thousands of pounds can be stopped by wind. You are a goddamm fool." Eventually, however, the truth dawned on railroad managers, especially after it was drummed in for several decades by a fanatical ex-Civil War chaplain named Lorenzo Coffin. So convincing were Coffin's arguments that in 1893 he pushed through Congress the Railroad Safety Appliance Act, which made both the air brake and the automatic coupler mandatory.

New safety devices arrived in a cascade during the 1870s and 1880s. Many early operational problems had been solved by the introduction of the "block" concept of train governance. The block system, first tried on the Camden and Amboy by Ashbel Welch in 1863 to deal with the heavily traveled stretch of track

between Trenton and New Brunswick, involved the concept that
space rather than time was the best method of governing the
movement of trains. By 1872, a patent was issued for a battery-
operated track circuit to control signals automatically within a
block. The use of electric block signals, with semaphors or colored
lights, did not spread rapidly among the railroads, and the idea
did not endear itself to tightfisted railroad managers. Many of
these felt that a manual block system using telegraphic communication between stations or signal towers was perfectly adequate.
And so it was—up to a point. But in time, the heavily traveled railroads running fast trains in close order came to see that automatic
block signals provided the fullest form of protection for train
movements.

From the perspective of railway passengers and the traveling
public generally, an even more obvious kind of improvement took
place in the 1870s and 1880s. This was the practical unification of
the rail system. Before the Civil War, lines in the eastern part of
the country were sufficiently unified for economic purposes that it
was possible to speak of a railroad infrastructure or network linking all major areas of the Union. But the unification had not yet
produced tangible benefits for the traveling public. In actual fact,
the eastern states possessed a great many lines which could and
did exchange passengers and freight, but the necessary exchanges
were still cumbersome and inconvenient. A person wanting to
travel between, for example, Boston and Buffalo could make the
trip on the Boston and Worcester to Albany, and then on the New
York Central from Albany to Buffalo, but there was no railroad
bridge crossing the Hudson River between these two lines.

Lack of railroad bridges over major rivers remained an enormous obstacle for many years. No railroad bridged the Missouri at
Omaha, so, indeed, in a sense, the famous "transcontinental" railroad was not that at all until well into the 1870s. People who wanted to travel westward from Chicago would have to be ferried
across the Mississippi from one railroad terminal to another. Nor
was there a railroad bridge across the Ohio River. Railroad maps
of the epic north-south Illinois Central Railroad show that you
could travel between Chicago and New Orleans in the years after
the Civil War. Chicago to New Orleans was definitely on the
timetable. The truth was, however, you could not actually make a
through trip wholly by rail until the completion of the great

bridge over the Ohio River at Cairo, Illinois, a structure that wasn't completed until 1889!

Even in the heavily traveled urban corridor between Boston and Washington, the idea of "through" train service was little more than a fantasy. In 1870, a person wanting to go between Boston and Washington would doubtless take the Old Colony boat train to Fall River and then an overnight steamer to New York—a pleasurable trip still remembered in song and legend. One would then take a ferry boat across the Hudson River and board the cars of the Camden and Amboy (soon to be absorbed by the Pennsylvania Railroad) for the trip to Philadelphia. From there, one could proceed by other lines not yet completely absorbed either by the Pennsylvania or the Baltimore and Ohio to Washington. Altogether a trip of several days, not the eight hours or less of today's Amtrak Metroliners.

The longer trip between New York and Chicago, or Philadelphia and Chicago, was an even greater nuisance and it meant to the human passenger several changes between lines, often the necessity of stopping for meals at train restaurants of inconsistent or dubious quality, with usual night-time stopovers at junction hotels. These hotels ranged from fair to good in quality, and a few were beloved of passengers making the trek across country. In any case, even the more shabby of them provided relief from the physical punishment of hours of traveling on the uncomfortable seats of wooden day coaches.

But there would be big changes in this chaotic, on-again, off-again style of train travel in the 1870s and 1880s. The major trunklines of the East eventually took possession of the connecting lines that were once their only access to territories beyond that of their original charters. For example, the Pennsylvania had enjoyed a long relationship with the Pittsburgh, Fort Wayne, and Chicago Railway, which provided railroad service between Pittsburgh and Chicago as early as 1858. But east-west passengers always had to change from Pennsylvania cars at Pittsburgh. In 1869, the Pennsylvania acquired the Pittsburgh, Fort Wayne, and Chicago under the terms of a 999-year lease, but it would still be several years before absolutely through service would be established.

A number of other carriers similarly expanded by acquisition. Commodore Vanderbilt, who had gained control of the New York Central to Buffalo for his New York and Harlem, quickly envisioned a through line all the way from New York to Chicago. To this end, he began buying up shares in the mostly unprofitable Lake Shore and Michigan Southern, which would provide him a water-level route between Buffalo and Chicago. This, of course, would become an integral part of the main line of the New York Central between New York and Chicago in the years ahead. The Erie, meanwhile, sought to draw nigh the city on Lake Michigan by acquisition of the Atlantic and Great Western, a road which shared its own six-foot gauge at the time of its original construction. On the other hand, unable to acquire an acceptable line by acquisition, John W. Garrett of the Baltimore and Ohio built his own line to Chicago across northern Ohio and Indiana, arriving at the windy city in 1874.

All of these railroad constructions and amalgamations would have a beneficial effect on the conditions of passenger trains and on the quality of long-distance travel. But probably no improvement in the immediate postwar period made a more lasting impression on the traveling public than the appearance on long-distance trains of comfortable and even luxurious sleeping cars. The sleeping car was hardly a complete novelty in 1870; indeed, a primitive sleeping car of sorts first appeared on the Cumberland Valley Railroad in 1836. In 1856, Webster Wagner, a New York stationmaster, fitted out a sleeping car which was used on the New York Central. Between that time and the end of the nineteenth century, there would be a number of sleeping car manufacturers working in the field. Eventually, one name came to stand out head and shoulders above the rest—Pullman.

The American sleeping car was largely the brainchild of George Mortimer Pullman, who eventually so completely dominated the field of sleeping car manufacture in this country that the very name Pullman was synonymous with "sleeping car" on American railroads. Of course, Pullman did not invent the sleeping car, and never pretended to, but slowly his method of construction and his way of operating his cars gained dominance in the field. Pullman was born in 1831 in Brocton, Chautauqua County, New York, in 1831. As a lad, he entered the contracting business with his father, who had made a tidy sum of money moving houses that were in the way of the expansion of the Erie Canal. Young George gained expertise in this business also, and in the early 1850s, while still in his early twenties, was invited to come to Chicago to perform some house-raising activities on plush Michigan Avenue, then virtually at water level. The street needed to have houses, mansions, and even hotels raised to prevent flooded basements. Pullman immediately came to dominate this field, his most remarkable achievement being the raising of the city's largest hotel, the Tremont. Using a thousand men and four thousand jackscrews, Pullman managed to raise the Tremont without even having to evacuate the guests. By the age of twenty-seven, he was one of the city's most prominent citizens, said to be worth twenty thousand dollars.

On numerous occasions during these years, Pullman had the need to travel back to his home state of New York, and like most travelers of the time he was unhappy with the rickety wooden coaches he rode with their inadequate heating and ventilating systems, with their inadequate springs and rough ride. He was equally displeased having to embark and disembark at junction points, lugging his baggage from one train to another, eating in station restaurants of unpredictable quality, and having to spend the night in seedy hotels. Pullman decided that what the country's railroads needed was a good, practical sleeping car.

Several years before the Civil War, Pullman contacted the Chicago and Alton Railroad with his idea to convert day coaches into sleeping cars. He converted two such coaches in 1858, and a third in 1859. The first overnight sleeping car trip by a Pullman car was made between Bloomington, Illinois, and Chicago on the night of September 1, 1859. While these early Pullman cars met with a small degree of success and patronage, the Alton did not order any more of them.

The early years of the Civil War found Pullman in the mining regions of Colorado, where he ran a general store. But he continued to have faith in the sleeping car idea and spent his idle moments sketching plans for new and improved sleeping car designs. During the war years, Pullman returned to Chicago, and approached the Alton with the idea of building a sleeping car from scratch—instead of merely reconverting existing coaches. The first all-new Pullman car, called the Pioneer, was put in service on the Alton in 1865. The car was divided into eight sections, with a washroom and two compartments on each end. To get all the fittings and luxuries that Pullman wanted in his car, the Pioneer had to be built longer and wider than all of the existing passenger coaches.

This expansion might have proven a fatal blow to Pullman's concept, since when the plans were viewed by Alton officials it was discovered that platforms, sheds, bridges, and other fixtures of the road would have to be changed to accommodate these greater dimensions. But luck of a rather macabre sort was on Pullman's side. After the assassination of President Lincoln, it was determined that the Alton would get the job of moving the president's funeral train on the last leg of its long journey between Chicago and Springfield. Accordingly, the Alton gladly made the necessary adjustments so that this luxurious car could be attached to Lincoln's funeral train. Thereafter, however, the car proved to be immediately successful, and it was in great demand by other dignitaries—for example, it was shortly loaned to General Grant, who was on a trip from Detroit to his home in Galena, Illinois, and this was another public relations coup for Pullman.

There seems little doubt that the immediate appeal of the Pioneer was its comfort and luxury. The car was built on sturdy and resilient springs. More importantly, however, the interior was elaborately designed with ornate decorations, influenced in some degree by the cabins and saloons of river steamboats. The interior was paneled in inlaid black walnut with framed mirrors between the windows. There was deep-pile carpeting on the floor. The seats were covered with embroidered cloth. Polished brass was used on toilet fixtures, lamps, and doors. The various fittings and accoutrements made the Pioneer by far the heaviest railway passenger car ever built. But railroads and their customers immediately found that the added weight and the added expense were worth it.

Besides the luxury features of his car, there were several technical innovations of design that accounted for Pullman's long-term success as a sleeping car manufacturer. In 1864, Pullman and his then partner, Ben Field (a boyhood friend from Albion, New York), were granted two patents, No. 42,182, for a hinged upper berth that could be stowed out of sight for daytime use, and No. 49,992, for hinging of back seat cushions so that a lower birth could be laid on top of seating when the passengers wanted to retire for the night. Both of these devices, with refinements, remained in use as long as the open-section Pullman cars were manufactured (and are in fact used in nearly all sleeping car designs to the present day).

This design allowed the Pullman car to be a highly efficient carrier of human cargo, while it also appealed to the public's taste for refinement and luxury. Some of Pullman's competitors were highly competitive as creators of luxurious and fanciful sleeping cars, but some of these involved designs that were so inefficient in their use of space that they could succeed only by charging exceptionally high rates to passengers. One of Pullman's early competitors was Col. William D'Alton Mann, whose Mann's Boudoir-Car Company produced highly luxurious cars with private sleeping rooms. But the great expense of these cars and the few passengers each could carry did not recommend them to American railroads, which would now be called on to provide sleeping facilities for thousands of passengers at reasonable rates. Pullman, unlike Mann (and other competitors, such as the Woodruff Sleeping and Palace Car Company and the Wagner Palace Car Company), produced sleeping cars that were comfortable and luxurious, but within reach of at least part of the traveling public. Pullman had figured out how to give Americans what they wanted—an elite sleeping car that could be enjoyed by the multitudes.[2]

Not that travel by Pullman was cheap—far from it. Few of the immigrant hordes that were setting out across the country could afford sleeping berths, and neither could many ordinary citizens. But the modestly affluent now had a touch of class in railroad travel, and they took to it with avidity. Pullman charged a hefty premium above railroad fare for his berths, but for most of his passengers this was paid with no complaint. After Pullman got into manufacturing his cars on a mass scale, which he did in the 1870s and 1880s, becoming himself one of the richest men in the nation in the process, he perfected and executed a system for operating these cars according to uniformly high standards. He developed a protocol for the operation and maintenance of his equipment that was envied throughout the world.

The Pullman "system" developed a method of efficient baggage handling. The company hired its own conductors to enforce company rules, such as the rule against wearing boots to bed—sometimes hard to enforce in the West in the early days, yet done nevertheless. Then there was the legendary "Pullman porter," who rendered courteous and efficient service to passengers and kept the cars clean. Cleanliness became a byword to the Pullman company. "Spotters" were hired to take note of soiled linen or less-than-gleaming washbasins. Each car was equipped with one hundred sheets and pillow cases, forty blankets, and towels of various types. All bedding was removed and cleaned nightly. No excuses for faulty or substandard service were permitted.

The sleeping car at last had made long-distance travel by rail comfortable and delightful. But the through sleeping car train would need another innovation to be successful, and that was the dining car. Here, too, George Pullman was in the forefront. Again, he did not invent the dining car, but as early as 1867 he introduced on the Great Western Railroad something he called a "Hotel Car," a modified version of one of his sleeping cars that had fewer berths, a small kitchen, and a place to set up tables for meals. A short time later, Pullman designed his first full dining car, calling it the Delmonico after the famous New York restaurant—a car that he once again pioneered on the Chicago and Alton. In due course, dining cars would be found on most long-distance trains, for example between Chicago and New York. For a number of years, the Pullman Company operated its own dining cars, but they were invariably unprofitable, so the function was passed along to the individual railroad lines, which continued to provide the service, although usually at a loss. This course of events proved to be a boon to the traveling public, since it invariably made food service available to all passengers, not only those of the first class.

With the coming of sleeping cars and dining cars, American railroad trains, at least on the trunklines, took on a much more elegant air. There was now a division of passenger classes, which seemed antidemocratic to those who were sensitive about such matters. On the other hand, the Pullman section sleeping car always had about it a tincture of democratic conviviality, since it converted into an ordinary, if elegant, coach with center aisle in the daytime. In later years, the Pullman company would introduce sleeping cars that contained compartments, bedrooms, drawing rooms and the like, but for a long time the democratic open section facilities predominated. Such a design never came into general use in social-conscious Europe, whose railways liked to provide private compartments, where members of the upper classes might be kept separate from hoi polloi. Indeed, when Georges Nagelmackers, the Belgian railway magnate who instituted the famed Orient Express in Europe (through his Compagnie Internationale des Wagons-Lits), came to the United States to investigate sleeping car devisings, it was the "boudoir" cars of Col. William D'Alton Mann that most appealed to him. Colonel Mann went to Europe as a consultant, but in America his own company (eventually absorbed into Pullman) specialized in making private cars for millionaires. His lush cars for regular passenger service never caught on.

During the 1870s, the railroads were not only beginning to offer more amenities and luxuries to the traveling public, they were becoming, on the whole, better run, better built, and better organized. The giant eastern trunklines were now large corporations, and they began to organize their managements according to standardized patterns—in essence the same sorts of patterns that are found in twentieth-century railroads. Coming onto the scene were accustomed officers and functionaries such as superintendents, trainmasters, right-of-way engineers, traffic managers, and auditors, as well as the line and staff officials of upper management that have characterized railroads ever since. Railroading rapidly became a profession, with professional people setting down procedures and protocols on everything from train movements to passenger relations, to signaling practices, to freight rate structures, to terminal management, and so on.

Standardization became the byword of the day, and it proved to be a great boon not only to the railroads themselves but to the society as a whole. During the 1870s, nearly all railroads of any significance were determined to convert to the now "standard" American gauge of four feet eight and a half inches. The once popular five-foot gauge of the South disappeared—most of the South's railroads needed rebuilding anyway. Even the eccentric six-foot gauge of the Erie had to be completely rebuilt to modern specifications in the 1870s. This was a terribly burdensome expense to the already financially troubled Erie, but now there was no choice; any railroad not conforming to the standard gauge would be consigned to oblivion; it could not exchange freight, and it could not tap the newfound national market for railroad service. By the twentieth century, all American railroads, with the exception of some small rural and mountain carriers, were built to the standard gauge.

Another form of standardization that the railroads imposed on themselves, and which then spread to society at large, was that of Standard Time. Before the Standard Time movement took hold, American time was as individual to a community as the style of the weathervane on top of the local courthouse. There were, for example, thirty-eight different times in the state of Wisconsin alone. In the realm of railroad scheduling, this could mean only one thing: chaos. In Pittsburgh, railroads ran on six different times. One station in Buffalo displayed three different clocks. Composing and reading a railway passenger timetable were acts of Byzantine complexity, and the confusion that resulted from this lack of standardization constituted a public nuisance of the highest order.[3]

The problem was solved in 1883, when a General Time Convention established by the railroads—a brainchild of William Frederick Allen of the staff of the *Official Guide of the Railways and Steam Navigation Lines*—put into effect four standard time zones that governed the whole of the continental United States. These time zones accepted by the railroads took hold everywhere, just as the railroads themselves were coming to dominate the tempo of American life. Ordinary people now found it most convenient to set their clocks by "railroad" time. The U.S. Congress, slow as usual in such things, did not officially adopt Standard Time until 1918, but by then it was hardly necessary—the railroads had done it for them.

The railroads were doing as much to improve themselves as they were to improve the general conditions of the national economy. Strong but light steel rails, used first on the Pennsylvania in 1863, were found on eighty percent of railroads by 1890. Old railway lines were often rebuilt with ballast, having gentler curves for safer operation and higher speeds. Punishing grades were reduced, new tunnels blasted through. All the great rivers were bridged, so that passengers (and freight, too, of course) could travel through without having to be cast out for ferry transfer. The major trunklines were almost all double tracked.

In freight service, well-developed urban terminals and transfer points began to make possible the fast and efficient movement of products and goods on a gigantic scale—far outstripping anything then realized in Europe or elsewhere in the world. In 1870, the average freight car on the Pennsylvania Railroad had a capacity of about ten tons; by 1880, that capacity had nearly doubled. There were many new kinds of freight cars available—boxcars, hoppers, cars for carrying timber, or livestock, or milk, every product customarily carried around the country in large quantities.

Not that the railroads were always the innovators. Sometimes customers and shippers demanded facilities for this or that kind of conveyance. Before the Civil War, railroads had resisted the development of milk traffic; after the war, they balked at the idea of shipping refrigerated meats. In the 1870s, an ex-Yankee meat packer named Gustavus Franklin Swift settled in Chicago and began talking about the possibility of slaughtering animals in the Chicago stockyards and shipping them as dressed meat under refrigeration to the East Coast. So daffy was he with the idea that his friends began calling him "that crazy man Swift." Swift failed to get any railroad to build a refrigerator car for him. A steer in the form of dressed beef weighed about forty percent less than it did on the hoof, so the carriers wanted no part of any scheme that would thus diminish their revenues. Accordingly, Swift designed and built his own refrigerator car, and shipped meat eastward over the Grand Trunk Railway, which had no livestock business.[4] The refrigerated meat arrived in much better condition than livestock buffeted for days in a cattle car, and all the major trunklines were soon forced to supply refrigerator cars.

But freight tonnage of every conceivable variety was increasing in the years after the Civil War. Ton miles of freight (that is, tons of freight multiplied by the number of miles they moved by rail) increased from ten billion in 1865 to seventy-nine billion in 1890. In one or two decades, the railroads brought about a complete transformation in the American economy. Anything woven, sewn, churned, or hammered out, any grains harvested or ore mined, could be shipped from one part of the country to another. Former luxuries of life became necessities, and with express businesses booming in these years a lady in Illinois could order a dress woven in New England or a gentleman in Minnesota could order a watch made in Philadelphia, and expect to have it delivered in a few days. In another decade or so, great catalogue merchants, men like Richard W. Sears and A. Montgomery Ward, now using

the railroads instead of the wagons of the erstwhile Yankee peddler, were able to place in American homes even in the most
remote locales everything from bobby pins to milking stools, from
children's toys to potbellied stoves.

The need for railroad services had grown so swiftly in these
years that the railroads themselves staggered under the burden of
competitive enterprise. In many areas, railroads were overbuilt—
there were too many lines serving the same territories—so something had to be done to keep the competing companies from
ruining one another. To dull the edge of competition, the railroads began to engage in pooling arrangements, which essentially
involved extralegal agreements to share traffic and earnings
according to an agreed upon formula. There were a great number
of competing lines between Chicago and Omaha, for example, so
a pooling agreement was hammered out there as early as 1870.

The pool idea worked fairly successfully for a few years. For a
while, so did the so-called Eastern Trunk Line Association, which
was made up of all the principal east and west roads as far as the
Mississippi. The Chicago-Omaha pool and the Eastern Trunk Line
association were both the conceptions of a German-born railway
executive named Albert Fink. Fink was highly regarded in the
industry, having formerly been a vice president of the Louisville
and Nashville Railroad, and he had arbitrated numerous disputes
among southern railroads. Furthermore, he was a man of both
philosophical and analytical cast of mind, and nobody refuted
him when he observed that "the railroad system has become so
extended and the business relations of so many roads to each
other have become so complicated that…there should be organized cooperation."[5]

Unfortunately, the task at hand proved to be too gigantic even
for the great mind of Fink. The pooling arrangements had no
legal status, and the railroads frequently cheated on them to get
the better of their rivals. In time, the pooling idea garnered an
unsavory reputation with the general public, and collusive rate-
making practices—indeed, all rate-making practices—gave the
railroads a bad name. Especially out in the grain states, rate practices would come to make railroads hotly detested for many years.
Hardly a farmer could be found who did not believe that the railroads set their rates in ways devilishly contrived to gouge him of
his hard-earned income. The problem, which the railroads never

successfully solved by themselves, would be the source of social unrest throughout the remainder of the nineteenth century.

In the 1870s, the railroads were getting a good deal of bad publicity for themselves in other ways as well. While becoming tremendously large institutions—while becoming "big business" in a nation that had not prepared for bigness, but only for the benign agrarian social order dreamed of by Jefferson—railroad finance and management went wild in the last three decades of the nineteenth century. In a land where neither law nor tradition had ample provision for controlling speculation, undisciplined business growth, and underhanded financial dealings, the America of the Gilded Age gave full rein to a generation of unprincipled business tycoons—the majority of whom lacked all sense of morality, all sense of the common good. Among these unprincipled players were some who today could only be called rogues, scoundrels, or even downright criminals.

One of the most prominent players with railroads in the postwar years, but no means the worst of the breed, was Commodore Cornelius Vanderbilt. Vanderbilt got interested in railroads rather late in life. He had been born back in 1794 and made a tidy fortune for himself in the steamboat business (thus, the honorific "Commodore"), and kept to this pursuit almost until the coming of the Civil War. In 1857, he gained a controlling interest in the Harlem Railroad, and in 1865 the Hudson River Railroad. A man of spectacular vision, within a few years he was thinking of a railroad line that would spread all the way to Buffalo, then all the way to Chicago. In his steamboat days, the Commodore was always of a monopolistic turn of mind, and it was impossible for him to get into railroads without somehow thinking of himself as controlling every railroad that came within his purview, at least every immediate competitor. By the late 1860s, he had designs on controlling the Erie, since it ran through "his" New York state. In this design, he was ultimately frustrated, but his financial maneuverings relating to the Erie had much to do with its subsequent financial ruin.

When Vanderbilt had designs on some property, he knew no scruples, and would use whatever means were at his disposal to gain his ends. By the 1860s, he was more than a little familiar with the trading practices of Wall Street, and his tricks could match the ingenuity of the best speculators on the street. He had learned from his steamboat days how you could find techniques to drive down the value of some stock you were hoping to acquire. But his principal concern was invariably acquisition rather than immediate profit; he fancied himself the ruler of a vast railroad system. And since his energies were fiercely devoted to that end, his goals were ultimately rewarded. By the time of his death in 1877, at which time he had become the richest man in American (the first American to die with $100,000,000 in his pocket), he had created the vast New York Central Railroad system, one of the great lines of the United States.

Once the Commodore had a tempting business conquest in mind, little could be done to thwart him of his ambition. Consider the case of the railroad line which ran through the central part of New York state, which was already called the New York Central Railroad. Vanderbilt did not own it, but only the railroads that led to it up the Hudson River from New York City. At Albany, Vanderbilt's Hudson River Railroad connected with the New York Central Railroad, and both passengers and freight could be transferred from one road to another. By 1866, traffic of both kinds was considerable. But the managers of the New York Central annoyed Vanderbilt, since they sent freight business his way only during the frigid winter months when Hudson River steamboats (including lines allied with the Central) were hampered by ice. This bypassing of his railroad rankled Vanderbilt, and one cold January day in 1867 he struck a blow. He suddenly halted train service on the east side of the bridge, forcing through passengers to stumble across the frozen bridge to the New York Central depot on the other side. Furthermore, the Commodore would not transfer either freight or freight cars: He simply dumped out the freight shipments at the end of his line.

This turn of events caused alarm among state officials in Albany, who called on Vanderbilt for an explanation. But the Commodore was ready for them. He showed them an old law, long completely neglected, which prohibited his trains from running across the river. By a kind of irony, the law had originally been sought by the New York Central in the early days when they were trying to prevent competition from any lines to the east. The legislators were left speechless—the law was there, it did exist.

But Vanderbilt was no man to be stymied by legal technicalities and loopholes. On other occasions, he reportedly said: "Law! What do I care about the law. Hain't I got the power?" So this charade was part of a well concocted and brilliantly orchestrated plan. Stock of the New York Central Railroad began to plummet on Wall Street, and the Commodore was prepared for it. He quietly began buying up stock on the cheap, knowing full well that this hostile connecting railroad would eventually fall into his hands. And it did—before the year was out. Vanderbilt had in one fell swoop acquired a great railroad system, one over which he could run his own through trains from New York to Buffalo.

With his intense dislike of competition and his love of monopoly, the Commodore shortly turned his eyes to another big railroad property, the Erie, which also spanned the state of New York farther south. Why should this line not be his also? And acquiring controlling stock did not seem on the face of it to present any serious difficulties. Since the 1850s, the stock of Erie had been bought almost exclusively for speculation, not for any intrinsic value it might have had. Wily old Daniel Drew, who had already lost several battles to Vanderbilt in the steamboat field, had been responsible both for the poor physical condition of the hapless Erie and for the extreme volatility of its stock. Vanderbilt began to buy quietly into Erie, and soon had a seat on the board of directors himself. Surely he and Drew must have eyed one another suspiciously in the boardroom, and there is little doubt that Drew had figured out what Vanderbilt was planning to do. He was going to buy up Erie stock until he had acquired control of the company.

Now Daniel Drew was certainly no more crafty than Vanderbilt, and his intellectual horizons were much lower. He had never been in the railroad business because he wanted to do some good for railroads—indeed, he regarded the Erie as nothing more nor less than a fruit tree which he might pick clean with impunity. Drew didn't really care very much who controlled the Erie, or who sat on the board; he was only concerned with devious trading in Erie stock so that he himself could take a profit. He was never more delighted than when the stock went down, since he was a short seller—an individual who hopes to see the price of a stock that he has already sold go down, so that he might buy it again later at a cheaper price.

During the war years, Drew had been relatively quiescent, and seemingly had not sought to plunder the Erie treasury to the limit; now, however, with his old archenemy Vanderbilt meddling in things, he became emboldened, and hoped to find a way to trap the Commodore in his own pit of greed. In this endeavor, he had of late acquired two partners who matched his own gift for skulduggery. These men were Jay Gould and Jim Fisk, two of the most blatant scoundrels of American record. Jay Gould was a much better educated man than either Drew or Vanderbilt, and perhaps as a financial manipulator he was craftier and more imaginative than either. Like Drew, he was a solitary individual who kept deals close to his vest. Like Drew, too, he was a pious church-going man who spurned a flamboyant life-style, so he did not give an immediate impression of a high roller, but he was a financial schemer on an exalted plane.

Henry Adams, the great social philosopher with strong roots in the older, tamer, more principled America, described Gould to perfection when he observed:

In character he was strongly marked by his disposition for silent intrigue. He preferred to operate on his own account, without admitting other persons into his confidence.... There was a reminiscence of the spider in his nature. He spun huge webs, in corners and in the dark, which were seldom strong enough to resist a serious strain at the critical moment.... It is scarcely necessary to say that he had not a concept of a moral principle."[6] Indeed, Gould was to have said after one of his intrigues went sour and was exposed to the public glare, "Nothing is lost here save honour."

The other rogue to link arms with Drew to thwart Vanderbilt's efforts to acquire Erie was Jim Fisk, Jr., a man of markedly different character from Drew and Gould. A flamboyant individual, son of a crafty Yankee peddler, he was completely unlike the quiet and gloomy Gould. As Henry Adams pointed out, he was "florid, gross, talkative, obstreperous." A giant man of considerable girth, he was nearly forty when he fell in with Gould and Drew, "but had the instincts of fourteen."[7] He caroused, chased women, lived sumptuously, arrived everywhere in a handsome carriage (Drew mostly walked to work, and Gould took public transportation). How these strange bedfellows were drawn to one another is a matter for conjecture, but it could be that Gould at least was aware of the limitations of his saturnine and crimped personality and accordingly profited from the dramatic and flamboyant qualities of Fisk.

The year 1868 was witness to one of the most memorable and

disgraceful episodes of American financial history—a battle for the control of the Erie Railroad between the so-called Erie ring (of Drew, Fisk, Gould, and their coconspirators) on the one hand and Vanderbilt on the other.[8] Vanderbilt had concluded that the Erie was in a shaky financial condition, which it was, and that certainly it was ripe for takeover. Previous deals had made him one of the wealthiest men in the country, and he felt that he was able to take on his crafty but not farseeing adversary, Drew. Immediately after the Civil War, Drew had once again begun shaking the Erie money tree for his own benefit. In 1866, he advanced his "favorite" railroad $3,500,000, taking 28,000 shares of unissued stock and three millions in convertible bonds. At the same time, he was going short on Erie in a rising market, then suddenly unloaded 58,000 shares. When the stock plummeted from 95 to 50 he made an enormous killing.

With Gould and Fisk on the board of Erie—Gould now as president and Fisk as vice president—the first order of business seemed to be to repulse Vanderbilt's attempt to take over Erie, which was intended to give him his New York state monopoly. Not that the Erie defenders cared that much for the financially ailing railroad, but rather they saw in Vanderbilt's avarice a way to make profits for themselves. Vanderbilt and his cohorts started buying Erie stock, but immediately they found that there was more of it available than they had ever dreamed possible. This is because Gould, Fisk, and Drew had gotten themselves a printing press and began to crank out reams of Erie stock certificates—all of it unauthorized—and the more stock the Commodore's forces bought the more of the new stock there seemed to be. Eventually, Vanderbilt sensed that he was being hornswoggled and he sought remedy in the law—the remedy he believed he never needed. Arrest warrants were issued for Gould, Drew, and Fisk, but they escaped to New Jersey, where they holed up in the Taylor Hotel in Jersey City, out of the jurisdiction of New York courts, but for safety's sake also surrounded themselves by hired thugs and ruffians armed with everything from shotguns to brass knuckles.

From the Hotel Taylor, which Jim Fisk started calling Fort Taylor, the Erie ring fought back, getting their own injunctions from judges whose pockets they had lined. In the war that followed, both sides used everything at their disposal, including the bribing of judges and New York state legislators. In the end, the

Erie ring triumphed, not because they had won the largest number of legal skirmishes but because they had already taken the Commodore to the cleaners and made such a physical and financial wreck of the Erie that it no longer seemed a very desirable takeover property.

Gould and Fisk remained in command of the Erie until 1872 (before that time, they had found a way to shove old Daniel Drew aside, leaving him on the road to bankruptcy). During their years at the top, the condition of the Erie continued to deteriorate. One would not have concluded this, however, from the look of the railroad's executive offices in New York. Gould and Fisk bought Pike's Opera House at Twenty-Third Street and Eighth Avenue in New York (later renamed the Grand Opera House) and built themselves a plush set of offices there amidst carved woodwork, stained- and cut-glass partitions, gilded balustrades, and frescoes on the walls and ceilings by the Italian artist Garibaldi. There were boudoirs available for the entertainment of Fisk's lady friends. Gould and Fisk rented this building to the Erie at $75,000 a year, and the railroad had to abandon its spartan waterfront headquarters at Duane and Reade Streets near the Erie's ferry to Jersey City.

Fisk was hardly the kind of individual suited to the arduousness of railroad management, yet he served as general manager of the road. Dubbed by the press "Prince Erie," he rode up and down the line in a resplendent private railway car, usually in the company of beautiful women. Not infrequently, he would bring whole trainloads of his friends to the Orange Hotel in Turners (now Harriman), New York, which housed a celebrated railroad eatery of the day. Here, Fisk's guests would dine, doubtless at the expense of the insolvent Erie, while tongues wagged and newspapers fumed. Fisk leant a certain amount of glamour and gusto to the careworn Erie, and many railroad employees regarded him as a heroic figure, probably little realizing that his only contribution was in draining the railroad's coffers and picking the worker's pockets. His influence on the road and his colorful lifestyle was cut short when he was shot by a young man who had stolen his favorite mistress, a third-rate actress named Josie Mansfield.

Jay Gould by himself, and with a certain amount of luck, might have succeeded in bringing Erie back to the forefront of American railroads.[9] He had the managerial skills to do it, and had in fact bought and restored to solvency the Rutland and

Washington Railroad in Vermont when he was a mere lad of twenty-one. Furthermore, after leaving Erie, Gould became one of the nation's most prominent railway magnates and showed signs of possessing talents beyond those of a mere financial manipulator. For a time, he controlled the Union Pacific Railroad, and before he died in 1892 he controlled the Missouri Pacific and other southwestern lines. He also owned the Western Union Company, and the entire system of elevated railroads in the city of New York. For years, he dreamed of owning his own railway system from the Atlantic to the Pacific. It was a dream that was never realized, but he became one of the most legendary railway capitalists of the nineteenth century.

But the wild period of speculation of the late 1860s and early 1870s infected Gould's blood for a long time. He was for years as dedicated to speculative intrigue as Daniel Drew—indeed, in 1869 he devised a scheme, which nearly succeeded, to corner the gold market, a story that has been told over and over again by historians of the American scene. Unfortunately, Gould's years with the Erie can only be regarded as a disgrace. Through all of the financial manipulations and dishonest dealings with Vanderbilt, he had left the railroad sixty-nine million dollars in debt. He had no time for the physical rehabilitation of the road, which he certainly must have known was necessary. While he sat in his luxurious gilded offices of the Grand Opera House, he struggled vainly to deal with the fact that the Erie had been plundered of all its assets. The rail was worn out; the locomotives were antiquated—a good third of them total wrecks; and passenger equipment was not fit for human conveyance. Accidents on the line were many, and employees were underpaid, often not paid at all. In the end, the directors of the line coalesced against Gould, urged on by many English stockholders who bought Erie stock when it was cheap, thinking it could go no lower. They finally ousted him as president.

The Erie Railroad never really recuperated from the assaults of men like Fisk, Drew, and Gould. It was never able to regain its place among the leading trunklines of the East because it took years to escape from its cruel debt and its physical dilapidation. The year after Gould left it, the Erie paid a dividend on common stock, but it did not pay another dividend for sixty-nine years: until 1942. For years, people would intone the old refrain that "icicles would freeze in hell before Erie declares a dividend."[10] The

Erie, like many other railroads of the time that had also been plundered of their assets, had been brought to ruin by the unbridled speculation and ruthless freebooting of the Gilded Age.

But it is fair to say there was always a bright side to these dark times of reckless competition and immoral speculation. The United States was in a period of such wild growth and expansion, such healthy and exuberant pragmatism, that any fair appraisal of the railroads of the time would have been forced to admit that most of the lines were better and more prosperous than they had ever been before. Even the Erie grew to be a much bigger version of its poor self. Formulas for managing railroads had been found and instituted, and, yes, practiced—even by the likes of Commodore Vanderbilt and Jay Gould. For all the excesses of the period, America's need for high quality, professionally operated railroads was being met. There might have been something terribly grievous in the rise of financial buccaneers like Gould and Vanderbilt, as thoughtful historians like Charles and Henry Adams ruefully told the nation at the time. There may have been dark fears that the old American republic was fading away. But the nation itself was too robust in the 1870s, moving too quickly, progressing too well, so most citizens simply didn't notice. Financial jackels may have looted railway treasuries, and many new railroad enterprises may have been built by crooks, even run by crooks, but the railroads themselves were doing well, providing better and faster service and doing it now with style.

C·H·A·P·T·E·R 8

THE COLONIZATION OF THE WEST

By 1870, it had become commonplace to say that the railroad was the agency that had made the United States a unified nation, that it had been the railroad which had drawn so many lonely and isolated communities into one national community. But the railroad's influence upon the trans-Mississippi West, the far West—sometimes picturesquely called the Wild West—was even more obvious and overpowering than it had been in the East. Here, it was not a matter of linking one tiny hamlet with another, or one isolated geographical region with the cities of the eastern seaboard; here, it was a matter of actually creating something from nothing. For a number of years after the Civil War, there were no hamlets to be linked—railroads jutted off into no-man's-land, into infinity, it was said. Tiny hamlets were not "reached" by the railroad; the hamlet was literally dropped down out of the railway cars. Where the railroad ran, there was something, or at least a pretense of something. Where there was no railroad, there was no civilization at all.

The building of railroads into the wilderness never ceased to be a puzzlement to European visitors. They saw the frenzied bustle and the manic optimism of Americans as the very height of lunacy. Why build railroads to places nobody wanted to go, why build railroads where there was no cargo to carry? Americans saw things differently, of course. For decades, they had been using the phrase "manifest destiny": This was their country, all of it, and they intended to settle and civilize the whole of it in due course. What's more, the far West represented a great challenge to the American imagination since the time of the Lewis and Clark expeditions— this vast territory inhabited seemingly only by buffalo and Indians evoked a deep passion and stirred the American spirit of conquest. For a long time, Horace Greeley in his New York *Tribune* had been trumpeting the slogan, "Go West, Young Man," and after the Civil War, a few who were not drawn solely by the lure of gold or silver heeded the cry. And these same years would witness a great influx of settlers from abroad, immigrants from the teeming shores of Europe hoping to enjoy the fruits of this bountiful land of opportunity.

Because the conviction was keenly felt, not only in Washington, but among the American people, that the West was now ready to reap some kind of rich harvest, there was no lack of railroad activity in the years after the completion of the transcontinental. There might well have been a cessation, since it was clear from the very first day of service that the transcontinental railroad was years away from making a profit. California had been linked to the Mississippi River and points East by rail, but there was little business for the railroad in the far West, nothing in any case that would spark the enthusiasm of any sane investor.

Still, even before the linking of rails at Promontory, there was much new railroad activity in the West, and plans for a number of lines were in the works. Indeed, the Union Pacific had had a competitor from the beginning—a line that stretched across Kansas and hoped to beat the Union Pacific in the race for the 100th meridian. When this railroad, actually called for a while the eastern division of the Union Pacific, lost the race, its directors petitioned Congress for permission to alter the survey of the original route, which called for it to turn northward and join the Union Pacific in Nebraska. It was now proposed to build straight west, up the valley of the Smoky Hill River and then on to Denver. The line, subsequently called the Kansas Pacific, was built, although not without the usual trials and tribulations of the day.

The scheme for the Kansas Pacific seemed more than reasonable, since it provided railway service to the growing state of Kansas, which had been admitted to the union in 1861. But more implausible, the post–Civil War era saw the beginning of construction on a railroad line across the northern tier of states—a territory that was not only unsettled but known to possess a hostile and perhaps unconquerable terrain. Still, this northern route had been discussed way back in the 1850s, and was one of those that Jefferson Davis had directed to be surveyed when he was Secretary of War in the cabinet of Franklin Pierce. The so-called Northern Pacific Railroad had actually been chartered by Congress on July 2, 1864.

This seemingly foolhardy act called for a railroad to be built from some point on Lake Superior either in Minnesota or Wisconsin, westward and north of latitude 45°, to or near Portland, Oregon. Not only was the distance vast and daunting (it needs to be recalled that the present state of Montana alone is bigger than the whole of Italy), but the proposed railroad would have to cross the Rocky Mountains, and there was not the least assurance that any railroad was equal to that task. Then there was the problem of raising the capital. Who would put money into such an enterprise in a territory even more wild and remote than that of the Union Pacific? The railroad was once again to get whopping land grants, although in the 1860s there seemed to be no prospect at all that profits were possible from their sale.

The problem of financing the Northern Pacific's construction seemed to be an insurmountable one until the famous Philadelphia investment banker Jay Cooke entered the scene. Cooke was a highly respected public figure, a man of commanding personality and great energy, possessing far more integrity than the typical financier of the 1870s. He had built a solid reputation by financing United States government bonds during the Civil War, and was, by all accounts, one of the great financial promoters and boosters of American history. The challenge of finding the money for construction of the Northern Pacific was daunting, since it was calculated that $100,000,000 would be needed to get the job done, and if it were not for Cooke's superb skills of salesmanship, the undertaking would never have been considered. Cooke began an aggressive advertising campaign to sell bonds, and in 1869, when construction began, hardly a week went by in the East when newspapers failed to have something to say about the construction of the Northern Pacific.[1] Cooke advertised that these lands, with their rich forests, were worth many times the $100,000,000 in gold bonds that were being offered—and here he was speaking the truth. But he also extolled the mild climate of the region, said to be comparable to that of Venice and Paris, and hinted that these mysterious regions might contain orange groves and banana trees—claims that were wild exaggerations, to say the least.

Work on the railroad continued, and Cooke managed to sell bonds both here and abroad. When the Franco-Prussian War broke out in Europe, however, some of his European deals fell through, and the American market began to sag also. In 1873, Cooke's banking house in Philadelphia failed, precipitating the greatest financial panic in the United States since 1837. Not only was work on the Northern Pacific stopped, but chaos reigned in all the nation's financial markets. Many other banks failed. The New York Stock Exchange was closed temporarily; the Gold Exchange, too, closed its doors. Thousands of American workers were thrown out of work; many industries were shut down for good; and construction on nearly all new railroads was halted for months, and in some cases years. Americans learned again the high price that must be paid for quick growth in financial deals that are too reliant on hope and expectation and not enough on tangible reality. The jubilant Northern Pacific dream would become a reality, but only after the passing of another decade.

A number of other railroad enterprises of the West antedated the Civil War in terms of actual inspiration. Around 1859, an Ohio lawyer named Cyrus K. Holiday who had moved West to Topeka, Kansas, helped stake out that town, served as its first mayor, guided it to become the state's capital, then started talking of a railroad that would follow the old Santa Fe trail to the southwest—the railroad that would eventually become the Atchison, Topeka, and Santa Fe, one of the great American railroads. The railroad was nothing but a Kansas project for many years, and by the time of the panic of 1873 the railroad had not been built beyond the state of Kansas. By the 1880s, however, with railroad frenzy again loose in the land, the Santa Fe route was completed to California.

And there were other railroad lines across the West which had been dreamed of for many years. One of these was the Texas and Pacific line, which southern senators had advocated before the war—a line that would follow the thirty-second parallel from Texas to San Diego. Thomas A. Scott, of the Pennsylvania Railroad, envisioned this route as a perfect adjunct to his great eastern trunkline, and in 1871 he acquired a charter and land grant for the construction of the railroad. He obtained the services of Grenville Dodge to lay out and build the line. Shortly into fierce competition with Scott would be Collis P. Huntington, who also dreamed of a line serving much the same territory, a line that came to be known as the Southern Pacific. It was perhaps inevitable that these two railroads would come into conflict, and they did. But even before that could happen, the Panic of 1873 had shattered the national economy, putting a heavy hand on both enterprises. Scott gamely moved forward for a while, and Dodge built the line across Texas using black prison laborers rented for a few cents a day from the state of Texas. But eventually he threw in the towel, and Jay Gould, always looking for a sick animal to "rescue," took over the Texas and Pacific, later giving it up to the powerful interests of the Southern Pacific.

Construction of railroad lines in the West was, it should be obvious, a cutthroat business at the very best. It was not for the faint of heart. During the 1870s, the opportunities for western lines were so meager, financing so uncertain and perilous, that the railroad scene was cluttered with instances of failure and unfulfilled opportunity. The western railroads fell prey to railroad jackels like Jay Gould, who, in addition to the Texas and Pacific also had his claws on the Union Pacific for a while, and probably had designs on almost every other railroad west of the Mississippi.

Furthermore, western railroads for years were exposed to every imaginable form of threat to their existence; everything from plague, to drought, to the attacks of Indians and wild animals. From the beginning, as trains began to carry express and gold shipments, they would be exposed to raids by train robbers and other desperadoes. Often, railroads could not be built unless under the protective guns of some militia, and once built could not be operated without similar support. There were a few times when to survive railroads had to declare war on one another. Such, for example, was the case in the late 1870s, when the Santa Fe had grown beyond Kansas and was stretching into Colorado, and now found itself in direct confrontation, indeed, in a state of war, with the Rio Grande railroad. Both lines wanted to get down into New Mexico by the Raton Pass—a place that clearly could not accommodate two railroads but which provided the only way to go. Both roads hired their own private militia, composed mostly of roustabouts and local idlers with guns. The Santa Fe got there first, and held the pass, but open warfare continued over this and other disputed territories for years afterward.[2] When the lines were not fighting things out in the Southwest, their attorneys were attempting to lay one another flat in courtroom battles, or their traffic men were exploring ingenious ways to kill off the hated competitor with rate wars.

Of course, the hardship conditions endured by western railroads were attributable not only, or even chiefly, to the fierce competition between lines. In the wide open spaces, competition and the lack of money were only minor impediments. Much larger problems than traversing the route or arranging for financing assailed the railroads everywhere they went. Since the territory that the railroads opened up was completely unsettled, the builders and operators of the lines had to deal with swarms of buffalo, ever-expected attacks by Indians, and the general lawlessness of the territory through which they ran.

It might be assumed that in their coming the railroads brought with them the first breath of civilization to the plains, but the truth is that as their lines inched forward they invariably planted a series of towns that were savage and undisciplined—blights on the once unspoiled landscape. For example, as the Santa Fe slowly extended itself across Kansas in the 1870s it created one repulsive and violent cow town after another. First there was Newton (often called "Shootin Newton"), then Dodge City, the most legendary of all the trail towns, later to become the setting of countless movie epics in our own century. Dodge City collected so many bad characters so quickly that it needed a lockup even before the railroad was able to bring in the lumber to build one. Dodge City's first jail was a huge hole dug in the ground, which, after the floods, could also double as a quick "drying out" spot for the town's drunks. These would be unceremoniously dunked in the muddy water. When "order" did appear in Dodge City, it was in the person of the lawless Marshal "Bat" Masterson, soon to be a hired gun of the Santa Fe in its battles with the Rio Grande.

And the cow towns did not become quickly civilized or gentrified as they grew in size. Abilene, on the Kansas Pacific, settled long before the shooting started in Dodge City, had become nothing but a bigger and uglier form of its earlier self. Said to be a town of forty saloons, it was regularly awash with whiskey; its highest forms of culture were gambling and the diverse ministrations of dance hall girls and prostitutes. Gunshots rang out by day and night, and no man who considered himself as such would be seen without a six-shooter at the ready in its holster. The railroad had created Abilene and Dodge City, as it would so many of their pale imitations, but once having created them it could do little to bring them to a state of civility.

Still, whatever there was of culture, or tradition, in the Wild West was, in a sense, the product of the railroad. Not that the railroad was the transporter of custom and tradition from elsewhere; rather, the railroad was the agency that allowed the West to develop its own myths and way of life. Consider the appearance of the fabled American hero known as the "cowboy." He was, according to western historian Dee Brown, strictly a creation of the railroad's extension into the territories west of the Mississippi.

The cowboy was a by-product of a particular set of economic circumstances that came about immediately after the Civil War. For some time, cattlemen in Texas had been raising longhorn cattle with the expectation of reaching eastern markets. And, as Brown pointed out, the markets were there: There was a big shortage of beef in the post-Civil War North. Unfortunately, there were no railroads in the south and none west of Missouri, causing the Texans to have to drive their cattle overland to the settled areas of eastern Kansas. Unfortunately, crossing these settled areas and getting their animals to railheads in Missouri was a deadly adventure for the cattlemen. The settlers of the area did not want their fences wrecked and their crops trampled, so they used force to keep the Texans from driving cattle across the territory. By the end of the summer of 1866, thousands of cattle were stalled between deadly Indian territory at the drovers' backs, and the nearest railroad line in Missouri. Many herds died or had to be abandoned before they could be sold.

The pushing of the Kansas Pacific westward to Abilene, however, was destined to bring an end to this standoff. Abilene was well beyond the settled farming country; furthermore, it was fairly convenient and easy of access to the Texans who could reach it by a trail pioneered by an old Cherokee trader named Jesse Chisholm. The Chisholm Trail gave way to a treeless plain leading to Abilene. By late summer of 1867, this route to Abilene had been worked out, and on September 5 of that year the first shipment of twenty cattle were rolling eastward over the Kansas Pacific. Before the season was over, thirty-five thousand cattle had been driven into Abilene. During the winter that followed, a Chicago livestock trader named Joseph McCoy sent agents across Texas to distribute circulars and to place advertisements in newspapers, urging cattlemen to drive their cattle to the railroad at Abilene. "The season of 1868 began early, with endless lines of Longhorns splashing across the Smoky Hill River into Abilene's loading pens. Each year the numbers doubled, the Kansas Pacific being hard-pressed to find enough cars in which to ship out the cattle."[3]

These legendary riders of the plains, actually nothing more than cattle drovers—sometimes known as that, sometimes merely called Texans—were usually emaciated and semibarbarous agricultural laborers, and earlier accounts written about them found nothing extraordinary in their profession. Laura Winthrop Johnson, who attended a roundup in 1875 and wrote about it for *Lippincott's,* found little to be praised about these men, saw no glamour in the "rough man with shaggy hair and wild staring eyes, in buttonwood trousers stuffed into great rough boots."[4] Shortly, however, imaginative visitors began to find something picturesque about these dusty men of the trail—perhaps it was something about their costume, which in time became more fanciful: the old Castilian sombreros, the gaudy jackets with many-colored braid and Indian beads, the open-legged trousers with rows of buttons, the blood red scarves imitating those of the matador.

Soon, the more direct and appealing name of "cowboy" was applied to these individuals, and with the help of figures like Buffalo Bill Cody, who held his first "Wild West" show in Nebraska in 1882, the cowboy nudged his way into the pantheon of American heroes. The cowboy became a stock character, a confection for dime-novel writers and commercial artists, just about the time that his occupation was being made redundant by the spread of the railroads throughout the Southwest. Done out of work as an itinerant laborer, the cowboy continued on as a legend. Without the railroad, however, the cowboy would not have made his appearance at all: He would only have been a stock handler on horseback. Without being set in motion by the faraway railheads, he would never have sung his lonely songs beside so many camp fires, would have met no dancing girls, would have encountered no intransigent town marshals, would have demolished no Bull's Head's Taverns or shoot-'em-up gambling joints. The railroad had given birth to the cowboy, as it had to nearly all the other human institutions of the West and Southwest, but what the railroad had given it also almost immediately took away.

The railroad's contribution to the West was due not only to the drama and color of the region, but to the very pulse of social life in the region. This was an area of the country where the railroad came before the settlements, so the railroad itself was the civilizer, the settler, the builder of communities. The most important contribution of the railroads to the West was that of colonizer and land developer—indeed, the railroads to a large extent succeeded in doing what the much praised Homestead Act had failed to do: They brought people to the empty prairies; they used not only their land grants but all their powers of persuasion to populate and promote the desolate country through which they laid down their rails. More than anything else, colonization was the great railroad contribution to the far West.

The railroads found out that the only way they were going to be able to sustain themselves economically was to take an active part in colonizing the territories through which they ventured, and they tackled this effort with great energy and imagination. Actually, the idea of the railroad as a seller and settler of land began even before the railroads ventured beyond the Mississippi River. The Illinois Central Railroad pioneered this activity as far back as the 1850s, when it began building its lines across mostly uninhabited prairie land. Indeed, the very intent in building the railroad was to settle and populate the state of Illinois.

In truth, a desperate need for "population" was apparent to the Illinois Central managers long before the first tracks went down. The railroad found in the early 1850s that it did not even have a sufficiently large labor force to construct the railroad in the short time allowed in the charter. When the company was formed in 1851, it had agreed to build approximately seven hundred miles of road in six years, the project to be financed through a federal land grant of 2,595,000 acres (the first of the large grants to railroads in the West) with the idea that the company would be able to finance itself by the sale of these lands. But how could seven hundred miles of railroad even be built without a gigantic labor force, which no western state possessed? "Experienced" railroad workers were especially difficult to locate, since the rapidly expanding railroads in the East had a virtual monopoly on them.

Roswell B. Mason, the resourceful chief engineer of the railroad, sent out inquiries as best he could, and even occasionally took out ads in newspapers. But in two years, he had assembled a work force of no more than three thousand men. He knew that these numbers were hardly enough to complete the line in the time required, so he was desperate to find new means of persuasion. Eventually, he had printed up circulars for distribution by the thousands in and around New York City, calling for laborers to be paid $1.25 a day and guaranteed employment for at least two years. He also arranged with other eastern railroads to transport willing railroad workers to Illinois at a special fare of $4.75. With not a small amount of hype, Mason extolled the virtues of Illinois, which he proclaimed to be the garden spot of the nation. It was, he said, "a rare chance for persons to go West, being sure of permanent employment in a healthy climate, where land can be bought cheap, and for fertility is not to be surpassed in any part of the Union."[5]

Mason's statements were labored truths. The land was indeed fertile, but only for those prepared for hard, sometimes brutal, labor in a harsh climate. As to being a healthy environment, the Illinois Central was continually impeded by serious, sometimes fatal, outbreaks of cholera, probably due to poor sanitation and tainted food supplies. Sometimes it seemed that huge crews were nearly decimated by virulent outbreaks of the disease. A gang working in the vicinity of Peru near the Illinois River lost 130 men in a two-day period. Still, Mason's efforts had brought in the labor force to get the job done, mostly Irishmen, although Mason eventually came to prefer the more temperate Germans, popularly called "Dutchmen." At its peak, the railroad would have about seven thousand men in the field, and a fair number of these would eventually settle permanently in the state of Illinois.

As the tracks went down on what was then called the "Chicago branch" (now the main line of the Illinois Central), stations, sometimes little more than shacks, were constructed, usually with little or no reason or justification, since not a single dwelling or human habitation could be seen anywhere. But near these stations towns would shortly sprout up. On the two branches north of

Centralia, many flourishing towns were born of impromptu railroad "stations," which occasionally were nothing more than piles of lumber. Among the Illinois towns created from nothing by the Illinois Central were Homewood, Harvey, Manteno, Peotone, Paxton, Rantoul, Onarga, Gilman, West Urbana (later Champaign), Ashkum, Kankakee, Arcola, Effingham, Mendota, Wenona, Oglesby, El Paso, Normal, Wapella, Moweaqua, Assumption, Pana, and Sandoval.[6]

Wherever railroads went during the nineteenth century, they gave themselves the prerogative of naming towns along the route, especially in places where they erected a station and nearly always when there was no settlement at all. Accordingly, throughout the West, one finds towns with the names of prominent railway magnates, engineers, financial backers, and the imaginative concoctions of some of those individuals. On the Illinois Central, many place names were and remain railroad inventions. Along the IC, there are towns named for early British investors who poured money into the railroad—Richard Cobden, Sir Joseph Paxton, William Gladstone (yes, the famous Victorian prime minister). There is a town named for Robert Rantoul, the Massachusetts senator who was a member of the formative company of the railroad. There is a Mason City, commemorating the railroad's great chief engineer Roswell B. Mason. The same practice naturally spread to nearly all of the later western roads.

When the initially proposed lines of the Illinois Central were completed, the state of Illinois was endowed with the most extensive railroad system in the land. Still, even though the population of the state grew steadily in the 1850s, most of the railroad's right-of-way was uninhabited, and the potential for railroad traffic of all sorts was disheartening. The state of Illinois itself, unlike other midwestern states (Wisconsin and Minnesota, for example), had not taken a strong initiative to populate its territory—perhaps because of its own bad experiences with land lot booms that led to the severe depression of 1837. It soon became clear to the Illinois Central management that the only way to drum up business was to settle its own territories by whatever means were at hand.[7]

As early as 1854, the railroad hired a land agent, Charles Du Puy, who went to work on the problem. DuPuy immediately began placing ads in newspapers in numerous eastern states extolling the vast agricultural potential of Illinois, touting the area as the veritable garden spot of North America. In addition to these advertisements, Du Puy made announcements in various "Emigrant Guides" that had wide circulation at the time, informing newcomers to the American shore of the cheap land prices in Illinois and the possibilities of starting life anew in this agricultural paradise. Lest potential urban wayfarers be missed, Du Puy also had ads placed in horsecars in New York City on the Second, Third, and Sixth Avenue lines.

The Illinois Central, like a lot of other Western railroads in the years ahead, was not above grossly exaggerating the quality of life on the frontier. They caused to be printed up what Stewart Holbrook called "fairyland pamphlets," showing snug farmhouses with gingerbread under the eaves, beautiful shade trees, babbling brooks, peaceful farms with mild grazing cattle, chickens, and vegetable plots, all suggesting that the area was already long settled and endowed with gentility. Illinois was, indeed, rich agricultural land, but the IC's puffery did not make clear to many potential newcomers that only cruel and backbreaking labor could wrest a comfortable and hearty livelihood from this stubborn prairie.

Du Puy's efforts slowly paid off, although perhaps not handsomely enough to please management; he was succeeded by another land agent named John Wilson, formerly a federal land commissioner, and apparently a world beater in this competitive game of colonization. Wilson continued to use the fairyland pamphlets, but he put many more agents in the field; they scoured the eastern states not for a single individual here and there, but for whole communities that might be convinced to move westward. These agents visited country fairs, attended public meetings, and talked to clergymen and town elders—all with the idea of stimulating mass movements of people to Illinois. In the rock-ribbed states of Vermont and New Hampshire, where farming was (and continues to be) a marginal occupation, large numbers of people began following the lure of the Illinois Central promoters. In spite of legends to the contrary, most Yankees were not lonely, misanthropic individuals clinging to their own isolated patch of land, but had a strong sense of community. The Illinois Central's men played up the idea that it would be possible for whole communities, whole parishes, perhaps, to move to this land of fertile soil, while keeping their own traditions.

Accordingly, out of Vermont two hundred families came to settle New Rutland, Illinois. Fourteen families from Massachusetts founded Rosemond. The Working Men's Settlement Association of New London, Connecticut, laid out the village of Lyman, Illinois, in 1856. Another New England group founded Boyleton. Nearby states also sent settlers into the Illinois Central's domain. The American Emigration Association of Louisville, Kentucky, took a good look at these fabulous land values in their neighboring state. A group from Ohio was largely instrumental in settling Champaign, County, Illinois.[8] The railroad was always generous in providing land for schools and churches, and was responsible for the establishment of churches whose denominations naturally matched the preferences of the settlers, whether Lutheran, Congregational, or other.

And there was another potential reservoir of settlers that the Illinois Central had not tapped before, but which became the target of Wilson and his minions—the many immigrants newly arrived in America, and the many more still abroad who might be induced to come. Ads were placed in foreign-language newspapers in New York and elsewhere, and in newspapers of European countries that were currently sending large numbers of people to the New World. Agents of the Illinois Central met arriving ships at Eastern ports and did all that they could to ease the way of imigrants to the Prairie State. In time, the railroad sent agents abroad to augment these efforts and perhaps steal a march on competing states. The railroad engaged Francis Hoffmann, a prominent German of the state who had served as lieutenant governor, to go to Germany and run an Illinois Central Land office in that country. Hoffmann took ads in German papers, hired runners in port cities, and distributed pamphlets and posters throughout the land. More than that, however, Hoffmann leveled his sights on already-established German communities in the United States. A good many Germans had already settled in Wisconsin, for example, since Illinois had earlier done little to attract them. In 1863, Hoffmann induced some of these Wisconsin Germans to purchase thirty thousand acres of Illinois land, usually in forty-acre tracts. Within a period of two years, he settled some two thousand German families in the Illinois Central territory between Mattoon and Centralia.

Swedes and Norwegians were not neglected either, for the railroad employed a gentlemen named Oscar Malmborg to do for the Scandinavian countries what Hoffmann had done in Germany. As a result of Malmborg's efforts, a fair number of Swedes came, and settled communities such as Big Spring and Neoga. The railroad gave the Lutheran church land in Paxton on which to locate a college—Augustana College, now located in Rock Island. Only a few Norwegians settled in Illinois, most of them preferring Wisconsin and Minnesota, states that more nearly resembled in climate and atmosphere the lands they had left. Some Swedes settled in Illinois only for a short while, then moved on to Wisconsin. But a small number of them stayed in Illinois.

The Illinois Central's colonization effort by any measure was an unqualified success. When the railroad began its colonization work, Illinois was a sparsely settled state—even Chicago was still a city of very modest proportions. But by the time of the Civil War, the state was a busy, bustling, and decidedly forward-looking region, accepted as a major state by its neighbors to the east. During the period between 1855 and 1861, the Illinois Central had sold one and a half million acres of its lands; the population during the decade of the 1850s had increased over one hundred percent, to a total of 860,481.[9]

The pattern of land settlement and all the methods of gentrification practiced by the Illinois Central were shortly repeated by railroads west of the Mississippi, with greater or lesser success, but in most cases with achievements that resulted in abundant traffic of all kinds for the colonizing roads. Few railroads were more aggressive in matters of colonization than the Burlington and Missouri River Railroad (later the Chicago, Burlington and Quincy), a road that for the most part developed soundly and auspiciously under the steady guiding hand of Boston financier John Murray Forbes. In the 1870s, the Burlington would do for Iowa and Nebraska what the Illinois Central had done for Illinois, and it would do so using the most sophisticated techniques of huckstering known to that day or ours.

The Burlington produced booklets, posters, and broadsides; it sent agents into eastern states and foreign countries; it advertised in newspapers; it made arrangements with other railroads to forward settlers to the Burlington at reduced rates; occasionally it helped immigrants from foreign lands with their ocean passage, and subsidized the transportation of household goods. The railroad made very strong and imaginative efforts to locate interested Europeans who might be suitable residents of these rich but tough-to-cultivate farmlands. For example, in 1870 the railroad had an agent named Edward Edginton stationed in Liverpool, England, where many émigrées took off for the New World, and boarded every ship leaving for America, visited every hotel and boardinghouse used by emigrants, handed out leaflets, published articles in local newspapers, posted handbills, and so on. Above all, the railroad never failed to play its trump card—the easy availability under generous terms of fantastically cheap farm acreage. In 1871 and 1872, the railroad was widely advertising lands being sold for twelve dollars per acre in Iowa, and eight dollars per acre in Nebraska, with interest rates at about six percent.[10]

The various Burlington promotional campaigns and advertising efforts were reasonably honest, although they frequently exaggerated the ease with which farms in these territories might be cultivated, and the salubriousness of the climate. They were not above making extravagant claims such that in the West of the United States, as opposed to the East, a man could earn more money and pay less for the necessities of life. Neither of these assertions was true, even though for the right individual at the right place, the great plains states did offer wonderful opportunities.

On the other hand, in various letters to potential immigrants, in booklets and letters to newspapers, the railroad took pains to explain that the newcomers needed in these new territories were those individuals seeking to make a living in agriculture and the mechanical trades. In the many handbooks produced for immigrants at that time, it was regularly underscored that the slogan "Go West!" was not intended for everyone. One booklet of the early 1870s strongly emphasized that what were needed were individuals with stout arms and indomitable character.

> Persons accustomed to living by their wits alone are not wanted.... Every one of the so-called learned professions is overstocked. There are more doctors, apothecaries, lawyers, literary men, architects, teachers, clergymen, and other men of liberal education in the United States than can make a decent living.... Even in the Western states, where their services are less required, the supply, though not

of high order, exceeds the demand....Clerks ought not to think of coming unless they have thoroughly made up their minds to lay down the pen and take up the spade or plough.[11]

It may seem a miracle to many students of American history that these rough and difficult plains could attract any settlers at all. Certainly states like Nebraska, the Dakotas, and Minnesota would not have been appealing to anyone who had achieved a modicum of success anywhere in the rapidly urbanizing East. This was the principal reason for the strong efforts made by the railroads to place Europeans on American farms in the West. But even the Europeans had to endure unspeakable hardships. Not infrequently, families that came to the West from Europe were bitterly disappointed with the harsh conditions they encountered— sometimes they wrote home to family members who remained behind, and their bitter accounts hampered later railroad colonization efforts. On the other hand, some immigrant families made clear successes of their new ventures. And even some of those who were disappointed or endured lives that were cruel, heartbreaking, and laborious, ofttimes enjoyed a sense of freedom and achievement that they didn't have in the old world.

Most immigrants who arrived in the West after the Civil War were leaving their homelands because of conditions that were lamentably bad, and had in many cases recently become worse. Many arrivals from Germany, for example, had come to America because of repressive political conditions that followed in the wake of the Revolution of 1848. Many came to escape conscription and army service that was long, strenuous, and degrading. After 1870, which saw the dominance of all Germany by Prussia with its relentless militarism, and opposition under Bismarck to democratic institutions, a steady stream of Germans continued to emigrate to the United States, and an increasing number would be drawn by the railroads to lands west of the Mississippi.

The reasons behind emigration from European countries differed from place to place, naturally. Sometimes the considerations were political, sometimes social, sometimes purely economic. For a long time, the search for religious freedom had been a strong motivation for emigrating to the land of the free. Without a doubt, poor harvests and the worn-out soil of Europe accounted for the arrival of many new citizens in the nineteenth century. But these were seldom the only considerations. In the Scandinavian countries, for example—and emigrants from these countries, particularly Sweden and Norway, added enormously to the population of the upper Midwest—no single set of circumstances was usually responsible for the extensive migrations of the 1870s and 1880s.

Most of the Scandinavian countries experienced bad harvests in the period between 1850 and 1880. In Sweden, there was a severe economic crisis in 1864 and 1865, and this period was followed by three years of near complete crop failures, bitterly remembered by Swedes for many years as the period of the "Great Famine." But there were more than enough other problems for Sweden's farmers, and nearly all the Swedes who came to the Midwest were farmers. The land was poor, usually stony: Nearly forty percent of Swedish soil was and is unproductive. Rents were high. Most Swedes who farmed the land were not too far removed from serfdom. Only those who owned their farms enjoyed anything remotely like comfortable circumstances. Sweden suffered from what was usually referred to as "title sickness"; good land hardly ever changed hands, and when it did the law of primogeniture prevailed. This caused many impoverished second sons to seek a living elsewhere.[12] Also, many people were in conflict with the state Lutheran church, which was seen as intolerant, petty, cold, and implacable, and not even above persecution. Emigrants to America hoped for a greater sense of religious tolerance, and for the most part they found it. (Curiously, the Swedes brought their Lutheranism with them, but transformed it to something warmer and more benign in their new homeland.)

Not all of the Scandinavians found what they were looking for in the New World. Many wrote home to family members complaining that railroads or local boosters had oversold them on the virtues of the Midwest. Many were fleeced by tricksters when they landed on the East Coast; many were sold bogus tickets by phony railroad agents; others were sold titles to nonexistent lands. And when they did get established, life was often every bit as hard as that which they had foresaken. Most of the Scandinavians lived in sod huts or houses that were little more than board shanties. Sanitary facilities were usually completely lacking, and many pioneers suffered from the "ague," "the itch," or conjunctivitis, an eye disease today easily curable, but then persistent and torturesome.

Ole Rolvaag, in his famous novels *Giants in the Earth* and *Their Father's God,* gives us some idea of the harsh conditions of life endured by his fellow Norwegian immigrants in northern Minnesota. Norwegians and Swedes suffered much attempting to deal with the elemental forces of nature in America, grappling with conditions unknown to them—plagues, locusts, dust storms, prairie fires, blizzards, malaria, cholera. Many of them failed; some perished. On the other hand, in the end, most of the Scandinavians endured and made a firm adjustment to their new homeland. Professor G. M. Stephenson, in his account of Scandinavian immigration, put the matter very well when he proclaimed that although most Scandinavians came from the lower classes, and their folk produced few eminent leaders, and perhaps few colorful personalities, they nevertheless, "with their qualities of industry, thrift, honesty, love of home, respect for law and order, religious nature, interest in education, and physical stamina …have played a respectable part in the development of American society."[13] They have provided much of the bone and marrow of the life of our upper Midwest.

The railroads, of course, were more than a little responsible for the ethnic settlement of the states west of the Mississippi, as they were of most things relating to the social life of the region. Human habitation in the West largely followed the path of the railroad in early times, and to this very day a look at any map will show that the principal population regions of the western states sprung up along the railroad lines. Nearly all of the cities in states like Iowa, Nebraska, the Dakotas, and Montana thrived because they were railroad towns; many had their inception at the moment of the arrival of the railroad. Their first settlements were literally thrown off newly arrived trains.

And once the route of the railroad was laid down, further settlement of the line was determined by the colonization efforts of the railroads, which sold such public lands that had been granted them and which they then attempted to promote and popularize. And in these colonization efforts, the railroads moved with a zealousness and a ferocity that is probably unmatched in American history. When the Northern Pacific Railroad got back on its feet again after the Jay Cooke debacle, its financial wizard for much of the 1880s was a highly cultivated and well-connected German intellectual named Henry Villard, who was more than a little interested in planting Germans in the states through which his railroad ran. This was also an especially tactful ploy since he had arranged much of his financing in Germany. The Northern Pacific advertised regularly in sixty-eight German newspapers and thirty-two Scandinavian papers. Furthermore, all over Europe it distributed maps, circulars, and a company magazine in several language versions. In the early 1880s, the railroad had 831 agents in Great Britain and 124 roaming through Norway, Sweden, Denmark, Holland, and Germany. All of these agents carried the company brochures, but they were also supplied with posters, photographs of available farmlands, and even stereopticans.[14]

Nearly all of the western railroads found their own favored target groups. An agent of the Santa Fe Railroad, one Carl B. Schmidt, a German who had settled in Lawrence, Kansas, was sent forth to explore the possibility of bringing groups of Mennonites from Russia (these Mennonites were Germans who had settled on the Russian steppes during the reign of Catherine the Great). Subsequent Russian czars had made things uncomfortable for these German-speaking people, and they were looking for a way to emigrate. As early as 1874, thirty-four families of Mennonites arrived in Kansas. The males, usually tall and bearded, clad in Russian blouses and billowing trousers, reminded native Americans of scarecrows, and many expressed astonishment that the railroad would bring such incapable looking individuals to America. But the Mennonites proved to be the best farmers that Kansas had: Their experiences in Russia made them familiar with dryland farming. But it was their industriousness that eventually endeared them to the natives. Wherever they went, they planted not only wheat, but orchards, hedges, and shade trees. And they instituted all manner of other agricultural experiments. When droughts came to Kansas in 1879 and 1880, the Mennonites had the know-how to survive and they took over farms abandoned by less hardy agrarianists.

So good were the Mennonites that other railroads tried to steal them from the Santa Fe. In later years, an agent of the Burlington confessed that he once met a trainload of Mennonites at Atchison, Kansas, for which a Santa Fe special train was waiting. He kidnapped the whole bunch and put them on his own train, which deposited them in Burlington territory in Nebraska.[15] Skulduggery of this and other sorts was quite familiar in the West.

Omaha, which was one of the most important gateways to western lands, had many railroad hustlers of this stripe. Men from the Union Pacific attempted to convince new arrivals that the lands of the Northern Pacific were cold, harsh, and infertile, and that their own lands were far more salubrious. However, as emigration from many European countries continued and increased throughout the 1880s and 1890s, all of the western states and all of the railroads got the settlers they needed.

For the most part, immigrants gravitated to the kind of territory that matched the experiences and the soils of their homeland. Swedes and Norwegians usually gravitated northward to Minnesota and the Dakotas. Many Germans wound up in Nebraska and Iowa—Germans in larger numbers would have settled in Kansas had not that state begun an experiment in prohibition very early in its history, an antisocial act that would have interfered with the Germanic need for *Frolichkeit*. In time, though, all of these vast lands, these millions and millions of acres, had plenty to offer all who wanted to come.

There are surviving photographs showing railroads like the Northern Pacific laying their tracks across lands that evinced no sign of life or human habitation, and there were many people connected with the western railroads who groaned at the implausibility of attempting to colonize these lonely places. Many of the pioneers themselves became disheartened, returned home, or perished. Many wrote to their native lands in a kind of grim mirth, and it was often repeated at the time that "nowhere on earth could a person look further than see less" than out on these plains. At any other time, it would have been thought the height of insanity to bring people here. In some countries, a summons to this kind of settlement might have seemed like a sentence to the wasteland of Siberia or the arctic tundra. But in America things were different. Optimism and expectation were always in the saddle, especially in the western states. The railroads believed that it was part of their destiny to build across these desolate places and then bring people to live in them. They built, and the people came.

C·H·A·P·T·E·R 9

ACROSS THE CONTINENT — 1875

The construction of the transcontinental railroad and other rail lines beyond the Mississippi brought more than homesteaders to the western states. Western railroading was not only a practical achievement, it was a heightened form of human drama, a clarion call to individuals everywhere who were looking for adventure, excitement, even danger. The spanning of the American continent was a milestone in the history of technology, to be sure. More important than that, it was an accomplishment that captured the imagination of people around the world. Newspapers in Europe were full of items about the transcontinental railroad for months, even years, after 1869, and the American West took on the legendary characteristic that it has retained to this day. Europeans aplenty—and not only emigrants—wanted to come to America and travel across the continent by train, to lay eyes upon herds of wild buffalo, perhaps to have some daring encounter with the Indians of the plains. Even though train travel in the West had more than its share of discomforts and dangers, it nonetheless held a fatalistic attraction for the idle rich, writers, adventurers, jaded baronesses—and sometimes just plain damn fools.

Within weeks of the opening of the transcontinental, publishers began turning out a flood of guidebooks to the railroad and to

the West generally. These books were sold in all the major terminals of the eastern cities, were hawked by news butchers on trains
themselves, and found their way to Europe, where they whetted
the appetites of countless adventure seekers. The biggest best-sell-
er of the lot was the *Great Trans-Continental Railroad Guide*, written
by one H. Wallace Atwell, who signed himself "Bill Dadd the
Scribe." The book's publisher, George Crofutt, claimed that his
firm sold a half million copies of this single title during the 1870s.
And there was plenty of competition from other publishers with
their own guidebooks. Strange as it may sound, such nonfiction
works, usually trailing items on a publisher's list, became objects
of intense interest and sales appeal.

The reason for this, no doubt, was that most of these guidebooks bore a rather close relationship to the dime novels and
penny dreadfuls of the period. Their authors painted a colorful
picture of the West that was often not far removed from the ficti-
tious. On the other hand, extravagant imaginings were not really
necessary. The West *was* exciting. The claims of potential perils
and discomforts, as well as delights, were not exaggerations. One
could shoot buffalo and cook the steaks out upon the prairie.
One's train *could* be threatened by herds of wild animals or
Indians, and would be, in a few years, by masked robbers. One
could find one's train derailed in some lonely pass, or isolated by a
blizzard or by a fog of grasshoppers or locusts. One *could* visit all
the "hell on wheels" towns that the railroad had only recently laid
down—towns like Julesburg, Benton, or Corinne. In these towns,
lawlessness still ruled, and this lawlessness stoked the fires of anyone with a passion for freedom and unconventionality. Here were
to be found everything one could want in the way of gamblers,
horse thieves, crooked sheriffs, cutthroat bandits, and prostitutes
of every stripe. Here, in short, was a land of epic proportions that
appealed to a European mind that had so long been cramped and
stultified by teeming cities and close borders.

Train travel across the United States was a daunting experience
in the decade or so following the forging of the transcontinental
link. The experience has been described by numerous foreign
journalists, by social philosophers of every variety, and by the letters and diaries of lady adventurers, to whom the wide open
spaces usually proved more than an ordinary treat. The many
early accounts of crossing the United States by rail also give a vivid

account of the American people, their common life, their daily burdens and intrigues. They give us an account of a nation that was still crude, careless, and disordered, but also bursting with energy and enterprise; a nation struggling to discover itself in the midst of conflicting values and fragile human institutions. The American was a fascinating human character because seemingly he had not yet fully discovered himself, but was frantically and steadfastly attempting to do so.

The railroad itself was a source of fascination to foreign visitors. Somehow, it captured the spirit of the American people; a train journey seemed to be a microcosm of the American experience. The flat, open, and democratic passenger cars in their tumult and disordered practicality expressed a portrait of a people whose nature had not yet crystallized, but whose superabundance of will and energy made all things possible. In the 1870s, the railroad, like the American nation, was crude, unfinished, waiting to happen—but still a clear manifestation of earthly glory.

In the 1870s, one could cross the nation by train, at least the guidebooks said so, although certainly not on one train or even two. The transcontinental trip was a model of capriciousness, complexity, and unstandardized whimsicality. East of Chicago there were several competing routes—as there were from Chicago to Omaha—but the virtues of all of them were unclear and subject to rapid change. No guidebook, no matter how fresh the ink, would be sufficient to tell a traveler how best to go, which railroad was the safest, which had the longest delays, which had the best eating places, which had the cleanest hotels. Whatever could be said to be true one week was likely to be a lie the next.

In the 1870s, most Europeans entering the United States arrived at the port of New York. By this time, Philadelphia, Boston, Baltimore, and Charleston had all faded by comparison as ports of entry. New York was now the place where the hordes of European immigrants arrived for dispersal around the United States. Many of these new Americans would, of course, take trips that had often been arranged for them by railroad agents to homesteads in Kansas, Iowa, or Minnesota; others would stay near the more thickly settled eastern states—although anyone wanting to leave New York City would invariably also reach his destination by train.

Arrivals to the port of New York were processed at Castle

Garden on the southern tip of Manhattan, the principal immigration station of the United States between 1855 and 1890, after
which it made way for a larger processing station nearby on Ellis
Island. In the 1870s, most newly arrived immigrants had sailed
into New York harbor from a variety of European ports, by far the
most important of which was Liverpool, England, but followed
closely by a number of others—Breman, Hamburg, Glasgow,
Antwerp, Rotterdam, Harvre, Londonderry, and Genoa.[1] At Castle
Garden, newly arrived immigrants were pointed the way to the
ferry sheds of several railroad lines, most of which were located
only a few blocks north on the Hudson River. From there, they
would travel to railroad terminals on the New Jersey side to begin
their journey across the continent.

In 1875, making a journey from New York to Chicago in a single
railway car was a near impossibility, although not quite an absolute
impossibility. The very first copy of the *Official Railway Guide* in
1868 showed that it was possible to enjoy a "Silver Palace Sleeping
Car" that traveled "without change" by means of the "Allentown
Line," linking New York and Chicago in thirty-eight hours.[2] This
sleeping car was apparently jointly carried by the Jersey Central
Railroad and the Reading through Allentown to Harrisburg,
Pennsylvania, thence on the Pennsylvania to Pittsburgh, and
finally between Pittsburgh and Chicago on the Pittsburgh, Fort
Wayne, and Chicago Railroad. Curiously, the great Pennsylvania
through line between New York and Chicago had not yet been
forged, nor would it be until the next year, when the Pennsylvania
acquired the Pittsburgh, Fort Wayne, and Chicago. This had long
been its western arm, but the Pennsylvania had carelessly failed to
absorb the line, and only did so when fears arose that Jay Gould
was planning to make a grab for it. Curiously, for a long time after
the Pennsylvania established a through route to Chicago, it still
required the vast majority of its passengers to change trains in
Pittsburgh.

These conditions were no different elsewhere. Commodore
Vanderbilt's New York Central did not run west of Buffalo until
near the end of the old Commodore's life in 1877, by which time
the Commodore and his son William had acquired the Michigan
Central and the Lake Shore and Michigan Southern for their
entrée into the city on Lake Michigan. The Erie, too, fumbling to
replace its antiquated six-foot gauge, was stalled in Buffalo until

1880, and offered only poor through service thereafter. Accordingly, almost anyone arriving in Chicago in 1875 had been forced to change trains once or several times, probably at Buffalo, Pittsburgh, or Detroit at the very least. The poor landed immigrants swarming around Castle Garden that year could probably not count on getting to Chicago in less than three days. Still, on any given day in the 1870s, a cluster of people, sometimes running into the hundreds, would be released from Castle Garden for rail journeys to various parts of the United States—an occasional few would then continue on the long trek across the country on the transcontinental railroad. Many of these individuals, especially the indigent, would shuffle on foot, sometimes on prearranged omnibuses, up West Street in Manhattan to the various ferry houses of the railroads, which had their terminals on the Jersey Shore—the Pennsylvania, the Jersey Central, and the Erie, later the Lackawanna. These dreary, barnlike ferry houses were not very far away in any case.[3] Some of the railroads maintained agents at Castle Garden, and these were responsible for dispensing tickets that in some cases had been subscribed in Europe. And they queued up others who had not been claimed by any railroad. The immigrant business was decidedly big business for the railroads in the 1870s, and a very competitive business at that, so all of the companies were anxious to shepherd as many newcomers to their own terminals as possible.

All the railroads running west from New York, and this included, of course, Commodore Vanderbilt's New York Central, whose trains departed uptown, had immigrant cars on their passenger trains in the 1870s. Sometimes, after the arrival of especially large boatloads, entire immigrant trains were gotten up. Such trains invariably contained the crudest passenger equipment on the railroad—wooden coaches with flat roofs, fitted out with hard wood benches, the typical middle aisle in the American style, with a pot-bellied stove in the middle and a "convenience" at the end. The convenience was of the "dry hopper" type—immigrant coaches did not have running water of any kind, although bottled water, as well as things to eat, could be obtained from the train butcher.

Not all of those arriving from Europe were herded onto immigrant trains or coaches. Well-born individuals with ready money in their pockets were able to purchase seats in regular coaches; those few supplied with the providence of gold coin were free to seek out sleeping accommodations, although such individuals amounted to only a small minority of people arriving from Europe. At the ferry houses, passenger and ticket agents were usually expert at sizing up their customers and separating the genteel classes from the huddled masses. Those who could afford to pay regular fares were expedited. This was democratic America, of course, and railroad agents were not social arbiters such as those of Europe. Persons who could pay would be sent forward in style if they had the money; for the most part, however, agents picked out the true immigrants by sight—there were the inevitable shabby clothes, tattered valises, or crudely wrapped bundles. Sometimes agents guessed wrong about whether an individual should be herded with the immigrant masses, most of whom were required to remain in the cold, dark ferry shed for a day or so if no immigrant train was scheduled. They occasionally sold cheap tickets to those who could afford to pay much more. English author Robert Louis Stevenson, who came to America in 1879 and made the entire transcontinental trip, was sometimes taken to be an immigrant and sometimes found to be a person of "worth," in which instance he was sold better accommodations.

Whatever route an immigrant train took in the 1870s, travelers could not expect to reach Chicago in less than two or three days. Inevitably, there would be poor connections and stopovers at places like Harrisburg, Pittsburgh, Buffalo, or Detroit. At such times, the well-heeled might be able to afford decent accommodations, while the lowly immigrant might be required to spend the night in station waiting rooms, or, in spartan "immigrant houses." Even the seasoned traveler possessing a guidebook could never be certain of the quality of accommodations in the 1870s; and he could have safely assumed that food at station lunchrooms was poor in quality.

The same thing seems to have been true around the world in the nineteenth century. The food in railroad refreshment rooms was invariably awful. Charles Dickens, who had lambasted the American railroads of the 1840s, did not stint in criticism of railroad restaurant food in his native England, which he maliciously described: "The pork and veal pies, with their bumps of delusive promise, and their little cubes of gristle and bad fat; the scalding infusion satirically called tea, the stale bath buns with their veneering of furniture polish; the sawdusty sandwiches, so frequently and energetically condemned."[4]

In the United States, things were equally bad in many places, although occasional station refreshment rooms had tolerably good food. But before the introduction of railroad dining cars, American travelers had other reasons to complain about the traumatic qualities of station eateries. They were usually too small, which resulted in many people going unfed and unquenched— the train whistle might blow as half of the throng was futilely attempting to elbow forward in the coffee line. Especially in the West, trains would sometimes suddenly creep out of the station without warning, leaving passengers in a perpetual state of panic and dyspepsia. Crews on immigrant trains were apparently especially sadistic and would sometimes start up after only five or ten minutes, without the slightest warning or signal to passengers, perhaps delighting in being able to leave part of their troubling horde for the next day's immigrant train.

As a matter of historical record, however, a few railroad hotels and a fair number of railroad restaurants achieved a modicum of praise in the nineteenth century. Even the careworn Erie had a few places that drew people from miles around. Its tattered station at Hornellsville had a restaurant noted for the quality of waffles it served—these being enjoyed with maple syrup from Dale on the railroad's Buffalo Division and sausage from Saegertown on the main line. The spot kindled a fond memory for many who traveled the southern tier of New York.

Changing trains in Chicago was an absolute necessity in the 1870s, and has been so throughout the history of rail passenger travel in the United States. In the 1880s, with the completion of the Canadian Pacific Railroad, it was possible to ride a single train in North America from the Atlantic to the Pacific, but south of the border this has never been possible, even in the age of Amtrak.[5] During the 1870s, with Chicago still recovering from the Great Fire of 1871, and with many of its railroad stations being rebuilt, or in a dilapidated state, the act of transferring from one railroad to another was a considerable nuisance. More often than not, a delay of a day or two could not be avoided either by immigrants or first-class passengers. The burden of changing trains in Chicago was eased somewhat by the existence of the marvelous transfer company of Franklin Parmalee, founded in the 1850s, and soon to become a gigantic enterprise that moved rail passengers and their baggage around Chicago with dispatch and high efficiency. The Parmalee Company and its teamsters and agents were known for their honesty and helpfulness, and the operation of this service was a noteworthy part of the Chicago railroad scene for nearly a hundred years.[6]

In 1875, only one transcontinental rail link existed, and that was the Union Pacific–Central Pacific route from Omaha westward to San Francisco. But more would be completed and others started in the next ten or fifteen years. The Santa Fe was busy building through the tumultuous Southwest, and in a few years, work would be resumed on the Northern Pacific. In the meanwhile, James J. Hill, a railroad builder of Herculean and epic proportions, would be pushing forward his Great Northern Railroad. Both of these northern lines would permit passengers to travel from St. Paul/Minneapolis to the wild and woolly Pacific Northwest. But those going West in the 1870s already had the choice of several routes from Chicago to the Union Pacific terminal in Omaha—the Chicago and Northwestern, the Rock Island, or the Burlington. Before 1872, when a rickety bridge was built across the Missouri River at Council Bluffs, one could not strictly enter Omaha by rail, so that the claim that there was a true transcontinental rail line had been a slight exaggeration. Even after, connections at Omaha were likely to be bad, and most passengers wanting to go through to California would find themselves faced with another delay of a day or more. The railroads east of Omaha apparently made no efforts to synchronize their schedules with those of the Union Pacific.

In 1875, Omaha was the place where the real West, the Wild West, began. If you came through Iowa or Missouri, you were still in civilization; as soon as you passed Omaha (or Kansas City on the Kansas Pacific or the Santa Fe), you were entering a territory that was often beyond the reach of the law, where anything could happen—and often did. Those who rode the transcontinental into Nebraska, Wyoming, and Utah were known to be putting themselves at risk; but, then, for countless adventurers of the day, that was the pleasure of it all.

Robert Louis Stevenson, traveling to join his beloved in San Francisco, was one of those who rode the immigrant train across the plains. There were regular trains as well, and even a few Pullman Palace cars en route to California, although fares on such cars were beyond the reach of all but a select few. There was no such thing as a sleeping car on the "immigrant train." Indeed, the immigrant train was what for years would be known in railroad parlance as a "mixed train." In the train taken by Stevenson, the consist included three coaches, all of them spartan and inelegant, with unbearable and poorly designed wooden seats in which sleep was never possible. The first coach was set aside for women and children, the second for men traveling alone, and the third for Chinese. Before the train departed, however, a number of head-end freight and baggage cars were added and a caboose brought up the rear.

The segregation of passengers was not scrupulously maintained during the journey except for the isolation of the Chinese. Men drifted into the women's car, and women and children felt no compunction about entering the men's car with its spitting and smoking. Stevenson was shocked to find, however, that the Chinese were keenly despised in the western states, and that their car was in essence a version of the Jim Crow cars that shortly would become standard on southern trains. Whenever the Chinese were discussed hereabouts, it was in terms of numerous stereotypes—their uncleanliness (they were in fact cleaner than most of the Europeans, although there was really no way for anybody to keep clean on this kind of train), their clannishness, their dishonesty, their cruelty, their deviousness, and their stupidity, since they spoke little or no English. Invectives were everywhere thrust upon the Chinese, mostly Stevenson concluded, because they posed an economic threat, "because their dexterity and frugality enabled them to underbid the lazy, luxurious Caucasian."

Before the train left Omaha, the coaches were visited by various hucksters offering for sale at scalper's prices such items as cushions, straw pallets on which one might hope to sprawl on bench or floor. After the voyage was underway, the cars were worked by news butchers, somewhat less avaricious in character, who would sell their usual line of newspapers, dime adventure novels, soda pop, cigars, soap, towels (these of scant use on cars in which the supply of water was almost nonexistent), coffee, tea, sugar, and tins of hash or beans.

As the train began its slow, laborious journey through Nebraska, none of the wildness of the West seemed to be apparent. For several miles, the train passed along the bluffs on which Omaha is built, then it broke out into open prairie land, which would continue mile after mile after mile. If there was any sensation of peril here, it was perhaps the sensation of being out upon an ocean or some great sea. Here, prairie grasses undulated in the wind like groundswells upon the Atlantic. Most travelers of the time commented on the monotony of the landscape. With the train moving at no more than twenty miles an hour, it seemed as though no change, no discernible landmark could be observed except endless vistas of sunflowers. Occasionally, very occasionally, there were small patches of trees, and at times passengers would spy at some great distance a few dark spots near the railroad, which, upon approaching, would seem to be a few cabins of a village. But for the most part, the horizon just continued to recede into nothingness, with every mile of progress unrewarded by any achievement or transformation. One felt lost out here; there was no moment of drama or even happenstance, just a feeling of perpetual loneliness. During the summer months, the prairie was soundless except for the persistent chirping of cicadas and the rustle of the wild prairie grasses, which most travelers found shorter than expected. In the winter, the same landscape could doubtless be even more desolate; in the fall, an element of drama might occasionally be introduced by a prairie fire. William Rae, a traveler during the first few years of the transcontinental line, proclaimed that "the spectacle of the prairie fire is one of infinite grandeur.... For miles on every side the air is heavy with volumes of stifling smoke, and the ground reddened with hissing and rushing fire."[7]

When the train reached the Grand Platte River, the passengers were overjoyed by the presence of this break in the monotony of the scenery. For miles now, the railroad would follow this river westward as did the wagon trains of earlier times. Still, there was nothing here either which suggested development, achievement, or anticipation; the sensation was always one of having reached the ends of the earth, a place where one does not drop over the edge, but progresses farther and farther into nothingness.

Some three times a day, and at hours that were never specified or explained to passengers, the train would stop at some eating place, usually looking like nothing more than a long shed. The

Pullman Company had placed one "hotel" car on the Union Pacific in 1870, but it was not scheduled for more than one trip a week, and these never on immigrant trains. The railroad "eating houses," as they were usually called, were seldom an epicure's delight. The food was uniformly undistinguished. William Robertson of Scotland found all three meals to be almost identical: "tea, buffalo steaks, antelope chops, sweet potatoes, and boiled Indian corn, with hoe cakes and syrup *ad nauseam*." Susan Coolidge of New York gratefully complimented one chef at Sidney, Nebraska, for serving "cubes of fried mush which diversified a breakfast of unusual excellence," but, by and large, on her trip west she found that it was "necessary to look at one's watch to tell whether it was breakfast, dinner or supper that we were eating."[8] And there was no little grumbling about some of the local comestibles such as prairie dog stew and sagebrush tea.

With few exceptions, the railroad eateries were crude and dirty, their proprietors and waiters unshaven, uncouth, and ill-mannered. "Civility is the main thing you miss," said Robert Louis Stevenson. The railroads themselves were largely responsible for this dismal state of affairs, since they did not operate the eating houses themselves but gave this work over to local entrepreneurs virtually without any supervision or regulation. By the mid-1870s, however, one of the most celebrated figures in the history of railroad dining was on the scene in Kansas, and things would soon take a decided turn for the better everywhere West. The gentleman's name was Fred Harvey—an Englishman by birth who had already had some experience running restaurants in small Kansas towns.

Harvey's estimable contribution to the gustatory annals of America began in 1876, when he approached Charles F. Morse, Superintendent of the Santa Fe, suggesting that if the railroad would give him space and supplies in its Topeka depot he would operate a restaurant that would do the railroad proud. Harvey scrubbed the place down, redecorated it, brought in new tablecloths, napkins, and silverware, and, most importantly, ordered good food, the cooking of which he supervised himself. No slatternly, coffee-spilling waitresses or filthy flapjack men for Harvey—his waitresses, whom he sometimes had to acquire from the East, were attractive, well-bred young ladies whom Harvey kept under close watch in a nearby dormitory. The Harvey girls wore clean, starched uniforms—a black dress with a bow and Elsie collar. Banished forever from these precincts were the loose women of the early "hell on wheels" towns. Harvey also put an immediate ban on cowboys entering his premises and putting their boots on the tablecloths, or slinging down their guns. He established these bans and he made them stick.

The Santa Fe was so pleased with this arrangement that it forged deals with Harvey to work the same miracle on other station restaurants along the line. Harvey, a gentleman to the core, never had a written contract with the Santa Fe or any other railroad—his every business deal was nothing but a handshake. By the time of his death in 1900, he owned and operated fifteen hotels, forty-seven restaurants, and thirty dining cars.[9] Without a doubt, Harvey's clean and civilized restaurants played a crucial role in the gentrification of the American West; it would be difficult to think of any other individual with a greater impact during the 1870s and 1880s.

When the transcontinental train entered Wyoming, nearly all the passengers began to evince a greater interest in the scenery; it was not, perhaps, a great deal more varied, but it was different. Those passengers who had been completely drained and enervated by days of sitting on wooden benches of immigrant trains were perhaps unable to appreciate whatever beauty there may have been. Robert Louis Stevenson claimed that he had been waiting patiently to get a glimpse of the Black Hills of Wyoming, but, once there, he found the scenery only slightly more variegated than that of Nebraska. It was the same dreary sameness of mood, although the setting was different—

> not a tree, not a patch of sward, not one shapely or commanding mountain form; sagebrush, eternal sage-brush; over all the same weariful and gloomy colouring, grays warming into brown, grays darkening toward black; and for sole sign of life, here and there a few fleeting antelopes; here and there, but at incredible intervals, a creek running into a canyon. The plains have a grandeur of their own; but here there was nothing but contorted smallness.[10]

Most of the passengers were getting in a more upbeat mood, and when the train passed into Utah, spirits were appreciably lifted by the Rocky Mountains, by the Echo and Weber Canyons, by tunnels, by crevasses, by towering pinnacle-like rocks, by fantastic shapes and profiles, by great pine trees. Even the place names, so well anticipated by the guidebooks, were sufficient to inspire awe and wonderment: Castle Rock, Pulpit Rock, Devil's Gate, Devil's Slide. Onward plunged the iron horse, passing territories through which the true equus would not have ventured, but which had been miraculously tamed by resourceful railway builders and engineers. Onward the train steamed, seemingly without effort, through darkened tunnels, along narrow ledge walls, with views down violent cascades and up to glittering towers and arches that suggested to some passengers the Alps of Switzerland. Many on board had read of the legendary Lewis and Clark expeditions, so that these were storied lands, and the object of excitement even to the most jaded world traveler.

By 1875, the element of danger had largely been eliminated from the transcontinental route, and the thrills achieved by the passengers in passing over this difficult and awesome terrain were mostly a product of the imagination—mostly, but not entirely. The guidebooks of the early days had placed much emphasis on the inherent dangers of passing through a country inhabited by buffalo and Indians, as well as other natural obstacles. In the first few years of the line, most of the dangers to passengers were from derailments and other purely technical mishaps. The first track had been laid down so quickly, and in places so haphazardly that derailments were common, and not many through passages were completed without travelers being thrown rudely out of their seats, sometimes with flimsy wooden cars sending splinters into their backs, while flames leapt up from overturned potbellied stoves.

There were always causes of delay attributable to the elements, even in the flatlands of Nebraska. Dust storms, swarms of locusts or grasshoppers, the smoke of prairie fires, could all bring trains to a halt for hours. In the winter, blizzards of a ferocity unknown to European visitors could completely shut down a line, and the job of keeping open the passes of the Rocky Mountains, where snow could pile up in drifts of fifteen feet, was daunting to the most skilled track crews. Even though these occurrences were routine, the railroad could not always be counted upon to clear the passes and keep on schedule. It was not unknown for whole trains to be stranded in the Rockies, sometimes for days on end. With food supplies running low, and with the inevitable remoteness of settlements, many winter passengers had reason to fear that they would ever make it through to California alive.

Almost all passengers wanted at least a tincture of danger, or perhaps adventure, and not many trips were made completely without mishap. A great many Europeans had heard that buffalo were numerous and that they frequently blocked the tracks or even attacked trains. Stories had circulated that it was possible any day to shoot buffalo from the train window, and many European sportsmen came with rifles in their luggage to do just that. By the early 1870s, buffalo herds along the Union Pacific right-of-way had been thinned considerably, and doubtless by 1880 many passengers would not get to glimpse a single one. Two hundred miles to the south, along the Kansas Pacific, there were still large buffalo herds, and Kansas Pacific engineers obligingly slowed their locomotives so that passengers with rifles could shoot from open windows. Sometimes they stopped completely, so that passengers could disembark and commence shooting wildly about. Occasionally, the engineers had to stop the train simply because swarms of buffalo were upon the track and refused to be frightened away by the hissing of steam or the hooting of whistles.

Another thrill expected by most passengers was to catch sight of a real live Indian. For the most part, this desire went unrewarded on the plains. During the building of the Union Pacific, General Grenville Dodge and his hardy band of military roustabouts had waged unrelenting war on the Sioux and other tribes who once lived along the right-of-way. For a time, the Indians fought back, derailed trains, and even scalped some passengers, but finally they let the despised "bad medicine wagon" have the territory. Furthermore, the horse Indians of the plains had been largely dependent upon the buffalo for their livelihood, and when the buffalo were pushed further north, the Indians moved out, too. Nonetheless, small bands of Indians or solitary figures in war paint or headdress could still be seen occasionally.

There were in the plains some occasional small bands of Indians, members of tribes that had gone over to agricultural pursuits, and a few of these could be seen in Nebraska. There were some Pawnees living on a reservation near Loup Fork, Nebraska, and these would sometimes approach the trains—to travelers from the East, they looked particularly fierce since the warriors among them still painted their faces and shaved their scalps to a tuft. The guidebooks announced that most of these warriors had rich collections of scalps dangling from their waists.[11]

All the travelers on the transcontinental in the 1870s were fascinated by Indians, even as Indian culture was being decimated and its traditions eradicated. Well-born European women seemed to be particularly enchanted by them. Lady Duffas Hardy was struck by the handsome males who were loading wood onto the tender of the locomotive on her train.

> "One especially attracted our attention....He wore a blue blanket wrapped around him, and on his head a broad-brimmed ragged felt hat with a mass of blue feathers drooping on his shoulders. The men stood in groups, solemnly regarding us with their big black eyes, still as statues; the women squatted on the platform or peeped at us from round corners. It was not exactly pleasant, but very interesting to find ourselves amid a score or two of this savage race, the men all armed with guns and knives.[12]

Passengers would get to see a good deal more of the Indians in Nevada before coming to their journey's end—the Central Pacific had encouraged the Indians and made a treaty with them, which allowed the braves to ride trains free; accordingly, many Shoshonis and Paiutes were to be seen loitering around every station, and many boarded the trains. In time, the Central Pacific found ways to restrict the Indians to immigrant cars, but they continued to hop onto the tops of tenders, baggage cars, or swing from the outside of boarding steps. In the far West, the Indians made good use of easy social intercourse with the travelers to sell tourists the inevitable Indian trinkets, baskets, blankets, and pottery. Such Indians had been tamed, but perhaps they were getting back a little of what was their due by this small trade with unwary tourists from lands far away.

Few passengers were threatened by Indians in 1875, but another menace had arisen about which there had been no word in the early guidebooks—the menace of the train robber. Wherever the railroad went in the West, it had absorbed nearly all of the territory's express business from the older stage routes, and regular trains often contained express cars that were known to hold ship-

ments of gold and bank notes. Such shipments, poorly guarded in
the beginning, became an obvious lure to individuals of a criminal
mind-set. It is not certain when the first train robbery occurred,
but as early as 1866, in the more civilized town of Seymour,
Indiana, a gang of ruffians in masks entered the express car
through an open door from the passenger car behind—in those
times no thought was given to shutting off the express car from
the coaches. Forcing the express messenger to open his safe, they
laid hands on some thirteen thousand dollars, pulled the bell
cord, and jumped off with the booty. This kind of assult on the
"money car" became typical of many train robberies in the years
afterward.

With the passage of time, train robbery became a much more
risky business, requiring a certain amount of finesse and specialized knowledge. The Wells Fargo Company, which undertook
most of the express business west of the Mississippi River, adopted
stringent measures to protect their shipments of valuables—securing their cars, hiring armed guards, and so on. Still, in states like
Kansas and Iowa, where the distances were vast and the long arm
of the law usually not all that long, an armed and formidable
group of men on horseback could still expect to pull off a successful train robbery with only a modicum of risk.

Some bands or gangs of individuals became adept at the art of
robbing express cars, disappearing for long stretches while they
lived off their ill-gotten gains, and then popping up again when
least expected, knowing that not all the western railroads could be
on the alert everywhere and all the time. One of the most successful gang leaders was Jesse Woodson James, a figure of such legendary proportions that he is one of the few professional criminals to command space in the pages of the *Dictionary of American
Biography*. James had been born in Missouri in 1847, was well-spo-
ken, and apparently not ill-bred, but his mind had been warped by
bitter experiences during the Civil War in the extremely anarchis-
tic conditions of his native border state.

James and his gang, which consisted of his brother Frank and a
varying number of others, had already had some experience as
bank robbers when they were first propelled to national notoriety
in 1873 by holding up a Rock Island train at Adair, Iowa, using a
new technique of wrecking the train by loosening a rail and
pulling it aside with a rope at the last minute before the engineer

could stop the train. In this first incident, the engineer was crushed to death when his locomotive turned over. Various members of the gang came out of the brush, subdued the remaining crew, worked over the express safe, and then went up and down the aisles of the passenger cars forcing passengers to put cash and valuables in a large grain sack. It was the classic train robbery of the kind that has since been celebrated by song and Hollywood legend.

Jesse James remained at large for many years, mainly because there were no known pictures of him, and probably, too, because he didn't strike often. He was killed at home in 1882 by a reward seeker, and thereafter his brother and other gang members left the trade. By this time, Jesse James was something of a folk hero, and the bounty hunter who shot him got nothing but disgrace and a fraction of the reward promised him. Like some other train robbers of the period, James was often polite to passengers, and engendered the idea that it was the railroad and not the robbers who were the villains. Virtually none of the train robbers of the 1870s and 1880s assaulted women; Jesse James was said to be kindly toward children and was said to have idolized his mother, so much so that when the Burlington providentially gave her a pass to ride on their trains, James never robbed the cars of that line.[13]

Obviously, even in the 1870s, train robberies were not a common occurrence; by the end of the 1880s, this notorious element of western railroading had almost entirely disappeared. So, too, had nearly all the manifestations of danger, natural hazzard, and hair-raising uncertainty that made western train travel so compelling during the early years. Of course, even by the mid-1870s, the last part of the transcontinental trip through California was mere froth for those who had come the whole way. Sacramento, in fact, was considered the end of the transcontinental line, because the Central Pacific had been built east from there. The rest of the trip, to the ferry at Oakland, which would carry passengers on the last lap to San Francisco, had become tame and unchallenging long before 1875.

And in another decade, even the wide stretches through Nebraska, Wyoming, and Utah would be relieved of their perils as western railroading outgrew its primitive frailties. By 1890, passengers traveling in animal-crib immigrant trains would be a thing of the past, and riders on the Union Pacific would enjoy the scenery from sturdy coaches. Pullman passengers riding in steel-frame cars could enjoy the precipitous canyons, the tunnels, arches, and hairpin mountain curves of the Rockies and the Sierra without surrendering the comforts of their own drawing room at home. True, the distances remained vast, and even in the twentieth century it was not unknown for the Overland Limited or the City of San Francisco to be stranded in some remote mountain pass during a winter blizzard. On the whole, however, advancing railroad technology and the rapid settlement of the western states had made these territories benign extensions of the nation to the East.

For a few brief years—years that storytellers and balladeers are never likely to forget—travel through the West was a great adventure, not unlike a safari to Africa or an ascension in a hot-air balloon. The railroad, of course, even from the beginning, had democratized these territories and made them a permanent part of the American experience. And even though America has become urbanized in the twentieth century, Americans seem to have retained a certain love of wide open spaces, an itch to explore lands where there are no noisy neighbors, where only the blue sky hovers overhead. Such longings have become marked traits of American character. With these traits has always gone a secret desire for places where nature is king and where law and order, administration and bureaucratic fussiness, have no sway; where there is at least the promise of adventure; where it is possible to cultivate a mood of recklessness and youthful abandon. While the West has now been absorbed into a uniform social order, those huge spaces between the Mississippi River and California offer a fervid reminder of what they were at the time of the first ocean-spanning railroad—a safety valve, a place for meditation, for dreams, for secret desires.

C·H·A·P·T·E·R 10

THE RAILROADS ARE VILIFIED

The transcontinental railroad had been the envy of the world, a technological marvel that had sparked admiration on every shore and brought genteel adventurers and sightseers across the American prairie who would not have dreamed of crossing such an uncivilized frontier a few years before. Similarly, by 1880, the feverish construction of railroad lines throughout the country had made the United States the leading railroad nation in the world, both in terms of mileage and technological achievement. The iron horse seemed now to rule everything in its domain. The complex network of rail lines, which had spread throughout every state in the union and throughout new territories even before they were admitted as states, clearly constituted the arteries and capillaries of the American economy.

Alas, all this should not suggest that everything was well with the railroad, or that the relationship between this vital infrastructure and the American people was a tranquil one. Just the opposite was true. Railroads were rapidly getting better, offering faster and safer services, but in their public relations aspects they were having trouble during the 1870s and 1880s. At no time in their history were railroads more bitterly hated, at no time were they more persistently objects of suspicion and distrust, than in these troubled years. Nor was this hatred and distrust regional, or limited to certain special interest groups—it was rampant everywhere in the land and infected all classes of society. The unrest that emanated from the railroad in those days spread to all industries and would have wide-ranging repercussions for the national economy and for the entire social order.

The railroads had been invested with a kind of demonology by the middle 1870s, had assumed a devil image. Curiously, this specter of evil had arisen first in the area where it might be least expected—in the farm states, the great grain states of the West, this area of the country that had so clearly been settled by the railroad, which for its sustenance and way of life had been so completely dependent upon the railroad. Almost without pause, however, the same seeds of discontent were sewn everywhere—in hard-luck factory towns, in coal towns, and above all in the railroad's own hiring halls, shops, yards, and roundhouses. The railroad was an industry, our biggest industry, and industrial discontent and labor unrest would soon be hard upon the land.

It may seem to be a quixotic footnote to history that a serious distrust of the railroads first arose in the newly settled farm-belt states. The farmers seemingly owed everything to the railroads—it had provided the wherewithal for them to enter the national market. The railroads made states like Illinois, Nebraska, and Iowa prosper, even as the old New England farmer on his stony and infertile upland pasture found his business shriveling up. Iowa was doing marvelously well because the railroads had allowed it to ship its grain to the East, and even abroad. But this total dependence on the railroad had put the farm business almost completely at the mercy of railroad rates and services. The railroad was the trunk and branches of the farm economy; individual farms were but the twigs and leaves.

Such a system, whatever its benefits, had done something to destroy the older concept of land and of the agricultural way of life. By the early 1870s, the farmer had become a completely different animal from the independent agrarianist dreamed of by Thomas Jefferson—the citizen-farmer working his own patch of land in self-sufficiency and high-minded isolation. The farmer-philosopher-democrat had been bedeviled, imprisoned by a kind of glorified serfdom, with his conditions of life determined wholly from outside. The farmer could be told that he was no longer a peasant, but rather a businessman. But this was small comfort if he had no control over his business. And by the 1870s, it was clear that he was not in control of his own business, that he was floundering, flaying about, caught in a cruel economic net not of his own making.

A big part of the problem was that America's newly discovered breadbasket was far larger than it needed to be. The West had been settled by thousands of new farmers from abroad, but by the 1870s it was apparent that the plains states were producing more corn and wheat than the nation could possibly consume. It is true that the populations of urban areas in the East were also growing tremendously, but not enough to consume all the grain produced in the vast acreage of the West. The price of grain began a slow and steady decline. No sooner had the new western farmers tamed their land and learned to deal with drought, grasshoppers, and dust storms, no sooner had they discovered the road to prosperity, than they found their incomes dwindling in proportion to their output.

Striking around for the source of their troubles, the farmers latched on to a number of wrinkles in the scheme of things, most of them related to the increasingly complex and ever-baffling economy. They believed that they were the victims of the middlemen who sold their grain, and of banks that mortgaged their farms and charged them exorbitant interest. Furthermore, they believed that marketing facilities were rigged against them. They objected to the money system and the hated gold dollar, and over the next few decades a cry for free coinage of silver could be heard everywhere in the western states. Westerners blasted the tariff, put in place to protect growing American industries from foreign competition, but also preventing farmers from marketing their superabundant harvests abroad. Above all, though, they blamed the railroads for their troubles, probably because the railroads were the most obvious and immediate tool of the national economy. The railroad annoyed them day in and day out.

That the railroad should be the chief source of the farmer's complaint is hardly a matter for wonder. The railroad was the only arm of big business and of the national economy that went everywhere. Land values were mysterious, and so was the price of gold, but the railroad—the railroad was here and now. In the 1870s and 1880s, the railroad was the only way that farmers could get their products to market. The whole system of western farming had grown up around the railroads. For years, nearly all profitable farms in the West were located within earshot of railroad locomotives. In Illinois, for example, nine-tenths of all farms could be found within five miles of a railroad."[1] What is even more relevant, the railroads themselves were forever meddling in the farm economy. Farmers came to believe that the railroads controlled not only *their* economy but the national economy as well.

The farmers were all aware, even as they settled their homesteads, that railroads had obtained millions of acres of land as a gift, that they had made big profits from the sale of such land. Furthermore, the land that they kept for their own purposes was held tax free, while the farmers themselves were having to pay exorbitant taxes on their properties. But this was not by any means the most important grievance against the railroads. The railroads had what amounted to a monopoly on grain traffic, and they exploited this monopoly to the full. The cost of shipping grain from South Dakota to Chicago was greater than the cost of shipping the same grain from Chicago to Liverpool. At one point, for example, when the rate of shipping grain from some Minnesota town to St. Paul was twenty-five cents a hundredweight, it would only cost half that much for middlemen to ship the grain the much greater distance from St. Paul to Chicago—in this case because there were competing railroad lines.[2]

To the great annoyance of farmers, railroads owned or controlled or influenced most of the local grain elevators. Operators of these elevators had the privilege of assigning a grade to the grain brought to them for shipment. Often, they would assign a grade to such shipments that were lower than the farmer would have received, say, at the Chicago exchange. Indeed, when the grain arrived at Chicago, it would probably be sold at the fair market value and the railroad would pocket the difference or share it with elevator men or dealers.[3] On the other hand, the railroads offered special low rates to shippers of commodities, but when these commodities arrived at the general store farmers were again gouged by high prices since there were few competing stores in small towns.

Furthermore, the railroads appeared to the farmers to be using a strong arm everywhere in the farm states. Railroads heavily subsidized local newspapers and owned many of them outright. Even more heinously, railroads seemed to have nearly all state legislators in their hip pockets. Farmers would elect individuals who promised to do their bidding, but a few months later they would seemingly be on the payroll of the railroad interests, riding back home on a pass or even in a private railway car. It hardly mattered whether the elected official was Democrat or Republican, the results were the same as far as the farmers were concerned. The railroads were always lining somebody's pockets—anyone who could assure the status quo, which is to say, would see to it that the farmer got the lowest possible price for his grain while having to pay the highest prices on everything coming into the farm community.

When the farmers began to organize in their own behalf, it is no surprise that railroad power was the first object of their attention. Over the years in the late nineteenth century, a number of farm political action groups came to the fore, the most important of these being the Patrons of Husbandry, popularly known as the Grange. This organization was actually formed shortly after the Civil War, and originally its purposes were avowedly social—it hoped to do something to bring farmers out of the isolation of their farmhouses, to provide a source of entertainment, to bring farm families together in a setting other than that of the church. Many farmers who remembered the Grange era in later years recalled most fondly the picnics, the suppers, and the gatherings of the local Grange Hall as the only source of community life available to western farmers in the nineteenth century. One of the most prominent literary sons of the middle border, Hamlin Garland, wrote nostalgically of one of the Grange picnics of his youth:

> It was grand, it was inspiring—to us, to see these long lines of carriages winding down the lanes, joining one to another at the crossroads, till at last all the granges from the northern end of the county were united in one mighty column advancing on the picnic ground, where orators awaited our approach with calm dignity and high resolution. Nothing more picturesque, more delightful, more helpful, has ever arisen out of American rural life.[4]

The Granger movement grew rapidly in the early 1870s: Between 1872 and 1874 some fourteen thousand local "Granges" were established, and by the latter year there were Granges in every state and nearly three-quarters of a million members nationwide. Its original objectives were to eliminate the isolation of the farmer, to provide solidarity and support, and these goals were met from the beginning. But when farmers turned out for fun and entertainment, it was inevitable that there would be talk, and talk would lead to action. Farmers discovered that they could band together and do things as a group that they could not accomplish singly. They established grain cooperatives, marketing organizations, loan agencies and even factories. To deal with the high prices in local stores, the Granger movement provided the impetus to the mail-order catalog business of Montgomery Ward. Most important of all, the movement began to look for ways to bring about reform of the railroads.

Eventually, the Grange became powerful enough politically to elect state legislatures that were independent of railroad influence, and these legislatures began to pass laws regulating freight and passenger rates. The first of these so-called "Granger laws" was passed by the Illinois legislature in 1873, and a number of other states passed similar legislation in the next few years. The railroads howled bitterly, claiming that all such laws were unconstitutional. Out in California, Collis P. Huntington roundly denounced these "Communists" who had attacked what he regarded as the sacred rights of property. Individual railroads attempted to punish communities that were known to be particularly strong Granger towns, sometimes eliminating or cutting back train service. Still, in spite of the powerful lobby of the railroads, the first of the Granger cases, which concerned establishing maximum rates for storage of wheat in railroad warehouses, was upheld by the U.S. Supreme Court in 1876.

Later Granger cases before the Supreme Court fared less well, and the overall regulation movement foundered when the Congress in Washington refused to establish a regulatory body. The rate regulation issue did not die, however, and was later taken up by nonfarm groups, which brought about the eventual establishment of regulatory commissions in some states and finally the Interstate Commerce Commission. The Grange was never entirely effective in creating anything like a "farm bloc" in Congress, and by the late 1870s membership declined greatly. However, the idea of unified political power did not disappear in the farm states. In 1880, many Grangers supported the Greenback Party, which that year nominated for the presidency James B. Weaver, a former Granger leader from Iowa.

An even more powerful successor to the Grange was the Alliance movement of the late 1880s. The Northwestern and Southern Alliance groups resembled the Grange in their broadly social aspect. They undertook numerous educational programs, circulated books like Henry George's *Progress and Poverty* and Edward Bellamy's *Looking Backward,* published newspapers and farm papers, sent out lecturers, and established farmers' institutes and study groups. In the early 1890s, these alliance groups, forming a union with discontented organizations from other parts of the country, including the Knights of Labor, Greenbackers, women's suffrage advocates, socialists, single taxers, free silverites, and others, formed the Populist Party and the broader "populist movement" that stemmed from it. The Populists gained strength by putting together farmers with laboring men of the East and reform groups of every stripe, although the party and the movement remained essentially agrarian in character, with Kansas seemingly a perpetual hotbed of Populist activity. From Kansas came Senator William A. Peffer, a wild-eyed reformer and orator who wore a beard as long as that of an Old Testament prophet; also the fire-breathing revivalist Mary Ellen Lease, who coined one of the Populists' most energetic slogans, "Raise less corn and more hell." The Populist movement, or at least some of its causes, flowed smoothly and imperceptibly into the Democratic party in the 1890s, most dramatically in the person of the movement's most powerful orator, William Jennings Bryan of Nebraska.

Specifically concerning the railroad, the various agricultural movements of the West in the 1880s through the 1890s believed that their ways of life had been deeply wounded by the economic effects of the railroad's monopolistic practices. On the other hand, farmers were also concerned with the passing of the agricultural way of life, which had long been an American ideal. The feeling was—and this mostly on the part of those with a strong philosophical and historical cast of mind—that the railroads had changed the nature and character of America forever. This point of view was put well and succinctly by Henry George as early as 1868 in an essay entitled "What the Railroad Will Bring Us." "The locomotive is a great centralizer," he concluded. It will cut the heart out of the traditional American way of life. "It kills little towns and builds up great cities, and in the same way kills little businesses and builds up great ones."[5] Such judgments and biblical-sounding prophecies revealed that the agrarianists had discovered first what the rest of the country would also learn by painful experience during the 1880s—that the railroad had changed the face of America, sometimes for the better, but that as an independent force it had taken control of America's destiny in reckless and irresponsible ways.

By the 1880s, the railroads were in the bad grace of citizens all over the country. The farmers were the most prominent group of shippers who felt themselves ill-used by the railroads, but there was a great deal of dissatisfaction with the gigantic railroad industry, much of it due, no doubt, to the realization that America had not encountered any industry on such a large scale before. Now, however, railroads were entering into combinations and cartels that were unprecedented in size and aggressiveness. At the same time, giant railroad companies were taking advantage of their excessive concentration of power to harass the workers of their own industry, suppressing wages, altering work conditions, and squeezing out, whenever and however they could, the last ounce of effort for a day's pay.

In some ways, the image of the railroads in financial circles had improved slightly. The fierce speculation in railroad stocks had abated since the time when Gould and Drew were attempting to knock off railroads as if they were baubles on a Christmas tree. Somewhat more disciplined financial management had come to the railroads, as had better management practices in general. Still, the Gilded Age was far from over, and in the last two decades of the nineteenth century the concentration of wealth became awesome, sometimes frightening, to Americans. This concentration was reflected in the ownership and amalgamation of railroads into bigger and more formidable enterprises.

On the other hand, the railroad moguls who came to prominence in this same period tended to be of a somewhat higher type than the rogues of the immediate post–Civil War period. The men who came on the stage now, men like James J. Hill and E. H. Harriman, were every bit as aggressive and ruthless as some of their predecessors, but they differed from them in a very important way: They were not mere freebooters who came to strip the railroads of their assets; they knew something about the railroad business; they wanted to capture railroads, but they also wanted to operate them well and efficiently. By the end of his life, even the rapacious Jay Gould was spending more time improving and upgrading his properties than he was ripping them off. Those who attacked the capitalist system in America, at that time and since, have complained that this system had no built-in restraints, and that only the guiding hand of government regulation could ever set things right. Perhaps so. On the other hand, history does show that the railroad moguls of this period, although they did get much richer than those who came before, also began acting more responsibly, and more intelligently.

Part of the reason for this may be that some of the latter-day railroad magnates were not just bent on destruction. They had grown up with railroads, had no small affection for the industry, and understood it from the inside. A good example of this was James J. Hill, whom historian Samuel Eliot Morison called our greatest railroad builder. Not that Hill had begun as a railroad worker or manager; instead, he, his railroad, and his territory grew together in a kind of symbiosis. The territory in question was the great Northwest, specifically, the states of Minnesota, North Dakota, Montana, Idaho, and Washington.

Hill was of Scottish-Canadian background, humble in origin, but of no mean education. In his youth, his eye had been put out by an arrow, but it became part of the legend of the Northwest that Jim Hill saw better with one eye than most men see with two. One thing that Hill had been keeping his eye on for a number of years was a little railroad that jutted out from St. Paul, Minnesota, euphemistically called the St. Paul and Pacific Railroad. Hill had been living in St. Paul since 1856, had kept a store there, and had worked as a freight agent for some steamboat companies and in the same capacity for the St. Paul and Pacific line. This railroad had once been part of the Northern Pacific, had been spun off, and had fallen into receivership in the Panic of 1873. Hill had come to believe in this little line, knew every inch of it, and was sure that great things were ahead for it. Everyone else thought it was a sorry joke.

In 1878, Hill was able to get control of the railroad with the help of three fellow Canadians—Norman Kittson, Donald A. Smith, an official of the Hudson Bay Company, and George

Stephen (later Lord Mount Stephen), president of the Bank of Montreal. These men, who helped Hill pay off the holders of the railroad's defaulted bonds (most of them in Holland), would later play an important role in the development of the Canadian Pacific Railroad. Their immediate reason for helping Hill was that they appreciated the value of having a railroad linking St. Paul and Winnipeg, since the latter lost its link with the Mississippi during the winter when the Red River was frozen over.

But Hill was thinking far ahead of this Canadian connection. Luck was with him from the start since the already built Minnesota part of the railroad, which he completely rehabilitated, became enormously profitable almost immediately. From this point, Hill moved forward with his vast intimate knowledge of the northwestern states (many of which he had visited by dogsled) to plan a route through this forbidding territory, even though everybody insisted it was hopeless to build a railroad there. The railroad, as it moved west, did not enjoy the bounteous land grants of the earlier western lines, yet Hill's line was prosperous every step of the way and never endured the disgrace and bankruptcy that had plagued the Union Pacific and the Northern Pacific. Hill's idea was to build slowly—and well—not laying any track that wouldn't pay off. Wherever Hill's railroad went (it would soon be called the Great Northern), there was business. Wheat in Minnesota and the Dakotas; coal and other minerals in Montana; lumber in Minnesota and in the far West. By the 1890s, Hill had made Minneapolis into the greatest grain-milling city in America; his railroad brought in the grain, and connecting railroads shipped it out as flour.

In the later years of his life, James J. Hill lived in baronial splendor in a castle in St. Paul, and before he died in 1916 at the age of seventy-seven he controlled not only the Great Northern but the Northern Pacific and the Burlington as well, this in partnership with the famous investment banker J. P. Morgan. But Hill was never merely a boardroom man or financial manipulator. He was a hands-on manager who followed his tracks westward in a caboose or handcar. His lines had been built without graft, bribery, and chicanery. Hill himself—a giant man with a giant temper—was always on hand to see that nothing was wasted. The story is told that along the right-of-way one day he discovered a new loose spike. He set off in search of the improvident road foreman who had let this spike get away. Luckily, the road foreman saw the parsimonious Scot bearing down on him and thought quickly: "Thank goodness you found that spike, Mr. Hill. I've had three men looking for it for nearly a week."[6]

Hill's ways were tyrannical and imperious, but his men were always with him. It is said that once in a blizzard when crews had been trying to clear the tracks for hours, the old man took a shovel himself and ordered the track gang into his private car for rest and coffee. For Hill, the railroad was not an object out there, something to be exploited, a plum ready for picking. It was a personal "empire," to be sure, and Hill was to become known in these parts as the "empire builder," but this empire was also a sacred trust, something built and managed with care and operated for the commonweal.

Another railroad magnate of the period—perhaps the greatest of all the American railroad financiers—was E. H. Harriman. Like J. P. Morgan, Hill's strong ally of the 1890s, Harriman was a Wall Street man, and was not above brass-knuckle warfare when he found it necessary to gain his ends. Yet in other ways, he was a financier on a much more exalted plane than the railroad raiders who had gotten the railroad industry such a bad name a generation before. Harriman was a man of substance with a firm personal conviction of how a railroad should be run; like Hill, he would come to intimately know the railroads he controlled, and he managed them with skill and finesse.

Harriman had begun his career as a messenger boy on Wall Street at the age of fourteen, but took some solid formal schooling at the Trinity School in New York City. In 1870, at the age of twenty-two, and with three thousand dollars borrowed from his uncle, Oliver Harriman, he purchased a seat on the New York Stock Exchange. A few years later, Harriman married Mary Williamson Averell, the daughter of a banker from Ogdensburg, New York, who happened also to be president of the Ogdensburg and Lake Champlain Railroad. Harriman's own interest in railroads began around this time, and soon, with the aid of the Averell family, he gained control of the Lake Ontario Southern Railroad. Harriman took it upon himself to learn the railroad business from the ground up. He renovated the track and rolling stock of the road, completely reorganized its management, then sold it at a huge profit to the Pennsylvania Railroad two years later.

Harriman's first experience in the railroad business taught him a lesson that he would never forget and which would be his guiding philosophy: "The only way to make a good property valuable is to put it in the best possible condition to do business." It was a lesson, alas, that Daniel Drew had never learned, and that dawned on Jay Gould only at the end of his career. There would not be any railroad that Harriman would control that was not infinitely better after it was touched by his hand.

The first major railroad transformed by Harriman was the Illinois Central, whose board of directors he joined in 1883. The Illinois Central, after its great triumphs in its native state, had never really fulfilled its destiny as a great north-south trunkline, but under Harriman's guiding hand the railroad was completed to New Orleans in 1892. So well financed and managed was the line by this time that it passed through the railroad panic of 1893 with hardly a ripple.

Shortly after this, Harriman was looking for bigger fields to conquer. By 1898, he was in control of the Union Pacific railroad, long a sorry and dilapidated line that had failed to respond to the touch of a succession of seasoned railroad managers, including Jay Gould. Within a mere three years, Harriman had put the Union Pacific on a sound financial footing and in the twentieth century no American railroad would be more synonymous with financial stability and sound management. For a while, Harriman had had to struggle for the Union Pacific with wily old Collis P. Huntington of the Southern Pacific. But Huntington had to retreat before this grand master; indeed, by 1901 Harriman also had the Southern Pacific in his empire.

Around this time, Harriman owned the largest collection of railroads ever under the control of a single individual in America; he envisioned a vast system of lines from coast to coast—in fact, he actually had such a system in place. In the early twentieth century, he controlled the Baltimore and Ohio (with its subsidiary links into New York, the Reading and the Jersey Central), and was a powerful player in the Erie for a number of years as well. For a time, Harriman wrestled with Jim Hill and J. P. Morgan for the Northern Pacific and the Burlington, and almost won the match. Much of his success was as a shrewd financial manipulator, but that was really only a small part of the story.

Harriman's interest in railroads was genuine; he was not the sort of man who failed to raise his sights above stock and bond certificates, or steel-engraved paper. Such paper symbolized tangible things to him—locomotives, bridges, terminals, the great possibilities of the American nation. In a sense, he was a hands-on railroad man like Jim Hill, and he perpetually rode up and down the lines he controlled. Harriman's two sons, W. Averell Harriman and E. Roland Harriman, who continued to run the Harriman empire after the death of the maestro in 1909, recalled taking trips in their father's business observation car, which was always attached to the *front* of an inspection train, and remembered the delight with which their father noticed and took in everything along the right-of-way. "He saw every poor tie, blistered rail, and loose bolt on my division," declared one superintendent.[7] And after Harriman was through with any railroad he had conquered, there *were* no loose bolts or blistered rails. He firmly believed that to be successful a railroad needed to be in tip-top physical shape, and the Harriman lines such as the Illinois Central and the Union Pacific were physical properties in meticulous condition.

Of course, by the early 1900s, the concentration of the railroads in the hands of a few moguls would be a serious concern to many Americans, and a public outcry against the Hills, Morgans, and Harrimans gave way to an era of trustbusting and of progressive reform. The railroad barons had in fact done a great deal to turn America's railroads into awe-inspiring physical properties and into successful money-makers, but in other ways, in these same years, the railroads continued to project a poor public image. However much the great men of capital had learned over the last several decades about financing and operating railroads, they had fallen far behind in their relations with their own employees. The American railway labor force had been pressed down into conditions of degrading and ill-rewarding toil, this in an occupation that had once seemed fun, had once provided a joyful participation in the material growth of the nation. The lot of railroad financiers, managers, and investors may have gloriously improved in the 1880s and 1890s, but the lot of the rank and file had not.

Accordingly, at the very time they were beginning to hear cries of injustice from farmers and from others who complained about their rates, railroads were entering a period of severe labor unrest. This unrest, like that in the farm states, would have the effect of giving the railroads a bad press in the 1870s, but, more importantly, it would bring a marked change to the American economy and to conditions of social life. The railroads would become the seedbed of the American labor movement, and although this movement was slow to find its voice and to realize its power, it would ultimately alter for good the conditions of living and working in America.

What were the immediate causes of disaffection among railway workers in the 1870s? There were a number. The railroads were becoming dramatically larger in this period, and the volume of traffic on most lines in the industrial states was increasing at a frightening rate. Railroads were changing work rules and otherwise attempting to squeeze more work out of the laborers they had. The occupation of railroad workers, whether engineer, brakeman, or telegrapher, was no longer the leisurely thing it had once been as a flood tide of new business coursed over the rails. Costs of living were increasing, but wages were not. After the panic of 1873, many railroads, fearful of their existence, actually cut wages. Furthermore, the increasingly competitive nature of the railroad, and the vociferous cries for lower freight rates, caused the railroads to look for ways to reduce their costs.

Since the labor supply was holding up well, railroad managers believed that they could always get good and willing workers at low wages. In the years between 1870 and 1900, there was a steady increase in immigration to the United States, most of this newer immigration no longer being from England or Ireland, but from southern and eastern Europe.[8] The newer immigrants from Italy, say, or Russia, seldom came from the educated classes and their typical inability to speak English condemned them, at least for the time being, to conditions of hard labor, and made them extremely vulnerable to exploitation. They also represented a willing and malleable work force that railroad managers could use to browbeat longtime workers already on the payroll.

Effective resistance to low wages and bad working conditions was very slow to arise in the 1870s, mainly because there was no way that workers could express their grievances. There were already in existence a number of railroad unions, but for the most part they were not like labor unions as we know them today. They were nothing more than fraternal and social organizations. In this respect, like the Grangers in the West, they had to find a way to become more than "fraternal" groups before they could have any leverage over their employers.

Still, the seeds of such a firmly knit organization were there. The earliest railway union was the Brotherhood of Locomotive Engineers, which had been established in Marshall, Michigan, in 1863 as the Brotherhood of the Footboard. This was followed by the Order of Railway Conductors in 1868, and the Brotherhood of Locomotive Fireman and Enginemen in 1873. None of these unions was begun with the idea of putting pressure on railroad managements for better wages or working conditions. Still, there was a small and well-publicized tradition of labor unrest in America, some of it surrounding the railroads or its auxiliary industries. In the anthracite mining towns of Pottsville and Mauch Chunk, Pennsylvania, a secret society of miners known as the Molly Maguires, in response to absolutely abominable working conditions, burned property and even murdered some of their bosses and their families. The Molly Maguires were stamped out, and some of their leaders hanged, but skirmishes of this sort doubtless impressed on workers in other industries the advantages of cohesive action.

The year 1877 was a turning point in the development of the labor movement, and it saw a sudden rise in the labor activism of railroad workers. The railroads, still smarting from the Panic of 1873, were leaning harder than ever upon their workers, and had already reduced wages several times, always to mute response or no response. Now, however, in June of that year, the Pennsylvania Railroad announced a ten percent wage cut for its employees, and a few other lines, the Erie, the Michigan Southern, and the New York Central announced a similar cut for July 1. The Baltimore and Ohio Railroad announced a cut of ten percent on all wages of more than one dollar a day, to be effective July 16. Wages had hardly been good to begin with—engineers and conductors were earning on the average three dollars for a grueling twelve hour day; firemen two dollars, and brakemen, a mere $1.75.

For some reason unknown to history, it was workers on the B&O who reacted first. On the morning of the day the pay cut was to go into effect, firemen and brakemen in Baltimore refused to work on freight trains heading westward. A similar resistance took place at the important junction town of Martinsburg, West

Virginia, where brakemen and firemen not only struck but refused to allow freight trains to move out of town. The state militia was requested by local officials and the governor of the state responded—indeed, he even expressed a willingness to lead the troops himself. However, the governor and other officials quickly found out that a great many people (and not only other railroad workers) were in sympathy with the strikers, so in the end the governor backed off and the West Virginia militia proved ineffective.

In the meanwhile, the Baltimore and Ohio had hired scab workers to replace those on strike and appealed to President Rutherford B. Hayes to send the army to do what state militias could not—or would not: keep the trains running. But when federal troops arrived at Martinsburg, they found a huge angry mob of some two thousand people, and these were only dispersed after soldiers fired into the crowd killing ten and wounding many more.

Needless to say, word of the fracas at Martinsburg spread like wildfire, and in the days that followed workers on other railroads began stoppages. There were strikes and acts of violence in numerous railway centers—not systematic and general, and usually carried on only by specific groups. Firemen and brakemen walked off the job at Hornellsville, New York, on the Erie. Firemen on the Lake Shore at Buffalo walked off. The Pennsylvania, which had announced the first cut, was hit hard at Pittsburgh. Following the usual procedure of the time, workers just left their trains and walked away. But they and their families and friends once again acted violently when the railroad attempted to hire scabs, so that eventually the state of Pennsylvania had to employ ten thousand troops to get the Pennsylvania trains running. Before things were over at Pittsburgh, five million dollars' worth of damage was done to rail and other property. Locomotives and cars were overturned and the roundhouse was burned. Chicago, already being the most important railway junction in the country, also reacted with street fighting so violent that for a time it seemed that the city might fall into anarchy. Mobs of discontented workers even roamed the financial districts of the city.

In the face of state and federal troops, and being unable to ignore the fact that railroads could draw from a vast pool of unemployed workers, the strikers eventually gave in and went back to work. They had lost—but only in a sense. Railroads were thereafter much more careful about slinging around wage cuts, and in the next several years there were fewer dramatic cuts. More importantly, however, railroad workers had at last come to see that there was more in unionism than fellowship.

Admittedly, not much was on the side of the labor movement during the 1870s and 1880s. Whenever labor unrest broke out, it was roundly condemned from pulpits and in the press. All politicians inveighed against union activity, making the public believe that it was inspired by "anarchists," "communists," or perhaps agents of some foreign state. These charges were patently false, but they were worrisome to a timid public, which didn't have the slightest idea of what a "communist" was. Except within the brotherhoods themselves, where the truth was known, the general public believed that strikes were the work of "incendiaries" or professional troublemakers.

But there were also a few natural forces at work in the United States that leaned in favor of labor during these tumultuous years. Since there had been no history of feudalism in America, there had never been anything like a fixed "laboring class" as there was almost everywhere in Europe. Making transitions from one job to another and from one income class to another was not only permitted in America but actually expected. And railroad workers were more fortunate than workers in other industries in being especially mobile. Even though railroads could threaten to hire unskilled laborers, the truth is that they always needed a large corps of trained and experienced journeymen, and such people could invariably find a good job someplace in an industry that was growing at a phenomenal rate. Railroad workers became highly mobile in the 1880s and 1890s—which gave rise to the term "boomer," used at the time for any itinerant worker, telegrapher, or brakeman who moved from railroad to railroad depending on pay and conditions of work. There was always strong competition for railroad labor, and this invariably kept conditions from getting completely insufferable.

The itinerant character of railway labor also added a certain attractiveness to what might otherwise be harsh working conditions. Even if the workday became longer and the pay was niggardly, most railroad workers continued to feel themselves better off than mine workers or factory workers. Being able to move from place to place gave railroad men the impression that ultimately they were footloose and fancy-free. They believed themselves to be uninhibited and unfettered souls, "knights of the road," so to speak. Accordingly, they found their ranks infiltrated by other still less inhibited souls—tramps, hoboes, vagrants, and others who liked the traveling life but would only work when really hard pressed. These "Happy Hooligans" and "Weary Willies," so beloved of a generation of cartoonists, added color and zest to the railroad scene, although many of these denizens of the railway demimonde were more given to riding the blinds, stealing, drinking, and lighting fires in boxcars than they were to productive labor.

Union organization among the "real" railroad workers continued throughout the 1880s and 1890s, although for years these organizations occasioned no violent outbreaks to match that of 1877. During these years, the last of the four major craft unions—that of the Trainmen—was established in 1883, begun in a sidetracked caboose at Oneonta, New York. But others were to follow shortly. The Order of Railroad Telegraphers was established in 1887; the Brotherhood of Railway Carmen in 1891; the Switchman's Union in 1894; the Brotherhood of Railway and Steamship Clerks, Freight Handlers, Express, and Station Employees in 1898; and the Brotherhood of Railway Signalmen in 1901.

Within another decade, starting around 1912, black rail workers also began to organize, establishing such unions as the Association of Colored Railway Trainmen and Locomotive Fireman and the Brotherhood of Sleeping Car Porters.[9]

The final years of the nineteenth century were not particularly notable for strikes in the railroad industry, but one further strike, in 1894, although by no means means as dramatic as that of 1877, had the effect of extending an era of bad feelings in the relations between the railroads and their workers. This strike was the famous Pullman strike of 1894, invoked by a recent union of a somewhat different sort, the American Railway Union, established the year before by Eugene Victor Debs. This union, of the vertical, or industrial, type, was formed under the assumption that individual craft unions couldn't succeed in the railroad industry.

Eugene Victor Debs was himself a product of the Brotherhood of Locomotive Fireman, once having been the grand secretary of that union and editor of the *Locomotive Fireman's* magazine. A native of Terre Haute, Indiana, the son of Alsatian immigrants, he left school at fourteen to work in the yards of the Terre Haute and Indianapolis Railroad and shortly thereafter became a fireman on the line. In his years with the fireman's union, Debs was on the conservative side, as were most railroad men at the time. He did not support the 1877 strikes. But he soon came to see that the only way that unions could serve their workers was through group solidarity. Thus, in the early 1890s, he resigned his job with the Locomotive Firemen and established the American Railway Union. He hoped this organization would include all railroad workers, operating and nonoperating, skilled and unskilled.

The ARU grew rapidly during its first year, especially early in 1894, when it staged a walkout against the Great Northern Railroad, and forced the stubborn and intractable Jim Hill to make major concessions. Flush with this success, the union planned a strike against the Pullman Company later that same year—an initiative that Debs himself was wary of, and one that proved to be disastrous. Once again, as in 1877, the central issue was a wage cut. The Pullman Company had suffered a slump both in its operating revenues and in its orders for cars as the result of the 1893 depression, and sought to reduce its workers' wages so that it could maintain profit margins. The employees were also unhappy with the working conditions of the "company town"— Pullman, Illinois—a uniquely designed enclave south of Chicago. Conditions in Pullman had deteriorated, rents had been raised, and workers believed that "Lord" George Mortimer Pullman was keeping them in conditions of feudal restraint, a judgment that was not far from correct.

Since the ARU was a nationwide union, members around the country shortly walked off the job on all railroads carrying Pullman cars. By 1894, this was nearly every major line. Naturally, within a matter of weeks, transportation, at least in the North and West, was paralyzed. Unfortunately, it was not a propitious time for a general strike against an entire industry, and an industry that was absolutely vital to the nation, so that forces against the strike quickly coalesced. The General Managers' Association of the railroads went into a high dudgeon and put in a trumpet call to plump Grover Cleveland, the Gold Democrat then sitting in tranquil eminence in the White House. Cleveland had his Attorney General, Richard Olney, draw up an injunction against the strike; what's more, he even sent federal troops to Illinois, even though none were requested by the governor of that state, the progressive-minded John Peter Altgeld. Altgeld, who upon becoming governor in 1892 had pardoned the remaining participants in the Haymarket riots of 1886, believed that things could be settled without force.

But the power of the federal government, and of national opinion, was too great: The American Railway Union was broken, and Debs and several of his "coconspirators" landed in jail. (While he was in jail, Debs turned his attention to socialism as a panacea for the ills of the world, and in 1900, and four times thereafter, was the Socialist candidate for president.) At first glance, the union movement was dealt a severe blow by the strike. On the other hand, it served to dramatically emphasize the plight of labor in these harsh and difficult brown decades, as Lewis Mumford so rightly called them. The Pullman strike brought into sharp relief the cruel divisions between labor and capital; it showed the general public—after initial fears wore off—that the government, and the courts, were for the nonce nothing more than dupes or handmaidens to big business. And interestingly, by the time of the 1896 election, the Cleveland faction was largely in disrepute in the Democratic party, and William Jennings Bryan, eloquent spokesmen of labor, of farmers, of silverites, took command of the party and gave it the progressive flavoring that for the most part it has had since.

In the railroad industry itself, the strike of 1894 provided a long residue of bitterness in the ranks; many years of ill-will and a dark reservoir of mistrust grew up between managements and the rank and file. The strike itself had not been without tangible benefits, since long-term solidarity of railroad laborers increased and their conditions of work did not further deteriorate. Many workers who had participated in the strike had been fired or lost their seniority; others were blackballed in subtle ways for years afterward. Still, the growing strength of the craft unions that were left made railroad managements somewhat leery of throwing mean curves at their men, and between that time and the Great Depression in the 1930s things improved for railroad workers, even if ever so slightly.

On the whole, after the strike of 1894 was over, it was the railroads and their managers who smelled bad and not the workers. The railroads had a great many indictments standing against them in these years. A movement to regulate railroads was gaining momentum; the Interstate Commerce Commission had been established in 1887 and was functioning, even though as yet it had few teeth. True, the Granger movement had had its wings clipped, at least in part, and the railway workers were still carrying their heavy burdens. But the public was now more than a little suspicious of the vast concentration of power in the railroads, and they looked with distrust on the empire building of men like Hill, Harriman, and Morgan. It was not surprising that when Frank Norris published his novel *The Octopus* in 1901, a railroad was cast in the role of villain. This was a notion and a truth that most Americans were by now willing to accept. The railroads, it was said, had grown too big, too powerful, too arrogant. Unfortunately, the times were still such that the villain could only be identified—not challenged.

C·H·A·P·T·E·R 11

TRAVEL IN THE GRAND MANNER

During the last several decades of the nineteenth century, the railroads were under repeated attack from reformers and social critics, and from those interest groups that believed themselves to be abused by the rates or foul business practices of the giant railway companies. But railroads as a common utility, as a mover of people, never lost their popularity among the common folk. The typical American always loved to bathe in the glory and the success of this great national enterprise. The carriers were sometimes despised in the abstract, and many people were hostile to the financiers, the manipulators, the stalled "malefactors of great wealth" who owned them. Many people were suspicious of whatever faraway agency of control there might have been standing behind the railroads, but this suspicion did not translate to the railroad as a part of social life, as a popular conveyance—certainly not as the most advanced form of land transportation known to history.

And, if anything, railroad services of all kinds were greatly improving during these years when railroads were heartily attacked for their concentration of capital or their collusive practices. By the 1880s, much old and primitive railroad equipment was passing quickly away, as were antiquated operating procedures. Flimsy wooden coaches with their dangerous potbellied

214

stoves were rapidly being replaced by steel cars of modern design. Block signals and air brakes were making rail travel much safer than it had been. Double tracking of major lines—indeed, in places, tripling and quadrupling of mainline tracks—were eliminating the frustrating delays so common in early times. Heavier and faster locomotives, improved roadbeds, and elimination of sharp curves now made it possible to run trains at higher speeds, so that travel times were steadily cut year by year. By the 1880s, it was possible to get between New York and Chicago in thirty to thirty-six hours. A decade or so later, the time would be reduced to twenty hours. Above all, as railroads offered better service, Americans took to them with avidity. Deep down, they loved railroad travel, which now more than ever they found to be an adventure in excitement and fantasy.

One thing about the railroads that appealed to Americans from the beginning was their individuality and eccentricity. The United States consisted of a great many railroad lines, all of which could trace their paternity to earlier lines that had once been small and primitive carriers. Many had now grown large, and to an extent their technology had become standardized. But in personality and peculiarity of style they had retained their individuality. Unlike the airlines of the present day, with their standardized reservation systems, check-in counters, and baggage handling systems, their microwave cuisine, and plastic curtains virtually identical from one carrier to another, the railroads in their heyday managed to keep some semblance of personal identity. Travelers had their own idiosyncratic reasons for traveling on this railroad or that when two or more stood in competition, and the diversity of services, of scenery, of accommodations were always topics of brisk discussion and debate.

The eccentricity and individuality of railroads went back to the early days, when locomotives and rolling stock, particularly passenger cars, were made to look as distinctive and peculiar as possible. As soon as American railway men declared independence from British pioneers, they began to experiment with a great variety of boiler arrangements, cab locations, and smokestack designs. American locomotives were fitted up with all sorts of strange appurtenances—cowcatchers, bells, whistles, huge storm lanterns, sometimes with paintings on their sides. Engine designers of an early time had surrendered to every imaginable flight of fancy—

cab windows of Gothic design, spokes of drive wheels painted in gold, elaborate brass fittings and trim on engines and rolling stock. Except in the first few years, when passenger cars were little more than tubs, railroads made every effort to see that their carriages, important as these were to the traveling public, were painted in distinctive colors and fitted out in the livery of the individual carrier. Often they bore scrolled lettering in gilded script or sported elaborate paintings of wild animals or notable landscape scenes from places along the route.

When American railroads began to build stations and other wayside structures, these, too, were as eccentric and highly individual as possible. Of course, as a young country with virtually no traditions in architecture, the United States was of necessity eclectic in its architectural devisings, and nowhere was this eclecticism more evident than in the proliferation of railroad station designs. Lucius Beebe, that great chronicler of railway mores and folklore, commented on the old Boston and Maine station at Salem, Massachusetts, which he declared suitable to be the castle of some Yankee Dracula, and on the Dearborn Street Station in Chicago, whose vaulted chambers he believed resembled those of a first-class Turkish hammam. Wherever one got off a train, remarked Beebe, there was an adventure in fantasy. Passengers "were set down in storybook settings, Grecian temples, Moorish arches, French chateaux, the tombs of Egyptian dynasts, Turkish mosques, Palladian porticos, Gothic castles, and Italian *palazzi*."[1] Even out-of-pocket railroads like the struggling Erie had their own picturesque stations: sometimes massive sheds looking like nothing more than the "depots" they were usually named, but sometimes exercises in Victorian fancy with curious pinnacles, dormer windows, French roofs, cheap but elaborate latticework, gingerbread, gableboard, or plaster fanwork.

Railroad workers, too—at least those who had regular contact with the public—appealed strongly to the fancy and the imagination. From very early times, the engineer was a kind of folk hero to Americans, and his place on the right-hand cushion of the locomotive was symbolic of a new kind of national priestcraft. The engineer was a hero to small boys and to station loafers everywhere, to many adults, to all those who came to memorize the names or numbers of locomotives as they chugged up and down the line.

In the early days, the locomotive engineer was a sufficiently important personage that he wore a top hat and cravat; later on, his apparel was closer to that of a workingman, but in the railroad's days of glory, this was not by any means lacking in style. On the celebrated White Train of the New York and New England, whose cars were all painted a cream color and whose very coal in the tender was whitewashed before each run, the engineer wore an all-white jumper, with white gloves, and sported a cap similar to those worn by race horse jockeys. And even the more lowly operational employees affected a distinctive appearance that could never fairly be called a uniform—the fireman's red suspenders were sufficiently inspiriting that for years copies of them were offered for sale on trains by news butchers and other hawkers.

Of course, train conductors of the nineteenth century—at first called "captains"—were also invested with style and romance. Like the early engineers, they, too, wore top hats, which proved totally impractical for the conditions under which they worked. They also sported frock coats, which eventually gave way to morning tailcoats in blue cloth with gold buttons. Conductors on cracklimited expresses or name trains wore flowers in their buttonholes to put them on an equal social footing with the men of affairs who rode their cars. And they had their own distinctive hallmark in possessing heavy, looped Albert watch chains of red or yellow gold.

Station agents and other nonoperating personnel seldom had this same kind of sartorial elegance, and never matched their counterparts in Europe where the "stationmaster," even in a small station, was a figure of some splendor. On German railways, for example, where there was a strong military tradition in railway work, and preference of employment was given to army veterans, stationmasters were known for their elaborate uniforms topped by epaulets, sometimes with gold trumpets hanging at their side and attached by fancy-braided cord. Such functionaries gave Germans the illusion of military dispatch and precision that they loved, and the populace warmed to stationmasters who sounded their trumpets, blew silver whistles, signaled trains to start with marshal's batons, and saluted everything in sight. (In Germany, even signal towermen and crossing watchmen saluted the trains.) The American station agent or telegrapher affected few airs, but he was nonetheless a sufficiently romantic individual to become a stock figure of melodramas and dime novels.

But railroads, and the people who worked on them, had been objects of public attention and romantic attachment since their first appearance in the 1830s. Now, however, in the 1880s and 1890s, when the reputations of the railroads were besmirched by scandal, by accusations of collusion, of combination, of frightening financial concentration, they were also getting better and more responsive to the demands of the traveling public. Train travel for the average American, whatever its thrills and promise of adventure, had, in the early nineteenth century, been plain, spartan, and tedious. Now, as with the wave of a wand, tedium would fly out the window. The railroads suddenly began to discover two qualities they had formerly neglected but which now began to whet the appetites of Americans everywhere. One of these qualities was a penchant for speed; the other a penchant for luxury. Throughout most of their early history, railroads had been looked upon as performing a singularly utilitarian function, even though this function might have been carried on with some zest and relish. Now railroads had the technical expertise and the prosperity to offer travelers a good deal more. They could move people faster, and they could move them in style.

These two new dimensions need not have developed simultaneously, but in fact they did. Of course, in the 1880s and 1890s, better track and equipment made faster journeys possible. But heretofore, train trips had always been broken up into numerous segments. It had been part of established practice to ride all day in a railroad coach and then stay overnight in a hotel. Even after the appearance of the Pullman sleeping car, dining service on trains was not commonplace, so stopping for meals (and usually for the night as well) continued to be an expected part of travel for many years.

There were a few other things that necessitated frequent stops for food or rest in the early days. Passengers on a train were, so to speak, cooped up in the car which they boarded. Because of danger to life and limb, they were not allowed to pass from one car to another. However, during the 1880s, with dining cars coming into regular use, it was imperative that passengers be able to move through the train. And the technical innovations to make this possible were now at hand. One development stemmed from the patenting in 1887[2] of the vertical end frame for passenger cars, which reduced the violent motions of the platforms and also the sudden jerk and rocking of the cars when the train started or stopped. Another equally important innovation was the development of vestibules that enclosed the platforms between cars and made it possible for people to walk between them without fear of being thrown overboard. The early vestibules were narrow, and did not enclose the whole platform, as on today's trains, but they accomplished their purpose. During the 1880s and 1890s, the slogan "Vestibuled Train" was a magic term to railroad publicity departments everywhere. More importantly, this development brought into existence the "train" in the sense we know it today— no longer a series of cars coupled together and pulling together, but a continuous unit for human uses.[3]

With these inventions, and with the birth of the single unit concept, the whole character of long-distance train travel began to change. The idea of the centralized dining car captured the imagination of the traveling public, and made it possible for railroads to run trains that did not make stops for meals. Over the next several decades, the old railroad eating houses and hotels of yore disappeared from the scene and a whole new way of thinking about rail travel developed. You could eat and sleep on trains and be delivered to your ultimate destination in only a fraction of the previous time.

As long as the old hotels and commissaries existed, there was really no impetus to move trains along faster; in fact, the train stops on long distance journeys had provided considerable charm and fascination. All of a sudden, however, the mind-set of the traveling public began to change; into public favor burst the idea of the express train or "crack" train, as it would soon be called. Not that the idea was born full-blown like Athena from the head of Zeus. The concept developed slowly over time in the late 1880s. In the 1890s, many once hesitant railroads became positively smitten with the idea. This advance could probably not have been avoided, since during this same time period railroads were having to think about trains as classified in numerous categories—local and long-distance trains, mail trains, accommodation trains, trains that carried Pullman or parlor cars, these latter obviously of a higher pedigree than others, which transported local passengers, or handled express and mail. It was inevitable that the trains of the highest pedigree should also be the fastest trains. Such a concept seems self-evident today, but

like so many other ideas, it took a long time dawning on railroad
managers.

In earlier times, speed was something that did not spark the
imagination of American railroad men. The annual report of the
New York Central and Hudson River Railroad in 1876 (the year
before Commodore Vanderbilt's death) gave the ordinary speed
of a passenger train at twenty-five miles an hour, including stops.
The average speed of an express train—such as it was—really
wasn't much faster: about thirty miles an hour, including stops.
The previous year, however, James Gordon Bennett, Jr., the reckless and improvident son of the founder of the *New York Herald,*
had gotten the idea that he could sell some of his New York
papers in Chicago if he could get them there in a day's time. So
he talked the Vanderbilts into providing him with a two-car speed
train for the trip. Bennett and his wife were on board the first
newspaper express, which left New York at 2:30 A.M. Sunday morning (after his newspaper was off the press), and then arrived in
Chicago thirty hours later. For this little stunt he paid the New
York Central one thousand dollars. He paid an identical sum for a
similar train over the next ten weeks so that Chicagoans could
have a New York Sunday paper on Monday morning.[4] The
Vanderbilts were not impressed by the shenanigans of this reckless
playboy, and as soon as he stopped paying for it the run was discontinued.

Seemingly, the old Commodore was never highly impressed
with the idea of fast trains—perhaps an expected response from
an old riverboat captain. In 1874, one George S. Bangs, who had
taken over the Railway Mail Service after the death of its founder,
George B. Armstrong, suggested that the Commodore put on a
fast mail train between New York and Chicago—a train that was to
carry nothing but mail and speed its way between New York and
Chicago in twenty-four hours. Doubting that the federal government would support such a venture, the Commodore warned his
son William against it. "If you want to do this, then go ahead,"
blustered the old man. "But I know the Post Office Department,
and so will you, within a year." And he was right. William spent a
lot of money building mail cars, arranging train schedules, and
the like, and after a year Congress cut appropriations for the "fast
mail," after which George Bangs resigned his position a crestfallen
man.

Still, the idea had caught the public fancy, and a few years later, under the direction of Theodore Newton Vail (later to become famous in the fields of telephone and telegraph), the fast mail was revived. A popular song was written about the idea of "fast mail trains," and shortly some plays as well. The position of railway mail clerk entered the pantheon of exciting American occupations. Youngsters around the country were intrigued by the notion of mail being sorted while a train was in motion. And, as the postal service developed stanchions at way stations so that fast-moving trains could collect the mail without stopping, a certain dramatic luster was added to the entire concept of "fast mail." At the same time, this concept of "fast mail" contained within itself the hint of "fast" passenger service as well, and eventually speedy passenger trains also got on the timetables.

Fast trains became fast, though, not initially because of their speed but because certain trains on long runs began making only a limited number of stops—such trains were often called "express" trains or sometimes "limited" express trains on timetables. In the beginning, these trains were not necessarily fast runners, except that the limited number of stops invariably resulted in shorter running times. But in time, these trains began to receive a certain favoritism from management in regard to equipment, publicity, and so on, and they accumulated a kind of luster which eventually translated into impressive running times.

Beginning in the 1880s, the passenger departments of the railroads started to become more aggressive about their limited express trains and began giving special attention to the task of choosing individual names for them. Passenger traffic managers were among the first "publicity men" to appear in American business, and they avidly explored new avenues to sell the services of their companies. Passenger services to resorts and to places at distant remove were promoted by means of coated-paper brochures, posters, maps, and decorative timetables. To go along with such promotional exercises, and facing stiff competition from rival railroads, it was only natural that the passenger service promoters would look for all kinds of ways to make their trains distinctive.

One such publicity gimmick was the naming of trains. This practice got off to a slow start, and did not become extremely widespread until after 1900. However, as early as 1889, the Pennsylvania had in service its Pennsylvania Limited between New

York and Chicago, and within ten years the railroad had five or six named trains in operation over the same route. Not all of the other major carriers immediately followed suit. There were few named trains before the mid-1890s on American railroads, although most of the flagship carriers listed in their timetables certain Vestibuled Trains, Solid Trains, or sometimes Limited Express Trains, which were otherwise unnamed. And when a number of such trains did begin to get names from company passenger agents, for a long time they were prosaic and unimaginative. Railroads to the east and west of Chicago had Chicago Expresses. There were so-called Atlantic and Pacific expresses. The time cards of the Pennsylvania for 1899 show that in addition to its Pennsylvania Limited, the other trains on the same route had much less inspiring names: Western Express, Atlantic Express, Day Express, Night Express, and so on.

In the 1890s, however, the passenger departments of the railroads began showing a lot more zest for the art of naming trains and squeezing the maximum publicity value out of doing so. Probably the greatest practitioner of this art was the rotund general passenger agent of the New York Central Railroad, George H. Daniels, who in October 1891 inaugurated a fast day train on the railroad's New York to Buffalo run, calling it the Empire State Express. The running time was as fast as the motive power of that day would permit, but once the public and railroad aficionados everywhere began focusing their attention on the distinctive qualities of this train, further efforts were made by management to make it a speed demon. In 1893, behind specially designed engine 999, the Empire State Express moved at a speed of 112 miles per hour. Nothing before had moved this fast across the face of the globe, and this speed record excited awe and admiration around the world. Of course, no such speeds were attained on regular runs, with the usual top speed of the 999 being no more than sixty miles per hour. But the New York Central had opened a floodgate of enthusiasm for speed, and it had craftily linked its speed trials with a "name" train, a practice that would be followed by major railroads thereafter.

George H. Daniels continued to be an imaginative namer of things. To howls of protest from other railroads, but in the true American booster spirit, Daniels began a campaign to call the New York Central the "Greatest Railroad in the World," a neat piece of hype that naturally could be neither confirmed nor denied. His greatest and most successful flight of fancy was the name he chose in 1902 for the railroad's candy train on the overnight run between New York and Chicago: the Twentieth Century Limited. It was a major coup, and one which the Pennsylvania tried—with only partial success—to counter with its own new train deluxe, the Broadway Limited (named, by the way, not for the street in New York City, but for the Pennsylvania's spacious four-track main line).

Not all of the carriers, even major lines, adopted the "train naming" practice with avidity. The Baltimore and Ohio, for one, was very slow to surrender to this vulgar salesmanship.

And for years the most famous train in America had been the Fall River Boat train, but the name as such never appeared on the timetables of the Old Colony Railroad or the New Haven thereafter—perhaps the name was too well known to be noted and a little Yankee understatement was itself a selling point. Other railroads had popular train nicknames that never actually got on the timetables. The Illinois Central's crack train in 1900 was the Cannonball. It was the train, incidentally, on which Casey Jones rode to his death. But no such name was printed in the timetables. The Illinois Central's publicity staff did not get busy in rounding up impressive sounding names until 1911, when they named the railroad's principal flyer the Panama Limited, to celebrate their growing freight traffic with Central America.

Most railroads kept their imaginations under wraps until after the dawn of the twentieth century, and when they did take to naming trains, the results usually tended to be pedestrian. For every Twentieth Century Limited, there were so many Erie Limiteds, Northwestern Limiteds, Lackawanna Limiteds, California Limiteds (on the Santa Fe), in addition to the usual carding of Fast Mails and Chicago Expresses. But the tendency to name trains slowly gained momentum. The legendary White Train was casting its exotic spell over the New England countryside at this time, and the Union Pacific's Overland limited was already on its way to becoming one of the great American trains of all time. The Chesapeake and Ohio cashed in on the "snob value" of its tidewater heritage, and in the mid-1890s its timetables already boasted the existence of the Famous FFV Ltd. and the Fast Flying Virginian.[5] Still, most railroads in this period were reticent and highly conservative in such practices. Around the turn of the century, there was a popular song called "The Wabash Cannonball," but the Wabash itself didn't bother to use that name for many years thereafter.

There were many other ways to attract passengers than the use of spectacular names, and in the 1880s and 1890s the railroads were discovering most of them. More important than stylish names, trains themselves were becoming stylish—stylish and luxurious. Year by year, passenger equipment got more solid, more comfortable, more ornate, more sybaritic. Every year, new technological advances were coming off the drawing boards of the Pullman company and other car manufacturers. The best new equipment was always consigned to a railroad's premier trains; accordingly, the Pennsylvania Limited was renovated and updated many times before it was superseded by the luxury Broadway Limited in 1902. In 1887, electric lights, powered by batteries, were used for the first time. In that same year thirty-six inch wheels replaced thirty-three inch wheels on passenger cars for much greater comfort. In 1889, cars on the Pennsylvania Limited began receiving steam heat from the locomotive, replacing the dangerous old systems for heating individual cars.[6] By 1891, company literature shows the Pennsylvania Limited as an all-Pullman train carrying a barber shop, a bath and valet service for gentlemen, and a ladies' maid for female travelers. There was a superb wine list in the dining car, and passengers could order the latest fashion in cocktails in the observation lounge car at the rear. Company literature showed a well-groomed train secretary with cutaway coat and boutonniere seated at an L. C. Smith typewriter ready to take dictation from an obvious man of affairs wearing a quilted smoking jacket and chomping an expensive looking cigar.[7]

The railroads outdid themselves in attempting to produce passenger equipment that was more luxurious and fanciful than whatever was offered by the competition. In railroad parlance of the time, passenger trains came to be known as "varnish," or sometimes "high varnish," so named for the expensive, exquisite, and highly polished woods used in their interiors. No effort or cost was spared to convince passengers that they were entering a realm of Lucullan fancy when they boarded a passenger car. In 1896, the Chicago and Northwestern Railroad put into service a wholly new Northwestern Limited—all the equipment outshopped at the Wagner Palace Car Company. Being in direct competition over the Chicago to Minneapolis route with excellent flyers of the Milwaukee and the Burlington, everything had to be of the best. The company publicity hounds of this Vanderbilt-controlled railroad exercised little modesty or restraint when they publicized the train as "The Best of the West." But it probably was. Certainly it was an example of the uninhibited approach to spending on passenger equipment that was typical of that day. A reporter for the *Minneapolis Journal* described the results with purple effusions:

> The world has been ransacked for costly woods; designers, carvers, upholsterers, and metal workers have apparently been given *carte blanche* in working out their ideas, with no limit placed on the cost of materials. Silken tapestries of Oriental richness, European refinement, and pleasing variety adorn the walls of the various rooms. Each compartment has its special scheme of color, upholstering, and decoration. Circassian walnut, San Domingo mahogany, English oak, vermillion wood, bird's eye maple, and rosewood, richly inlaid and highly polished, delight the eye.[8]

There are some historians who insist that the sleeping cars built by the Wagner Palace Car Company were the finest such general duty cars in the American record. Perhaps so; on the other hand, the railroads and the general public were most kindly disposed to the cars of the Pullman Company, which eventually secured a virtual monopoly over the manufacture of sleeping car equipment in the United States. In 1899, the Pullman Company purchased the Wagner Palace Car Company that had been providing sleeping cars to the New York Central and other Vanderbilt railroads,[9] and thenceforth the word Pullman became synonymous with "sleeping car" on American railroads, and remained so until the coming of Amtrak during the last third of the twentieth century.

What was it about Pullman that brought about this dominance of an entire industry—an untypical phenomenon in highly competitive America? The answer is to be found not merely in luxury or style—although to Americans long accustomed to travel in hard-seated, rickety, flat-wheeled coaches, the Pullman always represented a supreme achievement in luxury. Actually, the secret of Pullman's success stemmed from the remarkable economies afforded by the open-section sleeping cars, and from the various protocols in operating the cars themselves. For many years, the Pullman Company not only manufactured its sleeping and parlor cars, but it operated them itself, providing and training its own conductors, porters, and other personnel.

Whenever George Pullman was asked to explain the success of his company, he invariably replied that it was due to the institution which he called the "Pullman system." From early in his company's history, Pullman had decided to maintain and operate his equipment on a high level. He established and enforced standards and conditions of service right down to the smallest detail. The Pullman Company developed a system of smooth baggage handling. It hired conductors who enforced company rules and standards of decorum. One of the company's great contributions to railroad comfort and railroad lore was its invention of the Pullman porter, fully trained by a company school to render efficient and courtly service to passengers, to make up beds, and to keep the cars spotlessly clean.

The highest standards of cleanliness were always maintained both on the road and in company maintenance depots. The Pullman Company hired "spotters" to ride as passengers and take note of soiled linen or less-than-gleaming washbasins, and to report on disagreeable porters or conductors. Hygienic conditions were unexcelled, even in an age when the word "hygiene" was not much bandied about.

The open section Pullman car was an icon of American ingenuity. Not only did it permit the accommodation of the largest number of passengers in the smallest amount of space (using Pullman's own ingenious scheme of folding lower berths into seat partitions and upper berths into the ceiling for daytime travel), somehow it also appealed to potent instincts in the American's psyche. It allowed the traveler comfort and luxury, but it also administered to his love for sociability and conviviality. The open center aisle arrangement allowed passengers to wander up and down the aisles, and the new vestibules allowed them to pass safely from car to car. People could chat freely with one another in easy familiarity; children could be at play during daytime hours.

There were those who said that the Pullman berth was a constricting place, and some passengers complained of having to change into their night clothes while lying down. The open section Pullman did provide dressing rooms for men and women at opposing ends of the cars, so it was possible to change clothes in the dressing room and walk down the aisle in robe and slippers—an act of bravery that some modest Victorians of both sexes refused to do. The upper and lower berth arrangement had something gauche about it, and over the years a massive body of Pullman jokes and anecdotes developed around Pullman nights where a simple wrong step might result in a comical indiscretion. On the other hand, the vast majority of Americans believed these open sections to be safe and proper.

In the 1880s, when Col. William D'Alton Mann was attempting to sell some of his "boudoir cars" to European railroads, he leveled unflattering charges against Pullman sleeping cars. He alleged that they were wandering palaces of sin, claiming that women were frequently raped by their fellow passengers, that prostitutes were on board to provide services to tired businessmen, and that sexual trysts and lurid momentary assignations took place in these berths covered only by soft curtains.[10] This bad press in Europe never seemed to trouble Americans, however, even in Victorian times. Surely, those soft, rustling green silk curtains did on occasion conceal sexual peccadilloes, but the vast majority of Americans observed the conventions and limitations of Pullman travel and most acted in a responsible manner. The old scandalmonger Colonel Mann, whose American fortune was derived from a tattle magazine he published called *Town Topics*, and from some adroit blackmailing of society figures, could hardly say the same thing about the closed compartments of the Orient Express, which he designed and built in the 1880s. There were far more clandestine meetings and sexual trysts in these environs than in Mr. Pullman's communal and democratic sleeping car. By a kind of tacit agreement among passengers, the social mechanism of which can only be guessed at, and which perhaps was typically American, the Pullman car was mainly (if never exclusively) a place where the proprieties were adhered to.

Perhaps the sanctity of the old open sleeping car can be explained in part by its superlative cleanliness, even spotlessness—standards that were rare even in the best hotels of the day—as well as the crisp and highly professional performance of the Pullman conductors and porters, who ruled their domains like professional duennas. The porter, within easy call by electric bell, assumed permanent guard duty at the end of his car. Peeping regularly and stealthily down the aisle, few signs of trouble or malfeasance could escape his withering glance. Above all, though, the plushness and assured luxury of the sleeping car had a quieting effect on any bumpkin or crude adventurer who might have presumed to convert these corridors into his own domain. All such upstarts were brought to the quick and put on their best behavior by Pullman standards and proprieties.

From his very first car, fitted out for the Chicago and Alton in 1865, Pullman had attempted to lure passengers by an unmitigated appeal to luxury and even snobbery—the deep pile carpeting, the seats upholstered in expensive plush, the black walnut paneling embellished with marquetry suggestive of the first-class cabins of a riverboat or ocean sailing vessel. There were opulent, bevel-edged French mirrors of commodious proportions, elegant chandeliers, and curtains of heaviest silk and worsted—all of which had a calming, reassuring, civilizing, perhaps even somnolent effect. The fact that luxury could be combined with something considered as utilitarian as rail travel, something known to be at the beck of the sinews of commerce, surely appealed to both the playful and serious in the American psyche.

Combining luxury with utility was something that came easy to Americans, and it seemed to click immediately in the Gilded Age, which was itself a time of agonizing industrial and commercial growth. The same had not been true in Europe, where it had always been necessary to separate people of different social classes, and where the impetus was toward exclusivity and the hoarding of luxury. Throughout the nineteenth century, the Europeans never solved with easy grace the problem of getting different classes of people to ride on trains in harmony with one another. When the railroad made its appearance in England, people of the aristocratic orders could not seem to grasp the idea of a "common conveyance." At the primeval Euston Station, there had to be a special entrance and loading ramp for nobility and other genteel folk. And in the earliest days, British railroads had to provide flatcars, onto which carriages could be driven with their horses, with grooms standing behind, an amenity that assured lords and ladies that their status was not being compromised by this newfangled contrivance. Noble passengers, in other words, did not ride in railway cars at all in the beginning, but in carriages of their own accustomed design and appointment. This practice did not persist for long, since the English nobility would not conform to the time schedules of the railroads. Dukes and earls who booked passage on a particular train would arrive ten or fifteen minutes late, or sometimes even as much as an hour late, and expect the train to be waiting for them. When the railroads balked at this disruption, the nobility gave up on the trains and returned to dusty roads for several decades until at last they were forced to bow to the speed and convenience of rail travel.[11]

When travelers from Europe—even aristocratic travelers—arrived in America and took to our trains they invariably testified that Pullman travel was better than anything offered on European trains. Like most Americans, they were charmed by Pullman protocol. They were fascinated by the American appetite for convenience, for getting things done the easiest possible way, even though conventions and sacred practices had to be tossed out the window. An English traveler of the 1880s, W. G. Marshall, took delight in the Parlor Car, another contrivance of the Pullman Company. The Parlor Car was designed for daytime trips of various lengths, and equipped most usually with soft armchairs, sofas, and stocked with suitable reading materials, sometimes a magazine rack or small library. Every modern convenience had been thought out for passenger comfort. "In the parlor car we occupied today," wrote Marshall,

> a Negro presided over a pantry which was at one end of it and dealt out for consumption fruit, strawberries and cream, tea, coffee, milk, lemonade, gin, sherry cobblers, sour mash cocktails, gin cocktails, mint juleps and an immense variety of iced drinks. He seemed to have a ready and endless supply of everything in this line of trade.[12]

Pullman service provided a novel admixture of democracy, luxury, and convenience, but in the era of the robber barons—between 1870 and World War I—railroad travel in America was also witness to some expressions of opulence that might have seemed excessive even to the most patrician European traveler. During these years, American plutocrats took to a novel form of transportation—travel by private railway car. During the golden age of railroading, hundreds of such cars were in service, and their owners were usually men from the purple of commerce, although occasionally others indulged in the taste for private varnish: opera singers, baseball club owners, circus impresarios, or even burlesque queens.

Operation of private railway cars was, of course, prohibitively expensive, but at a time when Goulds and Vanderbilts maintained mansions with a hundred or more servants, enormous private yachts, and racing stables, the cost of upkeep of a private railway car was usually considered an ordinary business expense. Being privately owned, and merely operated by contracting railroads, there was no limit to the splurges of luxury that might be expended on these cars. They could be equipped with the most expensive woodworking and cabinetry, deep carpets, chandeliers, gold plumbing fixtures, wine cellars, fully stocked pantries, and servants' quarters. Invariably, there was a large salon, a private dining room, a master stateroom for the owner fitted up with a full-size bed; usually, there were several other staterooms for guests. Such cars often contained luxurious baths with showers or sunken tubs, and it has even been reported that a few owners attempted to install swimming pools.

Occasionally, the very richest of citizens traveled with several cars, including some specifically set aside for servants or other guests. It is said that at one time Jay Gould had a separate car for his favorite cow, which supplied milk for his bleeding ulcer. It was not unknown for millionaires to engage an entire special train for some specific purpose. J. P. Morgan once hired a whole train of Pullmans to transport a convocation of Episcopal bishops between New York and San Francisco.[13] Of course, in an age when there were no competing forms of long-distance travel, well-heeled Americans used the private railway car for everything from business travel to family vacations.

The private railway car was not unknown elsewhere in the world—Queen Victoria, the Kaiser, and the Pope rode in private cars—but they were never in such generous supply as they were in the United States, where literally hundreds of them were in service before World War I. After 1900, most of the cars in circulation in America were made either by the Pullman Company or the American Car and Foundry Company. A few, especially cars for railroad executives, were made in the railroad's own shops; a few others were made here and there under special contracts. When ostentatious display of wealth became a public indiscretion during the years of the Great Depression of the 1990s, the number of such cars being outshopped dropped considerably. After World War II, it seemed likely that the private railroad car would disappear completely except perhaps for the business travel of railroad presidents. Later cars that were made for railroad use were designed according to more spartan and utilitarian standards—often without drapes or tinted windows, lest railroad officialdom be accused of transporting parties of dancing girls, revelers, or lounge lizards—oft-heard complaints in days of yore. Interestingly, private railway cars did not disappear; in time, they made something of a comeback. There were more of them being operated in the 1980s than in the 1960s, and there is at present a spirited association for the owners of such cars, the American Association of Private Railroad Car Owners, which keeps the lingering enthusiasm for this phenomenon alive.

Back in the last years of the nineteenth century, when travel by private railway car was almost *de rigueur* among the truly wealthy, the railroads were also doing a great deal to bring the experience of luxurious rail travel to the lives of the ordinary citizen. In addition to the advent of famous named express trains, limiteds, high varnish, "white line specials," and so on, the railroads in these years were building spectacular stations, especially in the big cities, containing every manner of modern convenience and amenity. These large railroad terminals contained vast waiting rooms and concourses, sometimes with special retiring rooms for women travelers, often with fashionable shops and restaurants.

In 1896, the ever-inventive George H. Daniels of the New York Central introduced at the "old" Grand Central Station in New York the first "redcap" service in the United States.[14] A small corps of attendants was employed to help people with their bags—carrying them to the taxi ramp or even to the elevated railway or some nearby hotel. The service was free to passengers in the beginning, being paid for wholly by the railroad. Even though this situation was short-lived—not because the railroads became stingy in support of the idea but because Americans could not resist the impulse to tip—Daniels' "redcap" service became another one of the regular and expected niceties of rail travel in the glory days of railroading.

In more ways than one, the railroads became skillful at the art of "gentling" passengers. Most of the major railroads established ticket offices and travel bureaus in convenient locations—in downtown or posh shopping districts—so that it was not necessary for people to make a trek to the station or wait in long lines at the ticket counter. Such city ticket offices or travel bureaus were stocked (as are the offices of travel agents to this day) with coated brochures showing spas and resorts at distant remove. These bureaus were invariably supplied with maps of the railroad itself, sometimes containing scenic views of the right-of-way. The lowly timetable, which the railroads had completely neglected in the early years, now became a lovely work of art, doing its own part as a booster for the line. Railroads even began to issue magazines for release to the general public. Once again, George H. Daniels came to the forefront with his *Four-Track News,* a magazine that contained articles about many topics of general interest—much like today's airline magazines. In common with most of his competitors, Daniels also issued guidebooks, which effectively were advertisements for cities, towns, beauty spots, and historical sites along the New York Central Railroad. One of these, *Health and Pleasure on America's Greatest Railroad,* became truly encyclopedic. The 1896 edition contained 592 pages![15] More modest guidebooks of this kind were printed and distributed in the millions of copies.

Not only did the railroads aid people in reaching their destinations, whether for mundane purposes or for pleasure, they became seriously involved in promoting and developing destinations that responded to the public's fantasies. People wanted to see the scenic United States, and the railroad was the means that would enable them to do so. Accordingly, for many decades railroads were more than a little active in building up scenic spots, fine resort hotels, and fashionable vacation habitats as pleasing adjuncts to their regular service. It was only natural that the Northern Pacific would exploit its proximity to Yellowstone National Park and seek to bring hordes of travelers thence by means of advertisements and promotions. And every other railroad did likewise with its own natural wonders. The Great Northern promoted Glacier National Park; the Santa Fe, the Grand Canyon; the Lackawanna and the New York Central, Niagara Falls; and so on.

The very existence of the railroad had brought about the creation of many resort places from early times. Travelers were coming to Arkansas Hot Springs in the Ozarks even before the Civil War, later coming there over the rails of the St. Louis, Iron

Mountain and Southern Railroad. With the passage of time, many similar resorts came into existence and thrived because of their proximity to railroad lines. One thinks of such illustrious railroad resort spots as Saratoga Springs, White Sulphur Springs, French Lick, Poland Springs, Tuxedo Park, Newport, Palm Beach, Louisville, and Miami. Even a few places never actually reached by railroad were nonetheless railroad resorts—Bar Harbor, Maine, for example, the mother of the famous New England name train the Bar Harbor Express, and Hobe Sound, in Florida, which was as much the creation of the Florida East Coast Railway as was Miami.

During the glory years of passenger travel, railroads not only touted the resorts and glamour spots along their lines, they frequently owned properties in such places. The Chesapeake and Ohio Railroad owned and operated two of the most famous resorts in the eastern United States: the Greenbrier, at White Sulphur Springs, West Virginia, and the Homestead, at Hot Springs, Virginia. The Delaware and Hudson once had vested interest in hotels in Saratoga Springs, New York, and on Lake George and Lake Champlain. As early as 1879, the Southern Pacific Railroad purchased seven thousand choice acres on the Monterey Peninsula, for five dollars an acre,[16] and built there one of the grandest resort hotels in the American record—the Del Monte Hotel. (Nabobs from San Francisco were carried there by a train appropriately named the Del Monte Express.) In Florida, Henry M. Flagler built, and his Florida East Coast Railway operated, two justly famous luxury resort hotels—first the Ponce de Leon in St. Augustine and later the Royal Poinciana in Palm Beach. The Florida East Coast built a trestle across Lake Worth so that blue-blooded guests of the hotel could have direct access to the Royal Poinciana. And the hotel had its own exclusive railway yard, which during the 1920s would occasionally be filled to capacity with a multitude of private railway cars.

Some historians have insisted that railroads added nothing more to the Gilded Age than lining the pockets of so many financial buccaneers and freebooters. But such is a mean-spirited half-truth. During the period between 1880 and World War I, the railroads had so vastly improved their services, and offered so many new luxuries undreamed of before, that most American were willing to forgive them their varied transgressions. What is more important, railroads during these years fashioned a dimension of style and refinement to travel that added a great deal to the quality of American life, and their style and refinement could be afforded and enjoyed by the multitudes, thereby making a clear contribution to the welter of democratic life. The new railroad amenities and luxuries were also a strong buttress to the confidence of the rapidly growing middle class in America and obviously added a great deal to its most enduring institutions.

C·H·A·P·T·E·R 12

THE RISE OF THE RAILROAD SUBURB

The American railroads clearly did a great deal in the nineteenth century to develop and promote places of leisure—resort hotels, spas, national parks, scenic wonderlands. They made it possible for the ordinary American to take his rest at the seashore, at some cool lake, in the mountains—or at any place of some remove from the rapidly growing cities. But another contribution of rail travel had an even greater impact on society as a whole, and on everyday American life—the development of the bedroom suburb. Until the advent of the automobile in the twentieth century, individuals who wanted to work in the city and live somewhere else had almost no opportunities for doing so, especially if they were burdened by the necessity of being on the job five or six days a week. The railroad made travel of some distance between home and office a practical possibility. More than any other single agency, the railroad gave rise to what is now known as suburbia—both the place and the way of life.

Neither the idea nor the actualization of the bedroom suburb developed quickly. Few if any Americans thought of themselves as being suburbanites until long after the Civil War. On the other hand, the seed idea for the suburb goes back to the earliest days of railroading. The chug of the iron horse had not been heard for very long before some individuals wanted to use the convenience

235

and speed of the railroad to go back and forth between two places on a daily basis. It was this regular rail passage between two points that eventually led to the growth of the suburb.

Who was the first such regular rail traveler? History has not recorded, nor doubtless could it. There may have been a few people who regularly used the Charleston road, or the Baltimore and Ohio, or the Camden and Amboy in the incubator days of railroading. Most likely, the first use of the railroad for daily passage resembling what we today call "commuting" was on the New York and Harlem Railroad. A very early intention of this railroad, chartered in 1831, was to transport people up the elongated isle of Manhattan, much of it still unsettled and pastoral. The originally proposed line was to go up Fourth Avenue from Twenty-third Street to Yorkville and Harlem. As early as 1833, the railroad was carrying daily passengers back and forth between Twenty-third Street and Murray Hill, although the cars were horse drawn for the first few years. Due to the difficult terrain of Manhattan island and the necessity of drilling through bedrock between Eighty-eighth and Ninety-fifth Street, the original Harlem terminal was not reached until 1837. Steam locomotives were added in 1839, and thereafter the iron horse plodded its way up Fourth Avenue, terrorizing pedestrians, frightening horses, and bringing general chaos to the city environment.

The New York and Harlem Railroad (much later to become a part of the New York Central), was essentially what we would now call a street railway. The line was extended to lower Manhattan for a few years, but was later banned below Twenty-third Street because of the inherent dangers in the narrow, twisting streets. (Still later, of course, the railroad had Forty-second Street as its southern terminus.) By 1834, when the cars reached Yorkville, a regular schedule of service was maintained on the half hour. One-way fare was twelve and a half cents (in those days, there was a coin of that amount—one bit, the eighth part of a dollar),[1] no reduction being given for multiple rides. Clearly, the New York and Harlem was a passenger line that served the "suburbs," even though all of its suburbs have long since been swallowed up in the densely populated island of Manhattan and are suburbs no more.

New York was not the only city on the eastern seaboard that can lay claim to being the mother of commuter railroading. Boston and Philadelphia both have their partisans, and historians have given priority to each. Whichever way the dispute is resolved, both of these cities had service to suburban communities in the first decade of railroading. In Boston, three lines—the Boston and Worcester, the Boston and Lowell, and the Boston and Providence—were leading out of the hub of Boston by 1835, and there were daily passengers into the city from fairly early times. (Along the route of the Boston and Worcester, there had been daily commuting to Boston by stagecoach even before the coming of the railroad, and many conservative travelers at first were unwilling to give up the stages, which obligingly stopped right at their front doors.) In Philadelphia, the Philadelphia, Germantown, and Norristown (later part of the Reading Railroad) was completed to Germantown in 1832 and was carrying daily passengers to this nearby oasis shortly thereafter.

Precisely when commuting in the present sense began is a subject incapable of resolution. Actually, the very word "commutation" referred to the fact that railroads "commuted" the fares of regular riders, so that those who traveled every day of the week could get a reduced rate, encouraging and rewarding their regular patronage. It is not entirely certain when this idea was born, or whether it was the brainchild of the railroads themselves or of the passengers. Probably the idea of "commuted" fares began to take hold in the early 1840s. In 1841, a Mr. Lathrop of Madison, New Jersey, approached the Morris and Essex Railroad (predecessor of the Lackawanna) and offered to pay one hundred dollars for the privilege of riding the Morris and Essex between Madison and Newark for a period of six months.[2] Although it then took nearly two hours to get to Newark (and another hour to get to New York), the railroad granted the request, fully appreciating why one would want to work in Newark or New York and yet live in the lush hills of Morris County. In a year or so, the railroad was offering commuter tickets to a fair number of daily travelers. Similar arrangements were made around this time by the Boston railroads. The wily Boston railroad executives quickly decided to actively encourage suburban traffic, and by 1845 were offering promotional fares as low as one and a half cents a mile, an amount that would hardly cover their costs and which they would later come to regret when parsimonious Yankee commuters balked at even the most modest fare increases.[3]

Commuting by rail in the early years—that is, before the Civil

War—developed by slow degrees. In a few cities, the practice of taking the train to work became suddenly infectious; in other places, the idea just didn't seem to catch on. Invariably, though, suburban communities developed because the railroad already happened to be running trains in the vicinity. The railroad in these times did not build lines with the idea of encouraging a corps of daily riders; usually, there were railroad lines linking two distant points—Boston and Worcester, for example—and the people who lived a few miles out of Boston called for local trains to carry them to the city. In some cases, the railroads were reluctant to make such stops in the beginning, particularly because for a long time they might be asked to stop for only one or two passengers.

In Chicago, which today is one of the great railroad commuter cities of North America, regular travel to the city's core began almost as soon as the first railroads were in operation. But the volume of this traffic was originally microscopic. Passenger service in the Chicago area began in 1848, when trains started running on the old Chicago and Galena Union Railroad (later the Chicago and Northwestern), and doubtless the first year of operation saw a few individuals coming into Chicago from the Des Plaines River behind the diminutive wood-burning locomotive Pioneer.[4] Especially characteristic of what happened in Chicago was the early experience of the Illinois Central, which started laying its Chicago line in 1852. Shortly after operations began, the railroad received requests from a few individuals who lived several miles beyond the city limits (which was then located around Thirty-third Street) for a train to take them into the city. There was a delightful little pastoral community six miles from downtown, and one Paul Cornell, an enterprising young Chicago lawyer who owned land there, convinced the railroad to make a regular stop for passengers going into the city. Shortly, the railroad erected a small wood-frame station for the convenience of these passengers, and at Cornell's suggestion called the station "Hyde Park"—Cornell was thinking of London's Hyde Park, no doubt.

Hyde Park, apparently, was a delightful spot on high ground along the shore of Lake Michigan. It was interspersed with picturesque groves, and it is reported that in this vicinity "meadow larks sang in the clear morning air, and that at twilight the deep croak of the bullfrog was heard, with crickets, whippoorwills and

tree-toads joining in the chorus." After the little station was erected, a few individuals began using the train to Chicago on a regular
basis. There was enough traffic that in a few years the railroad
decided to put on a train especially for commuters—it was called
the Hyde Park Special, and went into service on July 21, 1856.
This was the first official recognition by the railroad that they were
running a suburban train service.[5]

Revenues from the Hyde Park Special were hardly encouraging
to the railroad, but the train was kept on, and in a few years was
extended to a more southerly neighborhood near what is now
Sixty-third Street in Chicago. Here, another small station was built
as well as a "wye" track for turning the train around. The railroad
called the station "Woodlawn," and it became, for a short time,
the new terminal of the Hyde Park train. What happened next was
rather characteristic in the ongoing saga of railroad commuting
both in Chicago and around the country. A mile or so south of
the Hyde Park station, a physician, Dr. J. A. Kennicott, built himself a beautiful home which he called "Kenwood," after his ances-
tral home in Scotland. The doctor's practice was in the city, and
he accordingly was a regular rider of the Hyde Park train. But he
didn't relish the long walk to the station, which could be more
than a little rugged in winter, so he importuned the IC to make a
stop closer to his home for himself and a few neighbors. This they
obligingly did. Later, when a few more people settled in the area,
a station was built, and, to honor the doctor, was called
"Kenwood." Kenwood and other hamlets along the railroad
(Oakwood and Woodlawn) were incorporated into Hyde Park in
1861. (Hyde Park itself, of course, has long since been swallowed
up by the city of Chicago.) But the pattern set here was typical.
Along railroad lines where people were quickly settling, trains
would be called upon to make frequent stops, stations would go
down every mile or so (and sometimes even closer than that), and
presto—a commuter line would come into being.

It was thus clearly the force and discovery of convenience that
brought the notion of "suburbia" into existence. Individuals such
as Paul Cornell and Dr. Kennicott, who had some identification
with the city and yet who desired to live in some pastoral glen
beyond the city's edge, discovered that the speed of railroad travel
would make it possible to conveniently make a professional life in
one place and a personal life in the other. Of course, not every

suburban community sprang to existence because a railroad ran by. Very often, these were towns or hamlets already in existence, and the building of a railroad line merely helped to transform them into full-fledged suburbs. This was especially the case in the years after the Civil War, when trains became faster, lines were double tracked, and all phases of service were vastly improved.

In the Chicago area, for example, Evanston was a substantial community to the north with a recognized independent existence, but it was pulled into the orbit of Chicago by the coming of the Milwaukee Road (later sold to the C&NW). When the Burlington built its own line into Chicago because the C&NW would no longer carry its cars, it followed a familiar old stagecoach route that already had a smattering of small towns between Chicago and Aurora—towns like La Grange, Downer's Grove, and Naperville. These readily became Chicago suburbs, but the Burlington, like most other railroads, quickly got into the swing of things and plopped down stations betwixt and between. One of these new towns, Hinsdale, was named for a member of the road's board of directors. Another new community along the Burlington—Riverside—was specifically planned in advance as a genteel suburban community. Designed by America's best-known landscape architect, Frederick Law Olmsted (who designed Central Park in New York, as well as some eighty major parks and thirteen college campuses around the country), Riverside avoided the grid pattern that had spelled monotony for so many midwestern communities, opting instead for winding streets and homes placed at irregular angles. The meandering Des Plaines River helped create a countrified mood, as did the planting of some sixty thousand shrubs and trees in a well designed, aesthetic pattern.

For the most part, railroads did not resist the proliferation of suburban traffic along their lines. Why should they? The traffic developed along existing lines—sometimes along main lines, such as that of the Illinois Central and Burlington in Chicago, or the Pennsylvania west of Philadelphia, or the Old Colony and the Boston and Albany in Boston. In the beginning, the railroad merely had to provide some additional stations on the line and perhaps an accommodation train or two. With the passage of time, the trains became many in number, sometimes locals and expresses. Shedlike stations were torn down and replaced by more commodious and pleasing structures. Suburban territories had to be double, triple, or even quadruple tracked, but by the time that such things came to pass, revenues from suburban passenger service were more than a little gratifying to the railroads involved, so they did much to encourage it.

Between 1880 and World War I, the pattern of railroad commuting to bedroom suburbs became a fixture of American social life. Nearly all cities of any size, most especially those in the East, gave evidence of some railroad commuting. Cleveland, Washington, Baltimore, Milwaukee, Cincinnati, Detroit, St. Louis, Pittsburgh, and New Orleans all developed some kind of suburban rail traffic by 1900. Although some may not believe it today, even San Francisco and Los Angeles in California showed signs of moving in this direction by the early twentieth century. Unfortunately, most of the western cities never developed the railroad suburb in the true sense, and rail commuting eventually withered away and died. Los Angeles didn't develop suburbia as it is understood in the East, in spite of the fact that for a while the Los Angeles area had a tolerably good system of interurban railroads. Because the eastern-style commuting suburb never appeared in Los Angeles, visitors and residents alike think of the suburban communities (even though they do have names and individual identities) as simply being a part of Los Angeles. What you have is essentially one gigantic urban sprawl, with linkages provided only by the automobile—a concept that is nothing like the suburbia so well known to easterners.

Four major American cities—New York, Boston, Philadelphia, and Chicago—developed vast and complex networks of commuter rail lines in the late nineteenth century, and in each of these cities the volume of suburban rail traffic continues to be heavy at the end of the twentieth century, even though now mostly under the auspices of state and regional transportation authorities. All of these cities were once served by a number of railroads, whose suburban lines poured in from every point of the compass. Boston was served classically by the Boston and Albany, the Boston and Maine, and the New York, New Haven, and Hartford, and their various predecessor companies. Philadelphia was the exclusive province of the Reading and the Pennsylvania. Chicago was host to five major railroads, all of which had extensive commuter traffic—the Illinois Central, the Chicago and Northwestern, the Burlington, the Milwaukee, and the Rock Island. At one time,

Chicago additionally enjoyed three important interurban lines built to near-railroad standards and had smaller commuter operations run by the Pennsylvania, the Chicago and Western Indiana, the Wabash, and the Alton.

New York, of course, was a gigantic beehive of commuter activity; everything here was on a truly massive scale. By the late years of the nineteenth century, suburban trains were pouring in from all directions, giving New York almost as much suburban traffic as all the other American cities put together. From the north came the various lines of the New York Central serving Westchester and Putnam counties and also the lines of the New York, New Haven and Hartford, reaching the New York suburbs of Long Island Sound such as New Rochelle, Larchmont, Mamaroneck, and Rye, and those farther up in Connecticut. This area contained some of the most lush commuting territory in the nation—Greenwich, Cos Cob, Stamford, Darien, Norwalk, Westport, and Fairfield, among others.

Hundreds of thousands of commuters would also be arriving by ferry boats from New Jersey. The Erie, the Lackawanna, the Jersey Central, the Pennsylvania, and the West Shore Division of the New York Central would all eventually have large fleets of ferry boats to transport suburbanites from many points in northern New Jersey to offices on lower or midtown Manhattan. On any given weekday, streams of office workers would pour forth from vast, creaking ferry sheds at Chambers Street, Liberty Street, Cortland Street, or Barclay Street and thread their way to the imposing towers of finance on Wall Street or Maiden Lane. All of the New Jersey commuter railroads had their own sovereign domains and their own breed of faithful commuters. The Lackawanna held sway in Essex and Morris counties, literally breathing life into the towns strung out on the first range of the Watchung Mountains: the Oranges, Maplewood, Glen Ridge, Montclair, Short Hills, Summit, then out into the fox-hunting preserves of Morristown, Far Hills, Peapack, Bernardsville, and Gladstone. The Erie, with a complex network of lines, dominated the many suburban communities of Bergen and Passaic Counties and Rockland County, New York. The Jersey Central had as its exclusive preserve the huge Raritan Valley south of the Watchung Range. The Pennsylvania had numerous commuting towns not only on its main line as far south as Princeton and Trenton but also down to the Jersey shore over the New York and Long Branch Railroad, which it owned jointly with the Jersey Central. In addition to its dense industrial areas of Essex, Hudson, and Passaic counties, northern New Jersey, as it encircled New York to the west, was one enormous web of bedroom suburbs.

Much the same can be said of the entire western end of Long Island, an area so densely packed that the Long Island Railroad that served it became the largest single commuter railroad in the United States in terms of volume of such traffic. The Long Island began serving the various communities of Brooklyn and Queens as early as the 1830s and 1840s (neither of these large territories would actually become part of New York until the founding of the Greater City of New York in 1898), and regular daily riders were almost immediately commuting on the Long Island between their homes and the railroad's ferry houses on the East River.

The railroad served the whole of Long Island, including such far-out enclaves of the super rich as Hampton Bays and Southampton. There is not a great deal of evidence that members of the four hundred rode the Long Island very often—Scott Fitzgerald's hero Jay Gatsby on his north shore estate seemed to prefer the conveniences of a high-speed motor car, but on the densely populated western end of Long Island the railroad was king. In parts of Queens and Brooklyn, the Long Island in later years seemed not very much different than a city rapid transit system, with closely scheduled electrified trains going to communities like Jamaica, Kew Gardens, Forest Hills, Hollis, and Douglaston. These, in spite of their individual identities, are essentially part of the City of New York. But beyond, in Nassau County, the Long Island came to serve dozens of bedroom suburbs. Five days a week, year in and year out, throngs of commuters would be railbound for New York from Great Neck, Glen Cove, Roslyn, Oyster Bay, Baldwin, Hicksville, Hemstead, Rockville Centre, Valley Stream, Syosset, Mineola, Massapequa, Wantagh, and countless other communities. It was the largest commuter operation run by a single railroad anywhere in the world; in the 1920s, sixty-two percent of all the rail commuters in the United States rode on the Long Island.[6] The railroad, apparently a good and reliable carrier until the 1890s, fell on hard times, and was taken over for a while by the Pennsylvania (which gave it access to the giant Pennsylvania Station in midtown Manhattan), but was never subsequently managed to the satisfaction of its passengers. Throughout all of its twentieth century existence as a private carrier, the Long Island was the Calamity Jane of commuter railroads. Nonetheless, even those who despised the threadbare equipment and the shabby service could hardly fail to express wonder at the enormity of the tasks undertaken.

The predicament of the Long Island gives some hint of the ambiguous and cautious attitudes toward suburban traffic held by railroad managements over the years. Commuter traffic was business, occasionally it became big business. It was never enormously profitable, although for years the railroads took pride in operating these commuter lines, perhaps realizing that the services had a certain intrinsic value in generating goodwill and public affection. A good many people living in suburban territories only knew their local railroads as commuter lines—doubtless, many people living on Long Island had no idea that their railroad also carried freight. The same might have been said about suburbanites living along the Lackawanna in New Jersey, many of whom never realized that their railroad was one of the nation's premier coal haulers or that profits from the coal business had paid for many of the improvements and refinements in the suburban territory during the first quarter of the twentieth century.

By the latter half of the nineteenth century, the railroads found themselves under constant pressure to improve and upgrade suburban services. They were not facing a new generation of passengers who noticed that this or that line passed through desirable neighborhoods and who were convinced that ministering to the daily needs of commuters was a major function of a railroad—an idea that the railroads at first had been slow to accept. City dwellers looking for new environments, or those already living in pastoral environments who wanted quick transportation to the city, got up petitions imploring railroads to build new stations, to put on more trains either local or express, and to assign better and faster equipment on suburban lines.

A very common circumstance in the late nineteenth century was that individuals who wanted train service to places near their home would actually finance the building of a station themselves if the railroad would agree to stop trains there. In the late 1870s, Stewart Hartshorne bought some land in what is now Short Hills, New Jersey, then an uninhabited spot on the Lackawanna's hard pull over the Watchung Mountain. He believed that this area could be a delightful retreat for New York bankers or businessmen, and even before many houses were built in the area he purchased a site near the railroad and spent $2,500 of his own money to build a station there. He later deeded this station to the Lackawanna with the proviso that it would stop trains there in the morning and evening for commuters. The Lackawanna obliged, and offered two trains a day each way.[7] Not too far away, in Glen Ridge, a well-to-do resident named A. G. Darwin built a beautiful station on an embankment above the Lackawanna's Montclair branch. He donated this station, resembling a large private home, to the railroad, and for many years it served as both station and post office.

Private construction of suburban stations resulted in some of the most comely and pleasing railroad stations built in the nineteenth century. In Hinsdale, Illinois, John and Alanson Reed, owners of Reed's Temple of Music in Chicago, living rather far away from the main station, built a small but lovely stone station called "Highlands" and donated this to the Burlington. It remains one of the most picturesque small stations in the United States. On the Pennsylvania "Main Line" west of Philadelphia, several stations were built by men of affairs who regularly rode the line. The Reading was especially fortunate in this regard. John Wanamaker, the famous merchant prince of Philadelphia, paid for several stations, including a "private" stop, Meadowbrook, near his own estate. An early Philadelphia developer, William Lukens Elkins, got himself on the map by building a station and naming it for himself—Elkins Park.

This kind of subtle pressure put on the railroads was not as important in the long run as the economic force provided by the growing number of daily riders and by the brisk activity of developers and civic groups. An extremely common phenomenon in the last three decades of the nineteenth century was for a developer to identify some geographical area that was clearly suitable for suburban development and then buy up large parcels of land for purposes of subdivision into residential properties. Almost invariably, it was the presence of the railroad that gave the impetus to these new developments, and more often than not the community was laid out with the railroad station and other commercial buildings being grouped together and constituting "downtown." The developers would then take on the chore of coaxing the railroad to build a station, or, if that failed, of building it themselves.

In a particularly pleasing area of Brookline, Massachusetts, with woods and gently rolling hills, Boston businessman David Sears laid out a subdivision called Longwood and saw to it that a handsome station and a Gothic parish building formed an architectural centerpiece of the community. Very often, areas that seemed suitable for daily commuting were quickly identified by developers and set aside for settlement as "exclusive" neighborhoods or preserves for the affluent and well-heeled. Riverside, Illinois, was one such community, but there were numerous others. Even before the Civil War, a New York real estate speculator and drug importer named Llewellyn S. Haskell bought forty acres of land under the Eagle Rock Cliff in West Orange, New Jersey, and began an elite suburban community there. By 1870, Llewelyn Park, as it was called, had increased to 750 acres and many large homes of architectural distinction were under construction there, mostly the homes of individuals who commuted on the Lackawanna into New York, a mere twelve miles distant. Llewellyn Park was maintained as a private enclave, with residents maintaining roads and parks cooperatively. With the passage of time, as the area of the Oranges became completely urbanized, Llewellyn Park had to be walled off from deteriorating neighborhoods and protected by fences and security guards, which would have been anathema to the original pastoral dream of Haskell. But in its heyday, Llewellyn Park was a place of great visual beauty and delight. In the late nineteenth century, the community's parks and gardens were witness to the first large-scale naturalization in the United States of many ornamental flowers such as the crocus, narcissus, and jonquil.[8]

Most of the nation's highly affluent suburbs tended to be a good deal farther from the city's core. Typically, they began in an arcadian setting, and never had to fear the encroachments of blue-collar neighborhoods or industrial blight. Chicago's most exclusive suburb, Lake Forest, began as a faraway retreat where a few privileged individuals took the breezes during the summer months. Being some twenty-five miles from Chicago, it could not have been a daily commuting town before the Civil War, although the first plans of the town from 1856 show the town to be laid out in immense lots with curved drives. In the early days, John J.

Farwell, a dry goods merchant, built a turreted baronial castle with a concrete exterior and an interior of black walnut and cherry. In the 1870s, a "Lake Forest Association" planned for a suburban community of some 1,300 acres amidst scenic moraines, steep, narrow ravines, wooded irregular lots, with tall bluffs looking out over Lake Michigan.[9] Within a few years, Lake Forest became home to members of Chicago's aristocracy—the Armours and Swifts—who could now make it into Chicago every day on express commuter trains.

It is not hard to see how suburban railroad traffic changed the American landscape in the 1880s and 1890s, how it forged a wholly new kind of link between the city's core and pastoral environs that had once been thought of as far away. It is a matter for deeper speculation how the development of suburbia changed the American way of life. In earlier days, many thoughtful observers were delighted to point out that the rise of bedroom suburbs answered some deep and enduring needs in the American psyche: the need for a relief from the clamor and strife of cities and the need for a patch of ground one could call one's own, an ideal that Thomas Jefferson had long ago insisted was essential for the survival of democracy. With the passage of time, numerous critics and social historians were less certain about the value of suburbia. Some pointed out that the suburb did not establish virtues of independence and self-reliance as did the frontier or the family farm, that suburbanites were deluding themselves that the presence of trees and well-kept lawns entitled them think of themselves as a new breed of hardy pioneers. Sociologists like David Riesman were quick to find some kind of relationship between the suburban life-style and "other-directedness," or conformity, all of which could lead not to an invigorating spirit in the common life but rather a stereotyping of manners and morals. In time, novelists like John Cheever, who gave a good deal of close scrutiny to suburban life, came to believe that there was something rotten at the core of it all, sometimes an ineffable rottenness, but rottenness all the same.

Whatever the results of such speculations, there is no doubt that the commuting life gave a much more standardized form to daily existence than anything that had been known in the more diffuse social world of the early republic. Daily travel by train meant travel by the clock—the 8:07 to the city in the morning; the 5:38 homeward bound in the evening. Office routines in the city were in fact adjusted to fit the times when railroads actually ran the largest number of trains on the most rapid schedules. During the morning "rush hour," as it came to be called, railroads accommodated suburban passengers not only by a large number of trains usually run in quick succession, but by expresses making few stops and thus greatly shortening the time needed to get to the office. Rush-hour trains would come to carry the vast majority of daily commuters, and would serve to enforce standardized hours for most office workers: the familiar, and formalized nine to five routine, for example.

The commuter very quickly became a creature of habit; trains, of course, had to be run on a schedule, and once these schedules were met and the commuter became used to them, there was strong pressure upon railroads to offer the same service at precisely the same time, six days a week, year in and year out. A look at suburban railroad timetables on some long-established lines in 1900, or 1930, or 1950, will show a strong tendency toward trains running at the same times and making precisely the same stops over these long stretches of time. In 1883, for example, the Lackawanna established a train popularly called the "Banker's Express," sometimes the "Millionaire's Express," and it left the railroad's Hoboken terminal at 4:15 every afternoon nonstop for Madison and Morristown. This train endured in the same time slot as long as the Lackawanna had its corporate existence. Many years later, it had lost much of its mystique (and its name) and had been electrified, but the schedule was identical within a matter of a minute or so.

An examination of the timetables of the neighboring Erie over a period of many years reveals much the same thing. Suburban timetables were not changed at all for thirty or forty years. At the Erie's Jersey City terminal, the railroad had painted signs on metal placards announcing the principal suburban trains and the stations they would stop at. These trains, with names like Ridgewood Express, Montclair Express, or Paterson Local, kept to nearly identical schedules for decades. A 1914 schedule for the Erie's Greenwood Lake Division shows a Montclair Express leaving Jersey at 6:14 P.M., first stop Montclair at 6:33—a timetable forty years later shows the same train with the exact same times! And the tatterdemalion Erie ran its trains on time to the shame of prosperous neighbors like the New Haven.

The uniformity of schedules probably brought about many other kinds of uniformity as well. Commuters somehow seemed to look alike, to dress alike. For years, before sartorial standards completely fell by the wayside, spring, summer, and winter attire of male commuters was nearly identical. Stetsons or homburgs would be replaced by straw boaters, usually on some tacitly agreed upon date in the spring. Brief cases, attaché cases, or other accoutrements went in and out of fashion over the years; they were highly stylized but uniformly accepted. The daily commuter's principal pacifier was the morning or afternoon newspaper, and any bystander looking up at a commuter train from outside would notice row after row of individuals similarly buried in copies of the *Wall Street Journal,* the *Chicago Tribune,* or the *Boston Globe,* all of which had been ingeniously folded to some suitably compact format. (The tabloid, convenient dimensions though it may have had, was seldom popular with commuters from more nobby suburbs—the *New York Daily News* and kindred papers of lurid substance more often offered their pungent daily morsels to bus or subway strap hangers than denizens of suburbia.)

Being crowded into long railway cars for thirty or fifty minutes twice a day gave few opportunities for amusement other than the daily newspaper, or in the case of the occasional female passenger, the pocketbook-ready dime romance novel. A few passengers stared passively out the window, perhaps using this interlude as a time to reflect on some complex issue of trade, or upon family uproars of the moment. Writer Max Eastman once observed that there appeared to be two kinds of commuters—the tough-minded and the tender-minded. The tough-minded commuter snapped open his paper the instant he boarded the train, his eyes eagerly scanning the bond quotations, then popped up, robotlike, as soon as the train got into Grand Central or Jersey City. The tender-minded commuter would, perhaps, dreamily look out the window, his mind drifting to a series of fleeting impressions; on the ferry boat across the Hudson, he would breathe deep of the salt air, watch the pigeons fly overhead, savor the welter of life, or meditate upon the ineffable qualities of things.

Perhaps there were more personality types among the railroad commuters than the tough-minded and the tender-minded, although it was in the nature of an habitual train trip carried on day after day, year after year, that the habits of commuters would invariably become routinized or stereotyped. It has been said that most men, when they shave, begin with the same side of their face every day, for no particular reason at all. Similarly, the vast majority of commuters would stand at the same place on the station platform day in and day out waiting for the train. Many would board the same car (second from the end, let's say) every morning, or try to get a seat on the same side—perhaps the *very* same seat. Particular commuter cars took on the characteristics of those who rode them—some were somber in mood, inspiring very little if any conviviality or conversation; others seemed to inspire more fraternization and garrulousness.

While it is true that the daily newspaper was the typical commuter's most characteristic preoccupation, the commuter passenger car was the scene of many kinds of social interaction over the years—even occasionally religious services! One of the most common diversions of commuters, especially of runs of more than half an hour, was card playing. Many commuter cars, especially with reversible seats, provided ideal circumstances for poker, or perhaps for Chicago bridge. Miscellaneous activities—from mandolin playing to political speech making—have been recorded. In recent years, women's self-help groups or assertiveness training sessions have been held on trains. Professor Lawrence Brennan, of New York University, offered a course in business letter and report writing to commuters on the cars of the Pennsylvania and Jersey Central on runs from the New Jersey seashore to New York.[10]

It is probably true that morning commuter runs were different from evening runs in mood and ambience. It is not surprising that Professor Brennan's course in writing was held in the morning and not in the evening, by which time few commuters would have been in a mood to be uplifted. In later years, particularly after World War II, many railroads put small set-up bars at the ends of commuter cars, so that passengers could enjoy some liquid refreshment before arriving home for their regular martini. On a few railroads, these bars were staffed by former sleeping car porters, whose jobs had been eliminated as long-distance trains disappeared. Overall, the sale of liquor on suburban trains probably added little to the quality of life aboard commuter cars.

Especially on railroads like the New Haven, where many years of inept management during that railroad's final decades caused regular and repeated delays, alcohol as a remedy for train frustrations was probably not a salutary influence. Doubtless, many an advertising account executive or media planner, already groaning under the yoke of a frenetic workday, arrived home in Cos Cob or Westport with "New Haven frazzled nerves," amplified by alcohol excess—greeting his loving wife at the station with crumpled tie, disheveled hair, perspiration-soaked shirt, and florid delusions of technological chaos.

For good or ill, commuting has been a way of life for well over a century, and continues to be today. When the railroads themselves (as opposed to state or regional authorities) operated commuter lines, a great deal was done to keep commuters happy—this was reliable business, even if never enormously profitable—and the railroads did much to publicize and glorify the service. Suburban passenger agents saw to it that the trains ran at favorable hours, and, insofar as possible, got people to work on time. They encouraged the development of suburban communities through advertisements, booklets, posters, and paeans of praise to the pastoral life of suburban communities. The passenger traffic manager and his assistants generally handled complaints with dispatch, attempted to recover articles left on trains (a frequent occurrence), issued easy-to-read timetables, and did whatever they could to solicit traffic in suburban territory, including special party movements or midday ridership. From the earliest times, the railroads issued monthly passes at reduced (or "commuted") rates, as well as weekly tickets, ten-trip tickets, fifty-trip tickets, or whatever formulations might gain wide acceptance.

Until the last few decades of the railroads' own operation of commuter lines, every effort was made to assign modern, clean equipment to suburban trains. During the day, when the coaches were in the yards awaiting the homebound riders at five o'clock, the windows were washed, the aisles swept down, the seats cleaned. The railroads always paid special attention to the major express trains which came in from far-out affluent suburbs. Usually, these got the best engines and the most senior crews. Almost all the major commuter lines had something that was the equivalent of the Banker's Express or the Millionaire's Express of the Lackawanna. More often than not these trains were only known by these hypertrophied nicknames to a select few—even the Banker's Express was never designated as such on the timetable. A few were named on timetables, of course, including the Erie's Tuxedo, which served its deluxe suburbs in Rockland and Orange County, New York—Tuxedo Park, Harriman, and so on—or the Reading's Crusader between Philadelphia and New York. Sometimes, the fancied appellations of commuter trains were known almost exclusively to railroad workers—such as the Illinois Central's express No.762, the fastest train between Matteson and downtown Chicago, called for years the Hot-Shot.[11]

Commuters themselves, of course, had a vested interest in the quality and the survival of suburban rail service. Sometimes, their concerns were expressed by commuter associations. Often, communities shared the responsibility of building or maintaining stations, making them scenic and habitable places. Over the years, many railroads provided special equipment for affluent commuters—parlor cars, club cars, and the like. Usually, such cars were on a subscription basis. That is to say, well-heeled individuals from Tuxedo Park, or Bernardsville, or Morristown, would arrange with the railroad to haul a private subscription car on a given train each day, usually the same time morning and night. Although available only to subscribers, such cars could be fitted out with deep wicker armchairs, swivel chairs or sofas. Some had libraries and took magazine subscriptions and were usually kept shipshape by a butler or majordomo, also charged with the responsibility of keeping stray lesser mortals from entering these sacred precincts uninvited. Occasionally, although seldom on a daily basis, suburban trains carried individual private cars. The Reading even had several private sidings for a few millionaires along its route. So, too, did the Lackawanna; for example, one built for Hamilton McK. Twombly at Madison.[12]

Many individuals who took the train to the city each day did so not only for years, but for decades. The railroads were sufficiently gratified by this extended patronage that they sometimes tendered banquets to loyal suburban passengers, occasionally bestowing plaques or gold watches. Starting in the 1920s, a number of the railroads of northern New Jersey started to become aware that they had individuals in their midst who had been traveling into New York since the 1870s or perhaps before, and they began newspaper campaigns to find "the oldest commuter" or the commuter with the greatest number of miles traveled. Addison Day, of Chatham, apparently won considerable national publicity in the early 1930s, as he celebrated a lifelong history of commuting that went back to 1868 and ended in June 1934, at which time he had logged nearly one million miles on the train. The Lackawanna threw him a party aboard the president's private railway car on his last trip home to celebrate sixty-six years of commuting. But all such records are hard to maintain, and within a few years, A. C. Wilmerding of Plainfield was touted as being the Dean of Jersey Central commuters with seventy years of ridership under his belt.[13] By 1970, the all-time record for commuting on the Lackawanna was held by W. Parsons Todd of Morristown, who commuted for seventy-two years, between 1898 and 1970.[14]

Engineers and train crews on suburban lines also shared some of this same glory. Most crews were regularly assigned, and some railroad employees racked up service records that were as impressive as those of the commuters. Samuel Johnson Snyder of Upper Montclair, New Jersey, wound up sixty-nine years as a conductor on the Greenwood Lake Division of the Erie in 1946: He had served 22,500,000 passengers and ridden 2,500,000 miles. Many regular crew members like Snyder were known by name and held in deep affection by the daily riders. Even the engineers were familiar personages in the days of steam. Ben Day, engineer of the Lackawanna's Banker's Express, was known for years to all who rode that famous train, and after he had been on the run for twenty years (in 1903), Day and his conductor Dave Sanderson were feted at a banquet and presented with gold watches; their wives were presented with cash purses of seventy-five dollars.[15] Over on the Erie, legendary commuter engineer Harvey Springstead had his name gilt lettered on the side of his cab, giving his run between New York and Suffern a special distinction and himself a nationwide reputation.

It was only natural that certain technological advances would eventually make great inroads in suburban railway operations. Chief among these was the automobile, which was little used for transportation from suburb to city before World War II, but increasingly became a factor thereafter. In the years after World War II, augmented funding of roads, intercity highways, beltways, and provisions for vastly improved suburban bus service were deeply injurious to the railroads' suburban revenues. Eventually, these developments and the general decline in railroad revenue would force the railroads out of the commuter business, with most of the still-existing lines taken over by regional or state transit authorities.

As late as the 1920s and 1930s, however, the railroads were still attempting to improve suburban service through the introduction of better equipment; automobiles and buses at that time had not yet made a drastic impact on the suburban lines, which continued to offer quicker and more reliable service. Electrification was one of the most important innovations during the first four decades of the twentieth century. Many railroads introduced clean, fast-accelerating electric trains, and this kept many passengers faithful to the train. The Long Island, because of heavy traffic on its western end in a totally urbanized environment, began experimenting with electrification as early as 1905. The construction of Penn Station and Grand Central Station in New York required both the Pennsylvania and New York Central to introduce some electric service to make possible the use of underwater and underground tunnels, and the experiments with electricity were sufficiently inspiring that the terminal electricity was greatly extended—the Pennsylvania even extended its electrified lines from New York to Washington and Harrisburg, Pennsylvania.[16]

Electrification was sometimes forced on the railroads by special conditions. In Chicago, the Illinois Central began electrified suburban operations in 1926, having been hectored by the city of Chicago to get steam trains from the beautiful lakeshore area of downtown Chicago. Doubtless a few decades later, diesel locomotives might have provided the same remedy, but over the years electrification worked splendidly for the Illinois Central and for the Chicago, South Shore, and South Bend Railway, an interurban line which came into the city on IC tracks. In the East, the Reading got into electrification because of the lack of capacity at its Philadelphia terminal (electric trains could be turned much more quickly and get out of the terminals much faster). The lack of space at the Lackawanna's Hoboken terminal caused that line to electrify a good deal of its suburban service between 1928 and 1931, although the Lackawanna had been upgrading its track and suburban stations with electrification in mind since 1910.

When the railroads began retrenching all passenger services in the 1950s and 1960s, commuter services, even though still subject to heavy demand, began to deteriorate badly. Equipment fell apart and was not replaced. Stations became shabby or uninhabitable, and continued to deteriorate because station agents or grounds personnel had been laid off. Many suburban stations were closed, causing passengers to wait on open platforms or under wretched lean-tos.

Eventually, it became obvious that allowing suburban train services to die was a terrible mistake. The state of Illinois built a number of massive expressways from the suburbs to Chicago after World War II, but these in turn became intolerable as people who abandoned the trains began clogging them. It did not go unnoticed that you could still get into the city faster on rickety commuter cars than you could on expressways with bumper-to-bumper traffic and many attendant accidents and delays. The equipment on the venerable Chicago and Northwestern Railroad had fallen apart by the mid-1950s, but when Chicago lawyer Ben W. Heinemann took over as President of the line in 1956 he concluded that he could get commuters back from the auto-choked, gas-fumed highways by putting on new streamlined, double-decker cars and push-pull diesel locomotives. Passengers came back in droves, and ridership on the old C&NW lines has remained strong since.

The situation in Chicago is perhaps typical of the other large cities where suburban rail traffic was traditionally important. All of the major commuter lines—those of the Illinois Central, the Burlington, the Rock Island, the Milwaukee, as well as the Chicago and Northwestern—were taken over by the Chicago Regional Transit Authority (now known as Metra). This quasi-public agency operates vital suburban services, usually over the tracks of the original railroads. Metra, like other such transit authorities, has worked hard to rehabilitate stations, provide new passenger cars, and keep them all clean.

With this infusion of public aid, suburban train service in the major cities where it once flourished—New York, Boston, Chicago, and Philadelphia—is probably a good deal better than it was thirty years ago. Train travel to the city's core through vast metropolitan territories continues to have obvious appeal. Even Los Angeles, which completely junked its system of interurban railroads after World War II, is turning its eyes to the development of a light-rail system using some abandoned rights-of-way. At present, no system seems better adapted than the railroad to fast transportation through congested urban areas.

Many state or regional sponsored transit authorities have done reasonably well with suburban train service. The New Jersey Department of Transportation offers better service today to New Brunswick and Princeton than the Pennsylvania did in the last years of its corporate existence, using fast electrified equipment. The cars assigned to this line (as well as other legendary New Jersey commuter lines—the old Lackawanna, Erie, Jersey Central) is spartan and unimaginative in design, and the New Jersey Department of Transportation doesn't seem to be able to keep the windows clean, so that whatever scenic delights New Jersey may hold are often invisible. But for the most part, the trains run on time, though perhaps not quite as unfailingly as the days of the 1930s and 1940s, when the suburban trains of the Erie and the Lackawanna ran on time ninety-eight percent of the time. Many older stations have been rehabilitated, and a few large stations— such as the beautiful art deco Penn Station in Newark and the Lackawanna's turn-of-the-century Hoboken terminal—have been lovingly restored.

It could be that something important was lost when the original railroads abandoned their suburban service to public control. Present-day operations are purely utilitarian, with few fripperies or aromas of distinct personality. The vine-covered stations of the Boston and Albany, lovingly maintained with garden patches and well-manicured lawns, are no more. Eccentric stations of individual design have given way to the erosions of time. And the ambience of new suburban stations is inevitably constricted and uninteresting. Often there is no agent, no newsstand, no shoeshine boy; sometimes no restroom; sometimes not even a place to sit down. Many older stations are converted to other uses, and instead of a comforting waiting room there is an antique shop, a real estate agency, or a boutique.

In their days of glory, the railroads operated their suburban lines with considerable individuality and panache. Public-sector suburban railroad services are largely unimaginative and standardized, although sometimes competently run. There are no suburban coaches of eccentric design and liveried colors. Gone are the Harvey Springsteads, Ben Days, and Samuel Johnson Snyders of the world—train crews are largely faceless toilers in the bureaucracy. Gone are the brightly polished, lovingly maintained steam locomotives that added charm and gaiety to commuting. There is no more Millionaire's Express, no electric Hot Shot, no Tuxedo Park Express. Private subscription cars with deep pile carpeting and wicker armchairs are a thing of the past. On the other hand, in the places where suburban railroading was once carried on in the grand manner (and now perhaps in one or two new places), the trains miraculously still run and do what is required of them. Nobody, in truth, has been able to think of a better way to get this particular job done.

It would be hard to say how many movies contained train arrivals and railway depot atmosphere. In Westerns, of course, the railroads were ubiquitous. In the 1952 classic *High Noon*, the ticking of the depot clock spells out the moment of truth for the town's only brave man—Gary Cooper *(Museum of Modern Art Stills Archive)*.

The open railway coach was peculiarly American and was ideally suited to the fluidity of our national life. "Sparking a girl" was a natural and everyday occurrence on the steam cars. Here, from the Paramount movie version of Theodore Dreiser's novel *Sister Carrie*, are Eddie Albert and Jennifer Jones in a ritual as old as civilization *(Museum of Modern Art Stills Archive)*.

Many of America's great resorts were literally creations of the railroad. Here, on March 14, 1896, a train has brought a covey of bluebloods and grandees to the Royal Poinciana Hotel in Palm Beach, Florida. Railroad magnate Henry Flagler erected a special railway trestle so that trains could reach his dream hotel *(Library of Congress)*.

This is the depot square in Wheaton, Illinois, in 1930. The coming of the train, as always, was a great social energizer in thousands of American towns. The clang of the bell, the puffs of smoke, brought everybody out of the stores, restaurants, and beauty parlors. When the trains came, things happened *(Chicago Historical Society)*.

One of the best-known public places in America, the concourse of Grand Central Station in New York, shown as it appeared in its glory years—in this case 1938. The great railway terminals of North America once gave people both a sense of grandeur and the notion that there could be uplifting places for all people *(New York Central Railroad)*.

Political campaigning by train was a regular ritual of American life during the golden age of the railroad. Here, campaigning for president in 1916, was Charles Evans Hughes and his wife posing for the photographer during the proverbial "whistle stop" appearance *(Burlington Northern)*.

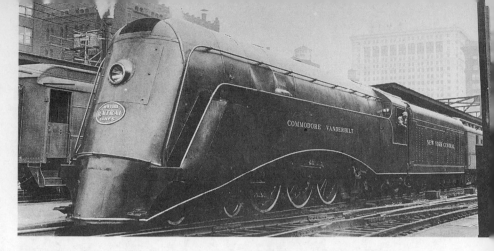

ABOVE: For the first half of the twentieth century, the major railroads ran passenger trains in high style—and on time. Herewith a newly streamlined steam locomotive (hopefully competition for the diesel) making its debut at the head of the New York Central's crack Commodore Vanderbilt in 1936 *(Bob Lorenz)*.

LEFT: As late as 1948, one railroad alone, the Pennsylvania, advertised fifteen trains a day between New York and Chicago. With the passing of a few years, and with a few spins of the airplane propeller, nearly all of these trains would be gone *(Author's collection)*.

BELOW: Midmorning train arrival on the Burlington at Hinsdale, Illinois, 1978. The comings and goings at the depot always produce a quickened pulse, a touch of human drama, a sense of the community of strangers.

Before there were jet airplanes everybody went by train—corporation presidents, baseball players, movie stars, grandma and Aunt Ida. Here on the open observation platform of the Pennsylvania Railroad's kingpin of the fleet, the Broadway Limited, was the King of Comedy, Charles Chaplin *(Pennsylvania Railroad)*.

The Turquoise Room of the Santa Fe Super Chief. This was one of the first private dining rooms on any regularly scheduled passenger train and characterized the pampering of passengers that prevailed on American railroads during the years of passenger travel *(Santa Fe)*.

RIGHT: Time was of the essence to the railroad; indeed the railroad probably created our present notion of time—social units measured in seconds and minutes. This enormous clock long presided over New York's legendary Penn Station *(New York Historical Society)*.

BELOW: For a long time railroads made special provisions for its female passengers, including "ladies only" cars in the early days. Shown here is the Ladies Lounge at Chicago's Northwestern Station newly remodeled (and for the last time) in 1947 *(Chicago and Northwestern)*.

ABOVE: A ritual as old as the railroad itself. These two little girls are putting a penny on the tracks to see what happens when the train passes by. This was once boys' work, but girls would no longer be denied life's simple pleasures. It was 1979 in the Chicago suburb of Palatine *(George H. Douglas)*.

LEFT: The United States never had true transcontinental trains like those of Canada. In the late 1940s such was proposed by railroad gadfly Robert Young of the Chesapeake & Ohio Railroad. But hard times were just around the corner for the railroads and the dream never really occurred *(B&O Museum)*.

The great Twentieth Century Limited left Grand Central Station from Track 29 for many years. This view from the 1920s offers ample proof that train travel was a stylish business as well as an essential part of the warp and woof of American life *(New York Central Railroad)*.

The commuting life. A scene familiar to millions of Americans in some of the nation's largest cities—the morning rush from train to office. Here surging forward are arriving passengers from two incoming trains at Chicago's Northwestern Station. With luck they will all be in their offices by nine o'clock *(Chicago and Northwestern Railroad)*.

If anyone suspects that railroad travel no longer casts a spell over the American psyche, they would do well to look at Washington's Union Station as it appears today, as fresh as a newly minted penny. Designed in the classical style by Daniel H. Burnham, the station has been completely renovated *(George H. Douglas)*.

It was an inspired idea to rejuvinate Washington's Union Station. It combines the railroad functions with those of a public mall containing boutiques, restaurants, recreational areas, and offices. The classic spirit and largesse of the original building have been retained, making a majestic space for the multitudes to enjoy *(George H. Douglas)*.

C·H·A·P·T·E·R 13

DOWN BY
THE DEPOT

The railroad had been the instrument that made suburbia possible; it had created commuting as a way of life for generations of Americans. The trip to the office on the 8:05 had a regular and recurring impact on the lives of millions of people: Perhaps it was the most frequent and habitual kind of relationship that the railroad would ever establish with the traveling public. But elsewhere in the nation, in thousands of small towns, most of them possessing only the slightest national significance, the railroad, if anything, had an even greater impact. The life-style of the commuter was standardized, routinized; his daily journeys to and fro were mostly lacking in drama or flourish. The suburban railroad station usually only provided a brief and fleeting impression to those boarding the trains in the morning and anxious to rush off to dinner in the evening. To the tired commuter, train travel quickly lost most of its color and distinctiveness. For over a century, however, the railroad and the railroad station were pregnant with meaning and high drama to people for whom the railroad continued to be a miracle—people strung out over vast lonely stretches of track.

For years, the railroad station, or railroad depot as it was usually called, was the locus of social activity in the majority of those small towns where the railroad played any role at all. The railroad station was not always at the geographical center of these communi-

269

ties. Indeed, as the towns grew there was always a strong tendency for people to move away from the tracks, to develop "better" parts of town removed from the sounds of the steam locomotive, from noisy switching activities, from the unloading of freight. But even where the railroad became relegated to its own quadrant, or to some industrial corridor, the railroad station and its immediate environment remained for a long time a highly important part of every community. And in many smaller communities, which had been nothing but creations of the railroad itself, the railroad station and right-of-way provided the most vital and dramatic presences of daily life. This was invariably the case because most small towns, by their very nature and locale, stood at distant remove from the cities and industrialized sectors of the nation. They remained isolated, becalmed, bucolic, even as the rest of the country gave up the rural and agrarian way of life. And many have remained so long into the twentieth century. Their location, "far from the madding crowd's ignoble strife," accounted for much of their charm, of course, but it also accounted for their social isolation and occasional inertia, for the slow and lonely pace of life. The railroad, however, provided the small town its link to the outside world—for nearly a century, sometimes its only link. More importantly, perhaps, it brought in some of the excitement, the quickened pulse of urban life. To the young of so many small towns, it afforded whatever there might have been of dreams of escape, of hope for an expansion of possibilities.

For this reason, whatever the placement of the railroad line, whatever the location of the station, the railroad environment and railroad doings figured prominently in small-town American life. Sometimes the railroad track paralleled Main Street from one end of town to another. Often the railroad and Main Street were one and the same place—in a great many towns the railroad was imbedded in an unpaved road as trains shared the right-of-way with wagons, wayward chickens, or cattle being driven to market. Nor did this distinction belong only to the smallest and most undeveloped of communities. Until well into the twentieth century, the Erie Railroad ran right down the middle of the main street in highly industrialized Passaic, New Jersey. So, too did the Pennsylvania Railroad in Xenia, Ohio.

Of course, many times the railroad skirted the edges of town; yet even when this was the case, the phenomenon that Freeman

H. Hubbard called "railroad avenue" held sway. Even when there were joint centers of focus—courthouse square or shopping district in one place, railroad in another—the railroad depot for a long time was the town's most dramatic and forceful center of activity. Some communities that grew up with the railroad made strong efforts to keep the tracks on the periphery, or relegated to a second-class neighborhood—this occasionally giving rise to the term "other side of the tracks," the sobriquet for run-down industrialized neighborhoods or shantytowns. Sometimes, the placement of the railroad was a matter of forethought and planning. In many western communities, the depot commonly appeared at one end of the main street. For example, the Grand Trunk Pacific (Canadian National) laid out many towns in the territories it developed, and these invariably used a standard plan with the principal street beginning right at the station's back door.[1]

Nearly always, though, the railroad station was a beehive of activity; its location was practically never a lonely part of town. If it started out as such, it would be swiftly brought into the human orbit. Nearly always, the railroad track and depot would have clustered around them other "service" facilities—livery stables, cafés, blacksmith shops, grain elevators, lumber and coal yards, mills, ice houses—and, as towns grew larger, factories and warehouses. Sometimes, the firehouse and the post office were located nearby. In the early days of railroading, before the coming of sleeping and dining cars, hotels were built near the railroad tracks for the accommodation of travelers—in fact, many early railroad lines were put down beside an already existing hotel or eating establishment. With the passage of time, the hotels across from the depot often became seedy, ramshackled places, while better hotels away from the tracks skimmed the cream of their trade.

Whatever configuration of buildings or service facilities may have existed near the depot in any particular town, the depot itself was a hub of activity, a focal point of energy and daily human contact. When trains were due, there was a noticeable flurry of directed motion as wagons, people expecting express packages, village loafers, and small boys were drawn to depot square as if by a magnet. The train track was the artery of small-town life, the station its heart, if never quite its soul. On the train, when it came in, was everything needed to keep life going, or at least, it seemed, everything that would provide life with some color or variety. Off the accommodation train in one grand dramatic moment were swept newspapers, mail, express. There was no federal parcel post until 1913, so before that time all packages shipped into town had to come by one of the express services and be picked up at the station. There were Sears Roebuck and Montgomery Ward catalogs, bank shipments, sewing machines, casketed human remains, students returning from college, blushing brides, muzzled dogs, hunting rifles, the new superintendent of schools, a soldier on furlough, jilted lovers and forlorn maidens, a salesman, or perhaps even a confidence man or seller of quack remedies. In one brief, shining moment, the whole town would be brought to rapt attention by this rich flourish of human pageantry.

The railroad station itself was always one of the most distinctive buildings in any small community. It was as easy to pick out by its style as the courthouse or (in later years) the post office. Not that small town railroad stations were architectural gems, but they had their own eccentric charm. Most of the small stations in America were built of wood, even well into the twentieth century. In the beginning, as befitting their utilitarian functions, many of them resembled nothing more than storage sheds, which, in essence they were. Beginning in the 1880s, however, and responding to the demands of local boosters and the traveling public, who called for stations that were something more than places to store freight, most railroads began to build small stations that were appealing to the eye and comfortable enough for human habitation. They may have continued to be spartan and wholly utilitarian structures, but their appeal was often augmented by flights of architectural fancy—classical or Gothic detail, romanesque clock towers, Chinese pagodas, eccentric bay windows, dormer roofs, and everywhere the ubiquitous laying on of Victorian gingerbread and tracery of every imaginable kind.[2]

Being essentially a utilitarian structure, the small-town railroad station tended to become stereotyped and standardized in its plan and layout, whatever freedom there may have been for eccentric variation in detail. So standardized did the layouts become that many railroads built hundreds of stations according to a few sets of specifications (A, B, or C plan, let us say—the one selected being determined by the size of the community and the expected use of the facilities). The very smallest of stations was sometimes nothing more than a shelter with a roof and three sides for protection against the elements. These were most often flag stations at which few trains stopped except on signal to the conductor or when passengers desiring to board operated a signal lantern to "flag" a train down. Slightly larger stations, without an agent, might be completely enclosed, although occasionally they might be maintained by a track walker or section hand.

Most typical of the small stations for the better part of a century was a layout that possessed, beside a general waiting room, a ticket and telegraph office, a baggage room, a men's room, and perhaps a special "retiring room" for women with toilet attached. Somewhat larger "combination" stations consisted of these facilities in addition to a room for incoming and outgoing freight. (When freight business in any town was voluminous enough, a separate freight station was built.) On the other hand, in countless small communities, all the important railroad functions were housed in one building, and the "agent" was a man of all work. That is to say, he sold tickets, assisted with the operation of trains by telegraph or telephone, handled baggage, mail, and express, and made out freight waybills.

The agent was a preeminently important individual in most small communities during the railroad era. Usually his "office" included a grilled ticket window facing the waiting room and more often than not a bay window on the track side so that he could look up and down the line for approaching trains. Most passengers thought of the agent as a ticket seller or baggage handler, but some were aware that he also had a vital function in the control of train movements. In the parlance of the Operating Department, the "agent" was usually called the "operator" because of his very vital function under the manual block system of operations where he served as the individual who manned the block and passed orders from the dispatcher to train crews. Many passengers were intrigued by this aspect of the agent's activities, and they were anxious to take a peek at his order board and the lamp in his bay window, which were essential for the orderly flow of traffic.

The station agent, above all, was a highly versatile functionary in the small towns of a century ago. He was the man to see about whether one's express shipment or the latest dress catalog had come in. Before the telephone, when the telegraph was the only means of swift electronic communication, he was often the only person privy to messages of vital human import—of storm and

stress, of floods and washouts, of birth and death—and he frequently had access through his apparatus to the news of the day
long before the city newspaper was thrown off the train. In some
communities, the agent doubled as postmaster, and it was not
unknown for him to be the barber, the seed dealer, or even the
dentist. A fair number of small towns used the station's waiting
room for church services, in which case the agent was a church
janitor as well.

Some agents took advantage of their pivotal position to order
needed goods from faraway places on a commission basis. Richard
W. Sears began his gigantic merchandising company as a station
agent in North Redwood, Minnesota, where, as a sideline, he sold
wood, coal, and lumber to nearby farmers and Indians. Later he
sold undeliverable watches that had been ordered from a firm in
Chicago, a business that became so good that he joined partnership with another watch manufacturer, A. C. Roebuck, creating
the enterprise which later burgeoned into the epic catalog business known to all Americans.[3]

In the typical small town, the agent was never a lonely individual, fingering his telegraph key and selling tickets in the short intervals immediately preceding train arrivals. The station was a hub of
activity all day long—sometimes all night long as well.
Accordingly, it was a magnet for persons of all ages and tempera-
ments. Naturally, when the train was due, the station attracted
those about to travel or those awaiting friends and relatives, but
more than purely utilitarian motives drew people to the station. In
many sleepy agricultural communities, the arrival of the steam
cars provided the day's only drama, the only evidence that there
were things in the world that transcended the humdrum and the
homespun. The coming of the train often cleared out the general
store or the barber shop or the apothecary shop—certainly whatever such establishments were located within easy walking distance
of depot square. In some communities, school was let out when
some crack flyer went by; in others, court proceedings were
recessed so that jurors (and perhaps even an accused murderer)
could partake of railway action. The whistle of an approaching
train seemed, as if by magic, to call to people from all points of
the compass, much like the musical notes of Hamlin's piper.
Whether those who pointed their steps to the depot were merely
onlookers or important functionaries—the drayman awaiting a

parcel or the village postmistress awaiting the dirty gray postal bag—train time was always a moment of heightened activity and intoxicating human interaction.

Even during the long quiet intervals between trains—and in many small communities these intervals could be excruciatingly long—the station tended to be a gathering place for hangers-on or loafers. The station was always the perfect spot for retired gentlemen, idlers of all kinds, champion talkers, crackerbarrel philosophers, out-of-work opinionizers, wine bibbers. And these, combined with whatever rail personnel may have gathered—track walkers, boomers, off-duty brakemen, even hoboes—provided the ingredients for a ready-made, and sometimes habitual, daily society. Some of these individuals muttered weak excuses that they were there to "help out" the agent in his regular chores, loading and unloading parcels or bags, perhaps. But for the most part, they were there because that is where the action was.

Probably no segment of the local population was more charmed and magnetized by the depot than the young, particularly young boys, and after school was let out in the afternoon scarcely a depot anywhere failed to be the second home to a gaggle of young lads drawn thither to watch the trains go by, to wave at the engineer, perhaps to live with the illusion of the more mature loafers that they were "helping out," or that they were somehow part of the railroad crew. Girls were less in evidence than boys, since the railroad was considered a dirty and dangerous place. Grant and Bohi, in their history of the country railroad station in America, pointed out that many families forbade their teenage daughters to hang around the depot since it might be frequented by traveling salesmen and other fast talkers.[4] (However true this may be, existing photographs of small-town depots record that not a few girls, like their brothers, were drawn the depot.)

But to boys, yes, to the American boy, the depot and its environs were a perpetual source of wonder and awe. There was nothing better in the small town. Loafing around the station, listing to railroad sounds, smelling railroad smells, this was the very zenith of boyish delight. Sometimes the agent would hand out small chores that were eagerly performed, gratis—the delivery of some package, the shoveling of snow from the doorway in winter. No boy could resist the golden opportunity when a train needed to be flagged to put the flag in its holder or hang out the lamp. Or bring in a pile of newspapers that had been hurled off a speeding express. It would have been a moment of consummate ecstasy to hand orders up to the engineer on an order hoop. But even if no chores were given out—and some agents had low tolerance for juvenile hangabouts—boys could always wave to engineers, walk along the rails, keep an eye on signals and switching activities, or be a passive onlooker of everything that transpired on the local railroad scene.

Boys could, of course, get into trouble and put themselves in jeopardy, which is why many agents and other railroad officials attempted to dust them off the property, but whatever efforts were put forward to diminish their presence was doomed to failure. Boys, being boys, would occasionally try to board slow-moving freights, climb onto boxcars spotted on a siding, climb up signal poles, scramble over bridges, teeter along the rails, play hopscotch on the ties, attempt to throw stones into coal cars, and sometimes play "chicken" with engineers by jumping off the rail at the last minute. And there was the inevitable penny or pebble on the track. Hardly a boy alive could resist the temptation to give this a try—perhaps it was a primitive David and Goliath impulse, perhaps a smug desire to bring a snorting, fiery dragon down to size, even though only in a symbolic way. The itch to discommode the monster (at least in the imagination) was irresistible. Curiosity, perhaps, was at the root of it. On the occasion of the inaugural run of the Boston and Lowell Railroad in 1835, one of America's primeval railroads, a small boy named Warren Teel stepped up to put a copper penny on the rail. As the lad himself told the story years later in the *Winchester Record,* he was admonished by a Colonel White standing hard by, who rebuked him with the warning that such an act might derail the train. But the stern colonel himself, or perhaps a lingering small boy buried deep inside himself, was smitten by the same curiosity and decided to try it himself, using a thinner silver sixpence. At the last minute, both boy and colonel leapt up to retrieve the coin, fearing dire consequences. After the steaming giant had passed by, the colonel proclaimed, "Sho! Might have put a silver dollar on the rail and done no harm."[5]

For boys almost certainly, perhaps for all depot watchers, there was something incomparably romantic and dramatic about the arrival of trains—this more than anything else engraved the railroad on the hearts of so many during its century-long reign. Stewart Holbrook, who spent much of his boyhood in northern New Hampshire near a little flagstop called Columbia Bridge on the Main Central, remembered above all else the nighttime arrival with the train whistling a mile down the track to foretell its arrival; then the light of the locomotive cutting through the night air like a knife, then the headlight trembling and rocking with the locomotive, then the engineer whistling for the stop, then the brake shoes being applied as the train came screeching to a halt. A routine visitation that doubtless was happening thousands of other places on this same day—yet every one of these arrivals always seemed to afford a never-to-be-forgotten moment.

> Once stopped, excitement mounted, for you know how it is when the fireman keeps ringing the bell, with its urgency to passengers to be spry and to get off and get on with speed and order. At Columbia Bridge as many as five persons might get off, but seldom more than two. Now and then a trunk came out of the mysterious recesses of the baggage car. Meanwhile we boys gaped up at the lighted windows, seemingly a full mile of lighted windows, strange heads and faces at each window—men, women, girls, babies, all strangers, all going somewhere, all impatient to get going again, some looking doubtless with amusement or condescension at the bucolics beside the track, quaint natives who still thought a train of steamcars a sight worth walking three miles to behold, even on a night dark and biting with cold. They were right, those amused or condescending passengers, those travelers who never knew Columbia Bridge except as a hick depot in the wilderness.... They were right, at least so far as I am concerned. Seeing a train of cars pass Columbia Bridge at night remains one of the greatest sights I ever saw. To watch a Constellation take off is as nothing in comparison.[6]

What was it about the passing of trains that made the small-town railroad depot such an exciting place? Undoubtedly, every small town had its events of greater excitement—its fairs, Fourth of July parades, its school jamborees, even perhaps its occasional scandals—but these were irregular high points punctuating long weeks or even months of routine and humdrum activity. The railroad drama was played out every day, and for the most part, with its evidence of technological muscle, it was a better show than most small communities could put on. The pageant of the passing of trains thus had a magnetic attraction for people of all ages and both sexes, not just small boys. As Holbrook's reminiscence makes clear, the arrival of trains was always a social event of considerable magnitude because it brought about contacts with the outside world that usually occurred in no other place and at no other time.

The depot, by a curious irony of history, not only had magnetic charms for humans, it seems to have cast its spell over animals as well. Over the years, the railroad depot seemed to be a gathering spot for man's best friend, the dog, and sometimes for other animals: cats, goats, pigs, even chickens. To be sure, some of these animals took root at the depot because they belonged to the agent or some other rail worker. On the other hand, many just seemed to have arrived on the scene and wormed their way into the daily routine by slow degrees. Agents or regulars might eventually confer mascot status on favored animals, but the record is also full of tales of animals who refused to leave after bidding good-bye to a beloved master who was off to war or the big city. The records are full, too, of stories of animals, mostly dogs, who became full-fledged rail workers, jumping up with order hoops or catching mailbags.

In an account of "rail dogs" in his book *Railroad Avenue*, Freeman H. Hubbard tells the stories of a great variety of these self-appointed railroad canines. There was the case of Shep of Ravenna, Nebraska, who met every train that arrived at the Burlington station there for fifteen years—he appeared mysteriously, as if from nowhere, whenever a train was due. When he died in 1943 of apparent old age, he was given a railroad funeral by the local agent, the section foreman, and switchmen. And there were dogs aplenty, apparently, who actually boarded trains and then returned to their base of operations. One of the most celebrated of such dogs was Admiral Dewey, who belonged to Miss Catherine J. Hughes, a New Haven agent at Rye, New York. Admiral Dewey took to leaping onto trains, and had to be returned to his owner by train crews. Eventually, Miss Hughes put a collar on the dog with the inscription "Pass Admiral Dewey to Rye." Somehow he would get back home, even though occasionally he would be gone for weeks at a time. Sometimes he would arrive at the Rye station, check on Miss Hughes to see that she was all right, and board the next train out of town.[7]

For animals, as well as humans apparently, the depot was a place of excitement and social interaction. It was not unknown for a number of animals to appear from several directions when trains were due. In the mid-1930s, P. J. Killen, agent of the Lackawanna at Oswego, New York, introduced his dog to the crew of the east-bound Lackawanna Limited, which stopped in town in the early afternoon every day. The dining car crew saved scraps and bones for the dog, which later was joined by others—sometimes as many as eight, and at one period this group included a cat that lurked off to one side but received a special handout. This ritual went on for fifteen years or more, even when the train became the stream-lined Phoebe Snow. The canine diners invariably showed up just before train time and were never disappointed.[8]

It must not be thought that the railroad depot was a place that only attracted those who were drawn hence by practical or worka-day pursuits, or others looking for excitement or sociability. Since in many small towns the railroad was the only representative of big industry, news of its functioning was carefully attended to even by those who had no time to hang out at the depot. In *Main Street*, Sinclair Lewis's satiric novel of small-town life, Dr. Will Kennicott, in spite of his busy medical practice, knew as well as anyone else the times of the trains. Hearing a whistle one morning on his rounds, he pulled out his watch and reflected: "No. 19. Must be 'bout ten minutes late." His wife, Carol Kennicott, a college gradu-ate who despised this small town of Gopher Prairie (assuredly based on Lewis's own home town of Sauk Center, Minnesota), for its intellectual sterility and standardized manners and morals, nev-ertheless regards the passing of the trains as "magic," perhaps the only magic available. She and her husband, like everyone else, knew everything about the railroad, even the names of its officers, probably in faraway St. Paul. As Lewis emphasized:

> To Gopher Prairie the tracks were eternal verities, and boards of railroad directors an omnipotence. The smallest boy or the most secluded grandam could tell you whether No. 32 had a hot box last Tuesday, whether No. 7 was going to put on an extra day coach; and the name of the president of the road was familiar to every break-fast table."[9]

Of course, none of this should be taken to mean that the rail-road was always a topic of unalloyed delight in the living and din-ing rooms of small town America. However much excitement and robust energy might have snapped and crackled with the passing of trains, and however brisk the environment of the station with its "live-wire" atmosphere, however much the railroad must have been invested with all the adventure of success in the realms of business and high finance, there was always a dark underside to the picture. It is perhaps fair to say that in so many of these small towns, so completely dependent upon the railroad for their subsistence and their contacts with the outside world, there was always a kind of love-hate relationship with the railroad and with depot square.

The reason for this was partly economic, to be sure. The railroad represented "big business," wealth, the machinations of faraway bankers and financiers. And, of course, the grain states had been witness to the very first violent animosities toward the railroad. The Grange and other farmers' organizations had taken aim at the collusive rate-making practices of railroads shortly after the Civil War. Naturally, farmers and residents of small towns did not hold *their* station agent, *their* familiar train crews, responsible for the excesses of the capitalists of New York or Boston, but the railroad as a business enterprise quickly became the object of derision in many small towns.

That wasn't all, however. There were many who felt that smoky steam locomotives and clattering cars disturbed the tranquility of rural communities and interfered with their traditional way of life. Many communities during the nineteenth and early twentieth centuries attempted to get railroads to relocate their rights-of-way, or to get them to move their rails away from the center of town, to eliminate yards, water tanks, sidings, workers' shanties, or whatever else there may have been of the railroad that was taken to be unseemly or tending toward pollution of the environment—the dumping of wastes, the emitting of smoke and flame. Some communities passed ordinances in an effort to curb railroad nuisances of one sort or another, and the town councils of numberless communities continually pestered railroad management for this or that improvement or abatement of nuisances. Usually railroads responded to such requests grudgingly, if at all. Sometimes they responded in vindictive or punitive ways. According to a famous railroad legend, the mayor of the town of Wayzata, Minnesota, got an injunction against the Great Northern Railroad in the 1890s and fined it for switching cars at night and whistling, which disturbed guests in a posh resort hotel on Lake Minnetonka nearby. Hot-tempered James J. Hill had the Wayzata station taken down and moved to the town of Holdridge a mile or so to the east. For about fifteen years, people in Wayzata had to hire livery service at fifty cents a head to reach the depot, and, of course, they had to use the same service to retrieve their way freight, which was also dumped off at Holdridge.[10]

And there were plenty of other grievances against the railroad. Many small towns resented the fact that the railroad often brought with it persons of unsavory character—the railroad worker himself was an "industrial" worker and not a bucolic, and in his wake might follow still less desirable citizens of the road—hoboes, tramps, bums, panhandlers, or others whose presence was considered deleterious. At division points and junctions, railroad workers had to be housed, and this not infrequently resulted in the presence of "shantytowns" and other neighborhoods thought to be of undesirable character.

The railroad was also considered a severe safety hazard. As towns grew, the intruding tracks had to be crossed by streets reaching out to new neighborhoods, and this invariably led to crossing accidents. By the early twentieth century, there were hundreds of thousands of grade crossings in the United States, and strong pressures were put upon railroads to reduce or eliminate these hazardous places. In urban areas, or areas of high traffic density, railroads did make determined efforts in this direction, but elsewhere the improvements were laggardly. The early diamond-shaped signs were eventually replaced by the now familiar crossbuck sign, sometimes augmented by crossing gates, an electric wigwag signal, and an alarm bell. At some busy crossings, railroads were required to supply crossing watchmen, whose penurious wages were probably less than the cost of providing grade separation. Out in the country, however, grade protection was minimal. In this, the United States differed markedly from most European countries, more densely settled and gentrified, where rails were carefully fenced and crossings much more elaborately protected. Accordingly, small-town America was constantly at warfare with the railroads, which were badgered to ameliorate crossing hazards. Local juries were sympathetic to families of persons killed or maimed in crossing accidents—of which there were thousands a year at one time.[11] This even though most accidents were the fault of the victims themselves, who disregarded the signals, attempted to bypass gates, or "raced the train" to the crossing. The railroad grade crossing was thus a constant source of ill will in many American communities.

But even beyond these sources of ill will, there were others, more deeply seated, more brooding, more fundamental. At the end of the nineteenth century, the old agrarian America was fading quickly away. The ideals of Jefferson and De Crevecoeur, according to which American civilization should rest on the healthy and idyllic existence of independent yeoman farmers and the cohesive and intimate force of small communities, had been cruelly eroded as America became a nation of cities and of mobile individuals and dispersed family units. The new American commonwealth that had arisen since the Civil War, teeming with immigrants from southern and eastern Europe, most of whom were drawn to cities and industrial pursuits, shifted the base of power in American society away from the farms to the big cities and industrial corridors. The small town was losing its grip on the American ideal, and it looked around for the sources of its discontent. Among the obvious and tangible victims of its wrath was the railroad.

It wasn't merely that railroads were big business, and sometimes a grasping big business that gouged the farmer of his profits. That was bad enough. But the animus toward the railroad in so many small communities was directed at something more dark and sinister. The railroad was a living symbol of this New World that had dared to take over American life—a lure, a Lorelei. It was the railroad that siphoned so many sons and daughters of countless remote farm cottages from the agrarian way of life and toward the big city. It was a veritable drain pipe that bled the human resources of these small towns; it was the evangelist, so to speak, that shouted all the virtues of city life.

It wasn't just that the railroad carried the members of the younger generation away to presumably greener pastures elsewhere, but that the railroad itself instilled the mores of travel, of mobility, of the sybaritic pleasures of "somewhere else." The railroad was in effect what John R. Stilgoe called a "metropolitan corridor," which is to say a conduit that made it possible for the younger generation to escape the rural homesteads and throw over their traditional folkways and values. The railroad itself was of this hated metropolitan world, not of the small towns that it merely served in cold disdain. But what is more important, the railroad was the only agency of the outside world that had the ability to beckon to the young, and offer promises of the more fulfilling world that lay beyond.

It was perhaps an oft-told tale—one remembers the old refrain of the music halls, "How Can You Keep Them Down on the Farm Once They've Seen Paree?"—the delights of city life sour the young on the "chores" of the farmstead: the early risings, the undependability of harvests, the slopping of hogs, the milking of cows, the locusts and other pests, the inexorable demands of a 365-day-a-year livelihood. And it wasn't only the harshness of farm life that drew the young away; it was the parched and sterile social life of the small community. There was so little to do there, and so much more to do in the metropolis. And somehow, this wider, more glamorous world was advertised, or at least hinted at, by the railroad and the bustling activity of the railroad depot.

It is not hard to understand why it was that the elders of so many small American towns had a smoldering fear and distrust of the railroad and often forbade their young to hang out down at the depot. The depot was the place where one learned of the outside world, of the city. Here it was that the kingdom of steam and electricity took over. At the hardware store, the ice cream parlor, or the general store, there was none of the sense of urgency, of scurry, of split-second timing that there was down at the depot at train time. Here there were clocks that gave time accurately to the second; here was the operator tuned into the outside world with his open telegraph key—"the live wire," as they used to say. And young boys who traveled to the place where the telegraph ended were themselves said to be "live wires," people of bustle and promise. They would forsake hickory shirt and overalls for a snappy broadcloth suit and bow tie; they would bristle with energy and with the desire to "make the grade" (another neat railway metaphor).

Even for those who were not tempted immediately away, there was always something beckoning, enticing, down at the depot, something of the promise of a brighter world. Was it the pile of newspapers thrown off the train giving vent to the pleasures and dalliances of the world outside? Was it the slick-coated brochures available in most stations luring one to distant resorts and places of leisured wonder? Was it the rack of timetables with the thousands of places one might visit? Was there something about the trains themselves? When the "limited" or "express" train made its grudging and half-hearted stop to discharge local passengers, the depot loungers could look up into the Pullman cars now lit by electricity (the vast majority of rural areas would not receive electricity until after World War I), the touch of luxury in the green silk curtains, the nickel-plated plumbing fixtures, the presence of painted, well-coiffured women looking down in disdain at the yokels slouching on their benches, corncob pipe in mouth. The Pullman car was the living embodiment of everything that was drawing the young away. It above all else, perhaps, caused the small town's reflective thinkers to abjure the effects of the railroad and refuse to allow their more suggestible daughters the freedom of the station platform. Yes, they might well be seduced by some fast talking drummer of trade or city slicker; even more likely they would be seduced by the overpowering call of luxury, of travel, and a better life.

A great many American writers who grew up contemporaneously with the railroad's golden age have given eloquent testimony to the sway that the depot and railroad ambience generally held over their youthful imaginations. This seemed to be especially true of so many midwestern writers, for whom the railroad represented the way and manner of escape from the dreariness of small-town life. F. Scott Fitzgerald, in his novel *The Great Gatsby*, remembered the Midwest of his boyhood through the power and high style of the railroad that delivered him from it. Hardly a small-town boy, having been brought up in St. Paul, Minnesota, he remembered most vividly the trains that carried him to and from college. He remembered the great metropolis, Chicago, "the old dim Union Station at six o'clock of a December evening…the long green tickets clasped tight in our gloved hands." There were "the murky yellow cars of the Chicago, Milwaukee & St. Paul Railroad, looking cheerful as Christmas itself on the tracks beside the gate." It was a smug, comfortable, stylish world, this world of the railroad when it got where it was really going—*out* of these small towns. "That's my Middle West—not the wheat or the prairies or the lost Swede towns, but the thrilling returning trains of my youth."[12]

Nearly the same emotion was expressed by Thomas Wolfe, who grew up in North Carolina, and remembered the railroad as somehow providing the way of escape from banality, the way to the sophisticated urban world beyond. His novels *You Can't Go Home Again* and *Of Time and the River* provide numerous scenes of travel aboard sleek luxury express trains, which magically transformed a person from the banal environment of the small town into a quite different world, one where the heart beats faster, the blood races, the glands do their work. In this other "swift" world, the senses are more acute, the sensibilities livened. "One looks at all the pretty girls with a sharpened eye and an awakened pulse. One observes all the other passengers with lively interest, and feels that he has known them forever." The passengers here seem to be so well dressed, so chic, their conversation is fluid and charming. They are seemingly possessed of aspirations and imaginative gifts. "In the morning most of them will be gone out of his life; some will drop out silently at night through the dark, drugged snoring of the sleepers; but now all are caught upon the wing and held for a moment in the peculiar intimacy of this Pullman car which has become their common home for the night."[13]

For not a few American writers, the train is not only an energizer of dreams but the only possible route of escape from a parched, sterile environment. A number of the characters of the stories of Sherwood Anderson, stunted in their personal lives and seemingly locked into their existence in some woebegone farm town, summon up the courage to run away, catch onto the back of some train as if their very lives depended upon it. Theodore Dreiser, another famous American writer, was himself one such a character. He had spent his teenage years in Warsaw, Indiana, and finding all avenues to success blocked there, suddenly announced to his mother one day, "Ma, I'm going to Chicago." His mother, astonished, asked, "When?" "Today" was the answer, and Dreiser was on the next train, as soon as he could get his bag packed, even though he had only confused and inchoate ideas of what he would do with himself there. His mind was awash with dreams of sitting in an office behind a rolltop desk, dreams that were impossible of realization in Warsaw.[14] In his autobiography, *Dawn*, Dreiser also recalled that one of his older sisters, a few years before, had gotten into the practice of hanging around the depot in another Indiana town where the Dreiser family had lived, and one day attempted to board a train leaving town. She was only prevented from doing so by a kindly agent who recognized her, sensed that she was running away, and successfully talked her out of going.

For so many of these sons and daughters of the middle border, the railroad train and the railroad depot represented just such a crucial and dramatic crossroads. The depot was the place where one said good-bye to family and loved ones. The minute one stepped on board the train, one could be renouncing one life and taking up another. As the train pulled out of town, and the wooden depot, the water tank were left behind, one could be on the way not only to another location but to another life. A curtain could suddenly be drawn across one's lifeline: One part of life's experiences would be in the past, another, eagerly awaited, would be yet to come.

For the eagerly expectant young, the "seeking young" as Theodore Dreiser called them—and in America most young are "seeking," striving to better and improve their lot—the railroad depot was the place where their quest began. It represented some great moment of truth. For their elders, for those clinging to the safety and security of small-town life, the station represented the threat of a slippery slope; the railroad itself represented the agency which could bring their way of life to a tragic end.

More often than not, these fears of the railroad were not consciously articulated, or only expressed in vague and amorphous ways. For even those who felt most threatened by this organ of the great world outside could not deny its importance to their own world, its supreme importance in sustaining the social and economic life of their community. Nor doubtless could they deny that the railroad quickened their own pulses and added some color and vitality to their own lives. Whatever there may have been to fear of the railroad, nearly all Americans in the late years of the nineteenth century and early years of the twentieth had at worst an ambivalent relationship with this the premier means of moving things from place to place.

This love-hate relationship with the railroad, if that it should be called, would of course change drastically in small-town America over the next several generations. Between the World War I and World War II, many thousands of towns lost their train service. Flag stops were dropped from the timetable; accommodation trains were eliminated. Express and mail service were dropped; agents were reassigned; the telegraph key grew silent. Many stations became threadbare and were boarded up. The erstwhile "live-wire" atmosphere of depot square receded into the happy pockets of memory. Another generation would be troubled more by the lure of the automobile than of the railway train. As the dominant force of the railroad faded, parents would be more grieved by their daughters dancing in roadside speakeasies, drinking wood alcohol, and spooning in the back of a roadster than by the beckoning hand of the Pullman car.

Accordingly, as the railroad depot assumed a progressively less important role in so many small towns across America, most people forgot that it had once been a place that inspired anxiety and distrust as well as excitement and high drama. With the passing of a few generations, the ambience of depot square would only be remembered fondly through a kind of mellow, amber haze. Still, those for whom the memory of the old-time railroad depot remains green now have a hard time recalling it as anything other than a place of unalloyed charm and delight—which, for the most part, it assuredly was.

C·H·A·P·T·E·R 14

THE GREAT
TERMINALS
IN CITY LIFE

There were tens of thousands of functional stations in the United States during the golden age of railroading, and they were a vibrant symbol of the railroad industry to generations of Americans. Their very existence and the day-to-day bustle of their activity provided the pulse of life to the many small towns strung out across America—some within easy reach of a great metropolis, some in the faraway hills or vast prairies—getting their strength and significance from the fact that they were linked together, part of a giant network, part of a great and cohering industrial force.

But as the United States became a highly urbanized nation after the Civil War, as large cities came to represent the dominant force in American life, most Americans came to think of the railroad as the tool of these great urban centers. The railroads had made these cities possible—and in some cases, Chicago for example, had built them from scratch. So most Americans came to think of the large cities as the places where all railroad lines began—and terminated. One boarded the train in Grover's Corners or Plainfield or Storm Lake, but one was *going to* New York, or Chicago, or Kansas City.

It had been this centrifugal force of the cities, this notion of the primacy of the metropolis, that had provoked a smoldering rage in the farmer, the small-town shopkeeper or lawyer, had fomented their suspicions of the long-distance luxury train, with its well-appointed, nickel-plated Pullman cars, its sleek, citified passengers. But the pull of city life was undeniable even to those most determined to resist it. And it did not take the railroads long to decide for themselves that they had given birth to what John R. Stilgoe called a "metropolitan corridor," a permanent lifeline between cities and other metropolitan or industrial centers.

With the establishment of these corridors, passenger trains would no longer be "way" trains or "accommodation" trains, but crack limiteds between New York and Chicago, or between St. Louis and Washington. As trains lost their local character and became the servants of these corridors, they began to take on the style and characteristics of the urban areas they so manifestly served.

Because cities and railroads were an integral and necessary part of the "new industrial America," few city folk questioned the presence of the railroad upon the urban landscape. For the most part, the railroad was taken for granted in cities, understood to be a modern necessity. There were good reasons for this. In its early days, when diminutive steam engines little bigger than toys thrust outward from cities like Charleston, or Boston, or Baltimore, the railroad was not intrusive; it represented only a convenience and, except to those frightened by the newness of machines, not a public nuisance. Also, in America, unlike Europe, cities grew up with the railroads, so that railroads seemed to be tied to the importance and prosperity of cities. Accordingly, little effort had been made to keep the railroad industry in harness, to keep tracks and railroad yards from blighting the urban landscape. In Europe, great pains were usually taken to keep rails on the periphery of cities, because cities were principally perceived to be places of residence, of parks and pleasure gardens, of sedate public buildings. There was no notion of some fundamental identity between city and industry of the kind that became seemingly self-evident in the United States.

Since railroads were considered necessary to the health and prosperity of urban life, efforts were not made to keep railroad tracks from the city's core. Except in a few isolated instances, railroad builders were allowed to lay down lines wherever they wanted. Giant, noisy, steamy railroad yards were constructed anyplace the railroad company could cheaply buy real estate. When the

Illinois Central Railroad was built into the city of Chicago, the city fathers permitted tracks to be laid right out on the beautiful shore of Lake Michigan; they even encouraged the railroad to build in that place that should have been left sacrosanct. Local authorities felt that the railroad, to maintain its position, would have to build dams, walls, aqueducts, and other structures that would also have the effect of protecting the ornate mansions then going up on Michigan Avenue. (Long-range planning seems to have meant nothing to city leaders at that time.) Curiously, even in places where there was some effort of planning, railroad lines were not excluded. In Pierre L'Enfant's plan for Washington, there were originally provisions for tracks and even a depot to be erected on the mall—a provision, luckily, that was never carried out.[1]

In the years after the Civil War, as America's cities grew to gargantuan proportions, few hindrances were put on the railroad as it built its lines into the very heart of the city. Occasionally, the cities balked and the railroad was banished from certain areas. Tightly packed New York eventually banned the steam cars of the all-powerful Commodore Vanderbilt below Forty-second Street, although once they had run to the southern end of Manhattan island. On the other hand, the famous "Chinese wall" built by the Pennsylvania Railroad in the center of Philadelphia, which made a frustrating puzzle of that city's inner core, took the better part of a century to come down. Even under the best of circumstances, the railroad was never banished very far. In New York City, railroad freight lines continue to run down the west side of Manhattan. And for years the numerous lines coming into New York from the west and east completely dominated the harbor of the city with their multitude of tattered ferry houses, freight terminals, coal stations, and livestock and produce warehouses. Their barges, tows, and lighters clogged the Hudson and East Rivers making the area unsuitable for recreational purposes.

Outside the city's core, the situation was, if anything, even worse. In these outlying areas were invariably located the factories, coke plants, refineries, steel rolling mills, and the many smelly industries that depended on the railroad for their raw materials and their trade. In the shadow of these unpleasant and untidy environments grew debased residential neighborhoods, many of which rapidly deteriorated further into slums, so that polluted industrial areas and the besmirched places of human habitation near them gave the fringe areas of most cities an unsavory character lacking in many older European cities.

In the twentieth century, reformers and city planners often looked back ruefully and lamented that things hadn't been done differently. Lewis Mumford, historian of cities and of technology, complained that allowing railroads the run of the cities brought about countless meaningless neighborhoods, with "shattered fragments of land, with odd shapes and inconsequential streets and avenues, left over between the factories, the railroads, the freight yards and the dump heaps." In the nineteenth century, in the complete absence of municipal regulation, railroads had been allowed to define the character of cities, and grab for themselves highly desirable locations for marshaling yards, coal dumps, and roundhouses. "Thus the railroad carried into the heart of the city not merely noise and soot but industrial plants and debased housing that alone could thrive in the environment it produced."[2]

The fringe areas of the great cities, the "railroadized" industrial corridors, became the most unseemly, sometimes the most revolting, parts of the national landscape. Utopians like Mumford believed that railroad yards and polluting industries should have been located in wide open spaces, but they were never able to explain how these areas would have been prevented from becoming "cities" with the same characteristics, because in an economy which is highly industrialized, the muscle of the economy cannot be separated from the heart; commerce cannot be separated from industry.

On the other hand, there was no doubt that the railroad defined the quality of the urban landscape, perhaps besmirching it in ways that might have been prevented with a modicum of planning. It is hard to deny a sameness, a gray uniformity, to these fringe city areas, and they had the power to lacerate the eye of the typical traveler riding the crack limited express train from more pastoral environs. In the 1920s, writer Edmund Wilson rode the Pennsylvania Railroad from New York to his suburban hometown of fashionable Red Bank, New Jersey. On emerging from the Hudson River tunnel, he noticed the drabness of the industrial marsh extending to Newark and beyond. Here, he remarked, even the presence of a church seemed to be out of place, even obscene. There were factories by the hundreds making everything conceivable in the world from paints, chemicals, fountain pens, mattresses, ketchup, and machine parts, to safety razors, umbrellas, fire extinguishers, and gum drops, and it all gave the impression of tremendous vitality and energy. There were human habitations, but they seemed to be lacking in love, and caring, and were besmirched with the same grime as the factories around them. There were "feeble-looking houses, unpainted and gray, which, but for an occasional line of clothes drying in the tainted air, would have seemed bleached to as complete a death as the sea they were islanded in."[3]

But the railroad was always more than "heavy industry" to American cities, and cities were never defined only by their industrial fringe. Americans were becoming an urbanized people at the end of the nineteenth century, and their cities were rapidly becoming places of sophistication, of convenience, of modernity. The railroad would have an important effect in making all of these qualities possible, so that whatever blight it might have brought to the urban landscape, it also helped create the metropolitan life-style that continues to charm and energize Americans in our own time.

The typical American, even in the early days of railroading, had good reason to be thankful for the convenience and proximity of the railroad and its passenger terminals. The railroads may have hogged some of the best real estate in town, but this invariably also provided the hitherto incredible luxury of permitting rail passengers to step on a train right in the heart of the city and travel to the heart of another city—perhaps going from a luxury hotel in one of these cities to another such in a distant city without having to go outdoors. Or one could board a train in New York, or Boston, or Chicago, be encapsulated in comfort and grandeur, and delivered in high style to one's own isolated hometown. This the railroad could do for them—a convenience forever denied to the woebegone airline passenger of the present day.

But it could do a great deal more. The railroad was the infrastructure that kept the nation together, so it provided a kind of human community, a bond of feeling and a commonality of interest. In spite of the constant fears that the railroad was an octopus whose tentacles reached out to strangle farms and hamlets, it was also a lifeline that made cities possible out of the roots of rural and small-town America.

Sometimes, the linkages provided by the railroad were not

merely suggestive but tangible. Helen Hooven Santmyer, who lived her entire life in Xenia, Ohio, recalled numerous train trips she took as a young woman to Penn Station in New York. There was a porter on the train named Noah who had come from Xenia, and the railroad wisely assigned him to the sleeping car on the train that went through Xenia. Mrs. Santmyer never forgot how pleasant it was both as a child and an adult to be remembered by Noah in the vast, monumental cavern of Penn Station.

> He knew everyone from his native town; he never failed to speak to a fellow citizen who came down the steps in New York and passed him on the way to the Pullmans. "Howdy, Miss!" he would say, and with a smile that showed all his teeth would lift his uniform cap: "Goin' home with us? How's your Pa? Ain't carried him for a long while."[4]

The city railroad terminals that were built in the last quarter of the nineteenth century and the first quarter of the twentieth were the most lavish and memorable symbol of the railroad to most Americans. As such, they were pregnant with meaning to people traveling to the great cities, and they did much to fix the quality of city ambience to those who had come to the city to make a new life there. Even more importantly, they were a gathering place for democratic man, a place where all manner of individuals, all classes of society, could mingle—their comings and goings, their motives, and their human purposes on display for all to see. If the railroad terminals were not the heart of a modern commercial society, they were clearly at least the lungs, a place of transpiration, of social metabolism, a place where the national way of living and of doing things became manifest.

The railroad terminal was one of the few universal public buildings that drew all citizens. It was as commanding in the typical city as the cathedral was in the Middle Ages, and even more important in daily life. There were few other buildings in the city's core that held meaning for everyone. The architecture was as recognizable as that of the public library, the courthouse, city hall, or the post office, but mostly those places drew people performing specialized missions. The railroad was always the largest, most pulsating, nodal point in the system that constituted the economic and social life of the nation.

The railroad terminal was also somehow a microcosm of city

life; scarcely another single place could make such a claim since the city by its very definition seemed to allow no small model of itself, no place where its essence could be summed up. But here in the great railroad terminal, one could see on display everything that made social life tick: urgency, mobility, response to desire and aspiration, standards of dress, habits of thought, peculiarities of speech, ebb and flow, joy and sorrow, motion and emotion, parting and reunion. Here was every manner of person: businessmen scurrying to conclude a deal; the failure returning home, that "place where when you have to go there they have to take you in"; soldiers and sailors going off to war; teary-eyed youngsters going off to private school, or to camp in summer; newly married couples beginning their honeymoon; the wife bidding her husband good-bye; the strained parting with the rejected lover; the traveling salesman or the cardsharp to whom the railroad train was lifeblood; immigrants with their bundles starting off on a wholly new life; an extradited suspect chained to the sheriff's deputy from some far-distant county. The same human pageant was to be seen as in the small-town depot, but here it unfolded on an epic scale, a veritable flood tide of humanity passing through the terminal's gates minute by minute and hour by hour.

The giant railroad terminal was not, curiously, quick to make its appearance. In the first three or four decades of railroading, there was little impetus to provide passengers more than crude, elemental, makeshift, uncomely, and basely utilitarian structures. Our experience thus was quite different from that of many European countries, where the railroad men immediately perceived the importance of having their stations, and above all their city terminals, stand as an ensign of railroad power and aspiration. In England, when the London and Birmingham Railroad was built— and today railroad historians have considered this the world's first "trunk railway"—it was immediately thought to be necessary to raise a monumental station in London. English poet and writer John Betjeman, who wrote a charming little history, *London's Historic Railway Stations,* opined that the line's builders perceived from the outset that the railroad station would be to the modern city what the gate was to the ancient city, and that, accordingly, the London and Birmingham "must be symbolized by a monumental entrance." This monumental entrance, Euston Station, built in the 1830s, was designed by a distinguished architect and Royal

Academician, Philip Hardwick. He was charged with the project of producing "a gateway from England's capital and heart, London, to her stomach and toyshop, Birmingham."[5] Alas, this magnificent edifice was torn down in the 1960s and replaced by an eye-lacerating monstrosity, proving that even the English don't always preserve their historical treasures. The point is, though, from the early days of railroading, they had immediately grasped the architectural significance of railway stations.

No such visions of architectural glory filled the minds of early American railroad builders. The city railroad station was not seen as anything other than a place to stop the train, to load and unload. From early days, city terminals, like all others, were called "depots," that is, places to store cargoes, including human cargoes waiting to board the train. Even in the cities, terminals were seldom more than enormous barns or sheds that provided a claustrophobic haven for passengers, goods, locomotives, and rolling stock; they were smoky, dirty, and uninhabitable places. Long after they gave up the practice of using old tollhouses or coach houses from a bygone era, railroads invested little money on stations even in large cities. When the Baltimore and Ohio extended its first line into Washington, D.C., the nation's capital, their station there was nothing but the back of a tailor's shop.

Architectural distinction was unheard of in the first two or three decades of railroading. Sometimes, as in the station built in Lowell, Massachusetts, in 1835, a feeble effort was made to copy classic architectural models. This structure resembled a Doric temple that carried the track through a colonnade, but the overall visual impression was that of a castle suitable for Count Dracula or one of his lesser henchmen.

The first terminal of any size to cater to the human needs of passengers was the station of the Old Colony Railroad in Boston, which was built in 1847. Officially called the Old Colony and Newport Depot, it was known to generations of Bostonians and other travelers as the Kneeland Street Station. From the outside, the station possessed little architectural charm, but at least the trains stayed out in back, where they properly belonged. The interior was the source of some comfort, since the station was built to exude some gentility to passengers of the great Fall River steamship line. The station had a high-ceilinged smoking room lit by gas and equipped with inside shutters. There were beautifully

wainscoted walls and ceilings, and, adding a proper note of gentility, there were a barber shop, telegraph office, newsstand, lavora-
tory, bootblack's stall, baggage room, lady's salon, and so on. In
1852, the Kneeland Street Station became the first station to
charge a small fee for checking baggage, in order to discourage
the habit of leaving parcels in the station for weeks at a time. The
response to this innovation among tight-fisted Yankees is about
what might have been expected: a storm of protest was raised
against such gouging.[6] But the practice persisted.

City terminals of more monumental size and importance began
to arise in the years after the Civil War, although the history of
civic architecture in America shows that it took a long time for any
kind of distinctive station style or design to emerge. For the most
part, barns just got larger or were attached to Victorian-style office
buildings. The early Van Buren Street Station in Chicago (later La
Salle Street Station) was of this type, as were early versions of the
Grand Central Station in New York. But in the newly affluent
America, architecturally "crafted" stations were soon called for.
Once again, highly refined Boston led the way. When the Boston
and Providence line proposed to build a station in the fashionable
Back Bay section of Boston, the resulting structure was specifically
designed to suit its sedate surroundings. This station, called the
Park Square Station, was the result of an actual architectural competition, and went under construction in 1872. The design and
materials resembled those of Memorial Hall at nearby Harvard
University, and there was no complaint that the building looked
unseemly in Back Bay. The building was of a gentle English Gothic
style, with a finely proportioned clock tower. In the large train
shed, there was an attempt made to imitate the famous pointed
arch of the great St. Pancreas Station in London. All on one level,
the structure gave a feeling of openness and airiness.

In one way, the Park Square Station was a great advance,
because it clearly recognized the importance of human comfort
and civility in a purely utilitarian structure. The building looked
as if it were inviting for human purposes. A librarian named Justin
Winsor wrote in the *Library Journal* in 1879 that the plan of the station would make a better library than any such then in existence.[7]
There was a lofty general waiting room with rose windows and
clusters of gaslights, and delicate iron tracery covered the steam
radiators. Above all, human comfort was being given prime con-

sideration. There was a reading room and a billiard room. A nostalgic Bostonian of the period remembered the station as the show building of Back Bay in the 1870s and 1880s: "Its gentle English Gothic exterior, its finely proportioned clock tower, its graceful facade, were the pride of our town, and the atmosphere of elegant social intercourse which pervaded its waiting rooms, its exclusive barbershop and even its refined washrooms was wonderful."[8] The station, alas, did not survive to the twentieth century. Like the Kneeland Street Station and two others, it was superseded by the great Boston South Station in 1899.

During the 1880s and 1890s, as passenger traffic increased and the demands on urban terminals became unrelenting, large and massive terminals were on the drawing boards of American architects, most of whom had been trained in Europe and eclectically followed traditional European styles. The most distinguished American architect of this period was Henry Hobson Richardson, who began using a Romanesque style in his large public edifices. The style he evolved, occasionally called "Richardson Romanesque," has been scorched by a number of later architectural critics, especially those of the "form follows function" persuasion, insisting that a railroad station should look like a railroad station and not a church or cathedral. Of course, this merely begs the question. What should a railroad station look like? Richardson's Romanesque-inspired stations somehow marvelously captured the age and symbolic significance of the railroad in the 1880s. The Richardson style of public building (and Richardson personally did not design any of the truly large terminals in his style, although he did create many lovely smaller models for the Boston and Albany Railroad) was massive, often with impressive towers. These buildings exuded an aroma of power and solidity, of comfortable self-assuredness. On the other hand, Richardson did not follow the Romanesque style slavishly, but molded it to its modern use. The architects who followed Richardson's inspiration, as, for example, in the great union stations of Indianapolis, Louisville, and St. Louis, and the Grand Central Station in Chicago, learned to play around with the style and adapt it to its new human ends. The solid masonry seemed somehow harmonious to railroad engineering generally, especially at this time when railroads were building massive bridges and viaducts of stone and reinforced concrete. Some snobbish architectural critics were to say that these buildings were squat and brutal looking. The truth is, they were not. Anyone who looks at the Union Station in St. Louis with its soaring, eccentric clock tower, and the diversity of its several segments, each of a different and whimsical nature, will see that American architects were coming up with something completely new on their own with this imported style.

If there are any doubts that these stations had as a principal function human adaptation and amusement, the interiors of most of these stations leave little doubt: Most of them continue to cast a spell over visitors a century or more later. The interiors of the Romanesque stations were, of course, awe-inspiring, enshrining the dominant force of the railroad in stone and marble. Jeffrey Richards and John M. MacKenzie, two English historians of the railroad station, found themselves much more impressed by some of these interior spaces in the Romanesque stations than their more sniffish American counterparts. Pointing specifically to the St. Louis Union Station of the 1890s, they commented:

> Every round-arched opening was made an excuse for a riot of sculptural detail spreading out into a great fan. Female figures with arms outstretched were a recurrent motif. The water fountain became an altar, standing on marble pillars and graced by its own fan design. The ticket office was surmounted by a great mural bearing all the symbols of engineering success, a multi-arched bridge, river steamers, and, of course, the steam engine arriving from the left and dominating all.[9]

As an architectural style, Romanesque seemed to have the advantage of tremendous versatility. Some of the stations may have emerged from the drawing boards as hodgepodges, as disorderly and eclectic monstrosities. But there were a number of obvious masterpieces. There seemed to be no limits to this basically good idea. In Canada, for example, American architect Bruce Price (father of famed etiquette authority Emily Post), designed for the Canadian Pacific Railroad two inspiring stations in Montreal, the Windsor Station and the Place Viger. These stations, which subtly incorporated the influence of French chateaux, gave birth to the so-called "Canadian Pacific" style of architecture, and can also be seen in some of the much admired Canadian Pacific hotels, such as the Chateau Frontenac in Quebec and the Chateau Laurier in Ottawa.

There were six large railroad terminals built in Chicago in the forty-year period between 1885 and 1925—more than in any other American city. Before the turn of the twentieth century, Romanesque styles prevailed and several stations in that mold were built. One of the finest examples of the style in the country was the Grand Central Station, opened in 1890, and for most of its history the Baltimore and Ohio's station in Chicago. Designed by architect Spenser Solon Beman, the station was hardly gigantic in size—its train shed covered only six tracks—but it is a fine example of how the Romanesque style was developed to serve the needs of the traveling public. The building was L-shaped, with a carriage court on the long side of the L, and the waiting room on the south side; the train shed fitted snugly into the angle between the two. There was a clock tower at the corner, with clocks facing in four directions (there were real chimes in the early days). The building was of Connecticut brownstone, brown-pressed brick, terra-cotta, Tennessee marble, granite, and iron.

How convenient it all was. There was a graceful porte cochere entrance on Harrison Street, the longest frontage, having three arches that looked small enough to be the entrance to a mansion, but that could actually contain a large number of omnibuses, cabs, and private carriages. The waiting room had floors and walls of marble; there were large and graceful arched windows of imitation Mexican onyx. The ticket office was easily accessible—only a few steps away. Another few steps away was a gracious restaurant, a few steps down marble stairs on the south end. The details and furnishings of the waiting room were reminiscent of a fine home. It was a warm and comfortable place. In addition to the marble floors and stained-glass windows, there was a massive fireplace, and, in the early years, rocking chairs. Even the doorknobs had scrolled floral pattern ornaments. The tracks were enclosed by fancy iron grillwork; the train shed, open on one side due to its small size, was light and airy.

In the early years, the station had in the basement a room that was fitted out pleasantly for mothers with children. Like so many stations of that day, Chicago's Grand Central had an Immigrant's Room, where newly arrived citizens could be cared for and given directions. Here there was a large bathroom where the dust of travel could be removed. Attendants dispensed fine and coarse brushes, soap, towels, water, and tubs (all at company expense), to allow foreign visitors the opportunity to spruce up before continuing their journeys. Altogether, Grand Central Station had a warm glow of human habitation about it—it was at the same time generous, commodious, yet easily accessible and compact.[10]

As the twentieth century dawned, in fact even before it dawned, city railroad terminals in America would have to become much larger in size, much more monumental and epic in their appearance. After the opening of the huge Boston South Station, no more gigantic overarching train sheds were to be built. They had presented enormous difficulties, and nearly all were eventually torn down. In 1907, the new train shed at the Lackawanna's terminal in Hoboken, New Jersey, designed by Lincoln Bush, and consisting of a series of continuous arches giving passengers complete protection from the weather but containing a slanting aperture for locomotive smoke to escape, spelled the doom for all subsequent monster sheds.

This perhaps gives some hint of the true genius of Americans when it came to their great city railroad terminals. During the first few decades of the twentieth century, huge and awesome stations would be built, mostly in the Beaux Arts tradition of monumental grandiosity using classical inspiration. Many people would continue to bemoan the fact that these stations lacked the beauty of their European counterparts in England, France, and Germany, and perhaps that was the case. But American engineers and architects (and railway passenger agents, for that matter) were always in the forefront when it came to figuring out how to do things in the simplest, most resourceful ways. In the area of orchestrating station plans, services, personnel, and conveniences into one great symphony, America took second place to none.

Sometime, perhaps in the 1890s, American railroad executives began to perceive that the railroad station was more than just a railroad structure that was plopped down in the midst of the city. It was more than just a building that should look impressive— although it should be that also. It was a place that should actually be integrated into city life, a transfusion point, a place where you were melded from one kind of environment—your home and office—to the world of travel, and then on to the place of your destination in one fluid movement. This was perhaps the singular contribution of the great American railway terminals.

When did it all begin? Was it in 1896, when George H. Daniels put "red caps" in Grand Central Station? Was it earlier, when the first immigrant rooms were installed in terminals? Was it when the railroads put in women's lounges supervised by matrons to look after mothers and their babies? Was it the artful handling of transfers between all the railroad depots in Chicago by the omnibuses of the Franklin Parmalee Transfer Company, whose operations were engraved on interline tickets for generations—an operation which at one time had 1,200 horses on the streets of Chicago? Was it when the planners of Penn Station in New York found a way to separate arriving and outgoing passengers on two levels, or when planners of the new Grand Central Station there had separate levels for suburban and long-distance passengers, two groups of people with obviously quite different needs?

There is probably no sense in attempting to find one particular point in time where a transition was made to a wholly new kind of philosophy about the railroad terminal, but probably at least by the 1890s, railroad men had become as firmly sold on the idea of building great terminals for public service as they had on the importance of providing fast and luxurious trains that caught the public's fancy. If trains like the Twentieth Century Limited and Overland Limited were flagships, banner bearers of a railroad's power and prestige, the city terminal became a fixed symbol of the railroad's role in the scheme of things. Even when such stations were true "union" stations owned by several railroads jointly, the belief was that the massive city terminal was a showcase for railroad power and glory. It ought not only look the part, but it should speak to the public in other ways as well, providing a bonding between the railroad and the general commerce and life of society.

Accordingly, the enormous stations that rose in the early decades of the twentieth century were more than just railroad stations, although they were clearly and emphatically that. They were temples of commerce and oracles of the American way of life, most assuredly of the urban way of life. Probably no great terminals built in America better illustrate the joint function of providing smooth and efficient service and forging a link between the railroad and the rest of society than the two terminals built in New York in the first decade of the new century—Penn Station and the "new" Grand Central Station, probably the most famous large terminals ever built in America.

A great part of the success of these two terminals was that they melded so smoothly and so unobtrusively into the city's heart. They were great human spaces like the enormous public squares of Florence or Venice. They were, in fact, among the few wholly public buildings in their city. They were open to everybody, unlike the department store, the huge bank lobbies, the theaters, and the skyscrapers, which only tended invitations to those who had business there. The great terminals were decidedly *public* places, located in the heart of the city (a distinction not enjoyed by the airports of today, which are by necessity at some remove from the city's core and thus not wholly integrated in the city's social metabolism). This basic harmony of the railroad terminal with city life was responsible both for their charm and their utility.

In the examples of both Penn Station and Grand Central Station in New York, an exceptionally smooth integration into the warp and woof of city life was made possible by a technological innovation—the development of the electric locomotive. Both of these terminals, which are planted in the very midst of busy commercial neighborhoods, give no indication of being anything other than grand public structures—the railroad tracks and all railroad activity is completely buried under city streets. Here one does not approach a railroad yard or a railroad shed, or any kind of railroad ambience; one moves from hotel or office or subway to one's sleeping car without trauma and without bother, and with a good deal of smug satisfaction over the manifest fruits of technology.

The very important advance in terminal design and philosophy was the product of a long-standing frustration on the part of executives of the Pennsylvania Railroad, most especially its president, Alexander J. Cassatt, who had long felt thwarted by his railroad's lack of access to the island of Manhattan. The mighty Pennsylvania, often called the "standard railroad of the world," had to dump its passengers for "New York" on the New Jersey shore of the Hudson River, from whence they would complete their journey to Manhattan by ferry boat. For years, the Pennsylvania had been chaffing at the bit, looking for a way to take its brass-knuckles conflict with the New York Central right to the home turf of the Vanderbilts. The only way to do this was to span the Hudson River, no mean undertaking. It meant either a tunnel under the river or a bridge. Pennsylvania engineers were thinking of both possibilities back in the 1880s, although either would have been a monumental undertaking with the technology available at that time. The tunnel was the best idea; alas, this presented a serious problem in that the operation of steam locomotives in such a tunnel was out of the question. Electric locomotives would have to be used, but in the beginning the electric locomotives available were not up to the task. By 1900 or shortly thereafter, new electric motors were available that could pull heavy trains, so it was decided to tunnel under the river and build a monumental terminal on the west side of the isle of Manhattan. The project became even more monumental when it was decided to make Penn Station a through station, bringing in the tracks of the Long Island Railroad (controlled at the time by the Pennsylvania) under the East River.

The Pennsylvania Railroad assembled a team of gifted engineers to complete this project, and engaged the architectural firm of McKim, Mead, and White to design a grandiose terminal that would be an affront to the empire of the Vanderbilts. The actual plan for the building was mostly the work by the firm's senior partner, Charles Follen McKim, one of America's most successful commercial architects of his time, perhaps of all time. McKim immediately grasped the idea that English architects had understood a long time ago—that a railroad terminal should be a monumental entrance to the city, much like the famous city gates of the Greek and Roman worlds.

Considering all of the engineering problems that had to be resolved in the building of Penn Station, the project was a stupendous one; the station itself was on a scale that had never been considered before. The tunnels, trackage, and electrical and signaling systems were things of enormous complexity, but building the station meant changing the entire face of New York City. Two whole blocks on the dreary West Side of Manhattan were commandeered for the purpose—eight acres in total—requiring the removal of as many as one hundred houses and several churches. A vast hole in the ground was dug that required the removal of three million cubic yards of earth and mica schist.[11] This gaping slice from the side of the city was watched by New Yorkers over a period of several years, and it was chronicled by the city's Ash Can painters, who squeezed all the human drama they could from this earthy yet epic undertaking.

When Penn Station opened in 1910, it was the largest through station in the world, a distinction that it never lost. On the Seventh Avenue side, the main entrance consisted of a massive two-block facade in the classical style—a large central element flanked by two colonnaded wings and end pavilions (the end pavilions were provided for vehicular entrances, the most common vehicle now being motorized taxicabs, which could deposit their passengers inside the station). The pedestrian entering the grand front entrance walked down a long barrel-vaulted arcade lined with exclusive shops, which led to an atrium, off which there was a restaurant and a lunchroom. From here, one passed by stairs or escalators to the main waiting room, a copy of the Tepidarium of the Baths of Caracalla in Rome; herein were contained the ticket booths and the information desk. Between here and the train concourse were two smaller waiting rooms, one for men and one for women. The main waiting room, of course, was awe inspiring in itself, but the train concourse beyond was almost stupefying in its dimensions. This single room of glass and iron construction, from which passengers would wait at their train gates, was 210 feet by 341 feet (with a breathtaking 150-foot ceiling), one of the largest rooms in the world, and could doubtless have held the whole army of the United States as of the year of the building's opening. This room could be entered from all sides, including from the side streets, and from the other waiting rooms below— that for the Long Island Railroad and for the arriving passengers. Except for the building's vast size, it was a model of easy accessibility. Without going outdoors, one could enter the Seventh Avenue (and later Eighth Avenue) Subway.

From its opening, Penn Station was a veritable city within a city. The building was only a block away from Herald Square, the city's busiest shopping center; but it also immediately developed its own cluster of buildings and activities. Not only was the station itself provided with room for stores selling everything imaginable to the traveler and nontraveler alike, early plans were laid to build two hotels connected by tunnels to the station. These hotels, the Pennsylvania and the New Yorker, were among the largest commercial hotels in the city at the time of their construction.

The city-within-a-city concept received an even more dramatic boost in the planning and development of the third (and last) Grand Central Station, which opened slightly two years after Penn Station. Grand Central Station was not simply the Vanderbilts'

answer to the Manhattan invasion of the upstart Pennsylvania, but
it was partly inspired by that act. The huge electrification project
of the Pennsylvania made New York Central officials see that they
had a golden opportunity to solve the long vexing problem of the
approach to their station on upper Fourth Avenue (now Park
Avenue). Trains of the New York Central and the New Haven
approached the old Grand Central by means of a partially covered
cut (before the 1880s, the tracks were at street level and provided
a constant hazard to pedestrians). The partially covered cut had
not been a complete answer, and operating steam trains in it had
resulted in several fatal accidents. Around 1904, the New York
Central's chief engineer, William J. Wilgus, was given the job of
planning for the complete covering of the tracks, an enterprise
that would also call for an entirely new station. Needless to say,
with a grandiose Penn Station on the drawing boards, the New
York Central was not going to spare any expense in building a terminal that would rival the Pennsylvania's station in grandeur and
modernity.

In a gigantic undertaking that took the better part of a decade,
the old open yards north of Grand Central were laid underground, and a new station with all tracks depressed was constructed (it would be a two-level station, the upper level for long-distance trains, the lower level for suburban trains). Electric locomotives would have to be employed, of course. For a few years, the
electric locomotives ran only to High Bridge; later, they ran to
Harmon, thirty-two miles from Grand Central.[12] The operation at
Penn Station was quite similar. For many years, the electric locomotives, after they went under the Hudson River, were taken off
in Harrison, New Jersey, at a place called Manhattan Transfer,
although this terminal operation was so successful that in the late
1920s the Pennsylvania undertook a massive project of
electrification which saw electric trains going on to Washington,
D.C., and Harrisburg, Pennsylvania. The New York Central's electrification made possible the development of the posh Park
Avenue section of New York City—an area that theretofore had
been a blighted neighborhood.

Not to be outdone by the architectural hubris of Penn Station,
the New York Central commissioned a station every bit as impressive, if not more so. Two architectural firms, Reed and Stem and
Warren and Wetmore, drew up plans for the building. The final

concept was mostly the work of French-trained Whitney Warren, whose design called for a station with the strong flavor of a French palace (the previous station had been in the French Empire style with mansard roofs—a typically Victorian edifice). The new station, which was built athwart Fourth Avenue with elevated roadways for through vehicular traffic around it, was somewhat less grandiose than Penn Station, but no less grand. Indeed, Grand Central Station lived up to its name—it was nothing but grand. The architectural niceties of the exterior gave some clue to its inner opulence. As a center crown, there was a monumental decorative statuary group forty-eight feet high representing Mercury, Hercules, and Minerva, arranged around a clock thirteen feet in diameter.

The interior of the station was both beautiful and striking in appearance, but also remarkable in its simplicity and ease of accessibility. There was an impressive waiting room that could be entered from Forty-second Street, and from this one could pass on to the grand concourse where tickets were sold, baggage checked, and trains boarded. However, since most people did not enter the station from the main entrance, but from a series of ramps and tunnels, the waiting room was a relatively tranquil place, usually spared the urgency of rush-hour pedestrianism. At each end of the main waiting room were separate waiting rooms for both men and women; these led downstairs to elegant marble-clad washroom facilities that offered every imaginable form of convenience to travelers, including rooms that were available with tubs, showers, and dressing rooms for those who wished to refresh themselves after a long journey.

The main part of the terminal, the grand concourse, could be reached by a short ramp from the waiting room, and was the ultimate expression of the playful opulence of the building. A room 287 feet long by 120 feet wide, with a ceiling 125 feet at its highest point, it was finished in Botticino marble and buff-tinted stone, getting light from three enormous arched windows on two ends. In a turquoise blue ceiling are depicted all the stars seen in the heavens between October to March, or Aquarius to Cancer, but here, too, were disguised some of the lighting needed to provide illumination for the nighttime hours.[13] A long bank of ticket windows ran along the wall opposite the train gates, but the focal point of the room was an octagonal information booth surmounted by a four-faced golden clock. Here, a large crew of information clerks answered thousands of questions a day, not only on train schedules, but on every imaginable topic of general interest: "Where is Canal Street?" or "How tall is the Chrysler Building?" The information booth was probably the most famous meeting place in New York City, and during the years of the station's glory, one of the best-known visual icons in the United States. Just as they used to say in Paris that if you waited long enough everybody in the world would eventually pass you at the Arc de Triomphe, so people said that if you waited long enough everyone in the world would pass you at the golden clock in Grand Central.

People moved in and out of Grand Central Station with meticulous ease. Many passengers entered the station from the west side, the taxi ramp on Vanderbilt Avenue, which led to a balcony that was always the best place to watch the throngs in the concourse. This place, dubbed the "kissing gallery" by local newsmen, was the place where many New Yorkers in the know arranged to meet their friends. Thousands of others entered the station from ramps and tunnels that came up from nearby office buildings and from a complex of subway stations. In numerous auxiliary concourses of the station were shops and services of every imaginable kind. Stores selling books, liquor, flowers, apparel, pipes, men's hats, and umbrellas joined the usual lunchrooms and snack bars. (Like Penn Station with its Savarin Restaurant, Grand Central had its premier eating establishment: the Oyster Bar.) During the years of World War II, there was a newsreel theater, a traveler's aid service, an art gallery, a gymnasium, locksmiths, cutlery stores, watch repair services, an emergency hospital with an attending physician and nurses—at one time nearly two hundred such stores and services.[14] Operating the station and its ancillary operations required a mighty force. The station had its own police force of forty-five men, quite adequate for a medium-sized city. During the hectic years of World War II, it took 3,100 people to run Grand Central Station, and this did not include any of the people working in shops, restaurants, and connecting hotels. Among these 3,100 were 285 redcaps, 60 parcel room attendants, and 335 janitors, window washers, and charwomen. It took forty-one information operators to answer phone calls. Sixteen information clerks manned two information booths (there was a second information booth on the suburban level). On one record day, July 3, 1942, these clerks responded to 17,313 calls for information.[15]

In the last three or four decades of the twentieth century, huge commercial malls have become among the most familiar landmarks on the American cityscape. Historians who have attempted to trace the origin of these complexes seldom go back beyond New York's Rockefeller Center of the early 1930s. Clearly, though, the "mall" concept was thriving as soon as the new Grand Central opened its doors in 1913. There is good reason for believing that the Grand Central Station beehive was not only the first of such grand bazaars, but the biggest and grandest. It was not the terminal itself that made the distinction—the railway terminal was merely the keystone in one of the most dramatic real estate developments of all time.

Sprouting up everywhere were gigantic hotels and office buildings. On land owned by the New York Central itself, two large commercial hotels, the Biltmore and the Commodore, served millions of people during the years of their prime. Both were connected to the station by lighted tunnels, so that there was no difficulty giving up your bag in your room on the Twentieth Century Limited and having it delivered by redcap and bellboy to your room in the Commodore (named, of course, for Commodore Vanderbilt). North and east of the station, on land once used for yards, the Grand Central Office Building was built, and another much taller office building, long a highly coveted New York address, the Graybar Building. Fitted in this tight space went the Grand Central Palace, one of New York's most important exhibition halls, a post office, a building for the Adams Express Company (later Railway Express), and a heating and power plant for the railroad. Finally, in the late 1920s, between Forty-fifth and Forty-sixth Streets, and serving as a centerpiece for the "new" Park Avenue, there was the New York Central Building, a thirty-four-story skyscraper crowned by a turreted roof that at night became a jeweled lantern.[16] All these buildings were connected to the station by lighted marble passageways.

Nearby the station, and easily accessible to it, other skyscraper office buildings went up during the 1920s. Among the first of these was the Lincoln Building on the south side of Forty-second Street. Then there were two art deco skyscraper masterpieces catercorner from one another on Lexington Avenue and Forty-second Street, the Chanin and Chrysler Buildings, the latter for a few years the tallest building in the world. Both of these were made accessible to Grand Central by underground passageways, making it possible for thousands of office workers to go to work in the city without having to go outdoors (and the hundreds of shops and restaurants in the Grand Central "city" could keep them completely encapsulated during their lunch hours as well).

Even buildings not connected directly to the terminal were essentially part of the web. This includes the new Park Avenue neighborhood north of Forty-seventh Street, which almost immediately became an area of luxury hotels and upscale office buildings. One of New York's most famous hostelries, the Waldorf Astoria, moved uptown from its original site on Fifth Avenue (now home to the Empire State Building) and built an impressive and opulent skyscraper building at Park Avenue and Forty-ninth Street. The Waldorf Astoria, built astride the underground tracks, received its own private siding from the New York Central, so that celebrated guests could take a hotel elevator to their private rail cars. President Roosevelt apparently did this on at least one occasion during World War II after a speech at the Waldorf.

Electrification had inspired tunnels—tunnels to everywhere, it seems. With the connection of the New York subway lines, all of whose adjacent stations were appropriately called "Grand Central," it was possible to go almost everywhere in Manhattan, or the city of New York for that matter. A Wall Street banker coming in from suburban Stamford or Larchmont would never need to expose himself to the elements until he left the subway at the lower end of Manhattan. Using the subways and the Hudson tubes, arriving passengers could go from Grand Central to the New Jersey harborside railroad terminals of the Erie or Lackawanna railroads or even to downtown Newark, ten miles away. Grand Central was the hub of a network the ramifications of which can hardly be calculated.

Some have called it a city within a city. The "magical city," it was called by others. Whatever it may be called, it is clear that this gargantuan urban complex is one of the wonders of the modern world. The image of the station itself has been tarnished with the decline of long-distance rail traffic, as we might well expect. But the station still gets heavy use, and has not lost any of its importance as a hub of human activity.

What is perhaps most important of all, Grand Central (and to a

lesser extent a number of other great city terminals) was a bold
expression of the possibilities of city life, especially in a democratic society. In recent years, there has been a great deal of criticism
of the quality of life in cities. But the great urban terminals, like
those in Washington, Boston, Philadelphia, New York, St. Louis,
and Chicago, have been among the city's most generous spaces,
one of the few places where people can move in freedom and exu-
berance.

Theodore H. Whyte, one of those observers and critics of city
life who lately have begun to express the view that cities are not
places where people are cramped, dismal, and unhappy, has insisted that much of the city's vitality is due to the fact that people, all
classes of people, can rub up against one another, look at one
another in action. Cities have a civilizing function because they
put all of life's joys and sorrows on display. The great railway terminals of North America made a singular contribution to city life
in that they provided an atmosphere in which all manner of people, people from every social class, may mingle, and do so in
spaces that are not restricting, not divisive, but filled with a kind of
grandeur. The great terminals were places that people could call
their own; they expressed the joys of freedom we accord to travel
and movement.

Among the best of such places were Grand Central Station and
Penn Station. Unlike the terminals of London, whose officials for
years went through unbelievable contortions to keep a duchess or
an archbishop from having to mingle with hoi polloi, at places like
Grand Central, every imaginable American type was on display. A
drifter or a pretty file clerk could come to watch them lay down
the carpet for the departure of the Twentieth Century Limited;
anyone could be there in the morning to watch Clark Gable or
Madeleine Carroll get off the train and go through the gate—just
like everybody else.

Above all, the great railroad terminals were places of human
assembly, a quality every city needs for its spiritual health. Airport
terminals, although they may have displaced railroad buildings in
the lives of long-distance travelers, are not, alas, the same thing.
They are not at the city's core. They are, by and large, not places
of architectural distinction. They do not strike much wonderment. Above all, they are not joyful places of assembly, but have
the feel of a moving platform that here and there has high-

ceilinged junctures. The railroad station of days gone by was altogether different. It expressed the grandeur and passion of the city and its people. It had a feel of openness and public hospitality often lacking in city life. As such, it performed for the people of the city a function that is as rare as it is wonderful.

C·H·A·P·T·E·R 15

ALL MANNER
OF BYWAYS

In the quarter century between 1890 and 1915, the railroad enjoyed its golden age. During those years, the railroad exercised a virtual monopoly both on intercity passenger traffic and on the transportation of everything except trivial quantities of local and long-distance freight. Virtually all manufactured goods, except the small amounts that could be sent by river barge, traveled by rail. Everyone who wanted to go between New York and Chicago, or between Baltimore and Atlanta, or Boston and Fitchburg, went by rail—at least if they valued even a modicum of comfort. And for luxury travel, there was simply no other way to go.

On the surface, at least everything was going the railroad's way during that golden quarter of a century. Trains ran on time; all of the expected services from the hauling of mail and express to the efficient and orderly management of small-town depots were handled with aplomb. Signals and switches worked. Railroads made money and they spent money, sometimes lavishily. The grisly accidents of times past declined in number, or at least they declined in proportion to the volume of the service. And this in an age when crack passenger trains were running at breathtaking speeds. In the 1890s, the railroads virtually invented the notion of speed. In May 1893, when Engine 999 pulled the Empire State Express at a speed of 112.5 miles an hour near Batavia, New York, it could honestly be advertised that no propelled vehicle had ever traveled so fast in the history of the world. Railroad speed was so dramatic and so esteemed by the public that the Post Office Department issued a two-cent stamp bearing an engraved likeness of the Empire State Express. Other stamps, and even banknotes displaying railroad subject matters, appeared in the next few years, acknowledging what everybody then knew: The railroad was not just part of the American infrastructure; it was the American infrastructure.

Nonetheless, the dawn's light of the twentieth century would cast dark shadows on the railroad's monopoly over transportation in America, and before the new century was half over the railroad's place in the scheme of things would be cruelly eclipsed. The twentieth century would see the introduction of new forms of transportation that, both singly and together, would put railroads in the shade. These new forms of transportation would take a long time gaining a foothold since they, too, had to pass through their technological infancy, but they were welcomed eagerly in places where they came into conflict with the railroad—the railroad, after all, had never managed to soften its harsh image as a tool of big business; had never removed the enmity of those who had been injured by monopolistic practices, collusive rate making, and all the rest.

The first challenge to steam railroads, and it was not to prove an effective one in the long run, was the rise of electric interurban railways—the phenomenon of the trolley car. As early as 1888, street railways in cities (formerly horse drawn) had been replaced by electrified cars operated from overhead wires, a concept pioneered in the late 1880s by Frank J. Sprague in Richmond, Virginia. After 1900, the streetcar idea spread beyond the city limits, and numerous entrepreneurs began building "light-rail" systems out into the countryside. The city street car began roaming around everywhere, even in arcadian glades. Between 1900 and 1910, hundreds of interurban lines were built, some of them in unlikely or obviously unprofitable places, taking advantage of the fact that capital expenditures were modest, with rolling stock usually consisting of a single car operated by a lone motorman. These trolley cars, or dinkies or doodlebugs as they were sometimes called, could haul people out to a picnic grove or amusement park for only a nickel—railroad fare for a comparable distance would probably be at least twenty-five cents. Furthermore, the trolley was used effectively for delivery of mail and packages to many places that had no rail service. The trolley, accordingly, gained the immediate and widespread affection of most Americans. Travel on these electric cars was quiet, leisurely, breezy, and fun. They were seen mostly in recreational terms as a good way to take the family on a Sunday outing or as a way to get to the ballpark, or a way to get to the next big town on the few pennies saved up in the cookie jar. The flimsy and poorly capitalized interurban companies were no real threat to the massive system of rail transportation, but they provided an irritating shock to the railroad in some places, and did lure away passengers in areas where the two forms of transportation went head to head.

For the most part, the railroads never really thought of the interurbans as serious competitors, and in some ways they seemed to be allies. They were usually not built as directly competitive lines; most had been laid down in places railroads didn't serve and had no likelihood of ever serving. A typical pattern in many communities was that the interurban line would set out from the local railroad station and carry transferring passengers—or mail and express—into new neighborhoods or to nearby towns not served by any railroad. Railroad managements were not strongly opposed to feeder lines with which they could exchange passengers or freight. Even where there was head-to-head competition, the interurban lines could offer service during off hours and at night when the steam railroads stopped running.

By 1915, there was a vast network of interurban lines in the United States, most densely concentrated in New England and the mid-western states. Indiana, for example, had an extensive system of lines, with Indianapolis as the hub. A large traction terminal was built in Indianapolis, and by 1914 it would serve some seven million passengers pouring into the state capital from every point of the compass. Many of these passengers were from communities that had no "rail" service. For a while, it was part of the American folklore that you could travel between Chicago and Springfield, Illinois, if you fancied riding on trolley cars; or even that a dauntless individual with a pocketful of nickels could go by trolley from Boston to New York, although with many changes of cars, needless to say. Some claimed that with ingenuity you could arrange to ride trolleys from New York to Chicago, but it is not absolutely clear whether this was actually possible.[1]

The interurban era in America was not long lasting. By the 1920s, most of these lines were dying or severely troubled. A few, like Chicago's North Shore and South Shore lines, both well capitalized and built over much of their length to near railroad standards, would last for many decades (the Chicago, South Shore, and South Bend continues to operate at this writing). Most of the little lines, few of which earned money for those who invested in them, were doomed by the first cough of the gasoline engine. When the automobile became a possession of the typical American household, the trolley as a way of getting out to the picnic grove or the ballpark quickly became a thing of the dead and dreamy past. Even in the cities, streetcars were doomed by busses, although urban street railways continue to make good sense, and cities that have preserved them (Toronto in Canada, for example) have had reason to be grateful for their presence.

During the last decade of the nineteenth century, new technologies for transportation were beginning to appear. Some of them provided only a minor annoyance to railroads; others were immediately threatening to revenues. One of the minor threats was the widespread proliferation of the bicycle in the 1890s. During the so called "gay nineties," Americans became positively wild about bicycles—adults and children everywhere were tooling around on bikes, entering six-day bicycle races, attending bicycle jamborees, taking bicycles with them on their vacations, and so on. Obviously, the bicycle, a local conveyance, was nothing more than an insect bite to railroads, but it was an annoying bite nonetheless. When bicycles were few, railroads carried them free in baggage cars, but when their numbers dramatically increased disgruntled railroad managers tried to slap a twenty-five-cent tariff on the service. But so great was the bicycle lobby in some states that laws were passed requiring railroads to carry bikes free as a part of a passenger's baggage.[2] Still, the bicycle never became anything but a minor irritation to the railroad industry even in the years of its greatest popularity.

So powerful was the monopolistic grip of the railroad on America's transportation system that it seemed for a long time as if there would never be a challenge to it. But bold competitors were just around the corner, and some of these would give railroads a really nasty jolt; one of them would alter the face of railroading forever. The interurbans had really taken few passengers away from the railroads, and they had done practically nothing to effect freight revenues, but by the 1890s there were incipient challenges to the railroad's complete dominance of the freight business.

Freight rates had been a source of annoyance for years, beginning in the grain states, so it is small wonder that many freight customers of the railroads would be looking for ways to throw off the yoke of railroad monopoly. In 1890, no group of rail shippers was more incensed by railroad neglect than the oil producers of western Pennsylvania. To counter the stranglehold the oilmen believed the railroads had upon them, they eventually developed pipelines—a technology that dealt a real blow to the rail monopoly. But this would be only the first of many blows that the railroads would suffer over the next several decades.

The biggest blow of all would come from the development of the automobile, which, like the interurbans, got its practical start in the 1890s. The automobile, by its very definition, was a distant cousin of the railway locomotive: Both devices had a common ancestor in early self-propelled vehicles such as the 1771 steam wagon of Nicholas Joseph Cugnot. (The original railway locomotive, after all, was essentially an auto-mobile.) By the 1870s and 1880s, French engineers were once again experimenting with self-propelled vehicles powered either by steam, electricity, or gas. Workable gasoline-driven vehicles were introduced in Paris in 1878 by two Germans, Gottlieb Daimler and Karl Benz, and their ideas spread to the United States by the early 1890s. In 1893, the brothers Duryea were startling their neighbors in Springfield, Massachusetts, by sputtering around town in their "horseless carriage" powered by a gasoline engine—machines sometimes called "motor wagons" or "motorcycles" in the early days.

For a few years, automobiles seemed to be amusing and entertaining vehicles. The Duryeas hand built a few machines for their friends, but they were generally considered to be of small practical value. It was not very long, however, before individuals would entertain the idea of manufacturing automobiles for sale to the general public. Before the 1890s were over, a steady stream of these novel vehicles were being made by Elwood Haynes of Kokomo, Indiana, Alexander Winton of Cleveland, Ohio, and Ransom E. Olds of Lansing, Michigan. By 1900, Olds was ready to launch a real campaign of manufacture and sales, and he put in production a light one-cylinder runabout with a curved dash. By 1901, the Olds Motor Works in Detroit, which later became the nucleus of the General Motors Corporation, would turn out over four hundred cars. The company's production schedule called for 2,500 cars in 1902 and 4,000 cars in 1903.[3]

These numbers, of course, were not really significant, and the toylike machines, which sold for $650, did not seem to be of compelling interest except to rich hobbyists and adventurers. To be sure, it would only be a few years before another Michigan tinkerer, Henry Ford, would produce a car that could be sold to millions of Americans, but in the first decade of the twentieth century, most people continued to think of the automobile as a kind of novelty or foolish extravagance. There was really not much you could do with these machines except amuse your friends on Sunday afternoons, typically with the adventure of getting the monster to cough its way to a start.

The principal reason that automobiles seemed to be no threat to the railroad in these early years was that there really was nowhere to drive them. They could be used for amusement, but not for transportation. This because the system of roads in the United States was really little better than it had been in the early days of the republic. In 1900, there was not a single mile of paved road anywhere in the United States outside the confines of cities and towns. Indeed, there would not be any concrete roads beyond municipal limits until 1908, at which time Woodward Avenue in automobile-minded Detroit was extended a mile out of town.[4]

When the railroads appeared on the scene in the 1830s, America lost all interest in road improvement, and, in spite of the efforts of such persuasive figures as Henry Clay, early dreams of a national road system had died. The National Road, once considered a vital project, was never completed to its projected length, and all federal aid to roads had ceased—even the idea of it had seemingly faded from memory. By the 1890s, however, the quality of roads once again became a burning issue. Bicyclists would clamor for better roads, and so within a few years would automobile owners and manufacturers. With the spread of a "metropolitan way of life," farmers complained bitterly about their isolation and asked for better roads to link them with the outside world. States began to pump a little money into roads at this time, and so-called "improved" roads, sometimes called "trunk roads," were built. Unfortunately, the better ones of these only connected important cities and towns. Accordingly, very little of the country was served by improved roads.

In 1903, when a young doctor from Vermont, H. Nelson Jackson, accepted a fifty-dollar wager to drive an automobile across the United States, the press called him "the mad doctor."[5] There simply were not enough long-distance roads to make such an idea feasible. Driving in a twenty-horsepower, two-cycle Winton touring car, the mad doctor managed to complete the trip in sixty-three days. He spent most of his time repairing tires, waiting for spare parts, and pulling himself out of mud and ditches. Ten years later, things were not much better, and people who wanted to cross the country by car found themselves spanning endless mud holes and streams without bridges, often having to be lifted from gullies with tackle blocks and dug out of desert sand—with the help of "real" horsepower.

One would think that the automobile age would have given an immediate spark to road construction, but such was not the case. Indeed, it was not until 1912 that any thought was given to the idea of building a transcontinental highway—a link of the sort that the railroads had completed over forty years before. When the idea came, it was the brainchild of a man connected with the automobile industry: Carl Graham Fisher, owner of the Prest-to-Light Headlight Company, and a prominent founder of the Indianapolis Speedway. Fisher was one of those big single thinkers, monomaniacs, with whom America has always been blessed, a man who simply wouldn't let an idea die—much like Theodore Judah, the monomaniac of the transcontinental railroad. Meeting with a group of automobile manufacturers at the old Deutsches Haus in Indianapolis on September 1, 1912, Fisher opened a campaign to raise funds for a coast-to-coast highway. Most of the funds would have to come from private donors (generally, they would be people connected with the automobile industry), although some state funding would also be involved. As one might expect, not all people, even those connected with the automobile industry, were enthusiastic about the idea—Henry Ford put forth nary a dime![6]

Fisher and his principal booster ally, Henry B. Joy, president of the Packard Motor Car Company, had hoped that the road could be finished in time for the San Francisco World's Fair in 1915; as things turned out, the road—eventually christened the Lincoln Highway—was not fully opened until 1923, giving some indication of the difficulty of obtaining funds and support for roads in those days. The truth was people were not of one mind where roads were concerned. A lot of people believed that money would be better spent on improving local roads than trunk highways that would serve only a few affluent people who could afford to take long trips. Perhaps Henry Ford was such a person. By 1915, most of the customers for his Model-T car were farmers and others whose main concern was getting to town in the "flivver." But the dramatic building of the Lincoln Highway caught the public's fancy and led to pressure being put on all levels of government to improve roads throughout the country.

States were the principal supporters of the highway boom, and before World War I most states were establishing "Highway Departments" and embarking on projects to upgrade existing roads and construct paved highways. Even the federal government, long hesitant, got into the act. Money spent on roads was supposed to be unconstitutional—or so early presidents and congresses believed—but in a populist democracy constitutional restraints are seldom allowed to balk the public will, so the federal government slowly began to sneak in funds for highways on the grounds that these monies were being used for "postal roads." Then, on July 11, 1916, President Woodrow Wilson signed into law a "Good Roads Bill," which carried a first-year appropriation of eighty-five million dollars. This proved to be the beginning of a long love affair between the federal government and the highway (and, by implication, gasoline-driven vehicles), which rose to a dizzying crescendo during the 1950s, when the federal government splurged on a vast network of limited-access interstate highways.

The industries that prospered with the growth of the nation's highways—the automobile and truck manufacturing industries, and the truck transportation industry—would thus be able to deal a sharp slap to the railroad business. The effect was not immediate, to be sure. Lengthy travel by car was not commonplace until the 1920s. Trucks, which first began to appear in 1904, were not really numerous for several decades. In the beginning, most trucks were local carriers; few were engaged in interstate commerce. By 1910, only ten-thousand trucks had been produced; five years later, there was an annual output of seventy-five thousand units, still not much to frighten the railroad. But by 1925, half a million trucks a year were being built and they would become a serious menace to the railroad freight business.[7]

The automobile manufacturing industry had been hopscotching along even before World War I, but during the 1920s it became the most wildly successful manufacturing industry of American history. There were 6,771,000 registered automobiles in the United States in 1919, but 2,000,000 new automobiles were manufactured that year alone.[8] A year later, Secretary of Interior Franklin K. Lane was able to report that the United States had more automobiles than all of the other nations of the world combined. Yet this was only the beginning. By the crash of 1929, the nation would have nearly four times as many automobiles as it did in 1920. The automobile, obviously, had gotten a vicelike grip on the American psyche; a car in the garage was no longer a luxury but one of the basic necessities of life. In their classic sociological study, *Middletown* (in reality Muncie, Indiana), Robert and Helen Lynd found that as early as 1923 this typical middle American town had two cars for every three families. Of 123 working-class families, 60 had cars, and of these 60, 23 out of 26 who lived in "very shabby houses" had no bathtubs, indicating that in much of the country the automobile arrived before the bathtub![9]

While the automobile industry was getting off to a flying start, the railroads were beginning to groan under the weight of lethargy and ineptitude. World War I was a total disaster for the railroad business. There were plenty of signs of trouble even before America entered the war in 1917. Little had been done to modernize management practices in the early twentieth century, and the response by railroad chieftains to the newer forms of competition had merely been to grumble about them. When the U.S. was called upon to aid Britain and France in 1915 and 1916, the railroads were clearly not up to the task. There were fewer freight cars in 1916 than there had been in 1914; terminal facilities were antiquated and inadequate, especially on the Atlantic coast, where they were desperately needed. In the months before the United States entered the war, the system seemed almost in complete gridlock. Freight rotted in yards. Because of the long-standing rail policy that freight cars couldn't be returned until there was something to fill them, there was a terrible shortage of cars in the Midwest. Thousands of empty cars huddled in eastern yards. A month before America entered the war, Samuel Rea, president of the Pennsylvania Railroad, actually admitted in testimony before the Interstate Commerce Commission that "the condition of the railroads today presents a menace to the country."[10]

During this same period, the relations between the railroads and their employees had greatly deteriorated. Wages for rail workers had not kept pace with those in other industries. In August 1916, Congress legislated an eight-hour day for railroad workers with provisions for increased pay for overtime, but management let it be known that they would not comply and would fight the provision in the courts. Clearly, railroad pay had not kept pace. In 1917, on the Erie Railroad, conductors were typically making $4.50 a day; baggagemen, $2.75 a day; and brakemen, $2.55 a day—with overtime for these same workers running from fifty-six cents an hour down to thirty-two cents an hour.[11] And there were other workers on railroads paid even less. There were crossing watchmen working thirteen hours a day seven days a week for a wage of no more than twelve dollars a week. Even on the more affluent Pennsylvania Railroad, laborers in the shops were making an annual wage of only $944.00 in 1916. With mileage rates and layover times, the railroad industry had long been able to whipsaw its workers, making published rates seem much more beneficent than they actually were. During the war and thereafter, some adjustments would be made in the hours and wages of railroad labor; on the other hand, many railroad men were working standard twelve-hour days as late as 1947, and the forty-hour week was a kind of agreed-upon myth for some years after that. Accordingly, in March 1917, a month before the declaration of war, the railroad brotherhoods served notice that they were going to strike.

When the war began, the government had no choice but to take over the railroads, a humiliating experience for the managers, since no other major industries received this kind of ignominious treatment. But after the war, when the lines went back to private hands, things were no better. There was an extended period of brutal labor unrest; there were an increasing number of complaints from shippers that rates were too high; and little had been done to improve the physical condition of the lines. By now, the railroads also had reason to complain about competition from trucks. They bellowed for relief and for assurance that their profits would not suffer from this new form of transportation, which clearly was being subsidized by public funds. The relief that was provided would only be temporary.

By the early 1920s, roads, automobiles, and trucks were beginning to make a strong dent in the transportation monopoly which railroads had enjoyed in America since the pre–Civil War period. The combination of the gasoline motor and publicly maintained roads free for use by all citizens would slowly but surely cut into the business of the railroads and eventually deliver a blow to them from which some believed they could never recover. The economic drain on the railroads was not immediately evident, and it would take more than two decades for railroad managements to realize that their wound had been potentially mortal. Even throughout the Depression years of the 1930s, when many previously healthy railroads fell into bankruptcy, few believed that the railroads could actually fold—all industries were in a sorry state in those years, after all. The World War II period, with its gasoline rationing, was a time of record-breaking earnings for the railroads, so this, too, temporarily disguised the economic woes of the industry. But conditions after World War II, especially the building of a vast network of interstate highways during the Eisenhower administration, would bring the railroads to the point of near economic collapse. And in these same years, the rapidly growing airline industry would almost completely ruin the long-distance passenger business.

Social changes emanating from all the newer forms of transportation began to be noticed as early as 1915, at which time perceptive economists could probably have perceived the slow decline of the railroad. Certainly by 1920, it was clear that America was making a transition to a new way of getting from place to place. Americans were now not only wild about automobiles, but everywhere they were demanding good roads to drive them on. Throughout the 1920s, the United States would spend a billion dollars a year building rural highways, and at least 400 million a year on city streets.[12] Some social changes derived directly from the economic drain on the railroad. Passenger service over rails declined everywhere. The interurbans, of course, rapidly disappeared unmourned, as people discovered the joys of taking their cars on jaunts to the picnic grove or the next town's ballpark. On the railroads, unprofitable branch lines were chopped off, ending services to many communities. Many "way" trains were discontinued as railroads concentrated on upgrading and improving long-distance services. Consequently, stations in small towns that once had regular train service were closed, or downgraded, or lost their agent, or otherwise fell into disuse. Towns thus neglected became still more dependent upon the automobile, and this led, in a kind of vicious circle, to still further abandonments, still further downgrading.

Of course, America's dependence upon the railroad did not die in the 1920s; the dominance of the automobile merely began to settle in on top of it and to create a wholly new way of looking at mobility, a wholly new way of getting about. The automobile created alternate patterns of urban and suburban living—even rural living. As the interurbans and city streetcars disappeared, many people began driving to work. New factories and places of business could now be located away from the city's core with disregard for the older means of transportation. New suburbs and other living areas mushroomed—especially in areas that had not been served by rail transportation. This, in turn, sparked the building industry, which provided a great deal of the boom to the economy of the 1920s. Industrial and commercial expansion was naturally explosive in these years, with new areas of cities bristling with office buildings, hotels, and skyscrapers. But residential construction during this time was mind-boggling. After 1922, forty percent of the building that went on was residential, most of this involving new-built homes in locales that would previously have been unfeasible because of inadequate transportation.

The new forms of transportation affected the way that people went to work. They even affected the way that people went to school. With school buses now available, especially in rural areas, "consolidated" schools could be built, and instead of the old "one-room schoolhouse," where a single teacher taught all students from kindergarden through high school, a number of teachers for different grade levels and with different areas of expertise could be employed in larger and better equipped schools. The automobile made it possible for people to wander afield for shopping and other commercial undertakings. In small communities, even in suburbs, the people who owned "downtown" no longer had a stranglehold on the purchasing habits of the populace. Ever more often, people were shopping in some other town, or "out along the road." The first decentralized shopping center, built mainly to lure automobile drivers, was the Country Club Plaza Shopping Center, which opened in Kansas City in 1922.

The automobile completely altered the way that people amused themselves. It brought about changes in the recreational habits of people unparalled in human history. It made possible the building of country clubs and golf courses, of road houses, of tourist courts and motels. The annual vacation and the "weekend" became a part of everybody's vocabulary and expectations. All Americans, not just the well-to-do, were looking for hunting and camping sites, picnic grounds, places to build a cabin. All of a sudden, everyone wanted to visit national parks and forests, and all the other scenic attractions along the way. In 1917, some 3,160,000 tourists visited the country's national forests; by 1920, the number had reached 4,832,671. Yet these figures would shortly be dwarfed.[13] Whole new areas of the country were opened up for recreational purposes. The automobile had created Florida as a resort paradise. Florida had earlier been the product of Henry L. Flagler and his Florida East Coast Railway, but the Flagler boom was as nothing when compared with the boom that was to come. This second boom, appropriately enough, was due largely to the efforts of Carl Graham Fisher, who, upon turning his attentions from the Lincoln Highway now became a booster for the "Dixie Highway,"[14] and subsequently one of the prime developers of Miami. But the growth of Florida's resort cities was not the main part of the story: The important thing was that the Florida boom could not have been possible in the 1920s had it not been for the automobiles, which deposited hordes of people at tourist courts, motels, bungalows, and even resort shanties or gaudily painted rooms over garages or roadside speakasies. In the 1920s, everybody said they wanted to get "off the beaten trail," but such was the freedom and mobility of the average person that the open road quickly became the cluttered road; the unspoiled paradise often became a more frantic place than the hometown that had been left behind.

The automobile was also the source of new and sometimes disquieting social trends. People loved their cars, but more reflective citizens had reason for concern over the new social mobility they brought. Long-established habits of churchgoing were broken as people used their weekends to take off on a jaunt or short holiday. Once tightly knit small towns lost their cohesiveness as people took off for neighboring communities, for the city, or for a short holiday someplace else. People everywhere now thought in terms not of the town square but of the "road" as the place where the action was. In 1920, when Sinclair Lewis published *Main Street,* the locus of American life was still "Main Street," but a few years later all this had changed. Lewis, himself a devotee of the automobile, would shortly advise a young writer to look for knowledge, and inspiration, and above all information, at the local garage. By the late 1920s, in his novel *The Man Who Knew Coolidge,* Lewis had a principal character embark on a trip for Yellowstone Park. But he never gets to the park, because before he travels very far on his way he is so caught up in the lure of the road itself with its stands and log hutches peddling every form of amusement, all kinds of knicknacks and gewgaws: miniature Mount Vernons, wigwams, pagodas—every trifle of which the commercial imagination is capable.

In the eyes of many traditionalists and moralists, the new culture of the automobile had a dark and sinister side. The automobile seemed to some to foreshadow the breakdown of old family values. Young people, particularly teenagers, used the automobile as a way of escaping the scrutiny of their elders. They now thought nothing of hopping in a car to attend a dance in some neighboring community, where their behavior would not be scrutinized. The car brought people to speakeasies, to unsavory roadside night spots. The car provided a new generation of bank robbers with "getaway" vehicles. The car seemingly brought liberation and "unrestraint" to young unmarried women, who were now free to dance without corsets, to drink too much alcohol, to smoke cigarettes without fear of discovery. The automobile had much to do with the shorter skirts of the 1920s, since the longer skirts of a few years before were a nuisance and a danger in car travel. Women shed them as they shed their long tresses. Above all, though, the automobile seemed to foster everything that was bad in the sexual revolution. The automobile transported one to lover's lane, and many elders believed that the car itself was nothing but a bordello on wheels. When the Lynds did their famous study of "Middletown," they spoke to a judge who claimed that of thirty girls brought before him charged with sex crimes, nineteen were said to have been committed in an automobile.[15]

It might have appeared that the automobile was more of a

threat to the sanctity of traditional values than the railroad had
ever been. In countless small towns across America, where the railroad was long thought to be a lure and a Lorelei, it was easy to see
the automobile as an even greater menace. The railroad had
threatened small towns, whose people felt that the train would
whisk their young away to urban ateliers of sin and depravity, or at
best to new and unconventional life-styles. But the automobile
permitted the young to enjoy their looser habits right in town, or
perhaps only a few miles down the road. On the other hand, the
automobile was advertised to the public as the ultimate democratic vehicle, and it clearly provided every bit as much a democratiz-
ing and "liberating" experience as the railroad had in the nineteenth century. Its power and popularity simply could not be
denied or counteracted. Accordingly, by the 1920s, the tattered
railroad depot, once thought to be the agency of big business and
of metropolitan lifestyles, now seemed by comparison with the
roadside speakeasy somewhat old fashioned, even comforting.
The glittering express trains might still glide by with their plush
and velvet Pullmans, but by the 1920s they no longer seemed to
foretell the loss of old ways. Old ways now had a new and more virulent enemy.

Very curiously, the replacement of railroad travel by automobile
travel did not have the salutary effect on rural and small-town life
that most people hoped and expected. Yes, the automobile was a
boon to the farmer who had long felt isolated in his farmhouse
and who reached Sunday church services or meetings of the
Grange only after strenuous and time-consuming effort. But the
town itself, the community, had lost much of its charm and cohering force, its ability to bring people together. The automobile fostered a new kind of independence, an individuality, but it was not
an individuality of neighborliness. Everyone was free to come and
go with the automobile —during the 1920s, Chevrolet copywriters
insisted that "every owner is in effect a railroad president, operating individually on an elective schedule"[16]—but that freedom was
not bound to any kind of corresponding sense of duty to one's
place of origin. A farmer hell-bent for Miami as soon as his crops
were in was less likely than ever before to share the views, the
habits, and the morals of his community.

Back in the 1880s, many sober thinkers were blaming the railroad for luring people away from small towns to the big cities.

Fathers were making dire predictions that their sons and daughters would be drawn away from home by the luxury of the Pullman car, by sophisticated life-styles—whatever might be at the end of the railroad line. Now it might be easier to see that the railroad depot—once taken to be an object of suspicion—was really woven somehow into the life of the community. The railroad itself fostered a sense of "place." The road, the highway, led only away from town—or, more precisely, it led to so many places that social life became splintered, diffused. The society brought about by the automobile was loose, attenuated, emaciated. It made people citizens of the world, but at the same time citizens of nowhere.

The railroad in its heyday had provided a sturdy lifeline, an artery, what John R. Stilgoe called a corridor. Towns and other places along the corridor got a certain amount of life's blood through this arterial passageway. Roads and even the most grand highways were not arteries at all but capillaries, minute vessels that permitted only weak social transfusions. Towns that had been on the railroad were somehow, as Stilgoe said, nodes, centers pulsing with life. When the railroad began to fade, the artery or the corridor weakened, in some places it seemed to die. The industrialized parts of the corridor perished ingloriously unmorned, creating a new kind of wilderness, with factories in decay, their windows smashed out by vandals, vulgarities spraypainted on their walls, their once spiffy and vibrating environs now dumping grounds and meaningless places of industrial clutter and visual pollution.

Other parts of the corridor did not suffer so grievously, but even in small communities the decline in the railroad meant the weakening of a civilizing influence—country stations lost their human functions, suburban stations lost their gardens to parking lots. As the trains themselves came off, there was a gradual weakening in the idea of public service. As express service faded away, you could still travel to some far distant place by car, but getting your trunk there was an altogether different matter. Above all, as railroad passenger service faded, thousands of communities had no public transportation services at all. Airlines when they came served only larger metropolitan areas; intercity bus systems, such as Greyhound and Trailways, when they appeared, served some smaller communities for a time, but never very many, and fewer and fewer with the passage of years. In 1910, ninety-five percent of the people lived within easy reach of a train station. There were indeed as many as 140,000 railway stations in the United States. The railroad in its day provided the only complete "public-service" network of transportation that America has ever had.

Above all, the railroad seemed to have provided a unity to our desires and endeavors. Even the small-town railroad depot, however humble, even the flag stop, was a gateway to some larger and more civilized world beyond. John R. Stilgoe suggested it was somehow a gateway to an ideal city, a city that was dedicated to service like the huge urban terminals. He quotes Henry James, who ordinarily did not find much that was civilized about America, discovering something calming and civilizing about travel on the Pennsylvania Railroad—an industrial corridor railroad if ever there was one. The railroad seemed always to open doors to something better than its intrinsic self:

> Absolutely, with a little frequentation, affected as better and higher than its office or function, and almost supplying one with a mode of life intrinsically superior; as if it really ought to be on its way to much grander and more charming places than any that happen to mark its course—as if indeed, should one persistently keep one's seat, not getting out anywhere, it would in the end carry one to some such ideal city.[17]

The railroad was thus always pregnant with promise and expectation; it offered the dream of the ideal city—a city where everything was planned, where everything was powered by electricity, where everything worked, where service and convenience were king. In its years of prime, the railroad had a civilizing and enculturing influence. It made of us a cosmopolitan people. As Henry James suggested, the railway seemed to lift people to a higher realm than any of the individual places it served. Perhaps most importantly, it bound these cities and towns together and linked the citizenry to communities and to the nation as a whole. It made of travel something decorous, elegant, convenient, and enjoyable. Alas, none of the other byways of the republic have been able to offer us half as much.

C·H·A·P·T·E·R 16

THE RAILROAD IN LITERATURE AND ART

For the better part of a century, the railroad was deeply rooted in the life of the American people. For most of these years, it was an integral part of the ancient rituals of birth and death, of change and transfiguration; it was a dramatic symbol of energy, of fate, and of power. Accordingly, it is hardly surprising that it was also a subject of abiding fascination for writers and artists, for intellectuals, and social philosophers, for all those who contemplate and relish the human pageant. In the late years of the nineteenth century and early years of the twentieth, the railroad regularly appeared as a subject matter of short stories, novels, plays, essays, poems, and ballads; it was also lavishly depicted in paintings, drawings, lithographs, posters, postcards, and other visual art forms too numerous to mention. The railroad, more than any other form of transportation in this country, has left us a rich legacy of cultural artifacts, and it is in large part through these that the railroad's presence continues to be so strongly felt.

American writers, especially, were powerfully drawn to the railroad in its golden years. Novels and stories, dealing as they so often do with conditions of social life, were regularly vehicles for the treatment of situations in which the railroad played an important role. But poets, too, were moved by the railroad because of its power, its symbolic significance, sometimes its strange eerie beauty. Railroad subjects were grist for the mills of versifiers and popular balladeers; but more profound expressions of railroad subjects could also be found in the nineteenth century in such serious poets as William Cullen Bryant, John Greenleaf Whittier, Emily Dickinson, and Walt Whitman. By the twentieth century, there were a number of poets who had actually worked on the railroad, and captured the rhythms and moods of the railroad environment in their work—Carl Sandburg was such a one. His father had been a longtime employee of the Burlington, and Sandburg himself was an itinerant railroad worker for a number of years.

American men of letters responded to the railroad as soon as the first lines were built in the 1830s. By the 1850s, the railroad was a major presence in American life, and we have already observed that writers such as Emerson and Thoreau saw the railroad both as a boon to democratic man and as an object of suspicion. The railroad could be and was a despoiler of nature; furthermore, in its manifestation of speed, and noise and clamor, it might be a despoiler of human nature as well. By the 1850s and 1860s, the great sages of New England were distrustful of the rapidly industrializing America of which the railroad was a leading force, and they were suspicious of the new generation of financial buccaneers on Wall Street—the Daniel Drews, the Vanderbilts, the Jay Goulds. And the deeply philosophical historians of the age, men like Henry and Charles Francis Adams, lamented the role that the new frenzy for business was playing in eroding the traditional values of the old American republic. And a few nineteenth-century American writers who were rooted in the old Puritan America—men like Nathaniel Hawthorne—believed that the railroad was the positive work of the devil. The strong pragmatic element in the American psyche did not allow this to be the prevailing view, but a distrust of industry and of business continued in the writers of the late nineteenth and early twentieth century.

For the most part, the literature in which the railroad plays an important role belongs to popular culture rather than to the realm of serious art. One thinks of melodramas, boys' books, thrillers, penny dreadfuls, lurid romances, and the like rather than novels of the first rank. But for a good many years, there were a few individuals in the United States, most of them with solid railroading experience behind them, who made a profession of writing stories and novels about railroading—works offering the ambience of stations, yards, roundhouses, trainmasters' offices, or locomotive cabs. In the railroad's years of prime, between 1890 and 1920, there were a number of popular authors who made a living writing such "railroad novels," and others writing juveniles of the same sort. These writers, who can genuinely be said to have created a "genre," although their names are now mostly forgotten, include Frank H. Spearman, Cy Warman, Frank L. Packard, Francis Lynde, Samuel Merwin, John Alexander Hill, and Alvah Milton Kerr. Among those who achieved success writing juvenile railroad stories were Burton Egbert Stevenson, Edward Sylvester Ellis, Allen Chapman, and Herbert Elliott Hamblen.[1] And these may be joined by an army of others who turned out railroad material for boys, from Horatio Alger to the multiple authors of the Tom Swift and Rover Boys stories. Most such authors, of course, have faded from living memory, but anyone who troubles to consult their fertile writings will still find a treasure trove of information about the place of the railroad in American life.

There is no major American novel in which the railroad is the predominant character unless perhaps one considers Frank Norris's *The Octopus,* in which the Southern Pacific Railroad is the titled creature which strangles the wheat farmers of California in its tentacles. On the other hand, any study of the American novel between the Civil War and World War I will discover the persistent and unmistakable presence of the railroad, will find over and over again references to the railroad as a creator of our way of life and as symbol of American energy, as a vehicle of all our social discriminations and nuances. The same may be said of the literature of Europe in the nineteenth century. Except for Emile Zola's *La Bete Humaine,* which has often been called the greatest novel ever to have been constructed around the railroad, few novelists took the railroad as their central focus. On the other hand, reading the novelists of England who lived in the railway age—one thinks of Dickens and Trollope, or in the twentieth-century, Kipling, H. G. Wells, and Arnold Bennett—the railroad is a vital character whose presence is deeply felt and seldom long out of view.

As American writers began to take the nation's social life as a subject matter in the years after the Civil War, the railroad became a persistent figure in the novels and stories of our major literary figures. This was particularly true of the realistic and naturalistic novelists who dominated American fiction between the 1870s and the 1930s. Nearly all of these writers were concerned with the ways that the railroad had transformed American society, how it had been intimately tied in with the American psyche, how it had become a symbol of the struggle for freedom and success, perhaps how it had created some of the looseness, the fragility, the instability of American social institutions.

Few American writers of the post–Civil War period were more interested in the railroad as an engine of social change than William Dean Howells, often credited by literary historians with providing the chief impetus to the movement called literary realism, the chief concern of which was, in Howells's own words, "the truthful treatment of commonplace material." Himself something of a restless man who began life as a printer's devil in Ohio, later settled in Boston, and then in New York, when it became the literary capital of the nation, Howells was an indefatigable observer of the passing scene. His best-known novel, *The Rise of Silas Lapham,* dealt with matters that would have been considered bad taste in the older romantic and genteel American literature: people's status in society and the morality of business.

The railroad and various railroad settings make regular appearances in the novels of Howells. A meticulous observer of life as it was lived in his time, Howells took note of the development of suburban commuters; he was concerned with the ways that the railroad broke down the barriers between the various sectors of the nation, how it sometimes created gauche or even hilarious human encounters, how it affected the surface of American life. Above all, the railroad always provided a new rhythm to American life, a new force in the domain of human relations. In his novel *A Hazard of New Fortunes* (1890), which concerns the move of a newly wealthy Pennsylvania-German named Dryfoos to New York, Howells treats the painful and difficult climb of the Dryfoos family up the ladder of New York society. At one point, Howells describes in some detail the then-open yards of the New York Central Railroad north of Grand Central Station. The railroad yard, with its smoke and inscrutable flashing lights, seems to be a metaphor for the disturbing complexity of modern life. At one point in the novel, several characters look down on the yards from a stopped elevated train and are intrigued by the "flare and tremor of the innumerable lights" and "the coming and going of the trains."[2]

Throughout his works, however, Howells is putting people in motion, showing Americans as a restless and peripatetic lot. Travel was one of his regular concerns—in fact, he published a number of travel books during his career—and in his novels and stories we discover what happens to people when they meet on trains, steamboats, or ocean voyages; how they interact with one another in hotels, museums, and libraries; what happens to them on their wedding trips and summer retreats.

None of Howell's novels have a predominately railroad setting as such; on the other hand, rather curiously, he wrote a number of plays—mostly melodramas and farces—in which trains or stations provide the principal setting. Few of these plays were ever actually put on the stage, although they are both readable and playable. They do show, however, how important the railroad was in Howell's mind as a blender and homogenizer of social mores. The titles of some of these farces—all very clever and ingeniously constructed—reveal the railroad setting: *The Albany Depot* (this being the station of the Boston and Albany Railroad in Boston), *The Parlor Car, The Sleeping Car, The Smoking Car.*

The plots of most of these plays are superficially frivolous, but nonetheless historically interesting. In *The Albany Depot* (1892),[3] a Boston gentlemen named Edward Roberts is asked to meet a new cook in the waiting room while his wife is out shopping. Not knowing what to look for, Roberts accosts a plump-looking lady who turns out to be the wife of a somewhat inebriated Irishman. The Irishman wants to pick a fight over the offense, and the farce builds up from that point. It is a peculiarly American social imbroglio—the kind of indiscretion that would doubtless never arise in a European setting. The point is that there was no limit to the number of shifting surfaces and raw materials for human comedy that are provided by the railroad station in a young democratic nation.

Around this same time, a great many writers from the Midwest and far West were beginning to make a strong impact on American literature. Sons of the middle border like Hamlin Garland, and transported westerners like Bret Harte and O. Henry, wrote about the railroad sometimes with bitterness and irony during these years when the railroad was the principal villain of western farmers and entrepreneurs. Few of the works of these writers took the railroad as their sole concern, but occasionally the railroad appears with eruptive force and monumental effect. One thinks of O. Henry's tiny masterpiece "Holding Up a Train," a work of brutal irony and keen human insight.[4]

Among these "western" works must be listed Frank Norris's *The Octopus* (1901), a novel projected to be the first part of a trilogy called "The Epic of the Wheat"—an epic never completed because of Norris's early death. *The Octopus* can be seen as a typical realistic novel of the time, but it must also be included among the progressive or muckraking novels of the early twentieth century, other specimens of which were written by Upton Sinclair and David Graham Phillips. The central theme of *The Octopus* is the harvesting of wheat in the San Joaquin Valley of California, an area seemingly dominated like a fiefdom by the "Pacific and Southwestern Railroad" (a thinly veiled substitute for the Southern Pacific). Norris portrays the railroad as being the absolute ruler of the town of Bonneville. It subsidizes and suborns Genslinger, the editor of the local paper. It also appears to control the state legislature and much of the industry of the area. The railroad's agent in the region, S. Behrman, influences prices, interest rates, and all local transactions. There is, of course, a great deal else in this long novel including a keen romantic interest, but the book can be taken as an accurate account of western hostility toward the railroad during these years.

Of America's naturalistic novelists of the early twentieth century, few treat the railroad with greater force and impact than Indiana-born Theodore Dreiser. It has often been said that Dreiser was one of the first of our literary figures to be "born on the wrong side of the tracks"—not a wholly precise assessment, although Dreiser did endure grinding poverty for a time in several Indiana towns where the Dreiser family lived, including Terre Haute, Sullivan, and Evansville. Dreiser was also haunted by the specter of unemployment as he jerked around the world looking for work as a naive and untrained newspaper reporter.

For Dreiser, the railroad represented something large, brooding, and fatalistic on the American scene; trips by train always seemed to represent a dramatic turning point in the lives of his characters. The intricate social ramifications of train travel were never lost on Dreiser, and he treated them with a keen sense of pity and largeness of understanding. *Sister Carrie* (1900), which some believe to be his greatest work, begins with the departure from home by the book's heroine, eighteen-year-old Carrie

Meeber, who in 1889 leaves her family in Wisconsin to seek a new life in Chicago. Dreiser was highly sensitive to the pain and wonder of such departures, since he had suddenly departed for Chicago as an adolescent and had himself been eighteen in 1889. No writer in the American record chronicled better than Dreiser the rootlessness and sense of expectancy inherent in train travel during these years, especially for young females, whose place in the scheme of things was perilous at best. Sister Carrie was being sent to live with her older married sister in Chicago until "something turned up." Accordingly, this train journey was a major turning point in her life, as Dreiser clearly saw. Where would it all lead? There was no knowing, but Dreiser captured the feel of this upheaval with deft precision.

> Whatever touch of regret at parting characterized her thoughts it was certainly not for advantages now being given up. A gush of tears at her mother's farewell kiss, a touch in the throat as the cars clacked by the flour mill where her father worked by the day, a pathetic sigh as the familiar green environs of the village passed in review, and the threads which bound her so lightly to girlhood were irretrievably broken.

> To be sure she was not conscious of any of this. Any changes, however great, might be remedied. There was always the next station where one might descend and return. There was the great city bound more closely by these very trains which came up daily. Columbia City was not so very far away, even once she was in Chicago. What pray is a few hours—a hundred miles. She could go back. And then her sister was there. She looked at the little slip bearing her sister's address and wondered. She gazed at the green landscape now passing in swift review until her swifter thoughts replaced its impression with vague conjectures of what Chicago might be. Since infancy her ears had been full of its fame. Once the family had thought of moving there. If she secured good employment they might come now. Anyhow it was vast. There were lights and sounds and a roar of things. People were rich. There were vast depots. This onrushing train was merely speeding to get there.[5]

As a longtime wanderer of America's urban corridors, few writers understood as well as Dreiser the tragedies of failed ambitions, the hopes and desires of the young as they hurled themselves against the hand of fate in search of some new life of luxury and high achievement. He understood how it was that the railroad symbolized the ups and downs of life's course, how it represented a kind of dramatic punctuation mark in people's lives, how it accentuated moments of life and death, success, and failure. A train ride could take you to the city, where you might succeed; it could bring you home again when your career was in ruins; it could bring home the remains of one's loved ones. Whatever there was about life that needed a heightened dramatic impulse, a trip by train supplied it.

Dreiser wrote several volumes of autobiography in which he frequently had occasion to make reference to the many times he was gripped by the enormity of change brought about by the railroad. His several trips to the "big city" of Chicago during his adolescence were some of these. Later, after working on a number of midwestern newspapers, he decided to attempt to "crack into" the newspaper field in New York. He traveled there by train, and at the old Pennsylvania Railroad terminal he got his first glimpse of the city framed through the huge arch of the ferry house—a city of hope and terror set upon a stage by a railroad terminal. Like many of his contemporaries, Dreiser understood how the railroad itself served as an energizer of desires, how it was the symbol of luxury and achievement for those rotting away in small towns. The railroad's main social function was that it reminded you of where you had come from, where you were going, what might happen to you in life. It fired up your psychic energies.

In the second volume of his autobiography, *Newspaper Days* (1922), Dreiser recounted the time that he quit his job as a reporter in St. Louis, thinking he might run a small-town paper in Ohio. He carried with him his meager savings of one hundred dollars and a few shabby bags. He slept fitfully. When he awoke in the morning, the train was passing "commonplace small towns" in northern Ohio, the stubble of cornfields framed in the window, the occasional protruding derricks of gas wells, the dreary cattle runs beside small-town depots. He thought of the dining car, which had always been a symbol of luxury to him, and determined to spend some of his fast-diminishing cash on an elegant breakfast, even if "it proved the last, pretentious, liberal, courageous deed of my life." The dining car could speak to his soul; it told him exactly where he was in life:

I have often smiled since over the awe in which I then held the Pullman car, its porter, conductor, and all that went with it. To my inexperienced soul it seemed to be the acme of elegance and grandeur. Could life offer anything more than the privilege of riding about the world in these mobile palaces? And here was I this sunny winter morning with enough money to indulge in a breakfast in one of these ambling chambers, though if I kept up this reckless pace there was no telling where I should end. I selected a table adjoining one at which sat two drummers who talked of journeys far and wide, of large sales of binders and reapers and the condition of trade. They seemed to me to be the most fortunate of men, high up in the world as positions go, able to steer straight and profitable courses for themselves. Because they had half a broiled spring chicken, I had one, and coffee and rolls and French fried potatoes, as they did, feeling all the while that I was indulging in limitless grandeur. At one station at which the train stopped some poor-looking farmer boys in jeans and "galluses" and wrinkled hats looking up at me with interest as I ate, I stared down at them, hoping that I should be taken for a millionaire to whom this was little more than a wearisome commonplace. I felt fully capable of playing the part and so gave the boys a cold and repressive glance, as much as to say, Behold![6]

The railroad appeared in so much literature during the early years of the twentieth century in just such a way—as an organ of social discrimination, as a guidepost on life's pathways. The railroad seemingly had the power to tell your future. If you were missing out on life's experiences, the railroad could tell you that, too (as in the familiar catchphrase "He missed the train," signifying the failure to make out in life's struggles). More than anything else, since the railroad provided the "metropolitan corridor" for the nation, it served as a transfusion point between all areas of the country and all levels of society.

For these reasons, it is not surprising to find the railroad as a regular presence in a large number of novels and short stories in the years between 1880 and 1930. And this is true of works by writers as otherwise diverse as Henry James, Stephen Crane, O. Henry, Mark Twain, Upton Sinclair, Owen Wister, Sinclair Lewis, Willa Cather, Edith Wharton, Zane Grey, Thomas Wolfe, and Scott Fitzgerald. The railroad makes frequent eruptive appearances in the novels and stories of Sherwood Anderson, much in the manner of Theodore Dreiser, as a beckoning hand of fate to those trapped in stifling small towns, those consumed with desire for success or luxury. John Dos Passos's rich novel *Manhattan Transfer,* which took its title from the marshy industrial place where for years the Pennsylvania Railroad changed its electric engines from Penn Station in New York, uses the railroad as a controlling metaphor for the complexity, the fragility, and the changeability of modern society.

To American writers, the railroad was always a dominant motif in the landscape both urban and rural. Nowhere is this more obvious than in the restless and biting novels of Sinclair Lewis. The railroad makes regular appearances in most of his major novels from *Main Street* to *Cass Timberlane*—this latter work containing an exceedingly funny Pullman car scene in which the book's principal character, a Minnesota judge, newly married to an attractive young woman, attempts to initiate his conjugal relations in an old-fashioned open-section sleeping car, a situation that had always been part of American folklore.

Like many writers of his day, Sinclair Lewis used the railroad as the most convenient way of evoking and explaining the American landscape. In his novel *Babbitt,* which is set in Zenith, Ohio, which Lewis proclaimed a generic city that could easily stand as the surrogate for any similar-sized city anywhere in the republic, the railroad is seen as defining the factory loop, the industrialized and smoky part of town, the "belt of railroad tracks, factories with high-perched water tanks and tall stacks—factories producing condensed milk, paper boxes, lighting fixtures, motor cars."[7] But in the wide open spaces of the great northern prairie states of Lewis's own boyhood, the influence of the railroad was supreme. In his novel *Main Street,* the central setting of which is Lewis's hometown of Sauk Centre (thinly disguised under the contemptuous name of Gopher Prairie), the railroad recurs throughout. Not only does Lewis make clear that all the residents of the town listen for the passage of the great limited express trains, they all know the exact arrival time of the way trains and the name of the president of the line.

The principal action of the novel begins when Carol Milford—a college graduate from a supposedly more sophisticated environment—arrives by train to marry a local doctor, Will Kennicott. The train that brings Carol Milford to Gopher Prairie—No. 7, the "way train"—not only offers a graphic summation of the landscape of the area in which she is to live, it paints as well a portrait of the people of these prairie towns. There are rolling clouds of the prairie, "towns as planless as a scattering of pasteboard boxes on an attic floor"; occasional glimpses of white farmhouses and red barns; faded gold stubble in a hot, dusty September. The slow way train grumbled its way up this thousand-mile rise from the Mississippi bottoms to the Rocky Mountains.

> There is no smug Pullman attached to the train, and the day coaches of the East are replaced by free chair cars, with each seat cut into two adjustable plush chairs, the head-rests covered with doubtful linen towels…. There is no porter, no pillows, no provisions for beds, but all today and all tonight they will ride in this long steel box—farmers with perpetually tired wives and children who seem all to be of the same age; workmen going to new jobs; travelling salesmen with derbies and freshly shined shoes.

> They are parched and cramped, the lines of their hands filled with grime; they go to sleep curled in distorted attitudes, heads against the window-panes or propped on rolled coats on seat-arms, and legs thrust into the aisle. They do not read; apparently they do not think. They wait.[8]

There was a grim monotony here, a stillness, a lack of civility. And what of these people who did not read, did not think? "It was a martial immensity, vigorous, a little harsh, unsoftened by kindly gardens." Still, in this big country, the mood was always ready to change, just as was the scenery out of the train window. One could never stay too long depressed, even on these most monotonous train trips. There was something big, of epic proportion here— perhaps something that could be forgiven after all.

> All this working land was turned into exuberance by the light. The sunshine was dizzy on open stubble; shadows from immense cumulus clouds were forever sliding across low mounds; and the sky was wider and loftier and more resolutely blue than the sky of cities… she declared. "It's a glorious country; a land to be big in," she crooned.[9]

These pages from Lewis's *Main Street* sum up about as well as possible the place that the railroad has had in the American novel. We Americans are a moody and mercurial people. We hanker after the sybaritic delights of the city; we violently switch our affections to nature and the wide open spaces. We are creatures of moods and diffused passions. We are rootless and have a disturbed notion of place, of family ties, of civic roots. No other form of transportation has better defined and accentuated these traits in ourselves than the railroad in its days of glory; accordingly, it is not hard to understand why for many years the railroad in its multitudinous settings was an enormous, brooding presence in the American novel.

But the railroad's appearance in American literature was not by any means limited to the novel and short story. The railroad was also a commanding presence in American drama, and a number of plays were written that either contained railroad action (sometimes hideously difficult to put on the stage) or railroad settings— stations, day coaches, dining cars, Pullmans. William Dean Howells has been mentioned in this regard, even though few of Howells's plays were ever actually produced. Other railroad plays were staged, however, some of them enormously popular. Among the plays that had a lasting impact on American culture was Augustin Daly's *Under the Gaslight,* which had its first run in 1867, when the conditions of stagecraft were very primitive indeed. The play actually called for the appearance of a flashing, snorting, hissing locomotive, which, alas, broke in two during one of the early performances.

Under the Gaslight was the very epitome of old-style melodrama. The third act of this play opened to reveal a railroad track running across the center of the stage as well as an array of switches, a shanty, a depot in the background, and other railroad devices. Here made his appearance, for the first but by no means the last time, the silk-hatted villain, prepared, with ropes and chains, to tie the hero to the tracks. "Heh, heh, heh," he snarls as he sneaks off into the trackside bush. "It is five minutes to midnight....The Lakeside Express is due on the hour." As a full moon floods the stage, the sound of a far-off locomotive whistle is heard, immediately alerting the audience to the big scene of the play—well foretold by the billboards and posters outside. The hero was about to be mangled by a giant steam locomotive. At the last minute, the heroine, whose honor, or virginity, or both, had been threatened by the villain in the first two acts, dashes onto the stage and with a courage improbable and an expertise surely impossible among the stock traits of Victorian womanhood, throws the switch at the last minute: The iron monster is sidetracked, the hero is saved. The villain slinks away, twisting his mustache in disgust.

Under the Gaslight was no isolated oddity on the American stage. In spite of the extreme difficulty of depicting railroad action on the stage, so many attempts were made that it might even be possible to write a book on the subject of American railroad drama.[10] In the 1890s, plays with a railroad setting hit the boards in merry profusion, and in 1892, when the miracle of speed was a constant preoccupation, there were three on the New York stage at one time: *The Limited Mail, A Mile a Minute,* and *The Midnight Special.* Perhaps the best and most successful of the railroad melodramas was Lincoln J. Carter's *The Fast Mail,* which was a smash hit both in New York and on the road. This play featured not one but two night mail trains and a great deal of heart-stopping action.

The better railroad plays combined vivid plots with a modest amount of believable human drama. In another play of Lincoln Carter's, *The Bride Special,* a railroad executive's daughter is spirited away from her suitor and kept captive in her father's private railway car. But the fiancé, who possesses some railroad expertise (expected of young males in those days) pursues the executive's special train with a switch engine and deftly lifts the young lady from the observation platform onto his locomotive.

After 1900, there were considerably fewer railroad dramas, but still not a scarcity. And a number of these were pretty good, including Rupert Hughes's *Excuse Me,* and Hecht and MacArthur's *The Twentieth Century.* There were a great many others with significant peripheral railroad interest, such as *Forty-Five Minutes From Broadway* by George M. Cohan, *Home Sweet Home* by Russell E. Smith, *The Little Journey* by Rachel Crothers, *Mrs. Wiggs of the Cabbage Patch,* and *Honeymoon Express,* the last of which featured Al Jolson's famous impersonation of a Pullman porter.

But if one considers American literature at the end of the nineteenth century and the first three or four decades of the twentieth century, references to the railroad are hardly limited either to the novel or the drama. Even the more elevated and rarefied art of poetry as practiced in those years contained railroad subject matters and atmosphere. At one level, there was a group of popular poets writing for newspapers and magazines who frequently produced poems or ballads (some of which were subsequently converted into musical form), and although most of them are forgotten today their work has merit, and their knowledge of and passion for their subject was genuine. Among these folk poets were

Arthur Crew Inman, Phineas Garrett, William Stanley Braithwaite, Strickland Gillilan, Cy Warman, and Harry Kemp. (The next chapter will treat the very large presence of the railroad in popular ballads and in folk music.)

Still, this hardly exhausts the picture where poetry is concerned. A great many poets whose place in the Pantheon are more secure also treated the railroad in their work. The gray eminences of the nineteenth century had done so, including William Cullen Bryant, John Greenleaf Whittier, Walt Whitman, and Oliver Wendell Holmes. In the golden age of railroading, the list of American poets who included railroad subject matters in their works, some serious, some light, could constitute an honor roll of American poetry: Carl Sandburg, Vachel Lindsay, Ambrose Bierce, Bret Harte, Edwin Arlington Robinson, Emily Dickinson, Joyce Kilmer, James Whitcomb Riley, Joaquin Miller, Archibald MacLeish, Christopher Morley, Edna St. Vincent Millay, Witter Bynner, Ogden Nash, E. B. White, Damon Runyan, Sara Teasdale, John Godfrey Saxe, Louis Untermeyer, and others.

Going into other departments of literature, the scope of achievement, if anything, is even more vast. In the nineteenth century, when we turn to the historians and social philosophers of the day, we find works of monumental achievement such as those of Henry and Charles Francis Adams. And there was a veritable flood of biographical works dealing with the giants of the railroad field—figures like Commodore Vanderbilt, Matthias Baldwin, Jay Gould, George Westinghouse, Eugene Victor Debs, E. H. Harriman, Jim Hill, Chauncey Depew, Jim Fiske, and many others. Travel writing, long considered a department of literature, flourished in the nineteenth century, and no account of the literature of railroading would be complete without mention of the many travel books written both by Europeans and Americans over the years. Many of the major English writers in the nineteenth century—figures like Dickens, Trollope, and Robert Louis Stevenson— wrote travel books as a sideline, and that practice was taken up by American writers like Howells as well. More prosaic and matter-of-fact, but still interesting, are enormous carloads of guidebooks to railway travel, about which an entire tome might be devoted.

The railroad has become the subject of much popular nonfiction writing over the years in the form of histories both formal and informal. But it has also been treated by numerous writers of considerable literary merit. The essay has never been as gracefully and consummately cultivated in the United States as in England; nevertheless, we have had our share of essayists who were fascinated by the railroad and who wrote charmingly on railroad topics. One who comes quickly to mind is Christopher Morley, a founder of the *Saturday Review of Literature,* who, in addition to novels and plays, wrote hundreds of delightful familiar essays in a distinctively personal style. These essays, many of which have been collected in book form, deal with topics as diverse as safety pins, doors, prayer books, thespianism, and book collecting. Morley was born in Haverford, Pennsylvania, in lush "Main Line" suburbia, and a considerable number of his essays deal with the commuting life, a subject he also pursued when he lived on Long Island and commuted to his job in New York as a book editor for Doubleday, Doran & Co. In his travels as a bookman, Morley became more than slightly acquainted with the trains of the New Haven between New York and Boston, as well as with the two great Philadelphia roads, the Reading and the Pennsylvania. Among Morley's railroad essays that have achieved a certain legendary significance are "The Paoli Local," "Broad Street Station," "Consider the Commuter," "An Early Train," "The Owl Train," "Going to Philadelphia," "A Package," and "On the Way to Baltimore." He wrote lovingly about those two great trains of the East, the Broadway Limited and the Twentieth Century Limited.

Although an easterner to the core, Morley published numerous essays dealing with experiences in other parts of the country as well as the railroads of Europe. One of his longer essays, "Notes with a Yellow Pen," gives an account of a trip to the west coast by the Chicago and Northwestern-Union Pacific route. And like a number of writers of familiar essays, he was not above breaking into light verse or even doggerel, dealing with the railroad scene in a funny, lighthearted way. In his "Adventures in the Middle West" he writes:

> We ride the old Rock Island
> That came from Denver's highland
> The rockety Rock Island
> That rolls through Ioway.[11]

Over the years, a great many other nonfiction writers have shown a strong interest in the railroad, although usually as one strong preoccupation among others. Falling into this category are historians, journalists, familiar essayists, travel writers, and commentators on the American scene. In this group may be included, among many others, Brander Matthews, Cleveland Moffett, E. V. Lucas, Frank H. Spearman, Joyce Kilmer, August and H. L. Mencken, E. B. White, Rogers E. M. Whitaker (whose railroad writings were issued under the name of E. M. Frimbo), Lucius Beebe, Edward Hungerford, Alvin F. Harlow, Oscar Lewis, Stewart H. Holbrook, Freeman H. Hubbard, Oliver Jensen, Garrison Keillor, and Paul Theroux.

If the railroad engaged the attention of some of our very best writers, it is probably fair to say that the history of American art has been somewhat less generous in its treatment of railroad subjects. At least it is probably safe to conclude that in the nineteenth century, when the railroad was at the height of its power and a commonplace of everyday life, few of the nation's greatest painters were drawn to railroad subject matters. Perhaps this is understandable when we consider the predominance of landscape painting in that time, and realize that American painters were still attempting to convey the notion of the American continent as an unspoiled wilderness. The romanticism and idyllic sense of bucolic landscapes kept several generations of painters away from the railroad. In England, on the other hand, the great landscape painters—the Turners and Constables—did not shy away from including trains and railroad lines in their landscape paintings. Too, in the latter half of the nineteenth century the great French Impressionist painters would use their art to capture the mood and feel of the Paris railway terminals, and the smoke and steam vapors of locomotives proved to be something that they could render with a keen sense of transcendent, iridescent beauty.

There were a few exceptions to this timidity amongst American painters. A few artists of the first rank did approach the railroad on rare occasions, gingerly perhaps. The famous landscape painter George Inness was commissioned by the Lackawanna Railroad in the 1850s to render on canvas the valley that in time became the city of Scranton, Pennsylvania, one of the great coal towns of North America. This valley, with encircling mountains so formidable looking that it is a wonder that the railroad could have penetrated them at all, had miraculously maintained its pristine beauty when Inness visited it, although the arcadian setting is interrupted by the presence of a roundhouse in the background in the heat and haze of a summer day, while a train works its way up the incline in the foreground. This painting, which now hangs in the National Gallery of Art in Washington,[12] is perhaps alone among American paintings in being able to present the railroad at peace and harmony with the landscape. It does not raise the question either in a crude and subtle way of whether the railroad is the villain that heralds the coming of an industrialized era. Instead, the railroad seems to be in harmony with its environment, as if it had verily created it, which in a sense it had. Probably the greatest of all American railroad paintings, it exists today as a reminder of the aesthetic challenges and dramatic possibilities that are inherent in the railroad but that went unrealized in nineteenth-century American painting.

Outside the landscape genre, there were several kinds of rail paintings that were frequently found in Europe in the nineteenth century but which did not become common in the United States during the same time period. English and French painters were assiduous in capturing the grand achievements of railway technology: inaugural runs, let us say, of the Stockton and Darlington, or the Liverpool and Manchester, the building or opening of the great railway terminals of London or Paris, which were considered to be monuments to national achievement; the presence and the undeniable appeal of graceful viaducts and bridges. American painters—resisting the inroads of technology—were seldom drawn to these momentous occasions, and were not taken by whatever aesthetic appeal or epic force there may have been in nascent technological development.

An interesting example of the American deficiency in this area was that neither the Union Pacific nor the Central Pacific commissioned a painting of the ceremonies at Promontory Point in 1869, even though the event was heralded in the news for weeks and months in advance. Nor did any painters undertake to chronicle the event on their own. There were, of course, newspaper illustrators on the scene, and when the two locomotives met before the public ceremony, a series of famous photographs were taken of the celebration by the construction crews, perhaps foreshadowing the coming importance of photography in railroad iconography. A painting of the official ceremony might never have been made except that Leland Stanford had been irked by the spectacular photographs: He didn't like the boozy celebration therein depicted, and he didn't like the fact that he himself wasn't in the pictures! Stanford commissioned an artist named Thomas Hill to produce an after-the-fact painting which included a great many people who were not even at the ceremony, such as Mormon leader Brigham Young, a few important political nabobs, even some dignified ladies who would not have allowed themselves to be found near such a spot, and, of course, Leland Stanford himself.[13]

Another kind of painting not well represented in the nineteenth century in America—at least where railroad subject matters are concerned—is what art historians have called genre paintings, that is to say, paintings which deal with everyday scenes, with people in natural environments, and treated in a realistic manner without idealization. In Europe, particularly England, one can identify a veritable treasure trove of such paintings, many of them found in the best museums—pictures of people rushing for trains, the bustle of the station platform, the drama of London terminals such as Waterloo or Paddington, sorrowful partings, the lover's kiss, great train robberies, anecdotal or narrative pictures of waiting rooms, train compartments, trackside scenes, and representations of all manner of humanity—children, brides, soldiers being shipped off to combat, confidence men, train guards, sweating porters, stuffy businessmen, London commuters, and all the rest.

It would not be entirely true to say that none of America's genre painters took the railroad to heart. A few did. Probably the best of the lot was Edward Lamson Henry, who in the middle years of the century produced some truly breathtaking scenes that captured the pulse and atmosphere of railroading as it was and as it touched the American people. Among Henry's paintings were historical accounts of some of the pioneer days of railroading—the inauguration of the Camden and Amboy, the first trip of the "De Witt Clinton"—paintings that were apparently painstakingly researched for accuracy and authenticity. Henry also painted a number of railroad scenes during the 1850s and 1860s that captured in profuse detail railroad ambience and the social content of railroad travel. Among his most spectacular successes was *The 9:45 Accommodation, Stamford, Connecticut* (1867). And there was *South Orange, N.J. on the Morris and Essex* (1864),[14] a richly detailed portrait of a town clearly poised between the old America and the new, between rusticity and suburbia. In this latter painting there is a diminutive diamond-stacked locomotive puffing up in the distance, an old-fashioned wooden depot with a few well-dressed travelers and a sprinkling of bucolics awaiting the train, a stagecoach and some buckboards hovering nearby. In the foreground there is a brisk looking lad of the Tom Sawyer variety hustling a flock of sheep across the tracks and out of harm's way in anticipation of the train's arrival. It would be hard to imagine a more lovely—and accurate—rendering of nineteenth-century railroading.

While it is true that American genre painters seldom took the railroad as a subject, it would be very misleading to say that the railroad was neglected by the world of art. The historical researcher has no trouble at all finding various pictorial representations of railroad scenes during the nineteenth century, although most of them, in the age before the dominance of photography, were created by pen-and-ink artists, lithographers, and artists employed by the popular press. There are literally thousands of such pictures originating in newspapers and in the various illustrated publications of the day such as *Harper's Weekly, Leslie's Illustrated Weekly, The Police Gazette, McClure's, Munsey's,* and so on. The journalistic pen-and-ink sketchers produced a veritable deluge of pictures of social scenes involving the railroad, as well as much gloom, catastrophe, romance, and intrigue, much of it of very high quality.

Publishers of prints and lithographs freely responded to a brisk and regular demand from the public that wanted to have representations of locomotives, stations, express action, and trackside melodrama of every conceivable sort. A number of such engraving firms responded with oversized prints suitable for framing. Undoubtedly the best-known firm producing prints of railroad interest was that of Nathaniel Currier and James Ives, whose printing plant on lower Manhattan turned out colored lithographic prints for sale to the masses. The firm eventually had over seven thousand different prints in production, and using a variety of artists, and selecting a broad spectrum of topics from ordinary life, they offered what was probably the first art in history aimed at mass consumption. A miracle of new lithographic and printing technologies made it possible to create art for "democratic man," and Currier and Ives prints, which usually sold for between thirty-five cents and four dollars, could be found hanging in the homes of fishermen and steelworkers as well as the affluent.

The railroad prints of Currier and Ives, usually, but not always technically accurate in detail, were keenly reflective of the railroad atmosphere and ambience of the day.[15] The railroad scenes were romanticized and dramatized renderings, showing express trains shooting their sparks into the night air, or views of the American landscape with trains moving through bright autumn landscapes, gliding over snowfields, across ravines and viaducts, through narrow mountain passes. There were prints of all the things that people wanted to see: train wrecks, robberies, snowbound trains, the shooting of Indians and buffalos from the front of a locomotive out on the vast plains. Many Currier and Ives prints were purely anecdotal or even cartoonlike treatments; as such, however, they represented the full range of human interactions with the railroad—the rush of passengers for the station restaurant, the stolen kiss in a dark tunnel, the high jinks and gaucheries of the sleeping car. The favorite comic topic of the Currier and Ives cartoon draughtsmen seems to have been the cowcatcher; in their most oft-repeated risible scenes, a cow manages to bump a train off the track—in spite of the cowcatcher.

In the twentieth century, the photograph became the predominate form of pictorial representation of the railroad, and one can only conjecture at the millions of railroad photographs that have been taken since the camera was put in the hands of amateurs. Interestingly, though, artistic renderings of the railroad did not dwindle away to nothing in the age of photography as one might expect. Indeed, there seem to have been more artists drawn to the railroad in the twentieth century than in the nineteenth. There continued to be a strong interest in sketches and pen-and-ink drawing in spite of the fact that in the 1890s magazines and newspapers acquired the ability to reproduce photographs by means of halftone plates. Even more curiously, in the twentieth century a larger number of painters became attracted to the railroad than ever before.

Certain developments in art history were partially responsible for this. Around the turn of the century, a younger generation of American artists, tired of stale academic painting and timid borrowings from European masters, began clamoring for revolutionary forms of art, demanding freedom from all of the older genteel inhibitions. By the time of the famous Armory Show in New York in 1913, a whole new group of artists was in the saddle, and some of them were strongly determined to render industrial America and scenes of everyday life in a resolutely incisive and realistic manner. One school of artists that came to prominence in the first decade of the twentieth century was subsequently called the "Ash Can" school[16]—an inappropriate label doubtless, but one which gives some indication of the urban focus of their work. A good number of the early group of Ash Can painters had been newspaper artists who worked together on papers in Philadelphia and then moved as a group to New York where they began painting cityscapes and other realistic scenes from urban life. Some of them, men like Robert Henri, John Sloan, Everett Shinn, William Glackens, and George Luks, had done their stint with pen-and-ink sketches, capturing for their papers railroad crossing accidents and other occurrences that would be of interest to metropolitan newspapers. But under strong prodding from Parisian trained Robert Henri, they took to the canvas and began rendering commonplace urban scenes as fine art.

Nearly all of the Ash Can painters were interested in railroad subjects and had numerous railroad paintings among their work. Most of them stalked the railroad yards that ringed the city's core. Everett Shinn did a series of highly moving studies of the New York Elevated Railroad. John Sloan did some canvases of the railroad ferries that worked the Hudson River for over a century—scenes that would have been a delight to Walt Whitman. Indeed, Sloan's *Wake of the Ferry* (1907) is such a haunting and lyrical depiction of the old railroad ferry crossing that it belies the meager labeling that has attached to such "realistic" works. In 1909, George Luks did a splendid portrait of the New York Central's roundhouses at Highbridge; Ernest Lawson, another member of the group, did a snow scene of the old Grand Central Station and its yards to the north.[17]

The next generation of realistic painters, men like Charles Burchfield, Edward Hopper, and Reginald Marsh, were, if anything, even more drawn to railroad topics than their teachers. Reginald Marsh spent a great many hours painting and drawing the railroad yards that sprawled in a tangled mass across the Hudson River in New Jersey. Of special interest to the social historian should be the paintings of Edward Hopper in which the railroad frequently appears as an instrument of spiritual alienation. There are cars on the New York Elevated, where people do not seem to relate; there are lonely and isolated freight cars and railroad bridges. In *Approaching a City* (1946), the upper Manhattan entrance to the tunnel to Grand Central is a gaping, meaningless hole carved under the metropolis, which, by the artist's own account, expresses "interest, curiosity and fear," the conflicting emotions of a person newly arriving in the city.[18] On a number of occasions Hopper sketched and painted train interiors, and these (like the 1938 oil, *Compartment C, Car 293*) express complex and indistinct personal feelings and social meanings.

In the twentieth century, as most are aware, art has fallen under the spell of many crusading forms and styles, some of them hardly lending themselves to treatment of the railroad. But in Europe, some of the surrealist painters depicted trains or railroad settings for their strange eerie purposes. One thinks of Paul Delvaux and René Magritte and above all the Italian Giorgio De Chirico, in whose canvases trains appear over and over again in lonely piazzas, peeping around unexpected corners, ofttimes expressing dream states whose meanings are doubtless unclear except to the artist. Some artists here and abroad took the railroad as a subject for abstraction. The American painter Charles Sheeler often depicted the railroad and various industrial landscapes in cool, analytical, cubist treatments.

For many years, there were also small numbers of painters who specialized in railroad paintings and illustrations for commercial purposes, but whose work in fact rises above the level of what is usually called "commercial art." The railroads themselves were partially responsible for this in that starting in the 1920s many of the well-heeled roads commissioned artists to paint canvases that could be used for calendars or posters, but whose originals could be hung or exhibited in art galleries. There thus grew up a small cadre of "railroad artists," whom it might be easy to demean if they had not been so good. The two mighty and competitive railroads of the East, the Pennsylvania and the New York Central, both commissioned works that would capture the flavor of their respective territories and ambience, and several artists came to be identified with one or the other of these railroads. For a long time, the work of William Harnden Foster, Walter L. Greene, and Leslie Ragan was identified with the New York Central; the work of Harold Brett and Grif Teller with the Pennsylvania. All these artists produced paintings that were both visually pleasing and dramatically electrifying.

Between 1920 and the 1960s, a good number of railroad

painters were working independently or on commission.[19] One thinks of Howard Fogg, often called the "dean" of railroad painters, who in a long career turned out not only paintings for posters and calendars but sketches for note stationery, book dust jackets, playing cards, Christmas cards, and all the rest. But there were a number of other excellent railroad artists: Otto Kuhler, Wentworth Folkins, Carl Ulrich, Peter Heik, Walter Krawiec, Gil Reid, J. B. Deneen, and George Gloff.

In the minds of most Americans, the railroad belonged to the shared culture, to everyday experience. Americans wanted their writers and artists to render the railroad both in depth of feeling and in dramatic intensity. The railroad has been well represented in the arts. But much more voluminously and zestfully it has been represented in creations and artifacts of the popular culture, and from these creations, more than any other, the railroad continues to be a living presence in American society, even though the railroad no longer touches the lives of the multitudes in quite the way it once did.

C·H·A·P·T·E·R 17

RAILROADS AND THE POPULAR CULTURE

For over a century, the railroad was close to the hearts and imaginations of the American people, and they expressed their affection for it in both literature and fine art. But the American love affair with trains and things concerning the railroad was never more fully expressed than it was in the popular culture. Americans loved to read about the railroad in their newspapers and turned with avidity to the front pages of the pulps and penny papers to read about the latest wreck, about the nefarious doings of Commodore Vanderbilt or Jim Fisk, or the heroic exploits of Kate Shelley or Casey Jones. For the most part, they did not turn to serious novels or lyric poems for their knowledge of the railroad but rather to dime novels, boys' books, penny dreadfuls, stage melodramas, posters, and prints. They liked to listen to the ballads and folk songs of the railroad. They liked to collect railroad memorabilia, much of which in the old days could be bought on the cars from the falsetto-voiced boy train butchers—railroad playing cards or engraved penknives. They liked to stow away and hoard timetables, ticket stubs, broadsides, and dining car silver from the Broadway Limited or the Super Chief. They liked picture books of trains; they heartily loved toy trains, scale models, and anything that would capture the imagination of children or recapture their own youthful fancies.

Over the years, no other popular art was more closely allied to the railroad than that of popular music. There was a natural affinity between music and the long steel rail—perhaps it was the fact that the clackety-clack of trains riding the rails had their own rhythm and thus provided an inspiration to the musical imagination of songsters. Perhaps, too, railroad folklore, with its heroes, villains, and romantic legends offered a vast repository of materials for balladeers. Above all, and perhaps most importantly, there were the traditions of the various wanderers of the rail—the tramps and hoboes—and of trackside laborers, particularly the black gangs who laid so many rails in the South and West and for whom singing as they drove in their spikes was as natural, and perhaps as necessary, as eating and breathing.

Celebration of the railroad in song goes back to the earliest days of railroading. In fact, two songs were written and published commemorating the building of the Baltimore and Ohio Railroad in 1828 even before a wheel had turned on that historical railroad. One of these songs was "The Carrollton March" by Arthur Clifton (granted a copyright on July 1, 1828, making it the first American railroad song to be recognized as such);[1] and the other was "The Rail-Road March" by Charles Meineke, dedicated to the Directors of the Baltimore and Ohio Rail Road and to singing the praises of their boldness in undertaking this ambitious project. The opening lines of "The Carrollton March" give some idea of the exuberant spirit with which the infant railroad was welcomed:

> O we're all full of life, fun and jollity,
> We're all crazy here in Baltimore.
> Here's a road to be made
> With the pick and spade,
> 'Tis to reach to Ohio, for the benefit of trade.

In the nineteenth century, it was common to celebrate any great national achievement with booster songs, many of which were published as broadsides for public enjoyment. Accordingly, a number of early railroads earned their own songs as did the telegraph when it arrived, the Atlantic cable, the sewing machine, the telephone, and the Brooklyn Bridge. But when the railroad became an exciting novelty to Americans, it was no longer necessary to commemorate the *building* of roads; song writers and balladeers began expressing the *excitement* of riding on the train.

John Godfrey Saxe's "Rhyme of the Rail," from the 1830s or 1840s, captured the joie de vivre of this new national experience:

> Singing through the forest, rattling over ridges,
> Shooting over arches, dashing under bridges,
> Whizzing through the mountain, buzzing o'er the vale,
> Bless me this is pleasant riding on a rail.

In a very short period of time, the railroad became a staple of song writers who took as their subjects the same sorts of things which fascinated the readers of dime novels and the penny press. There were railroad wrecks, the thrill of the lightning express, tales of valor and mischance, and every manner of human encounter touching the railroad—abandoned infants, sorrowful partings, burgeoning romances. Many popular ballads of the rails have been preserved because they were published either in broadsides or in pocket songsters of the day. Railroad courting songs, ending either in the joys of matrimony, or in failure and deceit, were legion in the early days. One widely distributed broadside from the 1850s, "Ridin' in a Railroad Keer," began:

> Suke Sattinet was a comely gal
> And loved her parents dear,
> Till she met slim Jim the miller's son,
> A ridin' in a rail road keer.

From the perspective of the twentieth century, it is probably easy to assume that blushing, bashful maidens were the principal victims of railroad dalliances, and a good number of the songs from these Victorian times chronicled tales of girls taken advantage of in long tunnels, hoodwinked by traveling salesmen or other slick talkers. Curiously though, gullible males were just as often taken advantage of by devious women. Beguiling young ladies managed to make off with the gold watches, fountain pens, or even the ready cash of the young men with whom they openly flirted. Not a few numbers in pocket songsters of the period were like one in Fred Wilson's *Popular Comic Songs No. 4* of 1866:[2]

> I travel for a firm in Wonsockett,
> In the cotton and woollen trade,
> And never had cause for a moment's woe
> Till meeting a fair young maid

Who served in a first class restaurant
On the Chicago and Alton line,
Refreshment room I ought to say,
But that mistake is mine.

In the years before the 1870s, much of the popular music concerning the railroad came from widely distributed songbooks that grew out of the minstrel show—a distinctly American contribution to show business history. Because it was a traveling institution, the minstrel show frequently moved by rail, and was thus more than a little prone to adopt railroad topics for its song and patter. On the other hand, a great many songs that had been popular for a long time were changed to reflect a railroad theme. A good example of this is "She'll Be Coming Around the Mountain," which Carl Sandburg claims had spread to railroad laborers in his youth and which he accordingly included among "railroad songs" in his *American Songbag* (1927). In nearly all its versions, there is a line about the team coming into town behind "six white horses," making it hard to classify as a railroad song, yet such it verily became.

By the 1870s and 1880s, the distinctive pattern and range of popular railroad songs had pretty much become established. Over the next century, most railroad songs seem to have been loosely classifiable into about half a dozen categories. One prominent category dealt with stories of a brave engineer or brakeman, or similar railroad figures like Kate Shelley, the fifteen-year old lass who tore off her bloomers to signal a train speeding toward a washed-out bridge. Many songs were of the "workin' on the railroad" variety—that is to say, ditties about the joys, the sweat, and the tears of railroad toil. Not a few of these were written by tarriers and gandy dancers who made a habit of singing while they worked—accordingly, some might be considered folk music in its purest form. Then there were the songs of tramps and hoboes, some of whom considered themselves to be "railroad men," although they may as likely have been social outcasts who merely used the blinds or boxcars as their favored means of travel.

And there were others. There were railroad blues songs—there were so many "freight train blues" and "train whistle blues" that they would be difficult to catalog. There were also numerous ballads of tragedy such as "He's Coming to Us Dead," and "In the Baggage Coach Ahead." On the other hand, there also tended to be a category of plucky upbeat songs about the joys of the railroad life, or about specific railroad trains and lines—songs like "A Railroader for Me" and "The Rock Island Line." Last, but by no means least, there were railroad spirituals such as "Life's Railway to Heaven" and "The Gospel Cannonball."

It is in the nature of all popular music that certain tunes will strike the public fancy for a while and then be cast into a realm of perpetual oblivion. Some railroad songs were very topical, dealing with a specific news item or an individual who enjoyed short-term notoriety. It is hard to imagine today that the rascally Jim Fisk was once the hero of a railroad ballad called "Jim Fisk, or He Never Went Back on the Poor," but the ballad was occasioned by Fisk's shipment of a train load of supplies to Chicago after the great fire in 1871. Fisk was given to making such florid gestures, and it is an ultimate irony that many laborers on Fisk's plundered Erie Railroad believed that "Jim" was one of them. He had, after all, worked his way up from poverty (as many at the time thought they could do), so it was easy to conclude that under Jim's flashy exterior there must have beat a heart of gold. There was no heart of gold in Jim, but he nonetheless became a hero to the struggling masses whose own aspirations could be so easily reflected off his diamond-studded shirt front.

If the song about Jim Fisk has been completely forgotten, other heroes of the railroad past have survived in good health. One is John Henry the "steel drivin' man," hero of a cycle of black ballads and tall tales. John Henry may have been a real individual or simply a composite (Louis Watson Chappell, a professor of English at West Virginia University, spent the better part of his life trying to trace the origins of the legend), but the essential John Henry story, that of a hard driving tarrier who won a battle with a steam-operated drill and then fell over dead, has never left the mainstream of American popular culture. John Henry remains a folk hero in much the same league as Davy Crockett and Paul Bunyan.

Another railroad hero who is still with us is Casey Jones—indisputably a real man who died in a railroad wreck on the Illinois Central at Vaughan Mississippi on April 30, 1900. By a curious set of circumstances, Casey Jones became the most legendary of railroad engineers without really doing anything newsworthy—indeed, he is generally believed to have been at fault in the railroad accident that killed him. Nevertheless, his heroic stature is justified by the fact that he was the only person killed in the wreck: He didn't jump clear when his crack express train plowed into a freight, but instead he stayed on to apply the brakes, which most likely saved the lives of many passengers.

Casey Jones became a household name in America as the result of a rather peculiar set of circumstances. The Jones wreck would most likely have been completely forgotten had it not been for Wallace Saunders, an unlettered black roundhouse worker at Canton, Mississippi, who, after the wreck, began singing songs about Casey Jones, perhaps in several versions. In his book *Long Steel Rail: The Railroad in American Folklore,* Norm Cohen presents evidence that even before Casey Jones's death Saunders was singing, and this perhaps in the company of a number of others, a group of "brave engineer" ballads—one for example, about a "Jimmy Jones"—but that when Casey Jones, whom Saunders knew, was killed, Saunders began transferring some of his words to this new hero, adding information about the Vaughan wreck. By some alchemy that defies rational description,[2] the Saunders song eventually got into the hands of two Tin Pan Alley song spinners, Eddie Newton and Lawrence Seibert, who in 1908 wrote their own version of the Casey Jones legend. This version, which played footloose with some of the facts, became a big hit. And it was this song, more than anything else, that was the origin of the Casey Jones legend.

Since most railroad heroes are now consigned to the recesses of history, and since most fabled railroad events like the Chatsworth wreck and the Johnstown flood are only feeble memories, one would think railroad popular songs would be completely unknown to the present generation of Americans. Such is not the case—railroad songs are still very much a part of American popular music. There are several reasons for this. A group of tunes that go back to the nineteenth century remain enormously catchy and are sung by barber shop quartets and other popular ensembles. It is hard to imagine that any American child who has gone to summer camp has failed to sing "I've Been Workin' on the Railroad," which is found in nearly every camp songbook ever published. More importantly, for well over a half century, railroad songs and legends have been kept alive by the enormously healthy and successful country and western music industry. Country and western stars and groups keep reissuing and revising railroad songs, and the public never seems to get tired of them.

The happy alliance between country music and the railroad probably goes back to the 1920s, when this kind of music was referred to as "hillbilly music," or occasionally "old time music." Around 1925, eastern record companies discovered that there was something of a market for hillbilly tunes, just as a few years earlier they had discovered a strong and steady demand for black folk songs. To be sure, there had been music in the hills of Virginia and Tennessee and other places in the South before the 1920s, although it had not been commercialized. For the most part, the white residents of these areas took their popular music from the folk songs, ballads and popular tunes of their English, Scottish, and Irish forbearers. Traveling up hill and down dale in the early years of the twentieth century solitary individuals sang to their own banjo arrangements or to those of small fiddle bands. They performed at county fairs, corn shuckings, tent meetings, school yards, and other local gatherings.

In addition to traditional nineteenth-century ballads, hillbilly singers at the beginning of the twentieth century performed tunes that came from Tin Pan Alley, but apparently when Tin Pan Alley turned its attention to the dance craze around 1915, the performers in the South began looking for their own material, sometimes composing new songs of their own. And they had a rich local heritage to fall back upon, not the least of which was black folk music. From their black neighbors, the country fiddlers learned to play the guitar; they picked up a number of the techniques of black music, most especially syncopated blues melodies with their flatted thirds and sevenths. But they also apparently picked up some of the favored themes of black songs, many of which were sung to the rhythm of the swinging hammer so well known to railroad construction gangs.

By the middle to late 1920s, there were a number of artists recording hillbilly music for major record companies, and some of the most prominent of these made highly successful hits with railroad songs. In this group were Vernon Dalhart and Jimmie Rodgers, and both hit the big time on the basis of their railroad tunes. They were not, in fact, the only successful figures on the scene in the 1920s, and some of the others—Fiddlin'

John Carson, Uncle Dave Macon, and the Carter Family—were also drawn to railroad songs and ballads.

Vernon Dalhart (his real name was Marion Try Slaughter) was born in Texas in 1883, but he had moved to New York hoping to carve out a career either in opera or light opera. A man with serious formal musical education (he had attended the Texas Conservatory of Music), Dalhart managed to find some minor roles on the stage in New York. He also did some singing in vaudeville and made out fairly well, perhaps rendering southern tunes and playing blackface roles. Around 1917, he found himself recording southern dialect tunes for the Edison Company, one of these being "Can't You Hear Me Callin' Caroline." By the mid-1920s, he was recording for the Victor Talking Machine Company, and one of his songs, "The Wreck of the Old 97," became an early hit of country music. Both the music and the words had been around for a long time; indeed, a number of other people (including Dalhart himself) had recorded it before without much success. However, when combined with another song called "The Prisoner's Song," hastily gotten up for Side B, this release of the "Wreck of the Old 97" sold over a million records in the next three years.

Historians of country music have pointed out that it was "The Prisoner's Songs," and not "The Wreck of the Old 97," which made the Dalhart disc so popular, yet "The Prisoner's Song" has been largely forgotten and "The Wreck of the Old 97" has gotten into people's blood and lives on. During the 1930s, the success of the record was such that intricate lawsuits were waged over the authorship of the words (a claim by a hillbilly named David Graves George twice went to the Supreme Court of the United States without any satisfactory resolution).[3] Perhaps it is something in the song's words that has given it an enduring popularity, perhaps it is the catchiness of the tune. The Old 97 was a Southern Railway "fast mail" and its wreck in 1902 was hardly unusual among railroad wrecks—only nine crew members were killed. But there was a poignancy about a speeding train catapulting to its doom, and the lines are easily etched in memory, especially the final lines of the engineer's gruesome death and the words of warning to wives of railroad men, and perhaps wives everywhere:

> He was going down grade making ninety miles an hour
> When his whistle began to scream;

> He was found in the wreck with his hand on the throttle
> And was scalded to death with the steam.
>
> So come you ladies you must take warning
> From this time now and on,
> Never speak harsh words to your true loving husband,
> He may leave you and never return.

Following his success with "The Wreck of the Old 97," Dalhart pressed a number of other discs featuring railroad songs, including the perennial "Casey Jones," "The Wreck of No. 9," "The Bum Song," "Billy Richardson's Last Ride," "The Wreck of the N & W Cannonball," and he made a permanent hit of the ultimate hobo song, "The Big Rock Candy Mountain."

A singer who was even more responsible for cementing a permanent bond between country music and the railroad was Jimmy Rodgers, whose brief but meteoric recording career between 1927 and 1933 has caused music historians to call him the "Father of Country Music." Mississippi-born Rodgers had himself been a railroad man, and his father before him had been a section foreman on the Mobile and Ohio Railroad. A frail youngster, whose career would later be cut short by tuberculosis, Rodgers grew up in a series of small Mississippi and Alabama towns—his father, too, was tubercular and died when Jimmy was only four. By the time he was in his early teens, he was a "water-boy" on the M&O, a chore he frequently shared with young blacks. Apparently the black railroad workers took a shine to Jimmy Rodgers and taught him how to pluck melodies from the guitar and banjo. Doubtless, he also picked up from them various work songs, moaning chants and crooning lullabies.[4]

As a young man, Rodgers held jobs on a series of railroads—this was the boomer era when rail workers customarily moved around a lot. But since his physique and stamina were unimpressive at best he never stayed employed for long and moved from place to place. Accordingly, he was as well positioned as any to empathize with hoboes, tramps, and other mournful castaways of railroad avenue and to sing their songs. Failing health eventually forced him to give up railroad work completely, and he took to performing. But he never stopped his wandering, which gave him a wide acquaintance with musical styles out of which he virtually created a wholly new tradition in music that we now call

"Country." He wedded together the styles of railroad and cowboy "wanderers"; he popularized a form of white blues music; and he borrowed freely from the sentimental ballads of Tin Pan Alley. Above all he learned to yodel, and yodeling quickly became an obligatory signature of the country singer. Younger aspiring singers, like Gene Autry, got to the top of their profession in the early 1930s because they could imitate Jimmy Rodgers's yodel.

It was probably not his musical innovations alone which caused historians to call Rodgers the father of country music—it was probably also his simple, straightforward style, the elemental humanity of the subject matters he selected for his recordings. He sang of home, of lost love, of "Mom" and "dear old Dad," and of course dug deeply into the firsthand experiences of his own lifetime, most especially as they related to the railroad. Trains and things connected with the railroad popped up everywhere in Rodgers's songs, and sometimes when adopting or arranging the work of others he intruded his own railroad yarns or flavorings. For example, his hit "Waiting for a Train" was a revision of an earlier popular tune, "Danville Girl." "Cowboy's Heaven" was reworked by Rodgers into "Hobo's Meditation."

During his brief but epoch-making recording career, Jimmy Rodgers released a number of hit songs with railroad subjects including "Ben Dewberry's Final Run," "Waiting for a Train," "Train Whistle Blues," "Hobo Bill's Last Ride," "Mystery of Number Five," "Hobo's Meditation," "Southern Cannonball," and "Let Me Be Your Sidetrack." But he also recorded or performed old-time favorites like "Casey Jones" and "The Wreck of the Old 97."

The presence of railroad themes and people in Jimmy Rodgers's music is probably responsible for the continuing preoccupation with the railroad among country singers and performers. Over the years, nearly all major country artists have recorded railroad songs; a number have even regarded themselves as specializing in railroad songs and have assiduously sought out fresh railroad material. One thinks, for example, of Roy Acuff in the 1930s, and Hank Snow in the 1940s and 1950s. Snow, a singer with a beautiful baritone and a hard professional competence, listened to Jimmy Rodgers records as a boy in his native Nova Scotia, and at the height of his career introduced a number of new railroad tunes to a now vastly increased radio audience. On the other hand, along with these few country singers who referred to themselves as "railroad" specialists—men like Roy Acuff and Hank Snow—nearly every major performer in the medium has recorded one or two of the old favorites; some have recorded a great many of them. The country-western enthusiast can easily find railroad songs on the records of artists as diverse as the Carter Family, Gil Tanner, Jimmy Davis, Gene Autry, Cliff Carlisle, Wolf Carter, Harry McClintock, Hank Williams, Ernest Tubb, Eddy Arnold, and Johnny Cash.

Over the years, popular songs concerning the railroad have come from many sources. Black blues singers have made vast contributions to the field, as have many performers from mainstream popular music. The 1940s saw the appearance of a number of catchy railroad tunes from the pop music field—there was "The Atchison, Topeka and the Santa Fe," and also "Chattanooga Choo Choo," played by the Glenn Miller Band in the movie *Sun Valley Serenade*. In release, "Chattanooga Choo Choo" sold over a million records. Nor does it seem likely that popular music has seen the end of railroad songs. One of the most beautiful railroad songs of all time, Steve Goodman's epic tone poem "The City of New Orleans," did not make its appearance until 1970; but it has subsequently been a favorite of many recording artists. And it is probably a good guess that there will be more such hits in the future.

The railroad's presence has been felt in a number of other popular media beyond those of song and ballad. The mass media of the movies and of radio and television have also shown themselves to be strongly attracted to railroad subjects throughout their histories. It is not at all surprising that the first film that historians have identified as discovering the potential of movies to entertain and tell a real story was *The Great Train Robbery*, filmed by the Edison Company in 1903. This film, only eleven minutes long, was shot by Edwin S. Porter, one of America's pioneer photographer-directors, and consisted of a single sequential short-action story. Porter was merely using an idea that was then being done to death by the various "Wild West" shows traveling the country, but he moved out of the studio in New York and filmed along the Boonton line of the Lackawanna Railroad, actually only a few miles from the towers of Gotham. Somehow, in the process, he made the territory look like the "Wild West."

Historians have testified that *The Great Train Robbery* taught Porter (and subsequent directors) how to cut, how to edit, how to place the camera in the establishment of scenes, how to get a story line to move. Movies had been so boring at the end of the nine-teenth century that vaudeville theater operators used them as "chasers" to get people out of the theater between shows. After *The Great Train Robbery,* and a few others like it, nickelodeons popped up in almost every neighborhood. As movie historian Arthur Knight has testified, "overnight, the movies became the poor man's theatre."[5]

Railroad trains and the movies seem to have been made for one another. In the train are speed, drama, action, and excitement— panting engines, billowing smoke, and great railway terminals that are a microcosm of urban life. Truth to tell, it was not *The Great Train Robbery* that first recorded a train on film. The Lumiere Brothers, who opened the first public cinema theater in Paris in 1895, included on their inaugural program a brief film entitled *Arrival of a Train at Ciotat Station.* In the years ahead, there would be literally thousands of such train arrivals in the movies. In the summer of 1991 the Museum of Modern Art in New York devoted several months to a cinema series entitled "Function and Journey: Trains and Film." This unusual tribute consisted of over one-hun-dred features, shorts, documentaries, and animated films from 1895 to the present, more than adequate documentation of the symbiosis between trains and film.

When one thinks of the relationship between the railroad and the cinema, the first thing that comes to mind are the many movies about trains that involve melodramatic action, especially that dealing with spies and international intrigue, often leading to murder, theft, abduction, or assault. The natural confinement of people on a train makes the railway car an excellent setting for plots that involve mystery, intrigue, suspense, and violent acts. European trains for some reason have always been particularly appetizing to movie makers, and any movie buff would have no difficulty reciting a list of thrill or action films involving trains from the continent of Europe. One could tick off the names of lit-erally scores of such films, some of them first rate: *Rome Express, The Lady Vanishes, Orient Express, Secret Agent, Murder on the Orient Express, Last Train from Madrid, Ministry of Fear, Van Ryan's Express, From Russia with Love, Terror by Night, Night Train to Milan, Istanbul Express, The Cassandra Crossing,* and many others.

Of the great film directors none seemed to be more convinced of the vast possibilities for suspense in trains and railroad stations than Alfred Hitchcock. Before coming to the United States, Hitchcock many times used trains as a location for perilous dramatic action with either British or continental settings. In the final years of his career in Britain, nearly all of his films had action in stations or trains, including *The Thirty-Nine Steps, The Secret Agent, Sabotage,* and *The Lady Vanishes.* When Hitchcock moved to Hollywood in 1938, he did not lose this interest; indeed, even before he visited the United States for the first time he developed a passion for American trains. He sent away for timetables of railroads and had such an uncanny knowledge of their schedules that he couldn't convince his friends that he did not have an intimate, firsthand acquaintance with the United States.[6]

During the next twenty years—the richest period of his Hollywood career—Hitchcock used trains and stations over and over again, vigorously milking all of their possibilities for suspense. Among these films were *Saboteur, Shadow of a Doubt, Strangers on a Train,* and *North by Northwest.* In this latter film, a kind of masterpiece in the genre of slick comedy-suspense, Cary Grant finds himself trying to escape the "bad guys," both at Grand Central Station in New York and La Salle Street Station in Chicago, where he implausibly disguises himself as a redcap. The scenes on the Twentieth Century Limited with Eva Marie Saint not only bring out the mood of suspense inherent in sleeping cars, but also a suggestive and steamy eroticism—the playful melange of which Hitchcock was a grand master.

American movie makers frequently used trains for purposes of suspense and intrigue, but far more frequently trains appeared in another kind of movie that was indigenous to the American soil, namely the Western. Classic movies with western settings were, for the most part, epics of the nineteenth-century frontier, and accordingly they could hardly have avoided the railroad even if they had wanted to. It is difficult to imagine a Western movie without railroad action—everything from train robberies, to cowboy and Indian encounters, shoot-out melodramas, and all the rest. Even at the present day, the Hollywood movie lot continues to be supplied with all of the props necessary to recreate the atmosphere of the frontier—diamond-stacked locomotives, wooden passenger cars, antique signals, water tanks, and country railroad stations, inevitably fitted up with a clattering telegraph apparatus. From the days of *The Great Train Robbery* and the films of William

S. Hart, there has probably been as much train action on Hollywood stages as there had been in the real old West itself.

A list of titles of Western films concerning the railroad would probably fill a small volume. A good number were excellent. To be sure, many took shameless liberties with the historical record, but a number were also carefully researched and offered authentic reproductions of real events. The building of the transcontinental railroad was the subject of several movies, including *Iron Horse* and *Union Pacific*. But one can also find a good amount of historical truth, or at least historical color, in *How the West Was Won, 3:10 to Yuma, Bad Day at Black Rock, Canadian Pacific, Last Train from Gun Hill,* and *Once upon a Time in the West*. There were at least a dozen movies featuring Jesse James, probably the best of the lot being an MGM release of 1939 with Tyrone Power and Henry Fonda as Jesse and Frank James. Paying little attention to the actual facts of the lives of the James boys, it was nonetheless a box office hit.

The classic Western *High Noon* with Gary Cooper offers a fully embodied sense of the place of the railroad in the life of the frontier. Director Fred Zinnemann repeatedly cut back to the station clock with seconds ticking away as town marshal Gary Cooper tries to raise a posse of timid townsfolk to combat the unruly local gang. The railroad station is accurately seen as the center of focus in the typical frontier town.

A number of Civil War movies also made good use of the props and mock railroad settings kept at the ready by the movie studios. The famous Andrews raid has been filmed several times. In *The Horse Soldiers,* John Wayne, playing an ex-locomotive engineer, leads a Union expedition to destroy a key Confederate railhead. *Gone With the Wind* has a very stirring and faithfully rendered scene at Atlanta's old Union Station.

Makers of comedies, too, have been drawn to the railroad over the years. Train-car chases and other slapstick sequences were vivid in the imagination of nearly all the silent directors and producers. There were Mack Sennett and Hal Roach, who led many a locomotive a merry chase during the 1920s. There was Buster Keaton's comic masterpiece, *The General,* and his *Our Hospitality*. There was Harry Langdon attempting to shave in a swaying Pullman car in *The Luck of the Foolish*. There was W. C. Fields stepping on and appropriating another man's ticket for a Pullman berth in *Poppy*.

There were Laurel and Hardy trying to go to sleep in the same Pullman berth in *The Big Noise*. There were the Marx Brothers chopping up railway cars for fuel in *Go West*. And there have been many other comic treatments of trains since the golden age of comedy. In a magnificent comic sequence in Charlie Chaplin's *The Great Dictator*, Adenoid Hynkel, dictator of Tomania, greets Benzino Napolini, dictator of Bacteria, at the railway terminal in the capital of Tomania. In more recent times, there were some choice sleeping car scenes in *Some Like It Hot* with Marilyn Monroe and Jack Lemmon. In the 1980s, *Trains, Planes and Automobiles* with John Candy and Steve Martin was seemingly dedicated to the proposition that "if anything can go wrong it will." This film contains railway mishaps so frequent and so unpleasant that Amtrak would not permit even the slightest glimpse of its logo.

In the now sadly departed genre of the great movie musical, there were a number of pictures with railroad settings or motifs, although there was no single musical built around a railroad theme. But some important movie musicals introduced popular songs elaborated from a railroad setting. There was *The Harvey Girls*, which introduced "The Atchison, Topeka and Santa Fe." Also *Sun Valley Serenade* ("Chattannoga Choo Choo"), *Dumbo* ("Casey Junior"), *The Jazz Singer* ("Toot Toot Tootsie Good-bye"), *Easter Parade* ("When the Midnight Choo Choo Leaves for Alabam"), *Forty-Second Street* ("Shuffle Off to Buffalo").[7]

It is not suggested that the movie industry used the railway only in light or frivolous treatments. Many European movies, especially, have used railroad settings to evoke serious human actions. One thinks of the French *La Bête Humaine* (based on Zola's novel), and the masterly British movie *A Brief Encounter*, directed by David Lean, in which a middle-aged couple each married to another, enjoy a few tender but futile liaisons in a railway dining room. But there are a great many other movies in which the strong bonding force of the railroad is evident: *The Last Journey, Metropolitan, Sullivan's Travels, Anna Karenina, Terminus, Night Mail, The Sting, The Manchurian Candidate, The Hucksters, Double Indemnity, Carrie, Death in Venice, The Railway Children, A Passage to India, Closely Watched Trains, The Train.*

Not all railroad films involve train action. The railroad station is often used for dramatic purposes, most especially for arrivals and partings. Small stations are used repeatedly in Western movies to punctuate or intensify the action—sometimes for dramatic shoot-outs, as in *3:10 to Yuma, Once upon a Time in the West,* and *Last Train from Gun Hill.* The great city terminals were equally useful as places to build up suspense and intrigue. Alfred Hitchcock used Grand Central Station in New York for scenes in two of his movies, *Spellbound* and *North by Northwest,* where the heroes (Gregory Peck and Cary Grant) are accused of murders and must lose themselves in the throng. Scenes of escape seem to come up over and over in movies placed in railroad terminals. In the recent movie *Witness,* a little Amish boy, witness to a gruesome murder, eludes two vicious drug dealers in the men's washroom at Philadelphia's Thirtieth Street Station. Even more often, the great passenger terminals were used for scenes of parting—especially in wartime, when soldiers had to take leave before joining their units. Actor Robert Walker put up with more than his share of such partings. In 1944, he had to leave the beautiful Jennifer Jones at Grand Central Station in *Since You Went Away.* The following year, he left Judy Garland at Penn Station in *The Clock.*

Throughout the history of the movies, the studios have used actual railroad terminals in their pictures, and it is hard to pass through Grand Central Station in New York, or Los Angeles Union Station, or Union Station in Chicago without seeing the sound booms and projection towers of some movie company. A number of times, it has been necessary to construct a movie set of a railway terminal when the story required very elaborate action or a great many scenes. MGM's *Union Depot* (1932) necessitated the creation of a set because all of its action took place in the station, and the screenplay by Gene Fowler wove together the lives of a number of serious and comic characters calling for a multitude of scenes that surely could not have been carried out in a station that was handling thousands of daily passengers. In the recent *Silver Streak* (the second of two Hollywood movies of this name), a mock-up of Chicago's Union Station had to be constructed because the directors wanted their speeding runaway train to crash into the headhouse of the station—a physical impossibility since the tracks go nowhere near the headhouse in the real station. Still, the model of the station was built with great care and attention to detail.

No mention of trains in the movies would be complete without some reference to city subway and elevated trains. Over the years, subway trains, tunnels, and stations have been used in hundreds of films, usually involving suspense, crime, or intrigue. So inviting has been the subway to the movie industry that the New York Transit Authority was required to put at the disposal of producers a station used solely for the purpose of making movies and television shows. The station employed for this purpose is the Court Street station in Brooklyn on an abandoned shuttle line. Even though the station is no longer in revenue operation, it possesses all of the things that movie makers require to produce a subway atmosphere—curves, a curtain wall, and switches.[8] The station is rented out to movie companies for realistic action shots (producers must also pay for train rentals, of course), and it is seldom idle for very long.

Subway action has been strongly appealing to filmmakers since the arrival of sound pictures. Usually, the subway has only an incidental relation to a film's story, but entire scenarios have been built around the subway on a number of occasions. One of the earliest, and best, was *Subway Express* by Martha Madison and Eva Flint and directed by Charles Erskin. Of the more recent such films, many will remember *The Taking of Pelham One Two Three,* a United Artist's film from the mid-1970s. The New York Transit Authority was not too keen on his film since it dealt with the seemingly implausible but dangerously tempting subject of the hijacking of a subway train. None too anxious to put ideas into the minds of criminally minded New Yorkers, the Transit Authority charged United Artists $275,000 for the use of the train and $75,000 for antihijacking insurance![9]

Many film directors have had a great itch to play around with the subway. The grand master of suspense, Alfred Hitchcock, had a good subway sequence in his movie *The Wrong Man* in 1956. In the movie, the hero, Henry Fonda, sits in an IND train that was supposed to be rattling noisily through the tunnel—actually it was standing still in the IND's Fifth Avenue Station. The New York elevated lines were also used dramatically in a number of films—the last Manhattan el was torn down in the 1950s, but filmmakers were subsequently able to make el films in Brooklyn or Queens. One of the best elevated sequences appeared in the first version of *King Kong* (1932). The monster ape from Africa busily rips up the tracks of the Third Avenue el line. A train coming down the line slams on the brakes. In one inspired scene, Kong's huge bloodshot eye peers in the windows at the passengers. Doubtless not liking these denizens of the urban jungle, the great ape throws the train down on the street and ties knots in it as if it were a sausage.

Either the subway or the el has appeared in hundreds of films. Among the others are *The French Connection, A Short Walk to Daylight, Beneath the Planet of the Apes,* Woody Allen's *Bananas, Union Station, Underground, The F.B.I. Story, The Young Savages, Practically Yours, Boys' Night Out, On the Town, The Bachelor Party, Bulldog Jack, Dressed to Kill, The Liquidator,* and a good many others with only minimal subway action.

When one thinks of American popular culture, it is natural to reflect first on the mass media of communication, and certainly these have always given their keen attention to things relating to trains and the railroad. But popular culture has provided many ways that a people can express their affinity with the objects, artifacts, and ideas that are a part of daily life, and because the railroad was for so long a ubiquitous part of American life, it is not strange that it has offered many expressive forms to the popular imagination. Long after the railroad moved from the forefront as a carrier of people, it has continued to inspire song writers, movie producers, novelists, and other creators of imaginative products. It continues to inspire, for example, the makers of toys for children. In the 1950s and 1960s, it seemed for a while that toy and model trains might disappear from the American scene, just as the passenger train itself seemed threatened. But this did not prove to be the case, and the interest in building and collecting these enchanting products now seems as strong as ever.

Toys are always an important part of any nation's culture, so it is not surprising that toy trains go back a long way in American history. It is not known with certainty when the first toy train was made, but it is most likely that the first mobile toy train was made in 1856 by a clock manufacturing firm in Connecticut. The locomotive had a spring mechanism to be wound up, but apparently it did not run on tracks. In 1868, the Ives Company opened for business, in this same Connecticut valley of clocks, and shortly began turning out a remarkable line of toy trains. In its plant at Bridgeport, which operated until the Great Depression of 1932, the Ives Company pioneered in the development of all kinds of toy trains, including those that ran on tracks, and even diminutive locomotives that were powered by steam.[10]

Electrically powered trains arrived on the scene fairly early, but none were built in quantity until after 1895. Before 1900, all quality toys were expensive, and only the well-to-do could afford mechanical devices that were intricate of construction. For much of the nineteenth century, the world looked to Germany for mass-produced toys—the Germans in the 1850s had found a way to fabricate toys using thin sheet metal. Accordingly, German toy trains were frequently found in the United States until World War I, after which a strong anti-German sentiment gave thrust to the American toy industry.

Electrical toy trains got a big boost after 1901, when Joshua Lionel Cowen started manufacturing them in New York City. The son of Russian immigrant parents, Cowen had earlier started to make electric novelties (Cowen claimed to have built the first battery-operated flashlight and the first electrically operated fan). Having looked at the electric toy trolley cars manufactured in the 1890s by the Carlisle and Fitch Company of Cincinnati, Cowen decided that there would be a vast market for electric trains among America's youngsters and he began putting them in production. Within a few years, he opened a plant in Newark, later Irvington, New Jersey, where millions of model electric trains were produced. At one time in Irvington Lionel had as many as two thousand people on the production line, building more railway cars and locomotives than there were full-sized versions of the articles.[11]

Other companies followed suit. Ives began making electric trains in 1910, and continued until its bankruptcy in 1932. Before World War II, Lionel had a number of competitors—Howard, Knapp, Voltamp—but eventually these disappeared. For a long time, Lionel's main competition was with American Flyer, which began making electric trains in Chicago in 1918. This company, bought up by the A. C. Gilbert Company of New Haven, Connecticut, in 1938, kept making toy trains until 1965, and had its own covey of loyal followers. The great success of the Lionel Company over the years was due to aggressive management and sales, but above all to the ability that Joshua Lionel Cowen had to divine the tastes of young boys who picked out trains in department store windows. Many of Lionel's trains were not scale models, and much of the auxiliary and scenic equipment—bridges, stations, watchmen's shanties, mountains, tunnels—were grievous-

ly out of proportion, but for that very reason they were highly stylized and full of the natural bravura that fires up a child's imagination.

The toy train industry enjoyed its pinnacle of success in the late
1940s and early 1950s, and then suffered a sharp setback. It was
said that model trains just couldn't be made to look glamorous on
TV; also, the declining fortunes of the railroad itself during this
period made many people believe that little ones, like their parents, weren't interested in trains anymore. For a while in the
1960s, some predicted that miniature trains would disappear for
good. The Lionel Company was sold several times; for a while, its
products were being made in Tijuana, Mexico. For a brief period
in the late 1960s, nothing at all was coming off the production
lines.

Suddenly, however, there was a renaissance of interest in miniature railroading—it came not so much from the young, but from
their elders, a generation of Americans looking for things to do
around the house. These elders took to scale-model railroad
building, or simply collecting. It had always been a part of the
American folklore that fathers bought model trains for their sons
so that they could play with them themselves—and this was doubtless true back in the great days of Lionel and Ives. But in the last
several decades, a whole generation of males (and a fair number
of females as well), have gotten interested in the nuances of
model train building, paying attention to intricate detail, elaborate scenery, and complicated layouts. Some of these hobbyists
construct models of once famous American trains from materials
provided by suppliers. Others have been able to purchase highly
detailed scale models from a variety of companies—German and
Japanese manufacturers have gotten into the field in a big way.
Magazines for model train aficionados are prospering mightily.
Model Railroader has a circulation of about 200,000, and when a
new publication for collectors called *Classic Toy Trains* made its
debut in the late 1980s, its premier edition of 35,000 copies sold
out immediately.

Even the old Lionel Company has been resuscitated and is
steaming on to new and unexpected glories. Bought in 1986 by
Richard Kughn, a Detroit real estate magnate and longtime model
collector, the new Lionel line is grossing fifty million dollars a
year. As many as 4,500 sets a day come off an assembly line in a

plant in Mount Clemens, Michigan, where two hundred members of the United Auto Workers Union (many of them women) produce once again the dreams of children out of die-cast metal and bits of plastic.[12] The profit figures on the model train industry and its various dependencies are bright in the extreme. Hobbyists and others spent more than 180 million dollars in 1987 as opposed to 133 million in 1983.

Model railroading and toy trains are only some of the areas where a fascination with the railroad seems to be intensifying in the last several decades. However gray the economic fortunes of the railroad since 1960s (and there have been many bright spots, too), large numbers of Americans seem to be as much in love with railroadiana as they were half a century ago, indeed probably more so. The last generation or so has seen no abatement in the number of fan rail trips. Dozens of railway museums, often with steam train rides, have been opened to the public in recent years. The phenomenon of the railway museum has spread throughout the country. Railroad ridership itself has been up sharply in the 1980s, with Amtrak scarcely able to meet the demands put upon it. The number of privately owned railway cars has increased, with many affluent individuals buying up old executive and private cars at a pittance.

The railroad has inspired collectors and hobbyists of every imaginable stripe.[13] A look through the classified ad pages of *Trains* magazine shows the great variety of items relating to the railroad that Americans want to buy and sell. Some collectors avidly specialize in highly arcane areas. There are people willing and anxious to get their hands on lanterns, signals, switch keys, bells and whistles, locks, baggage checks, ticket machinery, tickets, trainmen's badges and buttons, uniform patches, caps, engineer's hats, depot and train signs, dining car silver, linens, china from particular railroads, menus from famous crack trains, playing cards, sleeping car blankets and linens, ashtrays, posters, picture postcards, placards, railway maps, calendars, and advertising memorabilia. The marketing of printed material has long been a million-dollar industry in America. There are dealers who offer for sale items from an inventory of thousands of railway timetables going back to the early days of railroading. But many other kinds of printed materials exist to turn the fancies of the collector— sheet music, books, pamphlets, pulp magazines, annual reports, stock and bond certificates, rule books, and railroad literature of every imaginable sort. Without much effort, collectors of railroadiana can lay their hands on everything from the potbellied stoves of cabooses to the cabooses themselves.

Another million dollar industry that has grown up around the railroad in the last few decades is that of the video. Magazines for train buffs bristle with ads for video materials, which have almost completely shoved aside a smaller and earlier passion for records and audio tapes of locomotive and train sounds. Many of the videos on the market have been produced from old movies—some of professional quality, others of the strictly home amateur variety—but since the advent of video cameras a veritable army of filmmakers is in the field and on any weekend can be seen busy at work wherever train action may be on view. Some of the thousands of rail videos on the market are excellent in quality, although many are also poorly edited and weak on continuity—yet they still have a widespread appeal in spite of their steep price.

Even before the video came on the scene, the railroad drew to it the talents of a large number of still photographers, and it is an easy and safe generalization to say that no industry or activity in America has been so voluminously, fulsomely and lovingly photographed as the railroad. Many collectors of railroad memorabilia have collected photographs or books containing them. Many have toted along cameras for their own picture-taking exhibitions. Surely, millions of pictures have been taken of railroad scenes since George Eastman put his Kodak in the hands of amateurs. But in addition to the hordes of amateurs, there has always been a small cadre of professional photographers who specialize in railroad subjects, some of them possessing talents of the highest order. The works of these photographers have appeared in magazines, and many of them have been published in books. (Railroad photographers have themselves often become book publishers, or at least authors or producers of books). First-rate photographers were aiming their lenses at the railroad from early times—one can hardly forget Andrew J. Russell's plates of the great meet at Promontory Point in 1869. But with much quicker and more sophisticated equipment, the twentieth century has produced an army of highly gifted rail photographers whose works have graced many a magazine or book on rail history. Immediately coming to mind in the period between the late nineteenth century and the present are such names as J. Foster Adams, F. W. Blauvelt, William J. Landon, Gerald W. Best, Charles B. Chaney, Alfred W. Johnson, Richard H. Kindig, Philip Hastings, O. Winston Link, Jim Shaughnessy, Lucius Beebe, Charles Clegg, William D. Middleton, David Plowden, Richard Steinheimer, Ted Benson, Stan Kistler, Scott Hartley, Don Sims, John Gruber, and Don Ball, Jr.[14] During this same period, most of the major railroads employed their own professional shutterbugs, many of whom produced work of high quality.

A strong cohering force among rail fans over the years has been the publication of books, pamphlets, and magazines devoted to all phases of railroad activity. The publication of books for railroad enthusiasts has clearly been yet another industry generating enormous profits annually. Hundreds of new titles appear every year, some of them ephemeral, others serious works of history. Rail fans have long been disposed to acquire large folio volumes filled with photographs and there never seems to be a shortage of them on the market. Some of these books are carelessly yoked together collections of pictures, with poor editing and continuity (but still not modest in price); others are books of true merit. Some writers of illustrated railroad books (Lucius Beebe and W. D. Middleton are good examples) are able to provide historical continuity and serious reflective content in their work.

Railroad fans have also been well served by popular magazines over the years (these in addition to others that are directed to people inside the railroad industry). For a good part of the first half of the twentieth century, the dominant popular magazine was *Railroad Man's Magazine,* started as a kind of pulp in 1906. Ministering to the sorts of things the public then wanted to know about the railroad—stories of heroic brakemen, breathtaking rides, violent accidents—*Railroad Man's Magazine* devoted itself to "true-to-life" stories about the routines and adventures of working railmen. It ran poems and verse, and a great deal of material that we would now call "railway lore." It also ran nonfiction articles on objects of current interest to the reading public—articles about locomotive construction, signaling systems, railroad business, and so on. The magazine changed its name to *Railroad Stories* in 1932, and to *Railroad Magazine* in 1937, and although it continued to be well written and edited it slowly lost its luster as the leading railroad magazine.

Another major magazine came on the scene in 1940, when A. C. Kalmbach started *Trains*. Taking a different tack than *Railroad Magazine*, *Trains* jettisoned stories, poems, and railroad lore— doubtless all of the old "pluck and luck" tradition in railroad writing—and devoted itself exclusively to nonfiction reporting, and, above all, to good photography. Through skillful editing and decision making, *Trains* found its métier, and now rules as the premier rail fan magazine in the United States. With a sagacious mix of photographs, opinions, fact pieces, even though sometimes marred by gratuitous technical chatter, *Trains* has unwaveringly kept its finger on the pulse of rail fandom.

Mystery writer Agatha Christie, who frequently used the railroad in her own stories, once said that no form of transportation has been devised that possesses the charm and appeal of the railroad. On a train, she said, you are immediately confronted with everything that is exciting in life and nature. This is probably why the railroad has been kept so vigorously alive in the popular imagination. Even Americans who never ride the train harbor a lingering affection for things concerning trains and the railroads. They say that they'd like to ride a train again someday if only service could be improved.

In the meantime, they hearken to the sounds of the railroad and love to dredge up the noise of a steam whistle from some hidden memory; they jump in anticipation when a train flashes across a movie screen; they buy toy trains, they save old timetables. Cynical social critics have said that Americans are a people who live only in the present, a people who break all ties with the past. But in some brooding and elemental way, the strong link once forged between the railroad and the American people has never really been broken.

C·H·A·P·T·E·R 18

THE LINGERING PRESENCE

At the legendary New York's World's Fair of 1939–1940, several million visitors sampled a large and awesome exhibit that dramatized the manifold achievements of the American railroad. As befitted America's first great industry, the "Railroad Building" was the largest single structure at the fair. It contained a thousand-seat auditorium that allowed visitors to view an enormous diorama, which displayed five hundred pieces of equipment, and, in a forty-minute show, demonstrated every important function of modern railroading. But there were plenty of other railroad things to see at the fair: Twenty-seven railroads participated and offered exhibits of every imaginable sort. There was a veritable museum of British and American locomotives going back to the early days of railroading, including the Ross Winans of 1845 and the famous General of the Civil War.

A major goal of the exhibit was to demonstrate the historical contribution and solid paternity of the railroad. An extravaganza called *Railroads on Parade,* with music by Kurt Weill,[1] brought to life the great meeting of the rails at Promontory Point, Utah, in 1869. A cast of "thousands," and two accurately rendered but implausibly shiny work locomotives made their appearance as did Indians and troops of the U.S. Cavalry, reenacting the ceremonial driving in of the golden spike. The real stunners of the show, however, were the latest developments of railroad technology—sleek diesel locomotives and redesigned steam locomotives with aerodynamic cowling. The Pennsylvania Railroad exhibited a 140-foot long, 526-ton steam locomotive that came from the drawing boards of industrial designer Raymond Loewy. Weighing in at over a million pounds, this was the largest steam locomotive ever built by the Pennsylvania's Altoona shops. It was the pièce de résistance of the Pennsylvania's exhibit, and was kept continuously fired up and running on a roller bed at a speed of sixty miles an hour.

The emphasis of the exhibit was naturally on the power and dynamism of the railroad industry. Even more importantly, here was proof that railroads had a glorious future, that railroads were marching boldly ahead, and were expecting to reach the twenty-first century in a blaze of glory.

Not too far away in that glorious spring of 1939 were exhibits by a number of the railroad's modern competitors. A tiresomely large number of buildings were devoted to the automobile. There was also an impressive half-domed aviation building in which the latest aircraft were displayed suspended in a cyclorama. Everything about aviation seemed modern in the extreme in that now distant year on the edge of World War II. On the other hand, these great hanging birds still seemed to most fair goers to have something of the futuristic and fanciful about them. (The majority of Americans had never been up in an airplane in 1939.) So, too, did the exhibits of city planners, which showed sparkling intercity highways, limited access roads, sometimes of twelve lanes, in which automobiles sped to their destinations while bypassing spired cities with their brutal factory environs. The difference between these other transportation exhibits and those of the railroads was that the railroads seemed to have a firm grip on the immediate future, while these others seemed yet exploratory, tentative, idealistic. One thing was certain about the railroad—it was here, it was now; it was alive, it was healthy.

Or was it? When the World's Fair opened in 1939, the railroads, like most of the economy, had been through the worst depression in the nation's history. The railroads had had a rough time of it in the 1930s, and many had fallen into bankruptcy. On the other hand, the railroads had held up fairly well considering the terrible mess that they had been in during World War I, when many people believed that the entire rail network might collapse. By contrast, and as if by a miracle, the railroads managed to weather the storm in the 1930s—if just barely.

There were several reasons for this. Railroad managements had become more flexible, less hidebound; they were open to new ideas, receptive to new technologies. They didn't insist on doing things the same old way, as they had a generation before. There had been vast improvements out along the line. There was much new and improved rolling stock, both passenger and freight. Conditions of track and roadbed had been considerably upgraded. Railroads were much more efficient than they had ever been before, and they would become even more so. Certainly the most spectacular technological improvement of the decade just ending was the introduction of the diesel locomotive. Placed into passenger service by the Burlington in 1934 on the famous Denver Zephyr, the diesel locomotive would prove to be a boon to the railroads in the years after World War II, because of its unquestioned performance efficiencies.

Even though the diesel did not come into widespread use in the 1930s, the traveling public noticed vast improvements in railroad service during these years. There was plenty of evidence around that railroad service was retrenching. Many small, lightly used branch lines withered or died, and hundreds of small-town stations closed forever. On the other hand, where possible, the railroads attempted to find new solutions that would allow them to keep up service to lightly used lines. Even before the coming of the diesel, railroads had invested in gas-electric cars, sometimes called "doodlebugs," which allowed them to replace expensive and inefficient steam trains on branch lines and other places where only limited service was needed.

On major passenger runs of trunk railroads, service was markedly improved. Running times were greatly shortened due to better track and faster locomotives. Even before the appearance of the diesel, the railroads were placing in service bigger, more powerful, and faster steam locomotives. Fares were cut in the 1930s to attract more passengers. (During the Depression years, the average revenue per passenger mile sank to $1.90; commuters paid just over a penny a mile for their multitrip tickets![2] Most name trains were air-conditioned at this time—although the air-conditioning of private homes did not begin in a big way until after World War II. New and better passenger cars were being put in service, and after the introduction of the streamlined Zephyrs by the Burlington, many railroads placed orders for stainless-steel streamlined coaches. The two most famous name trains of the East, the New York Central's Twentieth Century Limited and the Pennsylvania's Broadway Limited, were both given streamlined consists in 1938.

Above all, with better equipment and better track, the railroads became a great deal safer than they had ever been before. The number of accidents of all kinds dropped sharply in the 1930s. In the years between 1923 and 1926, there had been over a hundred fatalities on the railroads each year. During the 1930s, the number of fatalities never exceeded forty except in one year—1938. Passenger safety was so vastly improved that the accident rate for the decade was cut by nearly fifty percent to just over .14 fatalities per 100,000,000 miles.[3] Railroad travel had once carried with it the threat of hazard and risk; now the typical American came to believe that train travel was by far the safest form of transportation. And clearly it was. With thousands of people being killed and maimed in automobiles, the railroad stood out in sharp contrast for its remarkable record of safety.

None of this meant that the railroads were healthy. From an economic standpoint, they were anything but that; they had been in a state of steady decline since 1916. This decline was due not to the appearance of younger competitors, for none of these (except the automobile) had yet gotten a firm foothold. The railroad by its very nature had built-in weaknesses, as well as some acquired infirmities that grew out of its unique American experience. One persistent weakness of the railroad in America was that insofar as it was a privately owned industry, it had always been obliged to sink a great deal of capital into its physical plant—roadbed, track, rights-of-way, fixed structures—and these costs from an economic standpoint were irrecoverable. Other kinds of businesses had much greater flexibility when it came to selling off unprofitable assets. If a particular venture didn't work, you just unloaded it and got into some other line of business. Railroads could not do this. Back in the 1880s and 1890s, the railroads had been clearly overbuilt, and their overextended plant would continue to plague them for the better part of a century. Indeed, this aspect of the railroad's troubles was manifest as early as 1893. The nationwide depression that began that year was mostly due to the fact that

British financiers dumped American railroad securities when they discovered that the damned fool Americans had built a great many railroad lines that could never possibly turn a dime's profit.

But there were plenty of other woes. Some of these also stemmed from sunk investment. The railroads were especially vulnerable to the gluttony of tax collectors of every stripe, and for many years, at least until the railroads were actually sick and dying, state tax collectors exercised their confiscatory powers to the full, flagellating the railroads at will, always under the assumption that the lines were fat and prosperous and could therefore underwrite any perceived public need. Furthermore—and this wasn't readily apparent in the nineteenth century—the railroad's irrecoverable investment also made it helpless before the demands of organized labor. In the 1890s, the railroads, with the help of government, had dealt with labor most cruelly. After World War I, and especially with the passage of several railway labor acts, the tables were turned, and labor, particularly the operating unions, exacted painful and potentially lethal tributes from an industry that no longer had the ability to fight back.

A few other weaknesses in the railroad economy had been present for a long time, but became evident only with the arrival of competition. From the beginning, there was an unavoidable taint of monopoly in the railroads' business which they could never seem to escape. This was manifested in collusive rate-making practices, with rates based on the value of service rather than costs. When the private trucking industry, which based its rates on costs, began competing with the railroads in the 1930s, the railroads were exposed to a kind of competition they would find difficult to combat.

The railroad's collusive rate-making practices had also let another evil genie out of the bottle back in the 1880s, and this would wreak havoc upon the industry for the better part of a century. The railroads could not handle the complexity of their own rate-making practices (although they certainly tried), and they had to call for relief from the government—the form of relief being the establishment of the Interstate Commerce Commission in 1887. The ICC set the rates, and brought a disarming kind of tranquility to the railroads, but it introduced many new kinds of regulation that in the long run had devastating consequences. Regulation meant a restraint on competition, and competition is supposedly at the heart of a capitalistic economic system. The railroads were thus restrained from effecting the kinds of adjustments to their business that alone makes for health in a free-market economy. They were trapped in a rigidity not entirely of their own making. Protection by the hand of bureaucracy kept them out of harm's way in the beginning, but later it condemned the industry to go through life as an overly large but sickly giant.[4]

Few if any of the underlying maladies of the railroads were obvious to the general public until after World War II, and they prompted little public debate until things began to look extremely grim for the railroads in the 1960s. On the other hand, during the 1920s and 1930s, there was plenty of evidence that newer forms of competition had cut into the railroad's near virtual monopoly of transportation. Most Americans were aware in the 1920s that the automobile and its various offspring (trucks and buses) posed a serious potential threat to the railroads. Most were aware that the automobile, with the earlier help of the interurban, had effectively wiped out railroad service to hundreds of small communities. The general public did not turn its attention to whatever problems the railroads might be having with trucks. In the 1920s, trucks posed only a small threat to the railroads as carriers of intercity freight. The trucking industry was a tiny one, small enough that it could have been taken over by the railroads. Indeed, such a step was actively considered by managements of the trunk line railroads in the late 1920s. Nor were buses a strong concern in railroad boardrooms in these years. Early buses were uncomfortable and generally regarded as unsavory by the traveling public. The national Greyhound network was established in 1929, but the roads available for intercity travel were poor. When it became possible to travel between New York and Chicago by bus, the trip took twice as long as a trip on one of the many comfortable express trains on that route. Accordingly, many years passed before buses made effective inroads into the long-distance passenger services of the railroads.

Still, every year throughout the 1930s, more and more revenues that once went to railroads were drained off to competing forms of transportation. Because most of these forms developed slowly, they did not seem to pose a really serious threat to the railroad's long dominance of the transportation scene. Most of the newer forms of transportation seemed to be nothing other than minor nuisances. The airline industry is an example. Throughout the 1930s, it remained diminutive. It had been kept alive since its founding in the 1920s by airmail contracts, this being only a mild annoyance to the railroads. Commercial passenger airlines appeared in the 1930s, but they gained only a tiny share of the market even on their strongest routes. Airport facilities, even in the largest cities, were meager. Chicago's municipal airport was Midway Field, its dimensions a mere postage stamp in the jet age—a single square mile. In the mid-1930s, however, Midway occupied only a quarter of this single square mile. A school was built on one part of its property and the field had railroad tracks running through the middle of it.

New York City had two commercial airports—Floyd Bennett Field in a very inaccessible part of Brooklyn, and North Beach Airport (later La Guardia), still poorly developed. Newark Airport in New Jersey handled most of the passengers for New York. By and large, flying was an unnecessarily complicated adventure before World War II.

When World War II arrived, the railroads had to carry the heavy burden of transportation almost single-handedly. Gas rationing made long distance trips by car a virtual impossibility. Air routes were severely cut back, and the only people allowed to fly were those who could demonstrate priorities in the war effort. Above all, of course, the railroad was the primary means of moving the armaments of war: It provided the wherewithal to transport troops to their ports of embarkation, while at the same time serving as the lifeline of the entire national economy. The railroads were accordingly called upon to perform a task of Herculean dimensions. And there was no repeat of their disgraceful performance of World War I. For the most part, the railroads put shoulder to the wheel and got the job done.

World War II proved to be a last hurrah for the railroads. It was the final period in our history when the railroad was able to interact with the lives of most people on a continual basis. It was a time when everybody who had to go anywhere once again rode the rails. There were families returning to their old home towns for Thanksgiving or Christmas, businessmen off on a junket to Buffalo, and, of course, there were soldiers and sailors, hundreds of thousands of them, crowded into Pullman berths, slumping down on aged coach seats, sometimes lying on cots in dining or baggage cars. There was an inconceivable surge of such human traffic—a traffic that, in this war, surged to both the east and west coasts.

During these years, the railroads prospered as they had not done for a quarter of a century. They were, it seemed, as by a kind of grace, as fully prepared for this war as they had ever been for anything. Even the surprise opening of the war for America—the attack on Pearl Harbor—was answered in a dramatic fashion by the railroads. On December 7, 1941, a number of aircraft intended for use by the Allies in the European war were loaded deep in the holds of a convoy of ships in an East Coast port. Four and a half days later, after a trip by rail across the continent, they were in the holds of ships bound for Hawaii.[5] All locomotives, even rusted out old tea kettles, were pressed into service. Boxcars and flatcars that in 1940 seemed as if they might be ready for the scrap heap were returned to service, patched up and made to do. The same was true of old passenger equipment. Hand-me-down coaches that had been idling away the hours in passenger yards were brought back to work hauling the thousands of young recruits going off to war and the hordes of private citizens hoping to settle their affairs or "go back home" one more time before the war effort was joined in earnest.

All of the statistics reflecting railroad service—and profits to stockholders—leapt off the page. Net railway operating income which had stood at $372,874,000 in 1938, with a rate of return on investment of 1.62 percent, rose to $682,133,000 in 1940, with a return on investment of 2.95 percent, and to $1,484,519,000, with a return on investment of 6.36 percent, in 1942.[6] All major railroads were making profits by 1942. Roads that only a few years before were being operated by trustees appointed by bankruptcy courts were paying handsome dividends. The passenger service of most lines, traditionally considered a deadweight, crept into the black and made money for their owners. Even the poor but grand Erie Railroad, which hadn't paid a dividend in sixty-nine years, and of whom it was said on Wall Street that "icicles will freeze in hell before Erie pays a dividend," finally paid a dividend on common stock in 1943.

Everyone was riding the rails in those years—soldiers, bankers, munitions manufacturers, babies. Coaches offered standing room only on many lines. Obtaining a Pullman berth or a parlor car seat was often a near impossibility. Platforms of stations everywhere were filled with milling throngs. On any given afternoon, the huge concourses of Pennsylvania Station in New York, or Union Station in Washington, spaces that had been designed to hold thousands of individuals with ease, could be found crowded with enough people to constitute a veritable army of a small nation. From these vast concourses, long chains of individuals passed down narrow stairways to trains that were crowded and smoky but often filled with a mood of camaraderie and gay resolve. The war and the dreadful attack on Pearl Harbor had galvanized the nation as had nothing before, and all travelers, perhaps even those taking up the seat of a soldier, were convinced that they were traveling in the war effort.

And it was not only travelers whose lives were touched by the railroad during the war. Railroad employment was up sharply with many new people brought into service. Older rail workers who a short time before had filled the unemployment rolls were pressed back into service. But there were many new workers—women especially. It had long been a tradition that railroading was strictly man's work, but during World War II women were found everywhere along the iron rail. There were women ticket agents, telegraphers, and conductors (sometimes called "conductorettes"), and even women brakemen on occasion. Women worked as clerks in freight houses, as telephone operators, "yardmen," signal operators, in all but the most strenuous or most highly skilled tasks. Down in the Southwest, the Santa Fe employed Mexican nationals and Indians from nearby reservations, placing them in track gangs that had been depleted by the draft.[7]

Naturally, the railroads lost a great many fit and able workers to the military services. By V-J Day, at least 350,000 rail workers had answered the call to arms. There was no choice but to tap previously unused pools of workers. Even teenagers, those below the draft age, were called upon to help. The Illinois Central Railroad established a "teenage" program to train sixteen- and seventeen-year-old youths to work as brakemen, firemen, switchmen, and the like. Between 1943 and 1945, when personnel needs were most desperate, the IC had in operation four railroad training schools (located in Chicago, Carbondale, Louisville, and Memphis), which graduated as many as four thousand youngsters and placed them in positions of responsibility.[8]

Alas, the vitality of the nation's railroads during the war cloaked a darksome and undeniable truth: The war was wearing them down. The basic economic ills of the railroads had not disappeared; indeed, they had become aggravated during the war and would grow worse shortly afterward. The heavy usage of the rails during the war, with the roads being forced to defer maintenance and unable to buy new equipment, would leave them in a perilous situation after 1945. Signs of the wear and tear were evident long before war's end. There were many more equipment failures than there had been previously. Along heavily traveled routes, trains were often late. Writer and critic Henry L. Mencken, who lived in Baltimore but who had commuted to New York once or twice a week for over thirty years, noticed that his trains now occasionally arrived late. In the 1930s he had ridden the Pennsylvania's crack flyers hundreds of times and had never been late. Now, however, there were equipment breakdowns, operational delays of one sort or another, usually not critical, but annoying nonetheless.

Even darker signs were on the horizon. On the very heavily traveled line that Mencken rode regularly, a line that put unprecedented demands on the Pennsylvania's tatterdemalion passenger fleet, there was a ghastly accident on September 6, 1943. A northbound advance section of the railroad's crack Congressional Limited derailed as it was picking up speed after its stop in North Philadelphia. The cause was a worn-out journal, and the failure violently thrust one car vertically up in the air. It was instantly sheared off by an overhead signal bridge and almost totally demolished as were several following coaches. The loss of life was heavy. It was the most deadly rail accident of the war years, with seventy-nine people killed. In the immediate aftermath of the accident, there was much talk of sabotage since captured German spies had long ago revealed that the main north-south Pennsylvania line was a principal target of sabotage plots. But a much more troubling truth emerged. This equipment, and much like it, was simply wearing out.

The heavy patronage of the railroads during the war years was amply documented in the newspaper accounts of the North Philadelphia accident. There were sixteen cars in the consist and several hundred passengers on board. Among those traveling that day, and mercifully uninjured, were newspaper magnate Roy Howard and Chinese philosopher Lin Yutang—adequate testimony to the variable and enormous load being borne by passenger trains during those years.[9]

Railroad business of all sorts began to decline as soon as the war was over. The decline was neither alarming nor precipitous at first. Indeed, the mood in the railroad industry was upbeat in the immediate postwar period. The railroads set about rebuilding their track and buying new equipment. Even the passenger service was not neglected. There was not the slightest talk of railroads giving up on passenger service, even though it was in a deficit again almost everywhere by 1946. A warm, optimistic glow bathed the railroads at least until 1950, as the newer forms of competition slowly inched forward. Characteristic of the upbeat mood of the late 1940s was an extravagant Railroad Show put on in Chicago in 1948 to celebrate the coming of the railroad to Chicago a hundred years before. All kinds of new equipment were on display—most of it streamlined and diesel powered—and the show's publicity hounds succeeded in establishing the idea that the railroads, and, yes, even passenger service, had a bright and glowing future. Expenditures for new equipment during the postwar period show that the railroads had every intention of digging in and meeting all forms of competition. By 1948, 250 new streamlined trains were in operation using 2,500 new cars, with another 2,000 cars on order for the near future. The Pennsylvania and New York Central Railroads, which had introduced streamlined consists for the Broadway Limited and Twentieth Century Limited in 1938—the work of prestigious industrial designers Raymond Loewy and Henry Dreyfuss—now purchased wholly new and, some said, even more beautiful trains. In 1949, the Great Northern Railroad revealed that it was spending nearly nine million dollars for sixty-six new cars to upgrade its Empire Builder, and later in the year the Burlington placed in service a wholly new California Zephyr between Chicago and San Francisco, a train that proved to be a howling success for the better part of a decade.[10]

There was a lot of talk in the late 1940s about completely revamping and modernizing the passenger service of the railroads. One of those who talked the most at the time was Robert R. Young, chairman of the Board of the Chesapeake and Ohio Railroad. A former Wall Street trader who got into railroads in the 1930s by taking control of the old railroad empire of the Van Sweringen brothers, Young took it upon himself to act as a gadfly for the railroad industry. In a well-orchestrated ad campaign, he complained of the various shortcomings of the passenger services of the major carriers—poor organization and promotion of the business, outmoded reservation systems (now coming into sharp conflict with the highly advanced systems of the upstart airlines), and any number of similar deficiencies. One of Young's ads, headed "A Hog Can Cross America without Changing Trains—But You Can't," made sport of a condition that hadn't changed in a hundred years. If you wanted to cross the country from New York to Los Angeles or San Francisco, you had to change trains in Chicago (or, alternatively, St. Louis or New Orleans). There was no such thing as through rail service.

Young's goading had the effect of causing some of the major transcontinental railroads to introduce through sleeping car service. You could now ride between New York and San Francisco without changing cars, but your car had to change trains, and very frequently the through service meant little more than sitting forlornly for a number of hours in a rail yard in Chicago—small comfort to most passengers. The United States had not (and has not under Amtrak for that matter) developed a transcontinental passenger service, although such was available north of the border on the Canadian National and the Canadian Pacific. A good many other reforms suggested by Young were never realized at all—a good reservation system had to await the coming of Amtrak in 1971.

Many of the proposals for upgrading passenger train service became moot after the mid-1950s, when the railroads got into serious financial difficulties and passenger operations sank deeper and deeper into red ink. The euphoria of the immediate postwar years quickly faded, along with all the hopes of railway managers that profits could be made from passengers. The railroad passenger business was now being done in by very effective competition from the airlines which quickly grabbed off the lion's share of the long-distance and transcontinental passengers. It was simultaneously threatened by the vast system of interstate highways provided at taxpayer's expense by the administration of President Dwight D. Eisenhower.

After the extensive experience with aviation in World War II, it was inevitable that the airline industry would turn into a giant in only a matter of a few years. And so it did. The major aircraft manufacturers—like Donald Douglas in Santa Monica, California, and William Boeing in Seattle, Washington—now had on their drawing boards large, comfortable and fast passenger airplanes. Fading into history now was the twin-engine DC-3, the workhorse of the 1930s, with which one might (weather permitting) take an all-day trip from coast to coast under trying, bumpy, and claustrophobic conditions. Now taking to the skies were giant birds that could move people long distances in comfort and safety. By 1954, the DC-6 was making a cross-country nonstop run in less than seven hours. And the jet airplane, which would cut that time drastically, was only three or four years in the future. The business of the commercial airlines burgeoned. Airline route mileage which had only been 39,000 in 1945 rose to 114,000 ten years later. Revenue miles rose from 32.6 million to 131.5 million in that same time period, and passengers carried rose from 475,000 to 3.4 million.[11]

Very readily, the airlines grabbed off a significant part of the passenger traffic between New York and Chicago, or between Detroit and St. Louis, or Chicago and Atlanta, all of which were overnight trips by train on major railway corridors. In the immediate postwar period, *both* the New York Central and the Pennsylvania had fifteen trains a day on their New York to Chicago routes, but many of these trains would come off within a decade. Robert R. Young, the great champion of passenger service, was stung by this decline when he took over the New York Central from the old Vanderbilt interests in a proxy fight in 1954. Only a few years earlier, he had been touting a completely revolutionized passenger service, but his subordinates quickly apprised him of the fact that the Central's passenger business was dwindling rapidly. Within a mere three years, Young would suffer the ignominy of presiding over the downgrading of the Twentieth Century Limited as that famous all-Pullman train was forced to take on coaches.

The New York Central, with Young's handpicked president, A. E. Perlman, was also stung at the same time by the construction of the New York State Thruway which paralleled the railroad's route between Albany and Buffalo. The Thruway dealt the same kind of crushing blow to the Central that the railroad itself had once dealt to the Erie Canal. Passenger traffic to the cities and towns of upstate New York fell off precipitously.

And the New York Central was not an isolated incidence of this trend. The number of passengers carried by railroads shrank alarmingly on every railroad in the country. In 1944, railroads had carried nearly 600 million intercity passengers. Already by 1949, with gasoline rationing off, this figure had dropped to 246 million; by 1959, it had fallen to 130 million, and by 1966 to 105 million. The railroad share of public carriage (not including commuters) dropped from 72.4 percent in 1944 to 15.2 percent in 1966.[12] By the early to mid-1960s, nearly all railway executives were talking in fatalistic terms about the future of passenger travel by train. There were active moves made to discourage passenger business—curtailment of service, downgrading of trains, slower schedules, closing of stations, elimination of dining or sleeping cars—and these had the effect of discouraging passengers all the more. By 1965, there were not a few prophets of gloom (and this included many railroad managers) who believed that in a few years there would no longer be railroad passenger service.

But the railroad's troubles were by no means limited to the passenger train. Intercity truck traffic was now making severe inroads into the railroad's primary business, the handling of freight. With a brisk competition from trucks using publicly financed interstate highways, many of the railroad's long-standing deficiencies were now revealed in a harsh light. The railroad suffered a much greater incidence of damage to cargoes than other forms of transportation. The slowness of rail freight became evident in the face of truck competition. Shippers who used trucks did not have to endure the long times needed to exchange freight cars to other lines, and in this newly competitive era the slowness and inefficiency of freight yards became apparent. Of course, as with passenger service, the decline of freight business was self-perpetuating. While revenues declined, railroads had smaller amounts of money available to buy modern equipment, to repair track and bridges, to upgrade yards, to automate systems, and so on. In the early 1960s, if not before, economists began to notice that the railroads were caught in what looked like a permanent and irremediable downward spiral. A few prophets of doom predicted that the railroad would be finished by the end of the twentieth century.

But such turned out not to be the case. The news about the railroads continued to be bad throughout the 1960s and 1970s—in the aggregate news reports always seemed to be of the progressive downsizing of railroad systems. Some once mighty railroads—the Lehigh Valley, for example—disappeared altogether. Mergers of formerly gigantic railroad companies became the order of the day. The Erie merged with the Lackawanna; the B&O with the C&O; finally, in 1968, in a move that nobody would have dreamed of a generation before, the Pennsylvania with the New York Central. And woe of all woes, the Penn Central merger did not save these two companies from having to go through the financial wringer: The newly merged company was in the bankruptcy courts a mere two years later, an event so catastrophic that many people believed that the railroad's day of apocalypse was near.

On the other hand, the railroads had been fighting back during the 1960s with technical innovations and improvements. They had thrown in the towel on their passenger business (although rescue was to come from the public sector), but they hadn't given up on their freight business. They determined to stay in the fray, and they did. During the 1960s, in spite of all their financial woes, in spite of all the talk of downsizing and merging, younger and more resourceful people in the business began experimenting with new forms of service. First, there was the advent of piggyback, which had had a modest beginning in the 1950s. Piggybacking was a system of carrying truck trailers on specially constructed flatcars, a system that gave the shipper flexibility and the railroads a renewed grip on the freight business. The piggyback concept was not really new. Shortly after the Civil War, P. T. Barnum, the great circus impresario, put his circus, menagerie, and sideshow on rails—fastening his wagons to the backs of flatcars. (Barnum's old circus never abandoned the rails—to this day, the Ringling Brothers, Barnum and Bailey Circus moves its two traveling circuses—the red and the blue—on forty-five-car freight trains.[13]) The Interstate Commerce Commission early approved the piggyback idea, which some trucking and labor interests opposed, and the railroads pushed the business with vigor. Between 1955 and 1960, piggyback climbed from 168,000 to 550,000 carloadings.[14]

By the 1960s, the railroads were aggressively instituting many other improvements in the freight business. Among the innovations coming in quick succession were the "unit train" and "rent-a-train" concepts, flexi-van and COFC—containers on flatcars— which can easily be transferred from flatcar to truck trailer to holds of ships. Such containers are sealed and locked to prevent pilferage. New and better freight cars, such as the "Big John" grain hoppers, were now put into service. At the same time, the railroads were buying heavily of computerized information systems for purposes of billing, locating, and tracing freight cars, and so on. They were automating freight classification yards and introducing any number of other labor-saving efficiencies.

The result was that the railroads retrieved a great deal of the business they had once lost. For example, putting in service a tri-level rack car for automobiles allowed them to get back something they had lost to trucks in the 1930s: the long-distance hauling of automobiles. This trade was aggressively pursued in the late 1950s by western lines, initially the Santa Fe and the Frisco. By 1961, half of all Class I railroads were offering this service; in 1965, the New York Central was running an entire daily train east out of Detroit, each trip carrying 1,800 new autos. By 1968, the railroad share of this new auto traffic was 5.4 million trucks and automobiles, about half of the annual production.[15]

In spite of the very grim outlook in the 1960s, even the passenger train was to enjoy a renaissance of sorts, although it was a long time coming. After many years of neglecting the railroad passenger service on the grounds that railroads were well-heeled and could afford to subsidize the passenger business, the public sector began to stir itself. States and municipal agencies now perceived the calamitous results of allowing major services to commuters to fail, and many of these were given needed support and later actually taken over by publicly administered agencies. In the halls of power in Washington, the attentions of thoughtful legislators and bureaucrats turned to methods of saving long-distance trains as well. Senator Claiborne Pell of Rhode Island published a very thought-provoking book in 1966 entitled *Megalopolis Unbound,* calling attention to the need for maintaining essential train services, especially in urban corridors where competition with airlines was feasible, and where relief of clogged highways was a paramount necessity. Even before his book was published, Pell was the moving spirit behind the High-Speed Ground Transportation Act of 1965, which laid the groundwork for the establishment of the famous Metroliner Service on the route between Boston and Washington, D.C. This service, which began early in 1969, offered trains traveling at speeds up to 110-miles per hour on continuous welded rail.

The Metroliner was an almost instant success. Its inauguration

at approximately the same time as the merger of the New York
Central and Pennsylvania Railroads seemed to be a good omen
for the merger's success. But the rapid decline of the Penn
Central into bankruptcy and the continuing hard times of many
other railroads only pointed out how important continuing government intervention was for the health of the railroads.
Accordingly, there was further talk about establishing a national
passenger service that would take this function away from the railroads and spread the success of the Metroliner service to other
parts of the country. In 1969 and 1970, a veritable hodgepodge of
"save-the-train" bills were introduced into Congress, and long
negotiations between Congress and a rather suspicious
Republican administration finally resulted in the passage of a bill
to establish a National Railroad Passenger Corporation. This corporation was to take over from the railroads all of the passenger
services of the country (except commuter) and run them without
regulatory interference of the Interstate Commerce Commission.
Called Railpax—later changed to Amtrak—the new entity was
brought into existence by the signature of President Richard
Nixon on October 30, 1970.[16]

Amtrak got off to a very shaky start. Congress did not supply
adequate funds to get the experiment off the ground in a healthy
condition. Amtrak, which began its life by pooling the existing
passenger equipment of the participating railroads, had to start by
dropping about half of the passenger trains still being run by the
railroads on May 1, 1971, its first day of operation. Some routes
were later restored, but Amtrak has subsequently operated a much
more diminutive system of passenger trains than the one operated
by the railroads prior to 1971.

The great hope, of course, was that the trains which remained
would be better run—that government sponsored passenger service would bid good-bye to nasty reservation clerks, flat-wheeled
coaches, uninhabitable stations, shabby dining cars and all of the
other deficiencies that had caused an outpouring of complaints
against the railroads for several decades. And to a certain extent,
these hopes were justified. Amtrak never got the money from
Congress that was needed to do the job right; it had to continue
using the tracks of the railroads which for the most part had been
downgraded for freight traffic. But it did manage to do about as
well as possible under these severe restraints. Many Americans

would continue to bewail the fact that in Amtrak the United States was not getting the modern high-speed passenger trains of the French or Swiss National Railways, or of the New Tokaido line in Japan with its "bullet trains." Amtrak from the beginning was a typically American political compromise—the kind of thing that would make no one totally happy. The curious mélange of public and private control would continue to raise troubling and refractory issues of public policy.

Amtrak did manage to muddle through some very hard years. It established a nationwide reservation system; it bought its own modern rolling stock; it developed laudable protocols of service; it modernized stations along its route. Some of its routes, such as the northeast corridor, already blessed with Metroliner Service when Amtrak took over, were outstanding successes from the outset. In other places, passengers returned to the rails when they saw that Amtrak was running pleasant trains and employing personnel who seemed to like people. To be sure, a sword of Damocles continued to hang over Amtrak, since there was always a lingering threat that funds would be cut off. In the budget-cutting mood of the early 1980s, there were threats from the Reagan administration that all funds would be cut off for Amtrak. Fortunately, these threats were never carried out.

And curiously, just as Amtrak came under some of its most serious threats, it was beginning to attract more passengers, some of them annoyed by the airline industry which had become "deregulated" under the very same Reagan administration. By the mid-1980s, airline fares were up drastically. Airlines were abandoning less profitable routes. They now seemed to be giving the public the same harried and indifferent clerks and flight personnel that once gave the railroads a bad name. Delayed flights, poor information, lost baggage, and deteriorating services of all sorts convinced many people who hadn't taken a train in years to try a ride on Amtrak. By the mid-1980s, nearly all the trains to the West Coast were booked up months in advance during the summer. There was a new generation of individuals who wanted to "see America," and who savored the long-forgotten pleasures of eating in a railroad dining car.

This does not mean to say that Amtrak is an unqualified success. It has done a great deal better than anyone would have predicted in 1971. Threatened regularly with oblivion by the withdrawal of federal funds, enough money has come in so that Amtrak has been able to keep pleasant, if not luxurious, trains in service. But there are ongoing problems with poor track many places that Amtrak goes, and when riders to the West Coast find themselves delayed up to eight hours because of slow orders, thereby passing the scenic part of their trip in the dark, Amtrak officials will hear more than enough of the complaint "Never again will I ride the train."

Amtrak has had to endure more than problems with insufficient funds and poor track; as a quasi-public institution, it has had to put up with the pork-barreling demands of congressmen whose votes are needed to keep it alive. Too, Amtrak has been saddled with unfavorable labor contracts and the extraordinary expense and inflexibility that goes with them. Passengers riding, say, the Southwest Chief, will find a large, helpful, seemingly unpressured onboard crew (attracted no doubt by highly inflated union wage scales); yet there is no one on board to clean out the washrooms, so that by the end of the trip across the country they are ofttimes in deplorable condition. Still, for the most part, Amtrak passenger service is tolerably good. Many passengers who were annoyed by the sniffish airs of the old Pullman porters and conductors find themselves soothed by the more democratically mannered attendants of sleeping cars and day coaches.

Amtrak has had by far its greatest success with the famous northeast corridor—Washington, Baltimore, Philadelphia, New York, Boston. Its fleet of trains there, powered by high-stepping 7000 hp B-B AEM7 electric locomotives pulling modern Amfleet coaches, is the showcase of the system. These trains have drawn so much patronage that Amtrak is now the top passenger carrier between New York and Washington, with seventy percent of the combined air-rail traffic. Unfortunately, Amtrak has not been as successful with the "corridor" concept elsewhere along its lines, which is to be regretted since the use of high-speed trains on corridors of medium lengths provides the best opportunity for modern rail technology, and probably the most favorable use of heavy rail passenger service in the United States. For example, Amtrak has not done a good job of capturing the lion's share of the traffic between Chicago and Detroit, or Chicago and Milwaukee, or Chicago and Indianapolis, objectives that would be within its grasp.

One further blessing conferred by Amtrak has been the salvation of many passenger stations. Amtrak has done a fine job of refurbishing old stations and in other cases constructing completely new ones where needed. Amtrak has played a major role in saving several great city terminals. For example, the rejuvenation of the old South Station in Boston, accomplished partly with local and state funds, not only saved this attractive anchor for the Amtrak corridor but preserved an historical landmark that is socially uplifting to the neighborhood in which it stands. The same may be said of the recent rejuvenation of the turn-of-the-century Beaux-Arts masterpiece, Washington's Union Station. Several earlier attempts to readapt the station for other purposes were failures, and there was considerable fear that it might have to share the fate of the monumental Penn Station in New York, leveled in 1963. In the 1980s, much of the old dignity and grandeur of Daniel Burnham's architectural masterpiece in Washington was restored by adapting it for multipurpose uses. Reopened officially at the end of 1988, the station has many of the features of a modern mall: Shoppers mingle with commuters, rail passengers, strollers, and visitors to the nation's capital, most of whom appreciate having a building they can call their own. The grandeur of the old railroad terminal has been maintained, and this gives the building a distinctive style and flavoring as a public place. But deftly insinuated into the complex are 120 stores, cafes, restaurants, boutiques, and a nine-screen cinema. Amtrak officials were sufficiently taken by it all that they moved in with their own executive offices.[17] The Union and South Stations bode well for railroad-centered urban revival projects in the years ahead.

It has been too often repeated that the last half of the twentieth century has witnessed the decline of the American railroad, and a weakening of its once strong bond with the American people. Between 1930 and 1980, the number of railway miles was cut in half. At one time, there hardly existed a community anywhere in the land which was not in reasonable proximity to a railroad line, even to a railroad station, but today there are many areas of the country where the clackety-clack sound of railroad movements and the shrill horns of diesel locomotives are never heard. There are millions of American young people who have never known that it was once possible to go home for Christmas to almost any town or hamlet by means of public carriage; that once upon a time you could send your trunk away to college by a railway

express service that would come to your house, pick up your
trunk, and deliver it safely to your college room by truck-rail connection two hundred or two thousand miles away. These same
youngsters probably cannot conceive that there was a time when it
was possible to look at a railway timetable and to ascertain that
you were to arrive at Philadelphia, or Des Moines, or Atlanta at
2:35 P.M. and that you would actually arrive at that time, and not
some other, even if your train had to slog through howling blizzard or torrential rain.

Still, it is remarkable that the railroad has managed to retain at
least some of the affections of the American people. Americans
are notorious for casting away practical contrivances that have
become outmoded. But there have been curious exceptions to
this. Radio, for example. Although radio was supposed to have
been superseded by television and many predicted in the 1950s
that it would disappear altogether, it hasn't. Reports of the railroad's death, too, were greatly exaggerated.

To be sure, some passion for the railroad has been maintained
by those of an older generation who remember the steam locomotive, who can recall the thrill of riding in a train behind this lovely
primordial monster. Much of the romance of the railroad faded
when the steam locomotive disappeared from the scene. Perhaps
there was something akin to human nature in these simple
machines, whose devisings could be so easily grasped. The steam
locomotive from the beginning had been likened to a horse,
which is to say, an animal, a comparison which gave it a natural
and personal element, something that could be understood and
kept under control. The diesel locomotive does not have this
attribute of kinship with conditions of animal life; neither does
the automobile nor the airplane. They are alien and impersonal
creatures.

The steam locomotive may have accounted for much of the
charm of the railroad, but not all of it. Since America grew up
with the railroad, the railroad was in a sense a part of our extended family, the family network we can never completely abandon.
The railroad defined us as a nation, it gave birth to our sense of
selfhood, it gave us our individual stamp. It had a great deal to do
with the formation of our national economy and our national culture. It was always a burning manifestation of local energies. For
most of its life, the railroad was an outward symbol of what we

were doing. For lumberjacks in the dark woods of Maine or northern Michigan, the chug of an approaching locomotive was not the sound of something foreign, something intrusive—it was never just somebody else's line of business. The railroad had pumped life into this remote land, was the obvious harbinger and measure of its success.

The railroad represented the can-do spirit and aroma of enterprise. And it did so in tangible ways. So much of what is called business and enterprise is cold, drab exchange—the heartlessness of paper transactions. The railroad on the other hand was always a manifestation of the tangible. It provided a lifeline, a way of connecting people and places who otherwise would be estranged from one another. Even Henry David Thoreau, who prized his solitude at Walden Pond, found that the railroad did something to make his heart beat faster, get his juices flowing, perhaps establish some sense of community with the rest of humanity.

As a form of transportation, the railroad was as nearly perfect as possible in its days of grace. Not only did it go everywhere—to 140,000 stations at one time—but travel by train was civilized and stylish. Slow by the standards of today, travel by train always had the mark of civility to it. On even the best aircraft of the present time, even in first class, one is not really a passenger, one is being shipped, like eggs in a carton. One is riveted to one's seat, with the activity of the nearby aisle uninviting and cramped. The train rider moved among his fellow man, rejoiced in an interpersonal environment. Rail travel also permitted him to keep his link with the world that lay beyond the window. He virtually became part of the railway scene himself. As Lucius Beebee once put it so well: "Romance and glory are implicit in outside motion, in side rods, crossheads, eccentrics, and the implacable rhythm of counterbalanced driving wheels reeling off the miles as the chapters of history were once written by the measured passus of the Roman legions."[18]

Because railroad tracks went everywhere and because giant railroad companies had their nodes and outposts everywhere in the land, the railroad was always closer to the people than any other industry. The railroad took on the characteristic of the places it served—it was a country gentleman or a slow-poke frontiersman as it threaded its way far beyond the urban centers. In the great industrial corridors, it took on the characteristics of cities and sprawling suburbs and exuded a character of bustle, of energy, high efficiency, and panache. The railroad was standardized in its technology, but not in its personality. Out where the way train dropped off its bundle of papers or solitary passenger, the railroad was one kind of being; in the city, often with thousands of passengers converging in some giant terminal, the railroad was something altogether different. The country station, often the very heart of the small town's social life, diffused and emboldened the railroad's functions. The great city's terminals were also centers of social activity, but here the railroad's presence was concentrated, plowed under, which is what city folk would have wanted. Trains crept slowly into huge overarching train sheds, and in more modern times slipped, electrically powered, into tunnels that began many blocks from the giant terminal, coming into town silently and unobserved—an unobtrusive but indispensable utility like electric and sanitary lines. Chameleonlike, the railroad adapted itself to its manifold localities and accordingly was buried deeply in the American psyche—was seen to be a part of America, not merely something spun out by technology.

Perhaps because the railroad had threaded the nation together, was once the nation's only infrastructure, because it was not just a utilitarian tool of our interests, but rather something imbedded in our psyche, we have never been able to shake ourselves loose of our infatuation with it. Something of an obsession with the railroad has stayed in our blood. Perhaps this explains why thousands of people annually visit the still growing number of railroad museums and avidly buy tickets for steam train excursions whenever they are available. Perhaps this explains why model trains—for adults and children—are selling better than ever. The toy train runs through scenic small towns with twinkling lights, through sylvan glades, over steel-arch bridges, past any and all of the scenic America that strikes our fancy: This is the America we like to know, in a kind of ideal and romanticized vision, always as something benign, something we believe can be kept under our control.

In the fall of 1989, a new luxury rail service mimicking that of the famed Orient Express was inaugurated between Washington, D. C., and Chicago. The train (called American-European Express) was no lightning express; indeed, it was nothing more than added equipment on Amtrak's regular Capitol Limited; yet its promoters were extolling the virtues of cars refurbished with mahogany woodwork, brass art deco lamps, a club car with a polished ebony piano and a black granite bar, a dining car that served stately seven-course dinners and had an impressive wine cellar; and sleeping cabins (including a "presidential cabin") with all the amenities. Although prices were steep, there was no shortage of customers for this kind of romantic adventure.[19]

Somehow, romance has always been closely allied to things concerning the railroad. Yes, the railroad has also been a business in America, sometimes a hated, sometimes a troubled, business. Yet there was to the railroad this other more highly personal side, this element of lingering romance. As Henry James put it so aptly, the railroad always held out the promise of being something more than its mere physical self. For we Americans, this "something more" was that the railroad charged up our psychic energies, made us realize our manifest destiny. The long steel rails running to the horizon invested the nation with a spirit of excitement and adventure, of vitality and eager discovery. The railroad always held the promise of romantic adventure because in a fundamental way it was identical with our own national yearnings; it gave birth to both our good and bad traits; it was one of the primal ways that we came to realize ourselves.

NOTES

Chapter 1

1. George Rogers Taylor, *The Transportation Revolution, 1815–1860* (New York: Harper & Bros., 1951), p. 7.

2. Wheaton J. Lane, *From Indian Trail to Iron Horse, Travel and Transportation in New Jersey, 1620–1860* (Princeton: Princeton University Press, 1939), pp. 64–65.

3. Van Wyck Brooks, *The World of Washington Irving* (New York: E. P. Dutton & Co., 1950), pp. 33–34.

4. Stewart H. Holbrook, *The Old Post Road* (New York: McGraw-Hill Book Co., 1962), p. 5.

5. John T. Cunningham, *New Jersey: America's Main Road* (New York: Doubleday, 1966), p. 129.

6. Malcolm Keir, *The March of Commerce* (New Haven: Yale University Press, 1927), p. 53.

7. Ibid., pp. 81–82.

8. Frances Trollope, *Domestic Manners of the Americans* (London: Folio Society, 1974), p. 246.

Chapter 2

1. J. B. Snell, *Early Railways* (London: Octopus Books, 1972), p. 5.

2. Kenneth O. Morgan, ed., *The Oxford Illustrated History of Britain* (Oxford: Oxford University Press, 1984), p. 451.

3. Arthur Elton, *British Railways* (London: Collins, 1945), p. 12.

4. Probably the best-known biography of the Stephensons is Samuel Smiles, *The Lives of George and Robert Stephenson,* originally published in 1861 (recent edition: London: Folio Society, 1975).

5. Howard Loxton, *Railways* (London: Paul Hamlyn, 1967), p. 32.

6. The Quincy granite railroad remained horse drawn until 1870.

7. Loxton, p. 32. Loxton's text shows a drawing of the *Orukter Amphibolos,* but one can only conjecture as to its authenticity.

8. Wheaton J. Lane, *From Indian Trail to Iron Horse, Travel and Transportation in New Jersey* (Princeton: Princeton University Press, 1939), p. 281.

9. Jim Shaughnessy, *Delaware and Hudson* (Berkeley: Howell-North Books, 1967), pp. 31–35. There is a drawing of the original Stourbridge Lion on p. 32, and photographs of the Century of Progress replica on pp. 33 and 342.

10. Seymour Dunbar, *A History of Travel in America* (New York: Tudor Publishing Company, 1937), pp. 943–54. This gives a good accout of all the Baltimore and Ohio experimental locomotive experiments up to the Tom Thumb. See also Edward Hungerford, *The Story of the Baltimore and Ohio Railroad, 1827–1927* (New York: Putnam, 1928).

11. Alvin F. Harlow, *The Road of the Century* (New York: Creative Age Press, 1947), pp. 12–14.

12. John T. Cunningham, *Railroading in New Jersey* (Newark: Association of American Railroads, 1951), p. 7.

13. Ibid.

14. Loxton, p. 22. This book contains extensive excerpts from Fanny Kembles's account of her first railroad trip.

15. Alvin F. Harlow, *Steelways of New England* (New York: Creative Age Press, 1946), p. 89.

16. From *The Western Sun* (Vincennes, Indiana), July 24, 1830; quoted in Dunbar.

Chapter 3

1. Wheaton J. Lane, *From Indian Trail to Iron Horse* (Princeton: Princeton University Press, 1939), pp. 273–74.

2. George Rogers Taylor, *The Transportation Revolution, 1815–1860* (New York: Harper & Row, 1951), pp. 79, 84.

3. Seymour Dunbar, *A History of Travel in America* (New York: Tudor Publishing Co., 1937), pp. 1067–68.

4. Clark Spence, *Montana* (New York: W. W. Norton, 1978), p. 7.

5. Edward Harold Mott, *Between the Ocean and the Lakes: The Story of Erie* (New York: John S. Collins, 1900), p. 98. For a full account of this day's activities, invited guests, speeches, etc., see pp. 94–109.

6. Edward Hungerford, *Men of Erie* (New York: Random House, 1946), p. 90.

7. For an account of many of these early accidents, see Robert B. Shaw, *A History of Railroad Accidents, Safety Precautions and Operating Practices* (self-published, 1978), pp. 13–21.

8. Charles Frederick Carter, *When Railroads Were New* (New York: Henry Holt & Co., 1910), pp. 169–70.

9. Ibid.

10. August Mencken, *The Railroad Passenger Car* (Baltimore: The Johns Hopkins Press, 1957), p. 10.

11. Ibid., p. 17.

12. John H. White, Jr., "Rails from Old World to New," *Smithsonian Book of Inventions* (New York: W. W. Norton, 1978), p. 95.

Chapter 4

1. Charles Dickens, *American Notes* (London: Oxford University Press, 1957; first edition, 1842), pp. 64–65.

2. Jeffery Richards and John M. MacKenzie, *The Railway Station: A Social History* (New York: Oxford University Press, 1986), p. 39.

3. Seymour Dunbar, *A History of Travel in America* (New York: Tudor Publishing Co., 1937), p. 1034.

4. Stewart H. Holbrook, *The Story of American Railroads* (New York: Crown Publishers, 1947), p. 354.

5. Dunbar, pp. 1037–39.

6. Edward Harold Mott, *From the Ocean to the Lakes: The Story of Erie* (New York: John S. Collins, 1900), p. 401.

7. Ibid., p. 400.

8. Alvin F. Harlow, *Steelways of New England* (New York: Creative Age Press, 1946), pp. 230–32. See also Lucius Beebe, *The Trains We Rode,* Vol. I (Berkeley: Howell-North Books, 1965), p. 308.

9. Holbrook, p. 402.

10. Ibid., p. 401.

11. Ibid., p. 301.

12. August Mencken, *The Railroad Passenger Car* (Baltimore: Johns Hopkins University Press, 1957), p. 22.

13. Mott, p. 409.

14. Thomas Curtis Clarke, "The Building of a Railway," in *The American Railway* (originally published in 1888; reprint, New York: Arno Press, 1976), pp. 45–46.

Chapter 5

1. For a description of the Grand Crossing accident, see Robert B. Shaw, *A History of Railroad Accidents, Safety Precautions and Operating Procedures* (self-published, 1978), pp. 95–102; the Norwalk accident is described on pp. 189–92.

2. George Rogers Taylor, *The Transportation Revolution* (New York: Harper & Row, 1968), p. 92.

3. Caroline E. MacGill, *History of Transportation in the United States Before 1860* (Washington: Carnegie Institution of Washington, 1917), p. 371.

4. Taylor, p. 96.

5. Ibid., p. 100.

6. *The Oxford Illustrated History of Britain* (New York: Oxford University Press, 1984), pp. 452, 455.

7. Stewart H. Holbrook, *The Age of Moguls* (Garden City: Doubleday, 1953), p. 22.

8. Matthew Josephson, *The Robber Barons: The Great American Capitalists, 1861–1901* (New York: Harcourt Brace & Co., 1934), p. 20.

9. An excellent recent account of Drew's Wall Street manipulations is contained in John Steele Gordon, *The Scarlet Woman of Wall Street* (New York: Weidenfeld and Nicholson, 1988).

10. Leo Marx, *The Machine in the Garden* (New York: Oxford University Press, 1967), p. 150. Another work that covers much the same ground as Marx but with more specific focus on the railroad is James A. Ward, *Railroads and the Character of America, 1820–1887* (Knoxville: University of Tennessee Press, 1986).

11. Henry David Thoreau, *Walden* (New York: The Heritage Press, 1939), p. 123.

12. Ibid., p. 122.

13. Nathaniel Hawthorne, "The Celestial Railroad," in *Twice-Told Tales*, selected and introduced by Wallace Stegner (New York: The Heritage Press, 1966), p. 163.

Chapter 6

1. *Eighth Census of the United States: Mortality and Miscellaneous Statistics,* 1860.

2. George H. Douglas, *Rail City: Chicago, USA* (San Diego: Howell-North Books, 1981). For an account of the contributions of William Butler Ogden to the growth of Chicago as a rail center, see pp. 9–26.

3. Russel Blaine Nye, *Society and Culture in America, 1830–1860* (New York: Harper & Bros., 1977), p. 282.

4. Henry V. Poor, *Manual of Railroads of the United States for 1868–1869* (New York: H. V. and W. H. Poor, 1868). See pp. 20–21 for the statistics on 1860.

5. Allan Nevins, *The Emergence of Lincoln: Prologue to the Civil War, 1859–1861* (New York: Charles Scribner's Sons, 1950), pp. 195, 305.

6. Stewart H. Holbrook, *The Story of American Railroads* (New York: Crown Publishers, 1947), p. 164.

7. John T. Cunningham, *Railroading in New Jersey* (Newark: Associated Railroads of New Jersey, 1951), p. 32.

8. Robert C. Black, III, *The Railroads of the Confederacy* (Chapel Hill: University of North Carolina Press, 1952), p. 23.

9. Ibid., p. 2.

10. For a brief account of the backgrounds of McCollum and Haupt, see Thomas Weber, *The Northern Railroads in the Civil War* (New York: King's Crown Press, 1952), pp. 135ff.

11. Robert Selph Henry, *This Fascinating Railroad Business* (Indianapolis: The Bobbs Merrill Company, 1946), p. 437.

12. Weber, p. 61.

13. Black, p. 31.

14. Ibid., pp. 29–31.

15. A good account of the Andrews raid appears in Oliver Jensen's *Railroads in America* (New York: American Heritage Publishing Company), pp. 74–77. Another good account is in Freeman Hubbard, *Railroad Avenue* (New York: McGraw-Hill Book Co., 1945).

16. Quoted in Dee Brown, *Hear That Lonesome Whistle Blow: Railroads in the West* (New York: Holt, Rinehart and Winston, 1977), pp. 71–72.

17. On Chinese immigration and employment in California, see Carl Wittke, *We Who Built America: The Saga of the Immigrant* (Cleveland: The Press of Case Western Reserve University, 1967), pp. 472–79.

18. For a popular account of the great race, see Brown, pp. 100–135. There is, however, a large literature dealing with the building of the transcontinental railroad. See, for example, Gerald M. Best, *Iron Horses to Promontory* (San Marino: Golden West Books, 1969); see also Barry B. Combs, *Westward to Promontory* (Palo Alto: American West Publishing Company, 1969); Wesley C. Griswold, *A Work of Giants: Building the First Transcontinental Railroad* (New York: McGraw Hill, 1962); George Kraus, *High Road to Promontory* (New York: Castle Books, 1969). Of recent interest is John Hoyt Williams, *A Great and Shining Road* (New York: Times Books, 1988). The classic text on the "big four" and the beginnings of the Central Pacific is Oscar Lewis, *The Big Four* (New York: Alfred A. Knopf, 1946). For an account of the Union Pacific construction, see Grenville M. Dodge, *How We Built the Union Pacific Railway*, U.S. Congress, 2nd Session, Senate Document 447 (Washington: Government Printing Office, 1910).

Chapter 7

1. U.S. Bureau of Census, *Historical Statistics of the United States, 1789–1945,* Washington, 1949, pp. 200–2.

2. For an account of the history of the Pullman Company, see Joseph Husband, *The Story of the Pullman Car* (Chicago: A. L. McClurg & Co., 1917). A more general account of sleeping cars is in August Mencken, *The Railroad Passenger Car* (Baltimore: Johns Hopkins University Press, 1937). See also John H. White's encyclopedic *The American Railroad Passenger Car* (Baltimore: Johns Hopkins University Press, 1978).

3. A good popular account of the standard time movement as it affected the railroads can be found in Stewart H. Holbrook's *The Story of American Railroads* (New York: Crown Publishers, 1947), pp. 354–59.

4. Cf. George H. Douglas, *Rail City: Chicago USA* (San Diego: Howell-North Books, 1981), pp. 161–65.

5. Quoted in John A. Garraty, *The New Commonwealth: 1877–1890* (New York: Harper & Row, 1968), p. 88.

6. Henry Adams, "The New York Gold Conspiracy," in Charles Francis Adams, Jr., and Henry Adams, eds., *Chapters of Erie* (Ithaca: Cornell University Press, 1956), pp. 104–5.

7. Ibid., pp. 105–6.

8. The classic account of the Erie raids is contained in *Chapters of Erie.* For a more recent account, see John Steele Gordon, *The Scarlet Woman of Wall Street* (New York: Weidenfeld and Nicolson, 1988). See also Edward Harold Mott, *Between the Ocean and the Lakes: The Story of Erie* (New York: John S. Collins, 1900).

9. For an account of the Gould presidency of the Erie, see Mott, pp. 161–200; see also Edward Hungerford, *Men of Erie* (New York: Random House, 1946), pp. 158–70.

10. Hungerford, p. ix.

Chapter 8

1. Eugene V. Smalley, *History of the Northern Pacific Railroad* (New York: G. P. Putnam's Sons, 1883), pp. 162–84.

2. Cf. Stewart H. Holbrook, *The Story of American Railroads* (New York: Crown Publishers, 1947), pp. 210–13.

3. Dee Brown, *Hear That Lonesome Whistle Blow: Railroads in the West* (New York: Holt, Rinehart & Winston, 1977), pp. 82–83.

4. Laura Winthrop Johnson, "Eight Hundred Miles in an Ambulance," *Lippincott's,* XV, June 1875, p. 695.

5. Holbrook, p. 103.

6. Carlton J. Corliss, *Main Line of Mid-America: The Story of the Illinois Central* (New York: Creative Age Press, 1950), p. 88.

7. Paul Wallace Gates, *The Illinois Central and Its Colonization Work* (Cambridge Harvard University Press, 1934), is the classic work on the colonization efforts of the Illinois Central in this period.

8. Holbrook, p. 107.

9. Ibid., p. 109.

10. Richard C. Overton, *Burlington West* (Cambridge: Harvard University Press, 1941), pp. 341, 360.

11. American Social Science Association, *Handbook for Immigrants to the United States* (Cambridge, MA: Riverside Press, 1871).

12. Carl Wittke, *We Who Built America: The Saga of the Immigrant* (Cleveland: Case Western Reserve University Press, 1967), p. 259.

13. Quoted in Wittke, pp. 291–92.

14. Brown, pp. 245–46.

15. Ibid., p. 250.

Chapter 9

1. *Official Railway Guide of the United States,* June 1868, p. 21.

2. Ibid., Table 132.

3. The Jersey Central ferry was eight blocks away at Liberty Street; the Pennsylvania nine blocks away at Cortland Street; the Lackawanna thirteen blocks away at Barclay Street; the Erie seventeen blocks away at Chambers Street.

4. Quoted in Jeffrey Richards and John M. MacKenzie, *The Railway Station: A Social History* (New York: Oxford University Press, 1986), p. 291.

5. In the 1940s and 1950s, through the efforts of Robert Young of the Chesapeake and Ohio, passengers could journey on sleeping cars that

were switched between railroads in Chicago, but no single trains of one name or number made a trip across the United States.

6. For a brief sketch of the Parmalee Company, see George H. Douglas, *Rail City: Chicago USA* (San Diego: Howell-North Books, 1981), pp. 143–47.

7. William F. Rae, *Westward by Rail: The New Route to the East* (New York: Appleton, 1871), p. 63.

8. Quoted in Dee Brown, *Hear That Lonesome Whistle Blow: Railroads in the West* (New York: Holt, Rinehart and Winston, 1977), p. 152.

9. A good account of the career of Fred Harvey can be found in James Marshall, *Santa Fe: The Railroad That Built an Empire* (New York: Random House, 1945), pp. 97–113.

10. Robert Louis Stevenson, *Across the Plains* (London: Chatto & Windus, 1913), p. 31.

11. Brown, pp. 149–50.

12. Ibid., p. 150.

13. For a good brief account of the career of Jesse James, see Freeman H. Hubbard, *Railroad Avenue*, New York: McGraw-Hill Book Co., 1945, pp. 105–23.

Chapter 10

1. Rodney Welch, "The Farmer's Changed Condition," *Forum*, X, February 1891, p. 693.

2. Oliver Jensen, *Railroads in America* (New York: American Heritage Publishing Co., 1975), p. 152.

3. Dee Brown, *Hear That Lonesome Whistle Blow: Railroads in the West* (New York: Holt, Rinehart & Winston, 1977), p. 273.

4. Quoted in Allan Nevins and Henry Steele Commager, *A Short History of the United States* (New York: Modern Library, 1945), pp. 374–75.

5. Henry George, "What the Railroad Will Bring Us," *Overland Monthly*, vol. 1, no. 4, October 1868, p. 38.

6. Jensen, p. 119. For a fuller account of Hill's life, see Joseph Pyle, *The Life of James J. Hill* (Garden City: Doubleday, Page & Co., 1917).

7. Quoted in John A. Garraty, ed., *Encyclopedia of American Biography* (New York: Harper & Row, 1974), p. 490. The classic biography of

Harriman is George F. Kennan, *E. H. Harriman*, 2 vols. (Boston: Houghton, Mifflin, 1922).

8. The proportion of British and Irish immigrants fell from 45 percent in the decade of the 1860s to 18 percent in the 1890s. That of the Italians, Russians, and South Europeans rose from .1 percent to 50 percent in this same period. Cf. Samuel Eliot Morison, *Oxford History of the American People* (New York: Oxford University Press, 1965), p. 768.

9. Stewart H. Holbrook, *The Story of American Railroads* (New York: Crown Publishers, 1947), pp. 257–58.

Chapter 11

1. Lucius Beebe and Charles Clegg, *When Beauty Rode the Rails* (Garden City: Doubleday & Co., 1962), p. 8.

2. This was patent #373098, granted to Henry Howard Sessions on November 15, 1887. The vertical end frame was developed by Sessions in the Pullman shops.

3. August Mencken, *The Railroad Passenger Car* (Baltimore: The Johns Hopkins Press, 1957), p. 34.

4. Alvin F. Harlow, *The Road of the Century* (New York: Creative Age Press, 1947), pp. 293–94.

5. *Official Railway Guide,* June 1893, p. 709.

6. Edwin F. Alexander, *The Pennsylvania Railroad* (New York: W. W. Norton, 1947), pp. 95–96.

7. Lucius Beebe, *The Trains We Rode,* Vol.2 Berkeley, CA: Howell-North Books, 1966), p. 525.

8. Quoted in promotional brochure, Chicago and Northwestern Railroad, 1897.

9. Mencken, p. 80.

10. E. H. Cockridge, *The Orient Express: The Life and Times of the World's Most Famous Train* (New York: Harper & Row, 1980), p. 25.

11. Lucius Beebe, *Mansions on the Rails* (Berkeley CA: Howell-North Books, 1959), p. 19.

12. From W. G. Marshall, *Through America* (London, 1882), quoted in Mencken.

13. *Mansions on Rails,* p. 18.

14. Harlow, pp. 408–9.

15. Ibid.

16. Lucius Beebe, *The Central Pacific and the Southern Pacific Railroads* (Berkeley, CA: Howell-North Books, 1963), p. 334.

Chapter 12

1. John A. Kouwenhoven, *The Columbia Historical Portrait of New York* (New York: Harper & Row, 1953), p. 166.

2. John T. Cunningham, *Railroading in New Jersey* (Newark: Associated Railroads of New Jersey, 1951), p. 95.

3. Lawrence Grow, *On the 8:02: An Informal History of Commuting by Rail in America* (New York: Mayflower Books, 1977), p. 133.

4. For a description of the origin and development of commuting in Chicago, see George H. Douglas, *Rail City: Chicago: USA* (San Diego: Howell-North Books, 1981), pp. 252–98.

5. Carlton J. Corliss, *Main Line of Mid-America: The Story of the Illinois Central* (New York: Creative Age Press, 1950), p. 347.

6. Grow, p. 81. The Long Island was the biggest commuter operation in North America, but South Station in Boston saw the largest number of train movements.

7. Ibid., p. 87.

8. Lida Newberry, ed., *New Jersey: A Guide to Its Present and Past* (New York: Hastings House, 1977), p. 352.

9. Harold M. Mayer and Richard C. Wade, *Chicago: Growth of a Metropolis* (Chicago: University of Chicago Press, 1969), pp. 84–85.

10. Communication with the author, April 15, 1979.

11. *Organization and Traffic of the Illinois Central Railroad* (Chicago: Illinois Central Railroad, 1938), p. 312.

12. Grow, p. 87.

13. Cunningham, p. 100.

14. Thomas T. Taber, III, *The Delaware, Lackawanna and Western Railroad in the Twentieth Century,* Vol. 1. (self-published, 1980), p. 203.

15. Cunningham, p. 100. For a fuller account of the career of engineer Ben Day, see Taber, pp. 365–66.

16. An excellent account of the Pennsylvania's massive and highly successful electrification effort is Michael Bezilla, *Electric Traction on the Pennsylvania Railroad, 1895–1968* (University Park: The Pennsylvania State University Press, 1980).

Chapter 13

1. H. Roger Grant and Charles W. Bohi, *The Country Railroad Station in America* (Boulder, CO: Pruett Publishing Co., 1978), p. 3.

2. For a discussion of the architectural element of American railroad stations, see Carroll L. V. Meeks, *The Railroad Station: An Architectural History* (New Haven: Yale University Press, 1956), the best general history of this subject, although not mainly concerned with small stations; H. Roger Grant and Charles W. Bohi, *The Country Railroad Station in America* (Boulder, CO: Pruett Publishing Co., 1978); Edwin P. Alexander, *Down at the Depot: American Railroad Stations from 1831 to 1930* (New York: Bramhall House, 1970); Randolph Bye, *The Vanishing Depot* (Wynnwood, PA: Livingston Publishing Co., 1973); Harold A. Edmonson and Richard V. Francaviglia, eds., *Railroad Station Plan Book* (Milwaukee: Kalmbach Publishing Co., 1977); *Waiting for the 5:05: Terminal, Station and Depot in America,* compiled by Lawrence A. Grow (New York: Main Street Press, 1977); Edward A. Lewis, *New England Country Depots* (Arcade, NY: The Baggage Car, 1973). An excellent discussion of the utilitarian functions of these structures is found in John A. Droege, *Passenger Terminals and Trains* (New York: McGraw-Hill Book Co., 1916).

3. Daniel Boorstin, *The Americans: The Democratic Experience* (New York: Random House, 1973), pp. 126–27.

4. Grant and Bohi, p. 9.

5. Quoted in Alvin F. Harlow, *Steelways of New England* (New York: Creative Age Press, 1946), p. 89.

6. Stewart H. Holbrook, *The Story of American Railroads* (New York: Crown Publishers, 1947), pp. 419–20.

7. For an extensive account of "rail dogs," see Freeman H. Hubbard, *Railroad Avenue* (New York: McGraw-Hill Book Co., 1945), pp. 262–94.

8. Thomas T. Taber and Thomas T. Taber, III, *The Delaware, Lackawanna*

and Western Railroad in the Twentieth Century, Vol. 1, (Muncy, PA: self-published, 1980), p. 166.

9. Sinclair Lewis, *Main Street* (New York: Harcourt Brace & Co., 1920), pp. 235–36.

10. Holbrook, p. 180.

11. According to the Interstate Commerce Commission, in 1902 nearly 4,000 people "struck by trains, locomotives or cars" died instantly or within twenty-four hours of collision; another 3,563 suffered injuries. Quoted in John R. Stilgoe, *Metropolitan Corridor* (New Haven: Yale University Press, 1983), p. 167.

12. F. Scott Fitzgerald, *The Great Gatsby* (New York: Charles Scribner's Sons, 1925), pp. 176–77.

13. Thomas Wolfe, *You Can't Go Home Again* (New York: Charles Scribner's Sons, 1940), p. 49.

14. Theodore Dreiser, *Dawn* (New York: Premier Books, 1965), p. 267.

Chapter 14

1. Henry Hope Reed, *American Skyline* (New York: The New American Library, 1956), p. 91.

2. Lewis Mumford, *The City in History* (New York: Harcourt Brace & World, 1961), p. 461.

3. Edmund Wilson, *The Twenties* (New York: Farrar, Straus and Giroux, 1975), pp. 22–23.

4. Helen Hooven Santmyer, *Ohio Town* (New York: Harper & Row, 1984), pp. 245–46.

5. John Betjeman, *London's Historic Railway Stations* (London: John Murray, 1972); p. 125.

6. Carroll L. V. Meeks, *The Railroad Station: An Architectural History* (New Haven: Yale University Press, 1956), p. 51. See also Walter H. Kilham, *Boston after Bulfinch* (Cambridge: Harvard University Press, 1946); Charles E. Fisher, *The Story of the Old Colony Railroad* (n.p., 1919), pp. 138ff.

7. Meeks, p. 101.

8. Quoted in Meeks, pp. 101–2.

9. Jeffrey Richards and John MacKenzie, *The Railway Station: A Social History* (New York: Oxford University Press, 1986), pp. 42–43.

10. Unfortunately, Chicago's Grand Central Station did not survive; it was demolished in 1971 in a wanton act of civic destruction. Another Romanesque station in Chicago, the Illinois Central station (called Central Station), was torn down three years later.

11. Cf. John A. Droege, *Passenger Terminals and Trains* (New York: McGraw-Hill Book Co., 1916); reprint, (Milwaukee: Kalmbach Publishing Co., 1969), pp. 151–52. See also Leland M. Roth, *McKim, Mead and White, Architects* (New York: Harper & Row, 1983), pp. 314–29, which contains an extensive treatment of the design and construction of Penn Station.

12. Alvin F. Harlow, *The Road of the Century* (New York: Creative Age Press, 1947), p. 415.

13. Droege, p. 168.

14. William D. Middleton, *Grand Central: The World's Greatest Railway Terminal* (San Marino, CA: Golden West Books, 1977), pp. 93–94.

15. Ibid., p. 120.

16. Harlow, pp. 416–17. For a detailed description of the Grand Central complex, see Middleton, pp. 81–129.

Chapter 15

1. For an extensive discussion of the interurban era, see William D. Middleton, *The Interurban Era* (Milwaukee: Kalmbach Books, 1967); and, by the same author, *The Time of the Trolley* (Milwaukee: Kalmbach Books, 1967).

2. Robert A. Smith, *A Social History of the Bicycle* (New York: American Heritage Press, 1972), p. 222.

3. Malcolm Keir, *The March of Commerce* (New Haven: Yale University Press, 1927), p. 316.

4. Joe McCarthy, "The Lincoln Highway: The First Continental Paved Road," *American Heritage*, June 1974, pp. 32ff.

5. For an account of this trip, see Ralph Nading Hill, *The Mad Doctor's Drive* (Brattleboro, VT: Stephen Greene Press, 1964).

6. McCarthy, pp. 32ff.

7. Keir, p. 323.

8. Department of Commerce, *Biennial Census of Manufacturers,* 1921, (Washington, 1924), pp. 1034–35.

9. Quoted in Frederick Lewis Allen, *Only Yesterday* (New York: Harper & Row, 1959), p. 136.

10. Peter Lyon, *To Hell in a Day Coach* (Philadelphia: J. B. Lippincott, 1968), p. 188.

11. Erie Railroad Company, *Rates of Pay and Rules for Conductors, Trainmen and Yardmen,* September 1917, p. 2.

12. President's Conference on Unemployment, *Recent Economic Changes in the United States* (New York, 1929), I, p. 246.

13. Burl Noggle, *Into the Twenties: The United States From Armistice to Normalcy* (Urbana: University of Illinois Press, 1974), p. 170.

14. Phil Patton: *Open Road: A Celebration of the American Highway* (New York: Simon and Schuster, 1976), pp. 44–45.

15. Allen, p. 83.

16. Patton, p. 81.

17. Henry James, in *The American Scene,* quoted in John R. Stilgoe, *Metropolitan Corridor* (New Haven: Yale University Press, 1973), p. 339.

Chapter 16

1. For an extensive bibliography of these writers and an account of some of their lives, see Frank P. Donovan, Jr., *The Railroad in Literature* (Boston: Railway and Locomotive Historical Society, 1940).

2. William Dean Howells, *A Hazard of New Fortunes* (New York: Harper & Bros., 1890), pp. 95–96.

3. William Dean Howells, *The Albany Depot* (New York: Harper & Bros., 1892).

4. O. Henry, "Holding Up a Train," in *Sixes and Sevens* (New York: Doubleday, Page & Co., 1911), p. 283, pp. 46–63.

5. Theodore Dreiser, *Sister Carrie* (Philadelphia: The University of Pennsylvania Press, 1981), p. 3. (The first edition was by Doubleday, Page & Co., 1900.)

6. Theodore Dreiser, *Newspaper Days* (New York: Fawcett World Library, 1965), pp. 300–1.

7. Sinclair Lewis, *Babbitt* (New York: Harcourt Brace & Co., 1922), p. 31.

8. Sinclair Lewis, *Main Street* (New York: Harcourt Brace & Co., 1920), p. 20.

9. Ibid., p. 25.

10. For an able survey of railroad drama, see Stewart H. Holbrook, *The Story of American Railroads* (New York: Crown Publishers, 1947), pp. 421–28. See also Russell E. Smith's "Railroads behind the Footlights," in *Railroadman's Magazine*, 1913. See also *The Railroad in Literature*, pp. 113–20.

11. Christopher Morley, *Christopher Morley's Briefcase* (Philadelphia: J. B. Lippincott Co., 1936), pp. 26–27.

12. A good reproduction of this painting can be found in Robert Goldsborough, ed., *Great Railroad Paintings* (New York: Peacock Press, Bantam Books, 1976), n.p.

13. C. Hamilton Ellis, *Railway Art* (Boston: New York Graphic Society, 1977), p. 48.

14. A good reproduction of this painting, which is part of the Chase Manhattan Bank Collection, is found in Oliver Jensen's *Railroads in America* (New York: American Heritage Publishing Co.), pp. 42–43.

15. Cf. Fred J. Peters, ed., *Railroad, Indian and Pioneer Prints of Currier and Ives* (New York: Antique Publishing Co., 1930).

16. The term "Ash Can" school first appeared in print in 1934, when Holger Cahill and Alfred H. Barr, Jr., used the term in their book *Art in America*. The term was not intended as a pejorative, but it has been used as such by some.

17. Bennard B. Perlman, *The Immortal Eight: American Painting from Eakins to the Armory Show, 1870–1913* (Westport, CT: North Light Publishers, 1979). The paintings by Luks and Lawson are found on p. 205.

18. Gail Levin, *Edward Hopper: The Man and the Artist* (New York: W. W. Norton, 1980), p. 47.

19. A good selection of the paintings of some of these individuals can be found in Robert Goldsborough, *Great Railroad Paintings* (New York: Peacock Press, 1976).

Chapter 17

1. Norm Cohen, *Long Steel Rail: The Railroad in American Folksong* (Urbana: University of Illinois Press, 1981), p. 41. Cohen's book is clearly

the most exhaustive scholarly account of railroad folk music in America.

2. Cohen, pp. 132–57.

3. For an extensive discussion of this litigation, see Cohen, pp. 211–17.

4. For a discussion of the career of Jimmy Rodgers, see Bill C. Malone and Judith McCulloh, eds., *Stars of Country Music* (Urbana: University of Illinois Press, 1975), pp. 121–41. See also Carrie Rodgers, *My Husband Jimmy Rodgers* (Nashville: Ernest Tubb Publications, 1985).

5. Arthur Knight, *The Liveliest Art: A Panoramic History of the Movies* (New York: Macmillan, 1978), p. 18.

6. Francois Truffaut, *Hitchcock* (New York: Simon and Schuster, 1966), p. 90.

7. Leslie Halliwell, *The Filmgoer's Companion* (New York: Avon Books, 1975), p. 759.

8. Stan Fischler, *Uptown, Downtown: A Trip through Time on New York's Subways* (New York: Hawthorne Books, 1976), p. 179.

9. Ibid., p. 180.

10. Charles Klamkin, *Railroadiana* (New York: Funk and Wagnalls, 1976), pp. 238–39.

11. A good popular account of Cowen and the Lionel Company is contained in Ron Hollander, *All Aboard: The Story of Joshua Lionel Cowen and His Lionel Train Company* (New York: Workman Publishing Company, 1981).

12. Robert Cross, "Railroad Baron Puts Lionel Back on Track," *Chicago Tribune,* December 18, 1986.

13. For a survey of the many fields of railroad collecting and memorabilia, see Klamkin.

14. An interesting account of the careers and achievements of some of these photographers may be found in John Gruber, *Focus on Rails* (North Freedom, WI: Mid-Continent Railway Historical Society, 1989).

Chapter 18

1. Stanley Applebaum, *The New York World's Fair, 1939–1940* (New York: Dover Publications, 1977).

2. John F. Stover, *The Life and Decline of the American Railroad* (New York: Oxford University Press, 1970), p. 203.

3. Ibid., p. 204.

4. For an extensive discussion of this complex and serious issue, see Albro Martin, *Enterprise Denied: Origins of the Decline of the American Railroads, 1897–1917* (New York: Columbia University Press, 1971).

5. Robert Selph Henry, *This Fascinating Railroad Business* (Indianapolis: Bobbs-Merrill Co., 1946), p. 448.

6. Peter Lyon, *To Hell in a Day Coach: An Exasperated Look at American Railroads* (Philadelphia: J. B. Lippincott, 1968), p. 175.

7. James E. Valle, *The Iron Horse at War* (Berkeley: Howell-North Books, 1977), p. 6.

8. Stover, p. 186.

9. Robert B. Shaw. *A History of Railroad Accidents, Safety Precautions and Operating Practices* (self-published, 1978), pp. 319–20.

10. Stover, p. 214.

11. Robert Sobel, *The Fallen Colossus* (New York: Weybright & Talley, 1977), p. 264.

12. Lyon, p. 229.

13. I owe this information to circus historian Tom Parkinson, personal communication. For more detail, see Tom Parkinson and Charles Fox, *Circus Moves by Rail* (Boulder, CO: Pruett, 1978).

14. Stover, p. 264.

15. Ibid., p. 268.

16. For a chronology of the events leading up to the founding of Amtrak, see Harold A. Edmonson, ed., *Journey to Amtrak* (Milwaukee: Kalmbach Books, 1972).

17. A detailed account of the rejuvination of Washington's Union Station, "Washington's Union Station Back from the Brink," is contained in *Trains,* May 1989, pp. 30ff. See also "Boston South Station Revival," *Trains,* June, 1989, pp. 38ff.

18. Lucius Beebe, "The Most Heroic of American Legends," in *The Lucius Beebe Reader* (Garden City: Doubleday, 1967), pp. 312–13.

19. John Skow, "Reinventing the Train," *Time,* November 13, 1989, p. 104. The American–European Express eventually became an irregularly scheduled excursion train.

BIBLIOGRAPHY

Books

Abdill, George B. *Civil War Railroads*. New York: Bonanza, 1961.

———.*Rails West*. Seattle: Superior Publishing Co., 1960.

Adair, Ward William. *The Lure of the Iron Trail*. New York: Association Press, 1912.

Adams, Charles Francis. *An Autobiography*. New York: Houghton, Mifflin Co., 1912.

———.*Railroads: Their Origin and Problems*. New York: G. P. Putnam's Sons, 1886.

Adams, Charles Francis, and Henry Adams. *Chapters of Erie*. Ithaca: Cornell University Press, 1956.

Album of Erie Railway Scenery. New York: Witteman, 1882.

Alexander, Edwin P. *The Collector's Book of the Locomotive*. New York: Clarkson N. Potter, 1966.

———.*Down at the Depot: American Railroad Stations from 1831 to 1920*. New York: Clarkson N. Potter, 1977.

———.*On the Main Line: The Pennsylvania Railroad in the Nineteenth Century*. New York: Clarkson N. Potter, 1970.

———.*The Pennsylvania Railroad*. New York: W. W. Norton, 1947.

Alexander, E. Porter. *Railway Practice: Its Principles and Suggested Reforms Reviewed*. New York: G. P. Putnam's Sons, 1887.

Alger, Horatio. *The Erie Train Boy.* United States Book Co., 1890.

———. *The Train Boy.* New York: G. W. Carleton & Co., 1883.

Allen, Frederick Lewis. *The Great Pierpont Morgan.* New York: Harper & Bros., 1949.

———. *Only Yesterday.* New York: Harper & Bros., 1959.

Alvarez, Eugene *Travel on Southern Antebellum Railroads, 1828–1860.* University, AL: University of Alabama Press, 1974.

American Social Science Association. *Handbook for Immigrants to the United States.* Cambridge, MA: Riverside Press, 1871.

The American Railway. New York: Arno Press, 1976. Reprint of 1888 edition.

Anderson, Elaine. *The Central Railroad of New Jersey's First 100 Years.* Easton, PA: Center for Canal History and Technology, 1975.

Anderson, Nels. *The Hobo: The Sociology of the Homeless Man.* Chicago: University of Chicago Press, 1925.

Anderson, Sherwood. *Winesburg, Ohio.* New York: Boni, 1919.

Andrews, Cyril. *The Railway Age.* New York: Macmillan, 1938.

Applebaum, Stanley. *The New York World's Fair, 1939–1940.* New York: Dover Publications, 1977.

Appleton, Victor. *Tom Swift and His Electric Locomotive.* New York: Grosset and Dunlap, 1922.

Athearn, Robert G. *Union Pacific Country.* Chicago: Rand McNally, 1971.

Atwell, H. Wallace *Great Transcontinental Railroad Guide.* Chicago: George A. Crofutt & Co., 1869.

Baker, George Pierce. *The Formation of the New England Railway Systems.* Cambridge: Harvard University Press, 1937.

Barger, Ralph L. *A Century of Pullman Cars,* Vol. 1. Sykesville, MD: Greenberg Publishing Co., 1988.

Baur, John. *Charles Burchfield.* New York: Macmillan, 1956.

Beebe, Lucius. *The Age of Steam.* New York: Rinehart & Co., 1957.

———. *Boston and the Boston Legend.* New York: Appleton Century, 1935.

———. *The Central Pacific and the Southern Pacific.* Berkeley: Howell-North Books, 1963.

———. *Mansions on the Rails.* Berkeley: Howell-North Books, 1959.

———. *Mixed Train Daily.* Berkeley: Howell-North Books, 1969.

———. *Mr. Pullman's Elegant Palace Car.* Garden City, NY: Doubleday, 1961.

————.*The Overland Limited.* Berkeley: Howell-North Books, 1963.

————.*The Twentieth Century.* Berkeley: Howell-North Books, 1962.

Beebe, Lucius, and Charles Clegg. *Great Railroad Photographs,* Berkeley: Howell-North Books, 1964.

————.*The Trains We Rode,* 2 vols. Berkeley: Howell-North Books, 1965–1966.

————.*When Beauty Rode the Rails.* Garden City, NY: Doubleday & Co., 1962.

Beers, Frank, *The Green Signal, or Life on the Rail.* Kansas City: Hudson, 1904.

Bennett, Arnold. *Your United States.* New York: Harper & Bros., 1922.

Benson, Lee. *Merchants, Farmers and Railroads: Railroad Regulation and New York Politics, 1850–1887.* Cambridge: Harvard University Press, 1955.

Best, Gerald M. *Iron Horses to Promontory.* San Marino, CA: Golden West Books, 1969.

Betjeman, John. *London's Historic Railway Stations.* London: John Murray Ltd., 1978.

Bezilla, Michael. *Electric Traction on the Pennsylvania Railroad, 1895–1968.* University Park: Pennsylvania State University Press, 1980.

Bierce, Ambrose. *Black Beetles in Amber.* New York: Western Authors Publishing Co., 1892.

Bishop, Mrs. I. L., *The Englishwoman in America.* London: J. Murray, 1856.

Black, Robert C. *The Railroads of the Confederacy.* Chapel Hill: University of North Carolina Press, 1952.

Bloodgood, S. Demitt. *Some Accounts of the Hudson and Mohawk Railroad.* Albany, NY: n.p., 1831.

Blumenthal, Albert. *Small-Town Stuff.* Chicago: University of Chicago Press, 1932.

Boorstin, Daniel. *The Americans: The Democratic Experience.* New York: Random House, 1973.

————.*The Americans: The National Experience.* New York: Random House, 1965.

Borkin, Joseph. *Robert R. Young: The Populist of Wall Street.* New York: Harper & Row, 1969.

Botkin, B. A., and Alvin F. Harlow, eds. *A Treasury of Railroad Folklore.* New York: Crown Publishers, 1953.

Bowers, Claude G. *The Tragic Era.* Cambridge, MA: Houghton, Mifflin,

Co., 1929.

Bowyer, Matthew. *They Carried the Mail.* New York: Luce, 1972.

Boy's Book of the Railroad. Multiple authors. New York: Harper & Bros., 1909.

Bradlee, Francis B. C. *The Boston & Lowell, the Nashua & Lowell and the Salem & Lowell Railroads.* Salem, MA: The Essex Institute, 1918.

————.*The Boston and Maine Railroad.* Salem, MA: The Essex Institute, 1921.

Brooks, E. L. *Rail Rambles.* Chicago: Occult Publishing Co., 1927.

Brown, Dee. *Hear That Lonesome Whistle Blow: Railroads in the West.* New York: Holt, Rinehart & Winston, 1977.

————.*The Westerners.* New York: Holt, Rinehart & Winston, 1974.

————.*The Year of the Century: 1876.* New York: Charles Scribner's Sons, 1966.

Brown, Walter Rollo. *I Travel by Train.* New York: Appleton, 1939.

Brown, William H. *The History of the First Locomotives in America.* New York: Appleton, 1874.

Bryant, Keith L. *History of the Atchison, Topeka and Santa Fe Railway.* New York: Macmillan, 1974.

Buck, Solon Justus. *The Granger Movement.* Cambridge: Harvard University Press, 1913.

Buder, Stanley. *An Experiment in Industrial Order and Community Planning.* New York: Oxford University Press, 1967.

Burgess, George H., and Miles C. Kennedy. *Centennial History of the Pennsylvania Railroad Company, 1846–1946.* Philadelphia: Pennsylvania Railroad Co., 1949.

Burr, Walter. *Small Towns: An Estimate of Their Trade and Culture.* New York: Macmillan, 1929.

Burt, Benjamin C. *Railway Station Service.* New York: John Wiley, 1911.

Bush, Donald J. *The Streamlined Decade.* New York: Braziller, 1975.

Butler, W. E. *The Engineer's View of the Promised Land.* New York: Fortuny's, 1939.

Bye, Randolph. *The Vanishing Depot.* Wynwood, PA: Livingston Publishing Co., 1973.

Byrne, Christopher. *Rhymes of the Rail.* St. Paul, MN: Rhymes of the Rail, Co., 1917.

Campbell, Edward G. *The Reorganization of the American Railroad System, 1893–1900.* New York: Columbia University Press, 1938.

Carr, Samuel, ed. *The Poetry of Railways.* London: Battsford, 1978.

Carter, Charles Frederick. *When Railroads Were New.* New York: Henry Holt & Co., 1910.

Casey, Robert J., and W. A. S. Douglas. *Pioneer Railroad: The Story of the Chicago and North Western System.* New York: Whittlesey House, 1948.

Cather, Willa. *Alexander's Bridge.* New York: Houghton Mifflin, 1912.

Cavalier, Julien. *Classic American Railroad Stations.* San Diego: A. S. Barnes, 1980.

Chambers, William. *Things as They Are in America.* London: n.p., 1854.

Chandler, Alfred D. *The Railroads: The Nation's First Big Business.* New York: Harcourt Brace & World, 1965.

———.*The Visible Hand: The Managerial Revolution.* Cambridge: Harvard University Press, 1977.

Chapman, Allen. *Ralph and the Midnight Flyer.* New York: Grosset & Dunlap, 1923.

———.*Ralph and the Train Wreckers.* New York: Grosset & Dunlap, 1928.

Clark, George Thomas. *Leland Stanford.* Stanford: Stanford University Press, 1931.

Clark, Ira G. *Then Came the Railroad.* Norman, OK: University of Oklahoma Press, 1958.

Clarke, Thomas C. *The American Railway.* New York: Charles Scribner's Sons, 1889.

Clegg, Charles, and Duncan Emrich. *The Lucius Beebe Reader.* Garden City NY: Doubleday & Co., 1967.

Clemens, Samuel Langhorne. *Punch, Brothers, Punch and Other Sketches.* New York: Slothe, Woodman & Co., 1878.

Cochran, Thomas C. *Railroad Leaders, 1845–1890: The Business Man in Action.* Cambridge: Harvard University Press, 1953.

Cohen, Norm. *Long Steel Rail: The Railroad in American Folksong.* Urbana: University of Illinois Press, 1981.

Coleman, McAlister. *Eugene V. Debs.* New York: Greenburg, 1930.

Coman, Katherine. *The Industrial History of the United States.* New York: Macmillan, 1919.

Combs, Barry B. *Westward to Promontory.* Palo Alto, CA: American West

Publishing Co., 1969.

Comstock, Henry B. *The Iron Horse.* New York: Galahad Books, 1971.

Condit, Carl W. *Chicago: Building, Planning and Urban Technology, 1910–1929.* Chicago: University of Chicago Press, 1973.

———.*Chicago: Building, Planning and Urban Technology, 1930–1970.* Chicago: University of Chicago Press, 1973.

———.*The Port of New York: A History of the Rail and Terminal System from the Grand Central Electrification to the Present.* Chicago: University of Chicago Press, 1981.

———.*The Railroad and the City.* Columbus: Ohio State University Press, 1971.

Cookridge, E. H. *Orient Express.* New York: Harper Colophon Books, 1980.

Cooper, Courtney. *Go North, Young Man.* Boston: Little Brown & Co., 1929.

Corliss, Carlton J. *The Day of Two Noons.* Washington: Association of American Railroads, 1959.

———.*Main Line of Mid-America: The Story of the Illinois Central.* New York: Creative Age Press, 1950.

———.*Trails to Rails.* Chicago: Illinois Central Railroad, 1937.

Craib, Roderick. *A Picture History of U.S. Transportation.* New York. Simmons-Bordman, 1958.

Crane, Frank. *George Westinghouse: His Life and Achievements.* New York: W. H. Wise & Co., 1925.

Crawford, J. B. *The Credit Mobilier of America.* Boston: C. W. Calkins Co., 1880.

Crump, Irving. *The Boys' Book of Railroads.* New York: Dodd, Mead & Co., 1921.

Cudahy, Brian J. *Change at Park Street Under.* Brattleboro, VT: Stephen Greene Press, 1972.

———.*Rails under the Mighty Hudson.* Brattleboro, VT: Stephen Greene Press, 1975.

Cunningham, John T. *New Jersey: America's Main Road.* New York: Doubleday, 1966.

———.*Railroading in New Jersey.* Newark: Associated Railroads of New Jersey, 1951.

Currier, Frederick A. *A Trip to the Great Lakes.* Fitchburg, MA: Sentimental Printing Company, 1904.

Dalhart, Vernon, and Carson Robinson. *Album of Songs*. New York: J. B. Haviland Publishing Co., 1928.

Daly, Augustin. *Under the Gaslight*. New York: T. H. French, 1895.

Daly, James. *The Little Blind God on Rails*. Chicago: Rand McNally & Co., 1888.

Danby, Susan, and Leo Marx, eds., *The Railroad in American Art*. Cambridge: The MIT Press, 1988.

Daniels, Winthrop M. *American Railroads: Four Phases of Their History*. Princeton: Princeton University Press, 1932.

Daughen, Joseph, and Peter Binzen. *The Wreck of the Penn Central*. New York: Signet, 1971.

Davids, Patricia. *End of the Line: Alexander J. Cassatt and the Pennsylvania Railroad*. New York: Neale Watson Academic Publications, 1978.

Davis, Richard Harding. *The West from a Cab Window*. New York: Harper & Bros., 1892.

De Golyer, Everett L., Jr. *The Track Going Back*. Fort Worth: Amon Carter Museum, 1969.

Dell, Floyd. *Moon Calf*. New York: Alfred A. Knopf, 1920.

Depew, Chauncey M. *My Memories of Eighty Years*. New York: Charles Scribner's Sons, 1922.

Dewhurst, H. S. *The Railroad Police*. Springfield, IL: Thomas, 1955.

Dickins, Charles. *American Notes*. London: Oxford University Press, 1957.

Diehl, Lorraine B. *The Late Great Pennsylvania Station*. New York: American Heritage Press, 1985.

Donovan, Frank P. *Harry Bedwell: Last of the Great Railroad Storytellers*. Minneapolis: Ross and Harmes, 1959.

————.*Mileposts on the Prairie*. New York: Simmons-Bordman Publishing Co., 1950.

————.*The Railroad in Literature*. Boston: Railway and Locomotive Historical Society, 1940.

Donovan, Frank P., ed. *Headlights and Markers: An Anthology of Railroad Stories*. New York: Creative Age Press, 1946.

Dorin, Patrick C. *Commuter Railroads*. New York: Bonanza Books, 1957.

————.*Everywhere West: The Burlington Route*. Seattle: Superior Publishing Co., 1974.

Dos Passos, John. *Manhattan Transfer*. New York: Harper & Bros., 1925.

Douglas, George H. *Rail City: Chicago U.S.A.* San Diego: Howell-North Books, 1981.

Drago, Harry Sinclair. *Canal Days in America.* New York: Bramhall Books, 1972.

Dreiser, Theodore. *Dawn.* New York: Liveright, 1951.

———.*Newspaper Days.* New York: Boni and Liveright, 1922.

———.*Sister Carrie.* New York: Doubleday Page & Co., 1900.

———.*The Titan.* New York: John Lane & Co., 1915.

Droege, John A. *Passenger Terminals and Trains.* New York: McGraw-Hill Book Co., 1916.

Drucker, James. *Men of the Steel Rails.* Lincoln: University of Nebraska Press, 1983.

Drury, George H. *The Historical Guide to North American Railroads.* Milwaukee: Kalmbach, 1985.

Dubin, Arthur D. *More Classic Trains.* Milwaukee: Kalmbach, 1974.

———.*Some Classic Trains.* Milwaukee: Kalmbach, 1964.

Dunbar, Seymour. *A History of Travel in America.* New York: Tudor Publishing Co., 1937.

Edmonson, Harold A., ed. *Journey to Amtrak.* Milwaukee: Kalmbach Books, 1972.

Edmonson, Harold A., and Richard Francaviglia. *Railroad Station Planbook.* Milwaukee: Kalmbach Books, 1977.

Ehrlich, Amy. *The Everyday Train.* New York: Dial, 1977.

Ellis, C. Hamilton. *The Pictorial Encyclopedia of Railways.* London: Hulton Press, 1956.

———.*Railway Art.* Boston: New York Graphic Society, 1977.

Elton, Arthur. *British Railways.* London: Collins, 1945.

Emerson, Edward Waldo. *Emerson in Concord: A Memoir.* Boston: Houghton, 1888.

Emerson, Ralph Waldo. *Essays: Second Series.* Philadelphia: McKay, 1892.

———.*Journals and Miscellaneous Notebooks.* Alfred R. Ferguson, ed. Cambridge: Harvard University Press, 1964.

———.*Nature, Addresses, and Lectures.* Boston: Houghton, 1884.

The Erie Route—A Guide to the Erie Railway and Its Branches. Author unknown. New York: Taintor Bros., 1875.

Faithful, Emily. *Three Visits to America.* Edinburgh: David Douglas, 1884.

Farrington, S. Kip, Jr. *Railroading: The Modern Way.* New York: Coward McCann, 1946.

Faulkner, Harold U. *Politics, Reform and Expansion, 1890–1900.* New York: Harper & Row, 1959.

Feid, Frederick. *No Pie in the Sky: The Hobo as American Cultural Hero.* New York: Citadel, 1964.

Ferguson, William. *America by River and Rail; or Notes by the Way on the New World and Its People.* London: J. Nisbit & Co., 1856.

Fischler, Stan. *Uptown, Downtown: A Trip Through Time on New York Subways.* New York: Hawthorne Books, 1976.

Fisher, Charles E. *The Story of the Old Colony Railroad.* n.p. 1919.

Fisher, Ralph. *Vanishing Markers.* Brattleboro, VT: Stephen Greene Press, 1977.

Fishlow, Albert. *American Railroads and the Transformation of the Antebellum Economy.* Cambridge: Harvard University Press, 1965.

Fistell, Ira J. *America by Train.* New York: B. Franklin, 1983.

Fitzgerald, F. Scott. *The Great Gatsby.* New York: Charles Scribner's Sons, 1925.

Flint, Harry M. *The Railroads of the United States.* Philadelphia: John E. Potter, 1868.

Flynt, Josiah. *Tramping with Tramps.* New York: Century, 1901.

Fogel, Robert W. *Railroads and American Economic Growth.* Baltimore: Johns Hopkins University Press, 1964.

Foner, P. S. *History of the Labor Movement in the United States.* New York: International Publishers, 1955.

Freidel, Frank. *America in the Twentieth Century.* New York: Alfred A. Knopf, 1970.

French, Chauncey D. *Railroadman.* New York: Macmillan, 1938.

From the Lakes to the Gulf. Chicago: Illinois Central Railroad, 1884.

Fuller, Robert Higginson. *Jubilee Jim: The Life of Colonel James Fisk, Jr.* New York: Macmillan, 1928.

Gabler, Edwin. *The American Telegrapher: A Social History.* New Brunswick, NJ: Rutgers University Press, 1988.

Garland, Hamlin. *A Son of the Middle Border.* New York: Macmillan, 1917.

Garraty, John A., ed. *Encyclopedia of American Biography.* New York: Harper & Row, 1974.

———. *The New Commonwealth: 1877–1890.* New York: Harper & Row,

1968.

Garrett, Phineas, ed. *The Speaker's Garland*. Philadelphia: P. Garrett & Co., 1885.

Gates, Paul Wallace. *The Illinois Central and Its Colonization Work*. Cambridge: Harvard University Press, 1934.

George, Charles B. *Forty Years on the Rails*. Chicago: R. R. Donnelley & Sons, 1887.

Goldsborough, Robert. *Great Railroad Paintings*. New York: Bantam Books, 1976.

Gordon, John Steele. *The Scarlet Woman of Wall Street*. New York: Weidenfeld and Nicholson, 1988.

Grant, H. Roger, and Charles W. Bohi. *The Country Railroad Station in America*. Boulder, CO: Pruett Publishing Co., 1978.

Greenberg, William T., and Frederick Kramer. *The Handsomest Train in the World*. New York: Quadrant, 1980.

Griswold, Wesley S. *Train Wreck!* Brattleboro, VT: The Stephen Greene Press, 1969.

————.*A Work of Giants: Building the First Transcontinental Railroad*. New York: McGraw-Hill, 1962.

Grodinsky, Julius. *Jay Gould: His Business Career, 1867–1892*. Philadelphia: University of Pennsylvania Press, 1957.

————.*Transcontinental Railway Strategy, 1869–1893*. Philadelphia: University of Pennsylvania Press, 1962.

Grow, Lawrence, *On the 8:02: An Informal History of Commuting by Rail in America*. New York: Mayflower Books, 1979.

————.*Waiting for the 5:05: Terminal, Station and Depot in America*. New York: Main Street Press, 1977.

Gruber, John. *Focus on Rails*. North Freedom, WI: Mid-Continent Railway Historical Society, 1989.

Hadley, Arthur T. *Railroad Transportation: Its History and Its Laws*. New York: G. P. Putnam's Sons, 1885.

Haney, Lewis H. *A Congressional History of Railways in the United States*. New York: Augustus M. Kelley Publishers, 1968. Reprint of 1908 edition.

Halliwell, Leslie. *The Filmgoer's Companion*. New York: Avon Books, 1975.

Hamton, Taylor. *The Nickel Plate Road*. Cleveland: World Publishing Co., 1947.

Hardy, Lady Duffas. *Through Cities and Prairie Lands: Sketches of an*

American Tour. New York: Worthington, 1890.

Hare, Jay. *History of the Reading.* Philadelphia: John Henry Strock, 1966.

Harlow, Alvin F. *Old Waybills.* New York: D. Appleton-Century Co., 1934.

———.*The Road of the Century: The Story of the New York Central.* New York: Creative Age Press, 1947.

———.*Steelways of New England.* New York: Creative Age Press, 1946.

Harte, Bret. *Poetical Works.* Boston: Houghton-Mifflin, 1896.

Hatch, Alden. *American Express.* New York: Doubleday, 1950.

Hawthorne, Nathaniel. *Twice-Told Tales.* New York: Heritage Press, 1966.

Hedges, James B. *Henry Villard and the Railways of the Northwest.* New Haven: Yale University Press, 1930.

Henderson, James David. *"Meals by Fred Harvey": A Phenomenon of the American West.* Forth Worth: Texas Christian University Press, 1969.

Henry, O. (pseudonym of William Sidney Porter). *Complete Works.* Garden City, NY: Garden City Publishing Co., 1937.

Henry, Robert Selph. *This Fascinating Railroad Business.* Indianapolis: Bobbs-Merrill Co., 1946.

Herr, Kincaid A. *Louisville and Nashville Railroad, 1850–1963.* Louisville: Louisville and Nashville Railroad, 1964.

Hill, Edwin Conger. *The Iron Horse.* New York: Grosset and Dunlap, 1924.

Hill, John Alexander. *Stories of the Railroad.* New York: Doubleday & McClure, 1899.

Hill, Ralph Nading. *The Mad Doctor's Drive.* Brattleboro, VT: Stephen Greene Press, 1964.

Hilton, George W. *Monon Route.* Berkeley: Howell-North Books, 1978.

Hilton, George W., and John F. Due. *The Electric Interurban Railways in America.* Stanford: Stanford University Press, 1960.

Hinshaw, David. *Stop, Look and Listen: Railroad Transportation in the United States.* New York: Doubleday, Doran & Co., 1932.

Hofsommer, Don. *Southern Pacific, 1901–1985.* College Station: Texas A & M University Press, 1986.

Hogg, Alex. *The Railroad as an Element of Education.* Louisville: Morton, 1897.

Holbrook, Stewart H. *The Age of Moguls.* Garden City, NY: Doubleday, 1953.

———.*The Old Post Road.* New York: McGraw-Hill Book Co., 1962.

————.*The Story of the American Railroads.* New York. Crown Publishers, 1947.

Holderness, Herbert Owen. *The Reminiscences of a Pullman Conductor.* Chicago: n.p., 1901.

Hollander, Ron. *All Aboard: The Story of Joshua Lionel Cowen and His Lionel Train Company.* New York: Workman Publishing Co., 1981.

Holmes, Oliver Wendell. *Complete Poetical Works.* Boston: Houghton-Mifflin, 1895.

Howard, Robert West. *The Great Iron Trail.* New York: Putnam, 1962.

Howells, William Dean. *The Albany Depot.* New York: Harper & Bros., 1892.

————.*A Hazard of New Fortunes.* New York: Harper & Bros., 1980.

————.*The Sleeping Car and Other Farces.* New York: Houghton-Mifflin Co., 1892.

————.*Suburban Sketches.* New York: Houghton-Mifflin Co., 1898.

Hubbard, Freeman H. *Railroad Avenue.* New York: McGraw-Hill Book Co., 1945.

Humason, W. L. *From the Atlantic Surf to the Golden Gate.* Hartford, CT: n.p., 1869.

Hungerford, Edward. *Daniel Willard Rides the Line.* New York: G. P. Putnam's Sons, 1938.

————.*Men of Erie.* New York: Random House, 1946.

————.*The Personality of American Cities.* New York: McBride, Nast & Co., 1913.

————.*The Story of the Baltimore and Ohio Railroad,* 2 vols. New York: G. P. Putnam's Sons, 1928.

Huntley, John. *Railways in the Cinema.* London: Allen, 1969.

Husband, Joseph. *The Story of the Pullman Car.* Chicago: A. L. McClurg & Co., 1917.

Industrial Chicago. Chicago: Goodspeed Publishing Co., 1894.

Inman, Charles Crew. *American Silhouettes.* New York: E. P. Dutton & Co., 1925.

Irwin, Godfrey, ed. *American Tramp and Underworld Slang.* London: Eric Partridge, Ltd., 1931.

Jackle, John A. *The American Small Town: Twentieth Century Place Images.* Hamden, CT: Shoe String Press, 1981.

James, Henry. *The American Scene*. New York: Harper & Bros., 1907.

Jensen, Oliver. *Railroads in America*. New York: American Heritage Publishing Co., 1975.

Johnson, Emory R. *American Railway Transportation*. New York: Appleton, 1905.

Johnson, Guy Benton. *John Henry*. Chapel Hill: University of North Carolina Press, 1929.

Jones, Helen Hinckley. *Rails from the West: A Biography of Theodore D. Judah*. San Marino, CA: Golden West Books, 1969.

Jones, Howard Mumford. *The Age of Energy: Varieties of American Experience, 1865–1915*. New York: Viking Press, 1973.

Josephson, Matthew. *The Robber Barons*. New York: Harcourt Brace & Co., 1934.

Kalisher, Simpson. *Railroad Men*. New York: Clarke & Way, 1961.

Kammen, Michael. *People of Paradox: An Inquiry Concerning the Origins of American Civilization*. New York: Alfred A. Knopf, 1973.

Keir, Malcolm. *The March of Commerce*. New Haven: Yale University Press, 1927.

Kelly, Ralph. *Matthias W. Baldwin*. New York: Newcomen Society, 1946.

Kennan, George F. *E. H. Harriman*, 2. vols. Boston: Houghton-Mifflin, 1922.

Kennedy, William Sloane. *Wonders and Curiosities of the Railway*. Chicago: S. C. Grigge & Co., 1884.

Kerr, Alvah Milton. *The Diamond Key*. Boston: Lothrop, Lea & Shepard, 1907.

———.*Young Heroes of Wire and Rail*. Boston: Lothrup, Lea & Shepard, 1903.

Kilham, Walter H. *Boston after Bulfinch*. Cambridge: Harvard University Press, 1946.

Kinert, Reed. *Early American Steam Locomotives, 1830–1900*. New York: Bonanza Books, 1962.

Kipling, Rudyard. *From Sea to Sea: Letters of Travel*. New York: Doubleday & McClure Co., 1899.

Kirkland, Edward C., *Men, Cities and Transportation: A Study in New England History, 1820–1900*. Cambridge: Harvard University Press, 1948.

Klamkin, Charles. *Railroadiana*. New York: Funk and Wagnalls, 1976.

Klein, Murray. *Union Pacific: Birth of a Railroad, 1862–1893,* Garden City, NY: Doubleday, 1986.

Kohlmeier, Louis. *The Regulators: Watchdog Agenies and the Public Interest.* New York: Harper & Row, 1969.

Kolko, Gabriel. *Railroads and Regulation, 1877–1916.* Princeton: Princeton University Press, 1965.

Kouwenhoven, John A. *The Columbia Historical Portrait of New York.* New York: Harper & Row, 1953.

Kratville, William W. *Steam, Steel and Limiteds.* Omaha: Barnhart Press, 1967.

Kraus, George. *High Road to Promontory.* New York: Castle Books, 1969.

Kuhler, Otto, and Robert Selph Henry. *Portraits of the Iron Horse.* New York: Rand McNally, 1937.

Lane, Wheaton J. *Commodore Vanderbilt: An Epic of the Steam Age.* New York: Alfred A. Knopf, 1942.

———.*From Indian Trail to Iron Horse: Travel and Transportation in New Jersey, 1620–1860.* Princeton: Princeton University Press, 1939.

Larrabee, William. *The Railroad Question.* Chicago: Schulte Publishing Co., 1893.

Larson, John L. *Bonds of Enterprise: John Murray Forbes and Western Development in America's Railway Age.* Cambridge: Harvard University Press, 1984.

Laut, Agnes C. *The Romance of the Rails.* New York: R. M. McBride, 1929.

Lee, Fred J. *Casey Jones, Epic of the American Railroad.* Kingsport, TN: Southern Publishers, Inc., 1939.

Lee, James. *The Morris Canal.* Easton, PA: Delaware Press, 1988.

Leverage, Henry. *The Purple Limited.* New York: Chelsea House, 1927.

Levin, Gail. *Edward Hopper: The Man and the Artist.* New York: W. W. Norton, 1980.

Lewis, Edward A. *New England Country Depots.* Arcade, NY: R. M. McBride, 1929.

Lewis, Oscar. *The Big Four.* New York: Alfred A. Knopf, 1942.

Lewis, Sinclair. *Cass Timburlane.* New York: Random House, 1945.

———.*Babbitt.* New York: Harcourt, Brace & Co., 1922.

———.*Main Street.* New York: Harcourt Brace & Co., 1920.

Licht, Walter. *Working for the Railroad: The Organization of Work in the*

Nineteenth Century. Princeton: Princeton University Press, 1983.

Lincoln, Joseph C. *The Depot Master.* New York: Appleton, 1910.

Lindsey, Almont. *The Pullman Strike.* Chicago: University of Chicago Press, 1964.

Lingeman, Richard. *Small Town America.* Boston: Houghton Mifflin, 1980.

Lomax, Alan. *The Folk Songs of North America.* Garden City, NY: Doubleday, 1960.

Lotz, Jim, and Keith MacKenzie. *Railways of Canada.* New York: Crown Books, 1989.

Loxton, Howard. *Railways.* London: Paul Hamlyn, 1967.

Lucas, Clinton William. *A Trolley Honeymoon from New Orleans to Maine.* New York: M. W. Hazen Co., 1904.

Lyon, Peter. *To Hell in a Day Coach.* Philadelphia: J. B. Lippincott & Co., 1968.

MacGill, Caroline E. *History of Transportation in the United States Before 1860.* Washington: Carnegie Institution of Washington, 1917.

Maiken, Peter T. *Night Trains,* Chicago: Lakme Press, 1989.

Malone, Bill C., and Judith McCulloh. *Stars of Country Music.* Urbana: University of Illinois Press, 1975.

Marshall, David. *Grand Central.* New York: McGraw-Hill Book Co., 1946.

Marshall, James. *Santa Fe: The Railroad That Built an Empire.* New York: Random House, 1945.

Marx, Leo. *The Machine in the Garden.* New York: Oxford University Press, 1967.

Matthews, Brander. *In the Vestibule Limited.* New York: Harper & Bros., 1892.

Mattson, Hans. *Reminiscences: The Story of an Immigrant.* St. Paul: D. D. Merrill Co., 1891.

Mayer, Harold M. *Chicago: Growth of a Metropolis.* Chicago: University of Chicago Press, 1973.

Mazlish, Bruce. *The Railroad and the Space Program.* Cambridge: MIT Press, 1965.

McAdoo, William Gibbs. *Crowded Years.* Boston: Houghton-Mifflin, 1930.

McAlpine, R. W. *The Life and Times of Col. James Fisk, Jr.* New York: New York Book Co., 1872.

McBride, Harry A. *Trains Rolling: Stories on Railroads at Home and Abroad.*

New York: Macmillan, 1953.

McCague, James. *Moguls and Iron Men: The Story of the First Transcontinental Railroad.* New York: Harper & Row, 1964.

McPherson, James Alan and Miller Williams. *Railroad Trains and Train People in American Culture.* New York: Random House, 1964.

Meeks, Carroll. *The Railroad Station.* New Haven: Yale University Press, 1960.

Meigs, Cornelia Lynde. *Railroad West.* Boston: Little Brown & Co. 1937.

Mencken, August. *The Railroad Passenger Car.* Baltimore: Johns Hopkins University Press, 1957.

Middleton, Philip Harvey. *Railways and Organized Labor.* Chicago: Railway Business Association, 1941.

————.*Railways and Public Opinion.* Chicago: Railway Business Association, 1941.

Middleton: William D. *Grand Central: The World's Greatest Railway Terminal.* San Marino, CA: Golden West Books, 1977.

————.*The Interurban Era.* Milwaukee: Kalmbach Books, 1967.

————.*The Railroad Scene.* San Marino, CA: Golden West Books, 1968.

————.*The Time of the Trolley.* Milwaukee: Kalmbach Books, 1967.

Milburn, George. *The Hobo's Hornbook.* New York: Ives Washburn, 1930.

Millay, Edna St. Vincent. *Second April.* New York: M. Kennerley, 1921.

Miller, David E. *The Golden Spike.* Salt Lake City: University of Utah Press, 1973.

Miller, Douglas T. *The Birth of Modern America, 1810–1850.* New York: Pegasus, 1970.

Miller, George H. *Railroads and the Granger Laws.* Madison: University of Wisconsin Press, 1971.

Miller, John Anderson. *Fares Please.* New York: Dover Publications, 1960.

Minehan, Thomas. *Boy and Girl Tramps of America.* New York: Farrar and Rinehart, 1938.

Miner, H. Craig. *The St. Louis-San Francisco Transcontinental Railroad.* Lawrence, KS: University Press of Kansas, 1972.

Mohr, Nicolaus. *Excursion through America.* Chicago: The Lakeside Press, 1973.

Moody, John. *The Railroad Builders: A Chronicle of the Welding of the States.* New Haven: Yale University Press, 1920.

Morison, Samuel Eliot. *The Oxford History of the American People*. New York: Oxford University Press, 1965.

Morley, Christopher. *Christopher Morley's Briefcase*. Philadelphia: J. B. Lippincott Co., 1936.

———.*Essays*. Garden City, NY: Doubleday, Doran & Co., 1928.

———.*Plum Pudding*. Garden City: Doubleday, Page & Co., 1924.

———.*Travels in Philadelphia*. Philadelphia: David McKay Co., 1920.

Morse, Frank Philip. *Cavalcade of the Rails*. New York: E. P. Dutton, 1940.

Mott, Edward Harold. *Between the Ocean and the Lakes: The Story of Erie*. New York: John S. Collins, 1900.

Mowbray, A. Q. *Road to Ruin*. Philadelphia: J. B. Lippincott Co., 1969.

Mowry, George. *The Era of Theodore Roosevelt*. New York: Harper, 1969.

Mullin, Glen Hawthorne. *Adventures of a Scholar Tramp*. New York: The Century Company, 1925.

Mumford, Lewis. *The City in History*. New York: Harcourt Brace & World, 1961.

Nebel, Frederick. *Sleepers East*. Boston: Little Brown & Co., 1893.

Nevins, Allan. *The Emergence of Lincoln: Prologue to the Civil War, 1859–1861*. New York: Charles Scribner's Sons, 1950.

Nevins, Allan and Henry Steele Commager. *A Short History of the United States*. New York: Modern Library, 1945.

Newberry, Lida, ed. *New Jersey: A Guide to Its Present and Past*. New York: Hastings House, 1977.

The New York and Chicago Limited. Pennsylvania Railroad, 1980.

Nock, O.S. *The Railways of Britain*. London: B. T. Batsford, Ltd., 1947.

———.*Railways of the U.S.A*. New York: Hastings House, 1979.

Noggle, Burl. *Into the Twenties: The United States from Armistice to Normalcy*. Urbana: University of Illinois Press, 1974.

Norris, Frank. *The Octopus*. New York: Doubleday, Page & Co., 1901.

Nye, Russel Blaine. *Society and Culture in America*. New York: Harper & Row, 1974.

Oberholtzer, E. P. *Jay Cooke: Financier of the Civil War*, 2 vols. Philadelphia: Jacobs, 1907.

O'Connor, Richard. *Iron Wheels and Broken Men*. New York: G. P. Putnam's Sons, 1973.

Organization and Traffic of the Illinois Central Railroad. Chicago: Illinois Central Railroad, 1938.

Overby, Daniel L. *Railroads: The Free Enterprise Alternative*. New York: Quorum Books, 1982.

Overton, Richard C. *Burlington Route: A History of the Burlington Lines*. New York: Alfred A, Knopf, 1965.

————.*Burlington West: A Colonization History of the Burlington Railroad*. Cambridge: Harvard University Press, 1941.

Packard, Frank Lucius. *The Night Operator.* New York: George H. Doran Co., 1919.

————.*Running Special.* New York: George H. Doran Co., 1925.

Packer, Eleanor. *The Silver Streak*. Racine, WI: Whitman Publishing Co., 1935.

Parkinson, Tom and Charles Fox. *Circus Moves by Rail*. Boulder, CO: Pruett, 1978.

Patton, Phil. O*pen Road: A Celebration of the American Highway*. New York: Simon and Schuster, 1976.

Pearson, J. P. *Railways and Scenery*. London: Cassell & Co., 1932.

Pell, Claiborne. *Megalopolis Unbound: The Supercity and the Transportation of Tomorrow*. New York: Frederick A. Praeger, 1966.

Pelley, J. J. *Railroads and the Future*. Washington: Association of American Railroads, 1946.

Perkins, Jacob Randolph. *Trails, Rails and War: The Life of General Grenville M. Dodge*. Indianapolis: Bobbs-Merrill Co., 1929.

Perlman, Bennard B. *The Immortal Eight: American Paintings from Eakins to the Armory Show, 1870–1913*. Westport, CT: North Light Publishers, 1979.

Perlman, Selig. *A History of Trade Unionism in the United States*. New York: Macmillan, 1922.

Peters, Fred J., ed. *Railroad, Indian and Pioneer Prints of Currier and Ives*. New York: Antique Publishing Co., 1930.

Pierce, Bessie Louise. *A History of Chicago*, 3 vols. New York: Alfred A. Knopf, 1937–1957.

Pittenger, William. *The Great Locomotive Chase*. New York: J. B. Alden, 1889.

Plowden, David. *The Hand of Man on America*. Washington: Smithsonian Institute Press, 1971.

Poor, Henry V. *Manual of Railroads of the United States for 1868–69.* New York: H. V. and W. H. Poor, 1868.

Prescott, De Witt Clinton. *Early Day Railroading from Chicago.* Chicago: D. B. Clarkson Co., 1910.

Price, Alfred. *Rail Life: A Book of Yarns.* Toronto: Thomas Allen, 1925.

Pyle, Joseph. *The Life of James J. Hill.* Garden City, NY: Doubleday, Page & Co., 1917.

Quaife, Milo M. *Chicago's Highways Old and New.* Chicago: D. F. Keller Co., 1923.

Quiett, G. C. *They Built the West.* New York: D. Appleton-Century Co., 1934.

Rae, John. *The Road and the Car in American Life.* Cambridge: MIT Press, 1971.

Rae, William F. *Westward by Rail: The New Route to the East.* New York: Appleton, 1871.

Railroad Jokes and Stories. New York: Wehman Brothers, 1924.

Rates of Pay and Rules for Conductors, Trainmen and Yardmen. New York: Erie Railroad Co., 1917.

Reed, Henry Hope. *American Skyline.* New York: The New American Library, 1956.

———. *The Golden City.* New York: Doubleday & Co., 1959.

Reed, Robert C. *The New York Elevated.* Cranbury, NJ: A. S. Barnes & Co., 1978.

———. *Train Wrecks.* New York: Bonanza Books, 1968.

Rehor, John A. *The Nickel Plate Story.* Milwaukee: Kalmbach Publishing Co., 1965.

Reilly, Thomas Sale. *Diary of a Roundhouse Foreman.* New York: Norman W. Henley Co., 1912.

Reinhardt, Richard. *Out West on the Overland Train.* Palo Alto, CA: American West Publishing Co., 1967.

Reinhardt, Richard, ed. *Workin' on the Railroad.* Palo Alto, CA: American West Publishing Co., 1971.

Reusing Railroad Stations. New York: Educational Facilities Laboratories, Inc., 1974.

Richards, Jeffrey, and John M. MacKenzie. *The Railway Station: A Social History.* New York: Oxford University Press, 1986.

Riegel, Robert E. *The Story of Western Railroads: From 1852 through the Reign of the Giants.* New York: Macmillan, 1926.

Ripley, William Z. *Railroads, Rates and Regulation.* New York: Longmans Green & Co., 1927.

Robertson, Archie. *Slow Train to Yesterday.* Boston: Houghton Mifflin, 1945.

Robertson, James Oliver. *American Myth, American Reality.* New York: Hill & Wang, 1980.

Robinson, Charles Mulford. *Suburban Station Grounds.* Boston: Boston and Albany Railroad, 1905.

Rodgers, Jimmie. *Album of Songs.* New York: Southern Music Publishing Co., 1934.

Rolt, L. T. C. *The Railway Revolution: George and Robert Stephenson.* New York: St. Martin's Press, 1960.

Rose, Joseph. *American Wartime Transportation.* New York: Crowell, 1953.

Rosenbaum, Joel, and Tom Gallo. *The Broadway Limited.* Piscataway, NJ: Railpace Co., 1988.

————. *The Seashore's Finest Train: The Blue Comet.* Piscataway, NJ: Railpace Co., 1983.

Roth, Leland M. *McKim, Mead and White, Architects.* New York: Harper & Row, 1983.

Russell, Charles Edward. *Stories of the Great Railroads.* Chicago: Charles H. Kerr & Co., 1912.

Sandburg, Carl. *The American Songbag.* New York: Harcourt Brace, & Co., 1927.

————. *Selected Poems,* ed. by Rebecca West. New York: Harcourt Brace & Co., 1928.

Santmyer, Helen Hooven. *Ohio Town.* New York: Harper & Row, 1984.

Saunders, Richard. *The Railroad Mergers and the Coming of Conrail.* Westport, CT: Greenwood Press, 1978.

Saxe, John Godfrey. *Poems.* Boston: Ticknor, Reed & Fields, 1849.

Scarborough, Dorothy. *On the Trail of Negro Folk Songs.* Cambridge: Harvard University Press, 1925.

Schivelbusch, Wolfgang. *The Railway Journey.* New York: Urizen Books, 1979.

Schlesinger, Arthur Meier. *The Rise of the City: 1878–1898.* New York: Macmillan, 1935.

Scott, James. *Railway Romance and Other Essays.* London: Hadden & Stoughton, 1913.

Sharlin, Harold. *The Making of the Electrical Age.* New York: Abelard-Schumann, 1964.

Shaughnessy, Jim. *Delaware and Hudson.* Berkeley: Howell-North Books, 1967.

Shaw, Milton M. *Nine Thousand Miles on a Pullman Train.* Philadelphia: Allen, Lane & Scott, 1898.

Shaw, Robert B. *A History of Railroad Accidents, Safety Precautions and Operating Practices.* Self-published, 1978.

Small, Charles S. *Rails to the Rising Sun.* San Marino, CA: Golden West Books, 1965.

Smalley, Eugene V. *History of the Northern Pacific Railroad.* New York: G. P. Putnam's Sons, 1883.

Smiles, Samuel. *The Lives of George and Robert Stephenson.* London: Folio Society, 1975.

Smith, E. Boyd. *The Railroad Book.* Boston: Houghton Mifflin, 1913.

Smith, Henry Nash. *Virgin Land: The American West as Symbol and Myth.* Cambridge: Harvard University Press, 1950.

Smith, Robert A. *A Social History of the Bicycle.* New York: American Heritage Press, 1972.

Snell, J. B. *Early Railways.* London: Octopus Books, 1964.

Sobol, Robert. *The Fallen Colossus.* New York: Weybright & Talley, 1977.

Southerland, Thomas C., Jr., and William McCleery. *The Way to Go.* New York: Simon & Schuster, 1973.

Spaeth, Sigmund. *Weep Some More, My Lady.* Garden City, NY: Doubleday, Page & Co., 1927.

Spearman, Frank Hamilton. *Hold for Orders: Stories of Railroad Life.* New York: McClure, Phillips & Co., 1901.

———. *The Mountain Divide.* New York: Charles Scribner's Sons, 1912.

———. *The Daughter of a Magnate.* New York: Charles Scribner's Sons, 1903.

———. *The Strategy of Great Railroads.* New York: Charles Scribner's Sons, 1904.

Spence, Clark. *Montana: A Bicentennial History.* New York: W. W. Norton, 1978.

Stanley, Henry Morton. *My Early Travels and Adventures,* Vol. 1. New York:

Charles Scribner's Sons, 1895.

Starr, John W. *Lincoln and the Railroads*. New York: Dodd, Mead & Co., 1927.

———.*One Hundred Years of American Railroading*. New York: Dodd Mead & Co., 1929.

Stevenson, Burton Egbert. *The Young Train Master*. Boston: L. C. Page & Co., 1909.

Stevenson, Robert Louis. *Across the Plains*. London: Chatto and Windus, 1913.

Stevers, Martin D. *Steel Track: The Epic of the Railroads*. New York: Minton, Balch & Co., 1933.

Stover, John F. *American Railroads*. Chicago: University of Chicago Press, 1961.

———.*History of the Illinois Central Railroad*. New York: Macmillan, 1978.

———.*The Life and Decline of the American Railroad*. New York: Oxford University Press, 1970.

———.*Iron Road to the West: American Railroads in the 1850s*. New York: Columbia University Press, 1978.

Streeter, Edward. *Daily Except Sundays*. New York: Simon and Schuster, 1938.

Swanberg, W. A. *Jim Fisk: The Career of an Improbable Rascal*. New York: Charles Scribner's Sons, 1959.

Swann, E. W. *Along the Line*. New York: Broadway Publishing Co., 1905.

Taber, Thomas T. *The Delaware, Lackawanna and Western Railroad in the Nineteenth Century*. Muncy, PA: Thomas T. Taber, III, 1977.

Taber, Thomas T., and Thomas T. Taber, III. *The Delaware, Lackawanna and Western Railroad in the Twentieth Century*, 2 vols. Muncy, PA: Thomas T. Taber, III, 1980.

Taylor, George R. *The Transportation Revolution, 1815–1860*. New York: Rinehart & Co., 1951.

Taylor, George R., and Irene D. Neu. *The American Railroad Network, 1861–1890*. Cambridge: Harvard University Press, 1951.

Taylor, Joseph. *A Fast Life on the Modern Highway*. New York: Harper & Bros., 1874.

Teasdale, Sara. *The Collected Poems of Sara Teasdale*. New York: Macmillan, 1937.

Thoreau, Henry David. *Walden*. New York: The Heritage Press, 1939.

Trollope, Frances. *Domestic Manners of the Americans.* London: The Folio Society, 1974.

Trottman, Nelson. *History of the Union Pacific: A Financial and Economic Survey.* New York: Ronald Press, 1923.

Turnbull, Archibald Douglas. *John Stevens: An American Record.* New York: The Century Co., 1928.

Turner, Charles. *Chessie's Road.* Richmond, VA: Garrett & Massie, 1956.

Turner, George E. *Victory Rode the Rails: The Strategic Place of the Railroads in the Civil War.* Indianapolis: Bobbs-Merrill Co., 1953.

Valle, James E. *The Iron Horse at War.* Berkeley: Howell-North Books, 1977.

Valley, Plain and Peak: Scenes on the Line. St. Paul: Great Northern Railway Co., 1898.

Van Metre, T. W. *Trains, Tracks and Travel.* New York: Simmons-Boardman Publishing Co., 1950.

Villard, Henry. *Memoirs,* 2 vols. Boston: Houghton Mifflin, 1904.

Wakeman, Frederic. *The Hucksters.* New York: Rinehart, 1946.

Walbourn, Charles Howard. *Confessions of a Pullman Conductor.* San Francisco: H. S. Crocker, Co., 1913.

Walter, Rush. *The Mind of America, 1820–1860.* New York: Columbia University Press, 1975.

Ward, James A. *Railroads and the Character of America.* Knoxville: University of Tennessee Press, 1986.

Ward, Martindale C. *A Trip to Chicago: What I Saw, What I Heard, What I Thought.* Glasgow: A. Malcolm & Co., 1895.

Warman, Cy. *The Express Messenger.* New York: Charles Scribner's Sons, 1897.

———. *The Last Spike.* New York: Charles Scribner's Sons, 1906.

———. *Short Rails.* New York: Charles Scribner's Sons, 1900.

———. *Songs of Cy Warman.* Boston: Rand Avery & Co., 1911.

———. *Tales of an Engineer.* New York: Charles Scribner's Sons, 1895.

———. *The White Mail.* New York: Charles Scribner's Sons, 1899.

Warshow, Robert Irving. *Jay Gould.* New York: Greenberg, 1928.

Waters, Don. *The Call of the Shining Steel.* New York: Chelsea House, 1928.

———. *Pounding the Rails.* New York: Chelsea House, 1928.

Waters, L. L. *Steel Trails to Santa Fe.* Lawrence, KS: University of Kansas

Press, 1950.

Wayman, Norburg L. *St. Louis Union Station and Its Railroads*. St. Louis: Evelyn E. Newman Group, 1986.

Weber, Thomas. *The Northern Railroads in the Civil War.* New York: King's Crown Press, 1952.

Weisberger, Bernard A. *New Industrial Society: 1848–1900*. New York: John Wiley, 1968.

Weller, John L. *The New Haven Railroad*. New York: Hastings House, 1969.

Weseen, Maureen Harley. *A Dictionary of American Slang*. New York: Thomas Y. Crowell Co., 1934.

Westing, Fred. *The Locomotives That Baldwin Built*. New York: Bonanza Books, 1956.

————.*Penn Station*. Seattle: Superior Publishing Co., 1978.

Wheeler, Keith. *The Railroaders*. New York: Time-Life Books, 1973.

Whitaker, Rogers E. M. ("E. M. Frimbo"). *Decade of the Trains: The 1940s.* Boston: New York Graphic Society, 1977.

Whitaker, Rogers E. M., and Anthony Hiss. *All Aboard with E. M. Frimbo.* New York: Grossman, 1974.

White, Bouck. *The Book of Daniel Drew.* New York: Doubleday, Page & Co., 1910.

White, James E. *A Life Span and Reminiscences of Railway Mail Service*. Grand Rapids, MI: Black Letter Press, 1973.

White, John H., Jr. *American Locomotives: An Engineering History, 1830–1880*. Baltimore: Johns Hopkins University Press, 1968.

————.*Early American Locomotives*. New York: Dover Books, 1972.

Whitman, Walt. *Leaves of Grass*. New York: Heritage Press, 1936.

————.*Specimen Days in America*. London: The Folio Society, 1979.

Williams, George H. *Life on a Locomotive*. Berkeley: Howell-North Books, 1971.

Williams, John Hoyt. *A Great and Shining Road*. New York: Times Books, 1988.

Williamson, Ellen. *When We Went First Class*. Garden City, NY: Doubleday, 1977.

Wilson, Edmund. *The Twenties*. New York: Farrar, Straus & Giroux, 1975.

Wilson, Neill C., and Frank J. Taylor. *Southern Pacific: The Roaring Story of a Fighting Railroad*. New York: McGraw-Hill, 1952.

Wilson, William. *History of the Pennsylvania Railroad Company*, 2 vols. Philadelphia: H. T. Coates & Co., 1895.

Windsor Station. Montreal: Friends of Windsor Station, 1973.

Winther, Oscar O. *The Transportation Frontier: Trans-Mississippi West, 1865–1890*. New York: Holt, Rinehart & Winston, 1964.

Wittke, Carl. *We Who Built America: The Saga of the Immigrant*. Cleveland: The Press of Case Western Reserve University, 1967.

Wolfe, Thomas. *Look Homeward Angel*. New York: Charles Scribner's Sons, 1929.

———.*Of Time and the River.* New York: Charles Scribner's Sons, 1935.

———.*You Can't Go Home Again*. New York: Charles Scribner's Sons, 1940.

Wood, Charles R. *The Northern Pacific: Main Street of the Northwest*. New York: Bonanza Books, 1968.

Woods, Katherine. *The Broadway Limited, 1902–1927*. Philadelphia: Pennsylvania Railroad, 1927.

Ziel, Ron. *Steel Rails to Victory*. New York: Hawthorne Books, 1970.

Periodicals

American Railway Journal	1832–1886
American Railway Review	1859–1861
Official Railway Guide	1868–
Pathfinder Railway Guide	various editions
Railroad Enthusiast	1834–1947
Railroad Gazette	1870–1908
Railroad Man's Magazine (with changes of title)	1906–1937
Railroad Magazine	1937–1979
Railroad Red Book	1884–1925
Railroadians of America	irregular annuals
Railway Age (with changes of title)	1876–

Railway and Locomotive Historical Society (bulletins)	1921–
Railway Chronicle	1873–1915
Railway Magazine	1897–1934
Railway Review	1868–1926
Railway Times	1849–1867
Railway World	1856–1915
Trains	1940–

I·N·D·E·X

ABOUT THE AUTHOR

George H. Douglas is the author of a number of book dealing with American history and culture. He is a professor of English at the University of Illinois, where his teaching interests are in American literature and studies, popular culture, and nonfiction writing.

The author of six books and the editor of seven others, Douglas is also the author of more than fifty articles in magazines and professional journals, most of these dealing with American people and places, with a special interest in social history.

Among his books especially relating to social history are historical/biographical studies of H. L. Mencken and Edmund Wilson—books that attempt to place the criticism of these men in a social setting. Two of his books, *Women of the Twenties* and *The Early Days of Radio Broadcasting,* are mainly social and historical portraits of the 1920s. His latest book is *The Smart Magazines,* a study of the rise of magazines for urban sophisticates.

Douglas has had a lifelong interest in railroad history and has written numerous articles on the subject. He is a member of the Lexington Group in Transportation History. As a young man, when train service was still thriving in America, he traveled throughout the United States by train. He possesses a large archive of pictures relating to the railroad in the United States.

Douglas is the author of *Rail City: Chicago USA*, an informal illustrated history of Chicago as a railroad town (Howell-North Books, 1980). This work, which went through several printings, is the only full-scale history of the railroad in Chicago: It received many favorable reviews in Chicago and throughout the United States.

For many years, Douglas has taught nonfiction writing and technical writing at the University of Illinois. He holds an A. B. degree from Lafayette College, an M. A. from Columbia University, and a Ph.D. from the University of Illinois.